THEORY AND METHODS FOR SOCIOCULTURAL RESEARCH IN SCIENCE AND ENGINEERING EDUCATION

Introducing original methods for integrating sociocultural and discourse studies into science and engineering education, this book provides a much-needed framework for how to conduct qualitative research in this field. The three dimensions of learning identified in the *Next Generation Science Standards* (*NGSS*) create a need for research methods that examine the sociocultural components of science education. With cutting-edge studies and examples consistent with the *NGSS*, this book offers comprehensive research methods for integrating discourse and sociocultural practices in science and engineering education and provides key tools for applying this framework for students, pre-service teachers, scholars, and researchers.

Gregory J. Kelly is Senior Associate Dean for Research, Outreach, and Technology and Distinguished Professor of Education in the College of Education at Pennsylvania State University, USA.

Judith L. Green is Professor Emerita of Education at University of California, Santa Barbara, USA.

Teaching and Learning in Science Series
Norman G. Lederman, Series Editor

Supporting K–12 English Language Learners in Science
Putting Research into Teaching Practice
Edited by Cory Buxton, Martha Allexsaht-Snider

Reframing Science Teaching and Learning
Students and Educators Co-developing Science Practices In and Out of School
Edited by David Stroupe

Representations of Nature of Science in School Science Textbooks
A Global Perspective
Edited by Christine V. McDonald, Fouad Abd-El-Khalick

Teaching Biology in Schools
Global Research, Issues, and Trends
Edited by Kostas Kampourakis, Michael Reiss

Theory and Methods for Sociocultural Research in Science and Engineering Education
Edited by Gregory J. Kelly and Judith L. Green

For more information about this series, please visit:
www.routledge.com/series/LEATLSS

THEORY AND METHODS FOR SOCIOCULTURAL RESEARCH IN SCIENCE AND ENGINEERING EDUCATION

Edited by
Gregory J. Kelly and Judith L. Green

NEW YORK AND LONDON

First published 2019
by Routledge
52 Vanderbilt Avenue, New York, NY 10017

and by Routledge
2 Park Square, Milton Park, Abingdon, Oxon, OX14 4RN

Routledge is an imprint of the Taylor & Francis Group, an informa business

Library of Congress Cataloging-in-Publication Data
A catalog record for this title has been requested
Names: Kelly, Gregory J., editor. | Green, Judith L., editor.
Title: Theory and methods for sociocultural research in science and engineering education / edited by Gregory J. Kelly and Judith L. Green.
Description: New York, NY : Routledge, 2019. | Includes bibliographical references and index.
Identifiers: LCCN 2018035430 | ISBN 9780815351894 (hardback : alk. paper) | ISBN 9780815351924 (pbk. : alk. paper) | ISBN 9781351139922 (ebk)
Subjects: LCSH: Science—Study and teaching—Social aspects. | Science—Study and teaching—Research. | Engineering—Study and teaching—Social aspects. | Engineering—Study and teaching—Research. | Next Generation Science Standards (Education)
Classification: LCC Q181 .T45 2019 | DDC 306.4/50721—dc23
LC record available at https://lccn.loc.gov/2018035430

ISBN: 978-0-8153-5189-4 (hbk)
ISBN: 978-0-8153-5192-4 (pbk)
ISBN: 978-1-351-13992-2 (ebk)

Typeset in Bembo
by Swales & Willis Ltd, Exeter, Devon, UK

CONTENTS

FIGURES AND TABLES

Figures

Tables

CONTRIBUTORS

Judith L. Green, University of California, Santa Barbara, emerita

Judith is an Emerita Professor in the Gevirtz Graduate School of Education at the University of California, Santa Barbara. As an Emerita Professor, Judith is engaged in developing new understandings with colleagues in pre-kindergarten through higher education contexts. Her research directions focus on developing understandings of how the Interactional Ethnographic approach supports research on social and discursive opportunities for learning and academic knowledge construction across disciplines through ongoing programs of research.

Elizabeth Hufnagel, University of Maine

Beth is an Assistant Professor of Science Education in the College of Education and Human Development at the University of Maine. Her research explores the ways learners and teachers emotionally make sense of science and learning through discourse in a variety of science learning settings. She teaches both secondary and elementary science methods courses as well as graduate seminars in science and mathematics education research.

María Pilar Jiménez-Aleixandre, Universidade de Santiago de Compostela, Spain

Marilar is an Ad Honorem Professor of Science Education in the Faculty of Education at the University of Santiago de Compostela, Spain. Her research focuses on students' engagement in argumentation and epistemic practices, through classroom studies and longitudinal designs. Her recent research explores the use of evidence by kindergarteners and the interface between critical thinking and argumentation on socioscientific issues. Outside science education Marilar is an award-winning author of poetry, fiction, and children's fiction and she has been recently elected for the Royal Galician Academy (RAG).

Matthew M. Johnson, Pennsylvania State University

Matt is an Assistant Teaching Professor with the Center for Science and the Schools in the College of Education at Pennsylvania State University. His research interests focus on how teachers learn about epistemic practices through in-service teacher professional development programs and how they provide opportunities for students to engage in them to learn disciplinary content.

Gregory J. Kelly, Pennsylvania State University

Greg is a Professor of Science Education and Senior Associate Dean for Research, Outreach, and Technology in the College of Education at Pennsylvania State University. His research explores issues of knowledge and discourse in science education settings. Greg teaches courses on teaching and learning science in secondary schools and uses history, philosophy, and sociology of science in science education. Recent research includes development of theories of epistemic cognition and analysis of engineering classrooms.

Kristiina Kumpulainen, University of Helsinki

Kristiina is a Professor of Education and Vice Dean for Research at the Faculty of Educational Sciences at the University of Helsinki, Finland. She is also the founding member and scientific director of the Playful Learning Center. Her research is grounded in sociocultural theories of human learning and development and interactional sociolinguistics. She investigates tool-mediated learning and communication in various settings, including early childhood centers, schools, libraries, science centers, and teacher education settings. She also addresses methodological questions in the analysis of social interaction in learning and education. Her current research centers on multiliteracies, STEAM education, play and learning, digital childhoods, learning across contexts, children's agency and identity, resilience, as well as visual participatory research.

Peter R. Licona, Elizabethtown College

Peter is Assistant Professor of PK-12 STEM Education at Elizabethtown College. Peter teaches courses on elementary, middle, and secondary science and mathematics methods and a course on cultural and linguistic diversity in PK-12 classrooms. His research program focuses on the intersection of culturally and linguistically diverse students and science education, with a focus on bilingualism.

Scott P. McDonald, Pennsylvania State University

Scott is an Associate Professor of Science Education in the College of Education at Pennsylvania State University. His research focuses on teacher learning, framed as professional pedagogical vision, of ambitious and equitable science teaching practices. He also studies student learning in Earth and Space Sciences, specifically learning progressions in Plate Tectonics and Astronomy.

Alicia M. McDyre, Pennsylvania State University

Alicia is an Assistant Professor of Education and Director of Curriculum and Instruction Field Experiences in the College of Education at Pennsylvania State

University. Her research explores the teaching and learning of science in early childhood classrooms, identity work in young children, and the authoring and positioning of girls during science instruction.

Rachel Mulvaney, Parkville Middle School and Center of Technology in Baltimore County, Maryland

Rachel is a Sixth Grade Mathematics and Science Teacher at Parkville Middle School and Center of Technology in Baltimore County, Maryland. Rachel teaches science topics such as ecosystem interactions, forces and motion, and earth and space science. Her special areas of interest include climate change within STEM education, particularly in a middle school setting.

Amy Ricketts, Purdue University

Amy is a Postdoctoral Research Associate in the Department of Curriculum and Instruction at Purdue University. Her research explores the complexities of supporting science teacher learning across the career span. Amy is a former K-8 science teacher of thirteen years, and has taught science methods courses for pre-service teachers. Recent research includes negotiating the (sometimes) conflicting learning goals of various stakeholders in a school–university partnership. Most importantly, Amy strives to learn with and from teachers.

Asli Sezen-Barrie, University of Maine (Orono)

Asli is an Assistant Professor of Curriculum, Assessment and Instruction in the College of Education and Human Development at University of Maine (Orono). Her research focuses on sociocultural dimensions of science teachers' professional learning while utilizing discourse analysis, interactional ethnography, and practices of climate science. Dr. Sezen-Barrie teaches courses on formative assessments, learning theories, and science teaching methods. Asli's recent research includes teachers' and their students' engagement into epistemic practices and the use of epistemic tools in science and engineering classrooms.

Audra Skukauskaite, Independent Researcher

Audra is an Independent Researcher, Research Consultant and Full Professor of Research Methodology, who teaches qualitative research as an adjunct for doctoral programs in Social Sciences and Integrated Medicine and Health at Saybrook University. Over the past two years, she has begun collaborations with the Lemelson-MIT program at the Massachusetts Institute of Technology, where she consults and conducts ethnographic research focusing on invention education. She also serves as a Senior Research Scientist for an EU-funded four-year project in health care education in Lithuania and a program chair for the Qualitative Methodologies section of the Measurement and Research Methodologies division of the American Educational Research Association. Audra's research, teaching, and consulting interests focus on learning, teaching, conducting, and publishing research in systematic and transparent ways. Her primary interest is in research methodologies, with the specific focus on how ethnographic epistemologies, discourse-based studies, and qualitative research enable studying and understanding complex social and learning environments within and across different fields.

Arzu Tanis Ozcelik, Aydin Adnan Menderes University, Turkey
Arzu is an Assistant Professor in the Department of Elementary Education in the College of Education at Aydin Adnan Menderes University, Turkey. Her research focuses on teacher learning of reform-based models of teaching, namely ambitious science teaching practices, and teachers' development of professional pedagogical vision around learning and teaching of science. Arzu teaches courses on physics, science teaching methods, and practices of science and technology to elementary and middle school majors. She also has studies on astronomy education and informal educators' instructional practices.

Carmen M. Vanderhoof, Pennsylvania State University
Carmen is a Graduate Research Assistant for Professor Kelly and pursuing her doctorate in Curriculum and Instruction (Science Education) at Pennsylvania State University. Her research interests are classroom discourse processes, elementary engineering education, STEM integration, group dynamics surrounding decision-making, multimodal literacy, multiple representations, and the intersection of multiple discourse analysis tools with multimodal and ethnographic perspectives.

FOREWORD

Meeting Methodological Challenges

María Pilar Jiménez-Aleixandre

The first paper authored by Greg Kelly that I read was published in 1993, when I was beginning my career in the University of Santiago de Compostela, moving from conceptual change towards the study of argumentation. Kelly, Carlsen, and Cunningham (1993) proposed, twenty-five years ago, to take into account the contributions from Science Studies – history, philosophy, and sociology of science – in science education research, framing it in a sociocultural perspective. That paper, together with Duschl's (1990) proposal and a postdoc visit to Peter Hewson in 1992, which gave me the opportunity of being inside Sister Gertrud Hennessey's classroom, changed my ways both of "seeing" events in science classrooms and of "seeing" science education research. As Galileo tells 10-year-old Andrea in Bertolt Brecht's play *Life of Galileo*, "to look is not to see." Andrea argues that he can see the sun moving, and that understanding the earth orbit is far too difficult for he is not yet 11, and Galileo replies that this is exactly why he wants Andrea to understand it.

For, since I began teaching in high school in the 1970s, I had been interested in learning and knowledge justification. In understanding how 11-year-olds learn science, in learning how to support them in "seeing" scientific phenomena through particular theoretical lenses. Graduating in biology in 1969, at a time when in Spain pedagogical training for teaching and science education research did not exist, I bought two books, Piaget's *The Origins of Intelligence in Children* and Neil Postman and Charles Weingartner's *Teaching as a Subversive Activity*, in an effort to learn some theory about education. During the five years of the biology degree, I only had the opportunity to enroll in one course about history of science and to read Benjamin Farrington's *Science and Politics in the Ancient World*. From Piaget I learnt that knowledge is actively constructed by the learner. In Postman and Weingartner's book I found ideas from Dewey, and a recommendation that school should develop in students the anthropological perspective, observing their own culture as if it were a foreign tribe, a suggestion that would be brilliantly developed by Latour and Woolgar (1986).

My trajectory can be representative, or in Heap's terms an example, of Spanish – and most European – science education scholars beginning to build research communities in the 1980s. Our background consisted solely of science concepts, methods, and approaches. Thus, many of the first research efforts were grounded in methods drawn from science. Heap (1995) pointed out that educational research – even when identifying itself as qualitative – often retained empiricist conceptions and criteria. In my context this trend was heightened in most of science education work, which attempted to legitimize science education research within empiricist frameworks. Different types of obstacles, epistemic, related to research traditions, experiential, and even affective, among others, needed to be overcome in order to engage in science-in-the-making studies, as suggested by Kelly and colleagues (1993). A few years later, after meeting Greg Kelly and cooperating with him in the first argumentation session in a NARST conference in 1997, I became familiar with Judith Green's insightful approaches. An influential example of their work together is the framework for examining students' discursive practices in a physics laboratory (Kelly, Crawford, & Green, 2001). Since then, scholars interested in what happens inside science classrooms, and how to account for it, have learnt much from both their theoretical contributions and their methodological proposals. Kelly and Green have developed insights and research methods to examine classroom discourse, and the book structure organized around eight empirical chapters illustrating specific methods gives it an innovative nature, while the rigor and depth of the contributions anticipate that it will soon become a classic.

Although I mentioned above science classrooms and science education, it needs to be noted that an original feature of the book is including engineering in its focus, which reflects one of Kelly's current research interest (Cunningham & Kelly, 2017a; 2017b), aligned with the *Next Generation Science Standards (NGSS)* (NGSS Lead States, 2013).

Methodology matters, and there is a thirst for robust reference books about it. Educational research about science and engineering has tended to have a stronger focus either on theoretical approaches or on empirical findings about learning and teaching. Methodological issues specific of these fields have, as a consequence, been given less attention. A substantial amount of scholarly work about science and engineering is grounded in domain-general research methods, from which we have much to learn but that are less suited to address some domain-specific issues. Domain-specificity is one of the methodological challenges that this volume seeks to meet, and which makes it a work of unique value. A second one is to tackle the three-dimensional learning, integrating core ideas, crosscutting concepts and practices, emphasized in the *NGSS*. A third challenge is to show

how rigorous qualitative research can make visible how science and engineering concepts, processes, and practices are socially constructed.

The volume is particularly strong from a methodological perspective, addressing issues that have been previously unresolved or understudied, or approaching more familiar problems in a new way. An instance is the construction of identities-in-practice of kindergarten girls as science learners, investigated by Alicia McDyre, in the Chapter 2. As she points out, most gender research in science has been about adolescents, and I will add that Early Childhood Education has received little attention. It should be noted, and praised, that gender is addressed in that early chapter, the first one reporting a study. Equity is also the focus of Peter Licona's chapter about the methodological decisions made in his study with bilingual students engaging in argumentation about the socioscientific issue of endangered species. The examination of emotional expressions, undertaken by Elizabeth Hufnagel in the context of environmental science and climate change, is another understudied issue. Hufnagel articulates a framework for the study of emotions in science classrooms, creating in the process the notion of *aboutness* to refer to the object of the emotion. Elementary engineering provides the context of two chapters: Johnson explores the joint social construction by students and teachers of failure and improvement in engineering design projects, and Vanderhoof carries out a multimodal analysis of engineering design, with a view towards transferability to other studies involving student–student interactions and a focus on student-produced artifacts. Asli Sezen-Barrie and Rachel Mulvaney tackle an original issue, how to build coherence among scientific concepts and related epistemic practices, in the area of climate science, through Informal Formative Assessments (IFAs). Learning science and engineering is dependent on how teachers teach, therefore on how teachers are enculturated, and two chapters propose new ways of looking at teacher education: Arzu Tanis Ozcelik and Scott McDonald focus on how pre-service science teachers develop what they term *professional pedagogical vision* related to ambitious science teaching, and the new challenges posed by the *NGSS*. Amy Ricketts analyzes a professional learning community, and how the teachers belonging to it developed a culture of reflective critique through conversations of a generative nature.

The emphasis on methodological challenges means that the focus of each of these chapters is a *reflection* about the process of research itself, discussing not only the final form of research questions, rubrics, or tools for analysis, but in particular the *decisions* made during the process, and even – as examined by Hufnagel – the changes in the logic of inquiry, as data were collected and analyzed. In other words, we get access to the science-in-the-making of these studies and dissertations, to the metaknowledge that went into this research, or that was generated during it. This explicit layout of reflections is another feature that makes this book unique. As Kelly and Green point out in Chapter 1, their goal is to make visible ways of developing and explaining processes involved in designing, conducting, and constructing warranted accounts from discourse analysis. Reflection about the research processes combines the three types of critical discourse identified by Kelly (2006): *critical discourse within group*, concerning developmental and definitional work regarding a research group's central theories, assumptions, and key constructs; *critical discourse regarding public reason* concerning the epistemological commitments of the field of education regarding research methods; and *hermeneutical conversations across groups*, designed to learn from differences across traditions.

The book offers a systematic approach to the study of educational events, an approach that is empirical and emphasizes methodologies, but that is also theoretically grounded; for methods have foundations on particular theories. The research reported in these contributions is grounded in a sociocultural perspective, bringing together approaches from discourse analysis, interactional ethnography, and epistemology, weaving them in a coherent whole. The qualifier "systematic" is relevant for, as Kelly and Green discuss in the Chapter 1, some qualitative studies suffer from problems such as lack of systematic sampling, lack of theoretically grounded approaches for the study of large data sets, or failing to situate instances of learning in ongoing sociocultural practices.

All scholars who have been extensively involved in reviewing manuscripts for refereed journals, in evaluating research proposals for National Agencies (such as NSF), or even in supervising doctoral students, know that most flaws of research proposals or manuscripts relate to methodological issues. This book will be useful for researchers, first because of its systematic approach to methodology, as illustrated for instance in the questions discussed in Chapter 1, ranging from asking ethnographic questions to recognizing relevant data sources, elaborating data representations, or finding patterns. Second, it will be useful for the book's range of examples, which develop all these questions and analyze a variety of dimensions about how the construction of science and engineering is accomplished.

An undercurrent running through the chapters is a commitment to equity, social justice, and a sustainable world. Two of the studies, Hufnagel's, and Sezen-Barrie and Mulvaney's, are situated in the context of climate change. In particular, Sezen-Barrie and Mulvaney take on the challenge of building coherence across concepts and epistemic practices utilized to justify the claim that humans are the main cause of current climate change. Denialism of anthropogenic climate change is an educational problem but, more seriously, it is a social and political issue impacting the earth's future. As Sezen-Barrie, Shea, and Borman (2017) point out, climate change skepticism is not scientific skepticism, but rather denial. This raises a theoretical issue: concerns are currently shifting from a focus on understanding the tentativeness of scientific knowledge towards a focus on epistemic education empowering students to face "post-truth." Chinn and Barzilai (2018) propose that a fully apt epistemic performance, on this dimension, would see abeyance as an option, but would judge that the scientific community consensus is sufficiently warranted. In order to examine such complex epistemic performances in classroom practice, we will need sophisticated methods, as those analyzed in detail in this book.

As Galileo Galilei – at least the Galileo imagined by Brecht – struggled to teach a 10-year-old to "see" beyond the apparent, and to uncover the relationships between earth and sun, so educational researchers strive to uncover how science and engineering are socially, conceptually, and discursively constructed in classrooms. In doing so they will find guidance in the accomplished scholarship brought together in this volume and, in particular, in the reflections about what the authors-ethnographers learnt from their analyses.

References

Chinn, C. A., & Barzilai, S. (2018). Teaching scientific thinking in a post-truth world. Paper presented in the AERA conference. New York, April 13–17.

Cunningham, C. M., & Kelly, G. J. (2017a). Framing engineering practices in elementary school classrooms. *International Journal of Engineering Education 33*(1B), 295–307.

Cunningham, C. M., & Kelly, G. J. (2017b). Epistemic practices of engineering for education. *Science Education* (online first). https://doi.org/10.1002/sce.21271.

Duschl, R. A. (1990). *Restructuring science education: The importance of theories and their development.* New York: Teachers College Press.

Farrington, B. (1965). *Science and politics in the ancient world.* London: Unwin University Books.

Heap, J. L. (1995). The status of claims in "qualitative" educational research. *Curriculum Inquiry 25*(3), 271–292.

Kelly, G. J. (2006). Epistemology and educational research. In J. Green, G. Camilli, & P. Elmore (Eds.), *Handbook of complementary methods in education research* (pp. 33–55). Mahwah, NJ: Lawrence Erlbaum Associates.

Kelly, G. J., Carlsen, W. S., & Cunningham, C. M. (1993). Science education in sociocultural context: Perspectives from the sociology of science. *Science Education* 77(2), 207–220.

Kelly, G. J., Crawford, T., & Green, J. (2001). Common tasks and uncommon knowledge: Dissenting voices in the discursive construction of physics across small laboratory groups. *Linguistics and Education 12*(2), 135–174.

Latour, B., & Woolgar, S. (1986). *Laboratory life: The construction of scientific facts.* Princeton, NJ: Princeton University Press.

NGSS Lead States (2013). *Next generation science standards: For states, by states.* Washington, DC: The National Academies Press.

Piaget, J. (1952). *The origins of intelligence in children* (M. Cook, Translator). New York: W. W. Norton & Co.

Postman, N., & Weingartner, C. (1969). *Teaching as a subversive activity.* New York: Delacorte Press.

Sezen-Barrie, A., Shea, N., & Borman, J. H. (2017). Probing into the sources of ignorance: Science teachers' practices of constructing arguments or rebuttals to denialism of climate change. *Environmental Education Research.* DOI: 10.1080/13504622.2017.1330949.

1

FRAMING ISSUES OF THEORY AND METHODS FOR THE STUDY OF SCIENCE AND ENGINEERING EDUCATION

Gregory J. Kelly and Judith L. Green

Introduction

The *Next Generation Science Standards* (NGSS Lead States, 2013) prominently feature three-dimensional learning—the integration of disciplinary core ideas, crosscutting concepts, and scientific and engineering practices. This tripartite emphasis raises methodological challenges for researchers and educators seeking to examine, and thus uncover, the ways in which science and engineering content, processes, and practices are ongoing social constructions in educational settings. The methodological challenges include understanding the cognitive, social, and interpersonal factors supporting or constraining the learning of these disciplinary ideas, concepts, and practices.

This volume brings together contributors who explore how science and engineering concepts, processes, and practices are socially constructed through coordinated interactions among students, teachers, curricula, texts, and technologies (Kelly, 2016a). Our goal in assembling this particular group is to make visible ways of developing and explaining processes involved in designing, conducting, and constructing research leading to warranted accounts of educational phenomena (Heap, 1995). A series of chapters that describe various dimensions of the construction of science and engineering make visible how, in what ways, for what purposes, and with what outcomes, science and engineering in educational settings are socially, discursively, and conceptually constructed.

This research approach takes seriously the ways that discourses and social practices are constructed over time by members of a sustaining social group. Such classroom cultures are formed through locally interpreted and recognized ways of talking, being, and knowing (Santa Barbara Classroom Discourse Group, 1992a, b). These reforms in science education emerged from a recognition, developed over fifty years of theoretical and empirical research on discourse processes and ethnographic studies of education (Green, 1983; Gumperz & Hymes, 1986; Hymes, 1974), of the important ways that educational experiences are created through discourse. This research tradition examines ways that educational and social experiences are shaped through discourse in and across interactions among actors in developing events and times (Bloome, Carter, Christian, Otto, & Shuart-Faris, 2005; Cazden, John, & Hymes, 1972; Heath & Street, 2008; Green, 1983; Green & Joo, 2016; Green & Bloome, 2004; Gumperz & Hymes, 1986; Hymes, 1974; Kelly & Chen, 1999; Lemke, 1990).

Early work on classroom discourse in science education focused on teacher talk. For example, Lemke's (1990) seminal work examined how and in what ways the thematic content of scientific knowledge was communicated. Such functional linguistic analysis showed how teachers came to frame science as difficult to understand and as accessible to only a cognitive elite by limiting classroom conversations to narrow conceptions of disciplinary knowledge. Since this early work, the field has greatly expanded to include a range of studies looking at issues such as student groupwork in laboratory settings, argumentation, assessments, uses of questioning, and studies of identity development (for review, see Kelly, 2014a).

Science and engineering education each have a history of ideas, recommendations, instructional design and practice, and suggested reforms. This book provides a set of selected studies, each of which examines some of the current practices in science, engineering, and teacher education. At the core of this volume is an understanding that, whether focused on students' engineering design challenges, identity construction as a scientist, or development of teachers' professional vision, everyday educational events are, and have always been, constructed through discourse processes, within the cultural practices of life within these and related settings (e.g., home, community, laboratories, social spaces).

The book's authors make visible ways of conducting ethnographically informed, discourse studies of science and engineering education as socially constructed in everyday life in classrooms (kindergarten through university). The research approach provides systematic ways to use large-scale video and qualitative data to examine salient issues for making sense of science and engineering. Chapter topics include argumentation, gender in science, engineering design, science accessibility for emergent bilingual students, the role of emotion in science learning, and teacher education.

Our review of the literature, and our experience as researchers, surfaced the need for a book providing multiple instances of systematic empirical studies of educational phenomena. Large-scale quantitative studies often lack the sensitivity to examine the ways that access to knowledge, affiliation and identity, and learning through design are constructed through social interaction. While such studies often report declarative statements about the current state, as measured within the boundaries set by the research instruments, they fail to explain why or how the current state was constructed. Alternatively, some qualitative studies do not utilize systematic sampling and/or theoretically grounded approaches for the study of large-scale video data sets. These studies often zoom to important instances of learning, showing how in such an instance learning occurred, but fail to situate the instance in ongoing sociocultural practices. In contrast, we seek to make transparent ways of systematic sampling and theoretically grounding approaches for analyses of large-scale video data sets or archived records (e.g., video, audio, written work by students). The approach lays out ways of recording, documenting, sampling, and analyzing video and artifact data through discourse analysis that addresses questions applicable to the understanding of three-dimensional learning (integration of disciplinary core ideas, crosscutting concepts, and scientific and engineering practices).

Epistemology, Methodology, and Educational Research

Educational research seeks to produce knowledge about learning, activities, people, institutions, and systems. Research methodologies are designed to produce new knowledge. Such knowledge is grounded in human perception, experience, practices, and identities. Thus, to the extent that research methodologies are about producing knowledge, they are epistemological. Like the study of knowledge (epistemology), research methodologies are concerned with the origins, production, evaluation, and limitations of knowledge (Boyd, Gasper, & Trout, 1991).

This book takes up the challenge posed by Kelly (2006) in an introductory chapter in the *Handbook of Complementary Methods in Education Research*. He identified three types of critical discourse with conversation metaphors for articulating, comparing, assessing, and improving research methodologies in educational research: *critical discourse within group, critical discourse regarding public reason*, and *hermeneutical conversations across groups*. We describe each of these critical discourses and explain how the chapters in this volume advance the challenge of building more rigorous, coherent, and transparent approaches to research methods in science and engineering education.

Critical discourse within group are conversations concerning developmental and definitional work regarding the creation, specification, and extension of a research group's central theories, assumptions, and key constructs (Kelly, 2006). Within-group critical discourse provides a forum for development of a research area's core theories and commitments. For example, in the subsequent section, *Discourse, interaction, and interactional ethnography*, we describe the central theoretical commitments of interactional ethnography and apply them to specific studies in the later chapters. In within-group conversations, there is a premium on the development of new ideas, metaphors, and redescriptions (Rorty, 1989). In these critical conversations, researchers create new vocabulary to make sense of our world. For example, notions such as "aboutness" (Hufnagel, this volume), "failure" (Johnson, this volume), and "professional pedagogical vision" (Tanis Ozcelik & McDonald, this volume) are re-imagined and re-articulated in science and engineering education in new ways that advance the respective conversations about emotions in science, engineering design, and teacher learning. We invite the readers to consider the ways that each chapter contributes to the creation of the substantive central theories, assumptions, and key constructs in the respective domains.

Critical discourse regarding public reason focuses on the development of epistemological commitments to assess the value of educational research within and across different research traditions (Kelly, 2006). These conversations concern the criteria used to judge research. Likely candidates for criteria would be insightfulness, empirical warrant, theoretical salience, consistency with other knowledge, transparency, and usefulness for practitioners. For example, later in this chapter we consider some critical methodological themes for research in education (Kelly, 2014b) as related to the empirical chapters (Chapters 2–9) in this book. Thus, critical discourse regarding public reason concerns the epistemological commitments of the field of education regarding research methods. What counts as valid and useful research in this area? What are the bases for decisions about the value and usefulness of studies of science and engineering education? How are studies of discourse, social practices, access, and equity across contexts and timescales valuable to engage the field in critical discussions about the epistemology of social science research?

Hermeneutical conversations across groups are conversations designed to foster learning from differences across traditions. They also consider the multiple audiences of research. There are many ways in which research in science and engineering education can contribute to conversations about educational research within and across research traditions. Based on this conceptual argument, we propose different directions for conversations about how research on science and engineering education ties into other traditions in the field. The first conversation supports consideration of how research on science and engineering can be informed by, and inform, the development of specific research methods for educational research more generally. Science and engineering represent compact disciplines, with relatively high degrees of consensus (Rorty, 1991; Toulmin, 1972). Each field represents unique ways that knowledge is generated, communicated, and applied. The uniqueness of some of the features of the disciplines of science and engineering presents models and challenges for educational research.

A second form of conversation can consider how different theoretical traditions within science and engineering education (cognitive, sociocultural) have examined substantive issues and how similar substantive issues articulated in the chapters of this book relate to that body of work. There are many ways that the social phenomena described in the chapters of this book could have been studied. By undertaking comparisons across traditions from linguistics, psychology, anthropology, and sociology about how key constructs are recognized, examined, and constructed in and through research, we can examine how these comparisons can inform hermeneutical conversations. A third form of hermeneutical conversation could explore how studies of discourse and sociocultural practices of science and engineering connect with studies across broad social phenomena beyond the specifics of these disciplines. Developing a research program addressing these problems may require examining how different approaches are mutually supportive and synergistic within and across disciplines in studying social phenomena. For example, studies of workforce development and policy can show how science and engineering interact with legitimizing institutions in society. At the center of these three forms of hermeneutical conversations, therefore, is a common critical theme—the understanding of relationships between research methodology and the production of knowledge through studies grounded in different traditions.

The connectedness of knowledge production and research methodology is made visible in each of the chapters in this volume. The selected studies adopt a common (although not identical) approach to the study of disciplinary knowledge, practices, and identities that permits ways of understanding the investigation of discourse from this epistemological point of view. Each author drew from, interpreted, and modified aspects of interactional ethnography. By holding the orienting theories for the study of knowledge construction constant, the collective work provides knowledge about how to research science and engineering ways of knowing, doing, and being. We now turn to an overview of interactional ethnography, which informed the subsequent empirical studies.

Overview of Perspectives: Discourse, Interaction, and Interactional Ethnography (IE)

Interactional ethnography is an approach to the study of culture. It considers the social contexts discourse uses as cultures-in-the-making. The orientation to understanding culture begins with the recognition of the importance of discourse processes, texts, and signs and symbols for the construction of norms and expectations; roles, relationships, and positionings; and rights and obligations as well as the construction of meaning among members. Interactional ethnography is informed by sociolinguistics, cultural anthropology, ethnomethodology, and critical discourse analysis.

Sociolinguistics investigates ways that everyday life is accomplished through discourse processes. Gumperz (1982) defines sociolinguistics as a "field of inquiry which investigates the language usage of particular human groups" (p. 9). Discourse is often defined as language-in-use that includes verbal exchanges, written texts, signs and symbols, and other semiotic resources (Jaworski & Coupland, 1999). These semiotic resources include contextualization cues, such as gesture, eye gaze, prosody, lexicon, grammar, kinesics, and proxemics (Bloome *et al.*, 2005; Gumperz, 2001; Green & Castanheira, 2012; Green & Wallat, 1979; Strauss & Feiz, 2014). To understand how specific discourse processes function, they need to be examined in contexts of use; thus, discourse studies are tied to ethnographic descriptions of what members of a social group propose, recognize, acknowledge, and interactionally accomplish as socially, academically, personally, and interpersonally significant. In such instances, interpretations of semantics and accompanying contextualization cues are highly culturally dependent. Meaning is derived from interactions that include the highly active interpretative nature of communication.

Cultural anthropology also informs interactional ethnography. Ethnographers produce data, from which texts about cultural processes and practices are constructed (Ellen, 1984). That is, anthropologists write culture (Clifford & Marcus, 1986). From this point of view, there is an active, participatory role of the ethnographer in the construction of the account of the putative cultural practices. Cultural knowledge is socially constructed through the languaculture of particular groups (Agar, 1994; Green, Skukauskaite, & Baker, 2012). This awareness of the reflexivity of the ethnographic point of view suggests the need for the analysts to make transparent the logic-in-use informing the methodological decisions of the study (Green, Dai, Joo, Williams, Liu, & Lu, 2015). Part of this orienting theory is the need to take an emic perspective to construct ways of knowing grounded in the local cultural practices. Green and Bridges (2018; following Heath & Street, 2008) identify what constitutes such an emic (insider) understanding, which includes suspending assumed-to-be-known categories of meaning to construct situated meanings from the local setting, recognizing differences between ethnographers' knowledge and that of the participants, and developing ways of representing what is known by the local (insider) actors. This awareness of the role of the ethnographer in the construction of the knowledge speaks to the need to engage in the critical discourses noted previously.

Ethnomethodology influences interactional ethnography in important ways. Ethnomethodology is the study of the ways that people accomplish everyday life. It is not a "research methodology"; rather, it focuses on the methods used to get through social contexts. In the study of scientific practices, ethnomethodology has attended to the products of science that emerge from interactional and discursively formulated events. Consider the following from Lynch (1992): "Ethnomethodology's descriptions of the mundane and situated activities of observing, explaining, or proving enable a kind of rediscovery and respecification of how these central terms become relevant within particular content of activity" (p. 258). Such respecification entails more than just producing declarative statements (empirical and contingent) of findings about the work of scientists. A different type of warranted claim is needed—ethnomethodology (and interactional ethnography) produces both logical and normative claims about the workings of social groups (Heap, 1995). Rather than empirical generalizations, claims are constructed through the study of culture and produce propositions revealing previous unrecognized patterns in everyday life. Although ethnomethodology presents the interactionally accomplished nature of everyday life and provides theoretical tools to understanding conversations, classroom discourse occurs in institutions and settings where power, control, and structures mediate the direction and nature of the discourse processes. This suggests a need to understand how power works in social settings.

Critical discourse analysis (CDA) examines how ideologies and power relations are manifest in ways that language is used in various contexts. In educational research, theories of power, culture, and social life inform ways that critical discourse analysis can be applied to life in schools (Rogers, Schaenen, Schott, O'Brien, Trigos-Carrillo, Starkey, & Chasteen, 2016). An ethnographic point of view recognizes that language and discourse entail meanings that have power for real people in real settings. Fairclough (2010) identified relational, dialectical, and transdisciplinary properties of critical discourse analysis (p. 3). First, the approach focuses on social relationships and the ways they use texts, genres, power relations, and institutions to establish and maintain these relationships. For example, science teachers have institutional power, established by their role as an authority in a classroom. Certain discourses afford teachers the ability to control others through the power instantiated by this role. However, the discourses of science, used by the teacher or texts of the classroom, may also be positioned to appear distant, objective, and unassailable. In this way, the genres of scientific explanation communicate an ideology.

Second, critical discourse analysis is dialectical. The uses of discourse and power in social relations and institutions are interconnected. As discourse is employed it creates consequences beyond that of mere discourse—that is, there are material consequences of ideologies. For example, academic success or failure has implications for who can participate in further debates about scientific or other matters.

Third, critical discourse analysis is transdisciplinary, drawing from multiple disciplines, such as sociology, linguistic anthropology, political science, gender studies, and/or education (Fairclough 2010; Rogers *et al.*, 2016). Interactional ethnography takes up Fairclough's (1992) three dimensions of critical discourse analysis methodology through analysis of text, analysis of text production, and social analysis of the discursive events, conditions, and consequences for participants. The application of interactional ethnography to science and engineering education in this book highlights different aspects of text, text production, and social analyses.

Taking an Interactional Ethnographic Perspective on Science and Engineering Education

Uses of discourse in the moment of interaction are always situated in a social and cultural setting. They are constructed in particular ways with conventions that align with the norms and expectations of the participants. And they have consequences for subsequent actions by the participants. Interactional ethnography begins by asking ethnographic questions, such as: What is happening here?

How are the norms and expectations constructed, developed, acknowledged, and legitimized? What counts as knowledge? For whom, under what circumstances, with what outcomes, with what consequence?

The process begins with an initial period of ethnographic research that seeks to understand insights into local communicative ecologies, discover recurrent communicative patterns, and identify how local actors define problems (Gumperz, 2001). These analyses become the basis for selecting sequentially bounded units or events, denoted by co-occurring shifts in content reference (spoken, written, or graphic/visual), prosody, or other stylistic markers, which are represented by transcripts. Thus, ethnographic description provides a basis for selection decisions and theoretical sampling in large ethnographic archives from which data sets are constructed (Gee & Green, 1998; Kelly & Chen, 1999). By drawing from the ethnographic descriptions, the detailed discourse analysis is informed by the broader contexts of use of the discourse processes in question.

To research the accomplishment of everyday life, a number of substantive assumptions define the orientation (Kelly & Green, 1998): As members of a group affiliate over time, social interaction helps them develop patterned ways of producing language-in-use (Bloome *et al.*, 2005). Such language use both shapes and is shaped by social order (Fairclough, 2010; Jaworski & Coupland, 1999), as social groups create particular ways of talking, thinking, acting, and being (Gee & Green, 1998; Santa Barbara Classroom Discourse Group, 1992a). These ways of acting come to define cultural practices, become resources for members, and evolve as members internalize the common practices and transform them over time. The cultural practices that constitute membership in a community are created interactionally through discourse processes. Local group members are also members of other groups, and thus bring frames of reference to each interaction, including experiences, beliefs, values, knowledge, and practices (e.g., ways of knowing, doing, interpreting, and so forth) that may match or clash with local ones (Castanheira, Crawford, Dixon, & Green, 2001; Kelly, 2014b). These substantive assumptions provide an orienting framework to examine three basic ways of investigating cultural practice: observing what people do, say, and make. Such assumptions about the construction of everyday life support the creation of common frameworks for interpretative research and are shared by research programs across academic disciplines (Baker, Green, & Skukauskaite, 2008; Bloome *et al.*, 2005; Green & Dixon, 1993; Kelly, 2014b). By supporting a common framework, we can build theory in education oriented to making knowledge accessible to learners. The framework is interpreted, modified, and integrated with other theories across the chapters of this book. In this way, the overall orientation demonstrates the importance of a common framework, but also the ways that such a framework can be taken up and at times extended to examine particular phenomena of interest to researchers across settings, perspectives, and topics in educational research.

Science and engineering are constituted by social practices, occurring in cultural contexts. Thus, through everyday practices of doing science or engineering, members of local communities propose, communicate, assess, and legitimize knowledge claims, engineering designs, and solutions to locally relevant extant problems (Kelly, 2016a, b). In professional and educational communities, the actions taken can become coordinated through concerted activity, thus developing patterned cultural practices of members for the group (Kelly & Green, 1998; Smith, 1996). Thus, through language use and other actions, social groups create meaning, and build identity and affiliation as well as academic knowledge and practices that contribute to larger societal needs. Rather than viewing science and engineering as disembodied knowledge, the authors in this book view disciplinary knowledge and practice as the products of concerted activity, and therefore subject to investigation through the study of the locally created, interactionally acknowledged and recognized cultural practices leading to the relevant knowledge and solutions to problems defined in such contexts.

Research Considerations, Approaches, and Methods

Interactional ethnography offers the possibility to build common frameworks for interpretative research to investigate the various ways that disciplinary knowledge and practice can be communicated in educational settings. There are multiple views of culture, and numerous approaches for how to define, do, or interpret ethnography. We find the distinction by Green and Bloome (2004) of (a) doing ethnography, (b) adopting an ethnographic perspective, and (c) using ethnographic tools to be especially helpful for the application of ethnography to school and other educational settings. Doing ethnography has traditionally referred to in-depth, long-term studies of culture often done by cultural anthropologists through extended field study. Within anthropology, adopting an ethnographic perspective means drawing from theories of culture and inquiry practices of anthropology to guide research in a given local setting. Using ethnographic tools refers to the methods and techniques employed in field work. For the most part, the examples in this book adopt an ethnographic perspective, viewing the local educational settings for research as open to interrogation through ethnographic questions (Heath, 1982; Bloome & Green, 2018). In each instance, the ethnographic methods employed are situationally defined.

In the next section, we provide an example of taking an ethnographic perspective from our previous work to illustrate some of the key features of interactional ethnography relevant to the study of science and engineering education. Subsequent chapters will further illustrate and elaborate upon these seven features. The example comes from a study by Kelly, Crawford, and Green (2001) where we examined the discourse processes of four groups of physics students studying oscillatory motion. The groups completed a series of tasks using force and motion detectors that graphed physical events instantaneously on a computer screen. The activity allowed students to vary aspects of the physical world and examine how these affected the graphical representations.

To apply an ethnographic perspective to these events, we engaged in the following types of research activity.

Asking Ethnographic Questions

Ethnographers ask questions. In this case, we asked: What's happening here? What are the roles and responsibilities as locally defined and construed by the students and teacher? What knowledge is relevant to completing the school task? How might the school task be related to disciplinary knowledge? Through data collection and analysis, the ethnographic research team refined the questions so that they were those most salient to understanding how knowledge was constructed, shared, and assessed (Kelly, Crawford, & Green, 2001). Thus, our set of ethnographic questions was emergent, relevant to our evolving knowledge of the students' construction of the physics, and open to debate and changes as we worked through the discourse analysis of the video episodes. In contrast, the study of physics often asks other sorts of questions; questions that do not consider science as culture and practice. From a cognitive perspective, researchers might ask a third set of questions, leading to different data and different results, thus showing how knowledge in social science is constructed, contingent, and informed by theoretical commitments. Cognitively oriented questions might include: What was the initial knowledge state of each of the students? What misconceptions about the physics of force and motion were addressed through the lesson? How did the students' self-efficacy lead to choices about solutions to the physics problems? How did the teachers' pedagogical content knowledge (PCK) inform choices about what to say to the students and when?

Identifying Sites for Knowledge Construction and Negotiating Access

To use interactional ethnography, the research team needed to identify sites and gain access for the study of knowledge construction. Much has been written about gaining access for qualitative research, for example, Corsaro (1985) and Emerson, Fretz, and Shaw (1995), so we will not elaborate here. For our physics study, we chose a site for research and thought about how to gain access to the sorts of data relevant to our research questions. We negotiated access with a high school teacher and her students. This involved learning about their curricular goals, understanding the content the students were studying, identifying areas of mutual interest (laboratory work with technology), and assessing the physical and technological constraints of the learning environment.

In this example, students needed to interpret the physical events (oscillating masses), symbols (real-time, computer-generated graphs), verbal and written prompts (teacher lab guidesheet, student talk), and embodied motion (student imitation of motion through physical movement of hands). Students based many of their knowledge claims in data acquired by the representation technologies. The computer-generated visual texts were a consequence of the live complex physical phenomena and offered sufficient interpretative flexibility (Knorr-Cetina, 1995) to provoke sustained conversation. This suggested to us the importance of creating a retrievable record of the events through video recordings and the collection of the lesson prompts and student-produced artifacts.

Recognizing the Relevant Data Sources for Interactional Ethnography

The video records of the events were relevant data sources because key features of the social phenomena included a series of knowledge claims made by the students. The series of student claims about physical phenomena often entailed false starts, changes in initial thinking, questioning, re-doing of data trials, rebuttals, and re-interpretations. Therefore, students' deliberation about the physical and representational phenomena was central to the activity. Relevant to the study of student discourse from a sociolinguistic perspective was consideration of the verbal and non-verbal communication, which included the signs and symbols, proxemics, and prosody of the conversations (Green, Weade, & Graham, 1988; Gumperz, 2001). Previous studies of scientific practice supported our methodological orientation. For example, Garfinkel, Lynch, and Livingston's (1981) study analyzed the "local, interactionally produced, recognized, and understood embodied practices" (p. 135) of astronomers as they discovered, named, and textually identified a pulsar. Much like the astronomers, the physics students made sense of the phenomena by proposing a series of claims that were considered and modified over time by the group members.

Discourse and Sociocultural Practices in Everyday Life, in Time, and in Space

The students' discourse processes in the small groups were not just constructed in the moment without referents, previous knowledge, or literary practices. Rather, knowledge claims made in the moment-to-moment interactions were embedded in speech genres, sociohistorical traditions, and ways of being that were drawn into and invoked in the local setting (Bakhtin, 1986; Bazerman, 1988; Kelly, 2008). For example, the data representations of the oscillatory motion stemmed from a long tradition of mathematical knowledge regarding ways of plotting variables for common understandings. The data acquisition technology concretized such knowledge and rendered visual images for the students to interpret. Such interpretation required not only making sense of the immediate displays, but also understanding the assumptions built into the mathematical traditions of data representation and graphing conventions. Thus, making sense of the oscillatory motion (displacement, velocity, acceleration, force) required drawing from knowledge of physics, but also a large number of conventions (i.e., ways of being and doing in science and mathematics) to render intelligible new constructions of meaning and, ultimately, new knowledge of the phenomena at hand. In addition, the relationship of the physical movement of the objects in space, the students' gestures, proxemics, eye gaze, and physical orientation, all influenced how the new constructions of meaning were developed. That is, the data inscriptions and their interpretation were physically situated in time and space, and the interpretation of the motions was dependent on, and embodied in, the students' physical movements.

The interpretation of the inscriptions required knowledge beyond what was made available in the moment of interpretation by the student groups. The discourse processes around the physics drew from, made reference to, and employed taken-for-granted knowledge of previously learned and understood knowledge of the relevant physics and conventions. As analysts we needed to draw on such knowledge to understand the sense making in the student groups. The discourse of the groups would be meaningless (or close to meaningless) without knowledge of the relevant sociohistorical knowledge and traditions (Vygotsky, 1978). To produce transcripts relevant to the events constructed by the students, teachers, texts, technologies, we needed to understand how the instances of discourse were part of larger cultural traditions from the discipline of physics, which informed the emerging taken-for-new knowledge of physics being constructed by the students in this situation.

Data Representation, Units of Analyses, in and over Time

Transcripts provide a means to render social actions and discourse accessible for interpretation and communication. The social phenomena in the Kelly *et al.* (2001) study required various forms of representation of the students' small group work—to make sense of the students making sense of the data representations of the physics, the analysts took an ethnographic point of view and constructed multiple representations of such sense making. These forms of transcripts and data representation took different forms to answer a set of increasingly specific ethnographic questions about the sociocultural phenomena.

After providing the reader a schematic of the layout of the physical arrangement and a sample of the student recorded data (Kelly *et al.*, 2001, figures 1 and 2), the authors provided a set of timelines depicting the phase units of activity across the four student groups. Phase units are demarcations of time and activity that mark the ebb and flow of concerted and coordinated action among participants and that reflect a common content focus of the group (Green & Wallat, 1981; Kelly & Brown, 2003; Santa Barbara Classroom Discourse Group, 1995). The phase units were part of the analysis of how the participating students constructed the activities: How the students took up and reshaped the assigned educational tasks framed by the teacher and guidesheet. In this instance, by looking across the constructed phases of activity, the analysts were able to ascertain how the groups devised strategies for accomplishing the educational tasks and identify different ways that the take-up of the task provided uncommon knowledge across groups.

After showing timelines and providing analysis of the phases of activity, subsequent transcripts brought the reader into the construction of group (who counts as a member), the negotiation of position and science content, and the construction of dissenting voices within the groups. These research topics were investigated through detailed transcripts that showed the interaction of the students' verbal communication, referents, proximal distance, eye gaze, and gestures. The driving research questions (also emergent in the analysis) required different forms of transcripts (Kelly *et al.*, 2001, figures 4, 5, 6, 7, 9, 10, 11, 12) to make visible different aspects of the sociocultural phenomena in question. In this way, the study identified and made visible the value and need for multiple types of transcript of the discourse processes. Answering the ethnographically oriented questions framing the study required a range of representations of the sociocultural activity.

Building Representations of Practice, Finding Patterns, Reaching Conclusions

Building data representations and examining data across units of analyses does not constitute an ethnographic study. Following this, important work needs to be done to find patterns in the data, look for disconfirming evidence, and reach conclusions. An ethnographic point of view entails asking questions of the data, examining the cultural phenomena, and re-examining initial results through recursive cycles of interpretation. For example, in the Kelly *et al.* (2001) study, the authors identified a number of patterns through the analysis of the classroom discourse. The analyses showed that through the social construction of the events, the students negotiated their roles within the small groups, assessed candidates for knowledge in the evolving public texts, and differentially defined the academic task. Interestingly, a number of factors mediated access to the science including the interactional demands for participation. The demands of the academic task required interpreting texts and instructions, posing answerable questions, drawing from an extant body of knowledge, conducting experimental data runs, connecting physical movement to two dimensional representations, interpreting data representations, drawing inferences from data, and weighing alternative constructs. These academic tasks occurred in small groups where the dynamics of the group supported and constrained who had access to what knowledge. A key finding of the study was that dissenting voices in the students' small group conversations afforded academic opportunities for the group—that is, the disagreements and articulation of alternative interpretations provided ways of making physics knowledge intelligible and members answerable to each other for knowledge claims. Across groups the valence put on dissent led the analysts to understand the ways that the small student groups constructed differential opportunities for learning.

Interpreting Results: Value of Studying the Construction of Knowledge and Practices

Science and engineering education have been studied from a variety of perspectives. Our argument in this book is that ethnographic perspective can provide unique insights into the disciplinary discourse, practices, and knowledge of these fields in educational settings. Different research approaches offer unique and often complementary perspectives on educational issues. The study of discourse practices aims to demystify science and engineering for students. Thus, the seemingly unassailable, ever-progressing knowledge of science and engineering becomes viewed as the work that people do. Our authors ask what counts as science, failure, emotion, argument, productive discourse, and so forth, highlighting that people construct science and engineering knowledge through action in the world. The accomplishments of science and engineering are truly astonishingly; however, from a distance, or in a textbook, complex equations and seemingly obscure theories appear mysterious to students. The effect is to make students feel that science and engineering are for smart people, people smarter than they are (Lemke, 1990; Carlone, Scott, & Lowder, 2014). Ethnographic studies of the everyday practices of science and engineering across settings (for reviews, see Kelly, Carlsen, & Cunningham, 1993; Cunningham & Kelly, 2017) illuminate how such knowledge is constructed through social, epistemic, and material processes. In education, the examination of the social construction of knowledge identifies learning opportunities; shows how to build access to knowledge; demonstrates ways that identity, affiliation, and emotion support learning disciplinary knowledge and practices; and makes visible how learning to teach can be understood as an iterative, enacted set of interpretative practices.

Overview of Forthcoming Chapters

Each chapter of this book describes research methods and illustrates them with examples of empirical analyses. Overall, they address issues about how to research reform-based curricula in science and engineering. These studies adopt a common orientation, which they apply, modify, and adapt to the methodological orientation of the situated study because each has a unique set of research questions, cultural practices, participants, and goals. The studies also refine the methodological orientation and develop new understandings of how to investigate science and engineering in educational settings. As noted by Bloome *et al.* (2005), "there is a dialectical relationship between a consideration of theoretical principles and their actual application" (p. xx). Thus, while each study provides an illustrative example of interactional ethnography, it also contributes to the cumulative knowledge of field through methodological and theoretical developments.

In "Making science and gender in kindergarten," Alicia McDyre studies the ways that gender and science interacted in a kindergarten class. This study considers how the three dimensions of the *Next Generation Science Standards*—core disciplinary ideas, scientific and engineering practices, and cross-cutting themes—are constructed for young learners by the classroom culture. The study examines the discourse processes constructing student participation in scientific norms and practices in kindergarten and the emerging identities-in-practice among students. Given the lack of interest among girls in later years of schooling, McDyre seeks to understand the norms of participation, the authoring and positioning of girls, and the identities-in-practice as constructed in this science classroom. Through the analysis of discourse practices and norms over time, the study identifies how identities-in-practice manifested differently across the various literacy practices and how students chose to take up science. She identifies important methodological issues for studying the construction of identities-in-practices that concern the situatedness of instances of discourse in the social norms of the classrooms. Interestingly, the author's understanding of such norms began with negotiation of access to the research site, teacher, and students. This negotiation was ongoing as the research questions and orientation changed over time. The construction of multiple types of transcripts and analyses demonstrates the need for detailed, careful study of the construction of discursive norms and practices that situate how gender and science are constructed through interaction.

A second study set in elementary schools, Carmen Vanderhoof's chapter, "Multimodal analysis of decision making in elementary engineering," examines ways that students make decisions regarding engineering design challenges. Vanderhoof considers how decisions were made within the semiotic fields constructed using the *Engineering is Elementary* (EiE) curriculum. She uses an ethnographic perspective to consider episodes of uncertainty (moments of doubt or disagreements) as rich data sources for understanding the construction of *what counts* as engineering knowledge and practices. Her research methods focus on the multimodal nature of meaning as constructed through talk and actions (Kress, Jewitt, Ogborn, & Charalampos, 2001). The visual and written elements of the interactions inform the interpretation of how uncertainty gets resolved in student groupwork around engineering design. Through careful, detailed analysis of the physical movements tied to the verbal exchanges, Vanderhoof demonstrates how engineering design allows students with varying skillsets opportunities to be seen as successful. Methodologically, the study offers interesting insights into how disciplinary features of engineering required a multimodal approach to understand how the materiality, gesture, and discourse processes were connected in the students' construction of meaning. Vanderhoof constructed detailed transcripts at the micro-level to understand and analyze how students' proxemics, eye gaze, and physical movement related to the material building and testing of objects during engineering design challenges. These transcripts show how Vanderhoof was able to render the decision making around uncertainty intelligible for herself as the analyst and for the reader by asking ethnographic questions of the data. This chapter complements the various meso-level transcripts and analyses provided by McDyre.

A common theme across the chapters is a focus on access to knowledge and equity for all learners. Peter Licona's chapter, "Translanguaging about socioscientific issues in middle school science," considers how emergent bilingual students engaged with socioscientific issues in a 7th grade classroom. In this classroom, the two teachers (Peter as visiting guest and researcher and Juanita, the assigned classroom teacher) constructed a set of learning experiences designed to engage bilingual students in conversations about criteria for deciding the status of endangered species. Licona needed to negotiate access and learn about the educational context through extended visits during the observational phase of his study. Much like the other analysts, this negotiation was ongoing and emergent. Over time the role of researcher, observer, curriculum designer, and part-time teacher in the classroom stabilized, allowing analysis of the students' learning and take up of argumentation practices. Through the analysis of the video record, Licona identifies how the science issues discussed in class entailed more than just knowledge about the animals and their environment; they also included considerations of the moral and ethical consequences of decisions about what counts as "endangered." The discourse processes around a set of epistemic practices identified what the students brought to bear on the decisions. To fully understand how the teacher sought to make accessible the processes of constructing and critiquing arguments around socioscientific issues, Licona draws on the notion of translanguaging. This refers to the ways that the teachers describe argumentation as an epistemic practice of science through the fluid use of English and Spanish, with a focus on communicating meaning. The transcripts show how such fluidity occurs in the processes of engaging the emergent bilingual students in scientific practices.

Engineering design challenges can provide unique opportunities for students to learn both science and engineering. Yet, designs often fail. Matthew Johnson considers how failure can be a learning opportunity in "Learning through improvement from failure in elementary engineering design projects." This study uses the *Engineering is Elementary* (EiE) curriculum (as did Vanderhoof) and considers the discourse related to responses to a variety of types of failure in design. The discourse of engineering includes a set of epistemic practices; one of these is how to improve from failure. In an analysis of two different approaches to civil engineering, Johnson investigates the nature of failure in elementary engineering designs, the teacher's reactions to failure in students' designs, and how the collective actions of students and teachers support or constrain improvement in engineering design. His analysis takes two forms. First, he engages in careful analysis of failure across cases through analysis of the video records of the events. Through the construction of event maps, transcripts, and process diagrams, he identifies how students learn to improve designs. Second, he develops an analytic rubric, based on the initial video analysis and also on knowledge of engineering design processes. He then applies the rubric to both video data and the students' written notebooks. The notebooks were part of the curriculum and offered specific prompts to the students. Johnson's analysis identifies key features after a perceived failure that led to improved design: appropriate attribution, aligned goals, and relevant strategies for change. Such improvement is fostered when students are given and take up the opportunity to improve, develop, and implement productive strategies, and make fair comparisons across multiple prototypes. This study shows how the written artifact, while the product of careful discourse analysis of the failure events, also offers a parallel and alternative assessment of the ways to learn to improve from failure.

Analysis of classroom discourse can contribute to understandings of in-the-moment assessment. Teachers use many types of assessment, some of which can be used to modify their discourse practices as they read and interpret the events in the classroom. In "An interactional ethnography perspective to analyze informal formative assessments (IFAs) to build epistemic and conceptual coherence in science learning," Asli Sezen-Barrie and Rachel Mulvaney analyze how a college mathematics professor sought to help students interpret inscriptions of climate data. The analysts were faced with the challenge of understanding how multiple actors, each with different roles and knowledge, can come together to improve the educational experience for the participating college students. The study draws on knowledge of the mathematics instructor, climate scientists, and educational researchers, each of whom understand the relevant phenomena (mathematical representations, climate science, classroom discourse) partially and in different ways. Through the use of event maps to situate the instructional conversations, the analysts come to see the importance of conceptual and epistemic coherence in instruction for providing access to the climate science. But how can such coherence be built in instructional conversations given the variability and lack of knowledge of students' knowledge prior to engaging in such an emergent conversation? Sezen-Barrie and Mulvaney address this by pointing to the need for informal formative assessment—assessments of students' knowledge emerging in the ongoing flow of meaning making. To understand the ways that informal formative assessment can be understood, Sezen-Barrie and Mulvaney draw from multiple disciplinary backgrounds and seek to make sense of the meaning making in the discursive construction of interpretation of climate science inscriptions.

While Sezen-Barrie and Mulvaney sought to understand students' conceptual and epistemic knowledge of climate change, Elizabeth Hufnagel takes a different perspective by focusing on students' affective responses to ecological crises. The three-dimensional learning of the *Next Generation Science Standards*, advocates for students learning disciplinary core ideas, crosscutting concepts, and scientific and engineering practices. This sort of learning may include engaging students in socioscientific issues, such as ecological degradation and other environmental issues with an emotional valence. In "Emotional discourse as constructed in an environmental science course," Hufnagel considers students' emotional reactions to climate change, a topic with serious implications for our planet. Unlike many ideological portrayals of science that situate science as objective and beyond the realm of emotion, Hufnagel takes seriously students' feelings for the consequences of climate change. She draws from sociolinguistics, social psychology, and the sociology of emotions to examine the social interactions supporting the construction of emotional expressions communicated in an undergraduate science course. Methodologically, the study identifies the need to consider the interactional, situated, intertextual, and consequential nature of emotional discourse across timescales. Hufnagel presents interesting findings about how students' emotions get evoked and manifest themselves, but to do so, she provides insight into her logic of inquiry—that is, the reasoning processes of her ethnographic perspective. She builds various event maps and constructions of classroom life from her large data set of the science classroom to find salient contrast points across perceptions, realities, and emotions. Her ethnographic orientation and the research methods permit her study to show how the "aboutness" of emotional expressions provides insights into students' perceptions of climate change as distanced, both temporally and spatially, from their lives.

Even for studies of student discourse, teachers of science and engineering play a key role in orchestrating the norms and expectations for how conversations get constructed. Arzu Tanis Ozcelik and Scott McDonald draw from Goodwin's (1994) notion of professional vision to consider how ways of seeing can be developed in preservice secondary science teachers. This chapter, "Discourse of professional pedagogical vision in teacher education," uses ethnographic methods to collect and analyze multiple data sources to investigate how preservice teachers develop professional vision around ambitious science. Although they focus on the emerging professional vision across contexts, Tanis Ozcelik and McDonald use participant observation and draw from multiple data sources such as ethnographic fieldnotes, video recordings of a teaching methods course, and documents and artifacts from the assignments and course materials. They apply a detailed coding scheme across the data set to show how professional pedagogical vision is negotiated both in the moment and over time in the discussions of teaching events. This study thus exemplifies the need to consider how knowledge (in this case professional vision), while emergent and contingent, is constructed in moment-to-moment interactions, each shaping and being shaped by the common understandings of the group. Further still, such moment-to-moment interactions are part of an ongoing cultural history of science, teaching, and teacher education. The study offers insight into the construction of professional pedagogical vision by providing examples of data inscription across time, events, and contexts. The authors render their thinking visible by providing insights into how their construction of the inscriptions of the educational phenomena made the emergence of aspects of professional pedagogical vision visible to them as analysts, and us as readers.

Developing ways of engaging students in science and engineering entails an ongoing process of learning and re-creation of oneself and one's knowledge and theories of learning. Developing such a reflective practice orientation takes time and effort and can be enhanced by professional development conversations. Amy Ricketts examines such issues in "Analyzing the generative nature of science teachers' professional development discourse." This study primarily concerns understanding how teacher communities can develop a culture of reflective critique. Building on sociocultural learning theory, Ricketts takes an interactional ethnographic lens to study the discourse of teacher learning. For the most part, sociocultural theories have informed studies of student learning; application of this perspective to research of teacher learning and knowledge has not yet been fully realized. Bringing such learning theory to the study of teachers in critical dialogue, Ricketts investigates teacher inquiry communities that build common, discursive practices that foster meaningful conversations. Ricketts sought and negotiated access to a setting that would get beyond assumptions about collegiality and surface agreements in teacher professional development settings. In this setting, Ricketts found professional conversations that aimed to develop ways of learning through probing, pressing, and challenging colleagues' ideas and claims. The study examines reflective critical discourse during sustained, professional development conversation over the course of an academic year. Bringing perspectives from the learning sciences and discourse analysis to the study of dialogues around evidence surfaced new methodological challenges. Ricketts identifies the need to re-examine how the interactional contexts are constructed and reconstructed in each instance of groups meeting, and even within the same meeting, and the need to consider the relevant unit of analysis for her emerging research questions. The salient issues supporting critical discourse included stance, availability of relevant resources, and tools. To understand the conversation routines of the teacher learning group, Ricketts looks across different units of analysis. In so doing, she was able to construct the meso-level analysis after looking in detail at the conversational moves.

Two scholars provide commentary on the book chapters. These authors were invited because of their knowledge of ethnography and discourse analysis and their experience working across perspectives in international education settings. Audra Skukauskaite provides a commentary in her chapter "Constructing transparency in designing and conducting multilayered research in science and engineering education." As a sociolinguist and outsider to the field of science and engineering education, she enters the analysis of the chapters by posing a set of ethnographic questions about the produced texts. This stance provides her a basis to ask of each of the chapters what was studied, how it was studied, and why such studies matter. In this way, she poses a set of ethnographic questions of the studies presented in the chapters. This ethnography of the textual representation of research provides a basis for her understanding of the ways the studies present exemplars of transparent research practices.

Kristiina Kumpulainen provides an alternative perspective on ways to read and understand interactional ethnography as interpreted and instantiated the studies presented in this book by drawing from Bakhtin's (1981) notions of chronotopes and addressivity. She applies understandings of chronotopes to examine "times and spaces through which particular types of educational processes and opportunities are made possible in the continuum of the past, present and future" (p. 257, this volume). Through an analysis of each empirical study, she identifies ways that the local cultures of science and engineering provide opportunities for engagement, learning, and identity development. Addressivity refers to the potential audiences that are addressed by the chapters of this book. Kumpulainen identifies a primary audience of educational researchers, but also recognizes the audiences of teachers, curriculum developers, and policy-makers interesting in learning about the situated nature of educational opportunity.

Critical Methodological Considerations for Research in Education

Studies of classroom discourse pose a number of methodological challenges, given the large data sets and need for detailed analysis. Across the chapters in this book, the authors take up these challenges and create plausible ways to investigate the construction of everyday life in educational settings. Through the process of explaining the research orientation and approaches, the authors make visible a number of critical methodological considerations proposed by Kelly (2014b):

(a) The importance of organizing research to situate discourse processes in sociocultural practices.
(b) The need to build ways of representing social action and practices to render transparent how and in what ways everyday life is constructed by participants.
(c) The value of making visible systematicity in analysis for the reader and interpreter of the research.
(d) The usefulness of research to inform and potentially change educational practices and policies.
(e) The recognition of the contingency of our own language (Rorty, 1989)—the intellectual humbleness and reflexiveness of each research tradition.

Across the chapters in this volume, the authors address these methodological considerations for research in education, making visible how they are relevant to the application of interactional ethnography and to the study of education more generally.

First, across the studies, it is clear that *discourse processes are situated in and lead to the construction of sociocultural practice*. This is an important dimension to the analyses. Although the uses of discourse in any one instance may be indicative of a practice, it is only through sustained use and concerted activity that the practice becomes established among members of a discourse community and visible to the analysts. Each instance of use needs to be examined in the relevant context of use. The examples in this book illustrate how to look over time and across levels of analyses. For example, Licona's chapter considers how the development of learning to argue occurred through numerous classroom events over time. His analysis considers the eventual products of research: Spoken and written student arguments about controversial socioscientific issues. Yet, the analysis began with fieldnotes of the classroom discourse norms, and moved to the acculturation processes of learning how to argue with evidence. Through a focus on the epistemic practices leading to the learning of how to argue, Licona came to recognize the importance of translanguaging as a pedagogical practice in the classroom that provided access for the students. In a second example, Ricketts recognized the multiple patterns over time that led to specific instances of generative teacher professional talk. In this case, an analysis of the emergent discursive practices of the professional learning group, including the uses of resources, tools, and situationally defined expertise, informed the interpretation of the conversation routines that support teacher generative talk and learning. In these examples and the others in the book, the specific situating of discourse processes in a broader context of use shows how discourse processes both shape social practices and are shaped by those practices.

Second, there are *different ways of representing social action and practices and rendering procedures transparent.* Analysts need to choose how to represent social actions to their audience. Each representation of an event, episode, or exchange entails the analysts making decisions about what and how to communicate with the audience of the research. We see in these studies ways of "zooming in" to understand instances of action, and "zooming out" to view patterns of activity. In this way, the reader or audience for the research is able to understand the evidentiary basis for the claims put forth. One illustrative example comes from the chapter by Tanis Ozcelik and McDonald. The analyses of the developing professional pedagogical vision spanned semesters in the teacher candidates' academic experience. The chapter examines how different experiences and discourse practices supported the development of coming to see teaching and learning in new ways. This study provided multiple representations of data selection, analyses, and conclusions (see Figures 8.2 and 8.3). By providing such examples, the authors offer insights into the logic of the analyses supporting the over-time study. An example of microanalysis, along shorter timescales, is provided in the Vanderhoof chapter. She sought to understand how the detailed conversation cues of students working in small groups could provide understandings of the ways that elementary students resolve uncertainty in decisions regarding procedural moves in engineering design. In this study, Vanderhoof, after situating instances of talk in ongoing practice, zoomed in and provides detailed sociolinguistic analysis of the construction of the academic tasks and engineering knowledge. Her study offers examples of how the physical orientation and eye gaze, as shown in Figure 3.3, and uses of photographs of the students, as shown in Figure 3.4, embody their proposed ideas and were central to understanding the social construction of the groups' engineering results. Across these and others examples, the reader is invited to make informed decisions about the nature of the research and what can be inferred by the conclusions.

Third, interactional ethnography, and qualitative research more generally, needs to *make visible and show how to make analyses systematic.* The complexity of classroom life suggests the need for researchers to be creative and adapt to events as constructed *in situ.* The required improvisation should include some degree of systematicity to develop credibility and render the analytic procedures transparent for other researchers. This is an important dimension to interactional ethnography. Events in everyday life can be interpreted many ways. A short clip of video may be misleading, or at least, suggestive of a particular interpretation from a particular point of view, under certain conditions. To address this concern, an interactional ethnographer often creates an anchor to explore the roots and routes of the observed moment by backward mapping across times, configuration of actors, and intertextually tied events. Thus, by tracing the histories leading to a particular moment in time, the interactional ethnographer constructs a local data set for developing theoretical warranted accounts of a particular interpretation or theoretical inferences assigned to the observed bit of life (Hymes, 1974). Looking across instances, finding patterns, and checking for discrepant events and interpretations build trust in the researchers' presentations. Examples of this systematicity can be found across the chapters in this book. For example, McDyre sought to understand kindergarten students' identities-in-practice. To make sure the instances of student authoring could be seen in patterned ways, she created extensive event maps across levels of analysis. These include building up from message units, to action and interaction units, to sequence units, and phase units (for details of the discourse units, see Green & Wallat, 1979, 1981; Kelly & Crawford, 1996; Brown & Spang, 2008; Appendix in this volume). Examples of data analysis showing this systematicity can be found in Figures 2.1 and 2.3. In this way, patterns of concerted activity and discourse practice can be seen as constructed across different units of analysis. Importantly, this allowed for the testing of initial interpretative claims (hypotheses) about the students' lifeworlds in kindergarten. In another example, Johnson built out a process to understand how to interpret responses to failure. He began with careful analysis of the video record, again building event maps denoting the teacher and students' activities over time for more than just instances of failure (Table 5.4). Through this process, and building from relevant literature from the empirical study of engineering, he developed a rubric to identify discourse events related to use of failure in the classrooms. He then could compare this to the students' written record in their notebooks. This demonstrates how a situated study of discourse practice can be made systematic, transparent, and potentially transferable to other engineering contexts.

Fourth, research in education has an obligation to provide thoughtful interpretations of educational phenomena, but also, to the extent possible, to provide ideas for social *change in specific educational settings*. These changes can be informed through the process and results of research. Interactional ethnography has much to offer the field, both through descriptive work and for building ideas for educational change. While interactional ethnography has merits in its own right regarding ways of developing understandings of the forms of life constructed in sociocultural situations, it also makes contributions that inform educational practices through research (Frank, Dixon, & Green, 1999). Each of the eight empirical chapters and two commentary chapters speak to the potential for implications for education. Two illustrative examples speak to a serious educational and societal problem: Human contribution to climate change. Sezen-Barrie and Mulvaney use discourse analysis to understand how knowledge from multiple disciplines can help researchers make sense of students' knowledge of climate change concepts during instruction in a college course. The analysis examines how the informal formative assessments provide ways for teachers to learn how to understand students' understanding "on the fly" in instructional settings. This allows them to change their teaching to reflect student understanding and learning. Hufnagel also addresses students' learning about climate change. Her study provides a new and unique approach to the examination of students' emotion by investigating how emotions are evoked and expressed in the everyday life of a college course. Her results make clear that students' emotions in science learning, particularly as related to (potentially overwhelming) ecological degradation, need to be taken seriously and built in to thinking about curriculum, instruction, and assessment.

Finally, interactional ethnography acknowledges the importance of reflexivity and how commitments to theoretical positions and choices about actions for research may lead to alternative interpretations of the phenomena. Rorty (1989) called this *recognizing the contingency of our own language*. Research takes a textual form in the context of presentation, and in doing so, commits to certain vocabularies and ways of conceptualizing phenomena. This perspective takes a view that meanings of knowing and categories of concepts "are created in the public domain in the context of collective situations and activities" (Toulmin, 1999, p. 58). Our research perspective, like all others, populates an ontology—a world of concepts that form the basis for thinking about educational phenomena. The objects of thought acquire properties by virtue of human activity (Bakhurst, 1997, p. 159), which includes social significance where meanings are constructed and interactively acknowledged (Bloome *et al.*, 2005). Such activity includes the discursive work of research groups and traditions where meanings are defined, evoked, and socially negotiated around purposeful activity aimed at understanding sociocultural phenomena. Such discursive work manifests in public texts—verbal, written, and symbolic—that inscribe an ontology of research meanings. Through ongoing conversations about research (Kelly, 2006), reference to previous public texts codify an ontology of a group (e.g., members of a research group, discipline, or sub-discipline) through use and shared assumptions of meaning (Wittgenstein, 1958). The concepts in a given ontology "are not simply dictated by the findings of the laboratory, or by any sort of sense-experience. Their origin is social and historical and represents some enduring human interest" (Lewis, 1929, p. 6). The ontology is populated by a set of concepts, emerging from human interests, and constructed by social groups with histories and common cultural experiences (Vygotsky, 1978). Examining ways that texts (verbal and spoken discourse, signs and symbols) are referenced, taken up, appropriated, and reinterpreted identifies how concepts populate an ontology (Kelly, 2016b).

From this perspective, each theoretical tradition builds an ontology of constructs put in place by previous scholars, interprets these constructs, and modifies or changes them as needed for the work at hand given the current constraints. Each time, texts are produced by drawing from and making use of previous texts and their interpretation; thus, intertextuality serves a method to identify socially salient concepts comprising an ontology of a research tradition. The studies reported in this volume recognize the contingency of such choices. Collectively, they make visible the importance of understanding the limitations of any one method or framework for observing, describing, analyzing, and interpreting processes, meanings, and practices in educational settings. These studies also demonstrate how interactional ethnography can support analyses of different phenomena, social contexts, and configurations of actors in particular social settings that shape what constitutes science and engineering in particular educational contexts.

References

Agar, M. (1994). *Language shock: Understanding the culture of conversation*. New York: William Morrow & Company.

Baker, W. D., Green, J. L., & Skukauskaite, A. (2008). Video-enabled ethnographic research: A microethnographic perspective. In G. Walford (Ed.), *How to do educational ethnography* (pp. 77–114). London: Tufnell Press.

Bakhtin, M. (1981). *Dialogic imagination: Four essays*. Austin, TX: University of Texas Press.

Bakhtin, M. (1986). *Speech genres and other late essays*. Austin, TX: University of Texas Press.

Bakhurst, D. (1997). Activity, consciousness, and communication. In M. Cole, Y. Engeström, & O. Vasquez (Eds.), *Mind, culture, and activity: Seminal papers from the Laboratory of Comparative Human Cognition* (pp. 147–163). Cambridge, UK: Cambridge University Press.

Bazerman, C. (1988). *Shaping written knowledge: The genre and activity of the experimental article in science*. Madison, WI: University of Wisconsin Press.

Bloome, D., Carter, S., Christian, B., Otto, S., & Shuart-Faris, N. (2005). *Discourse analysis and the study of classroom language and literacy events: A microethnographic approach*. Mahwah, NJ: Erlbaum.

Bloome, D., & Green, J. L. (2018). Ethnography. In B. Frey (Ed.), *The Sage encyclopedia of educational research, measurement and evaluation* (pp. 616–622). London: Sage Publications.

Boyd, R., Gasper, P., & Trout, J. D. (Eds.). (1991). *The philosophy of science.* Cambridge, MA: MIT Press.

Brown, B. A., & Spang, E. (2008). Double talk: Synthesizing everyday and science language in the classroom. *Science Education, 92*, 708–732.

Carlone, H. B., Scott, C. M., & Lowder, C. (2014). Becoming (less) scientific: A longitudinal study of students' identity work from elementary to middle school science. *Journal of Research in Science Teaching, 51*(7), 836–869.

Castanheira, M. L., Crawford, T., Dixon, C. N., & Green, J. L. (2001). Interactional ethnography: An approach to studying the social construction of literate practices. *Linguistics and Education, 11*(4), 353–400.

Cazden, C. B., John, V. P., & Hymes, D. (Eds.). (1972). *Functions of language in the classroom.* New York: Teachers College Press.

Clifford, J., & Marcus, G. E. (1986). *Writing culture: The poetics and politics of ethnography.* Berkeley, CA: University of California Press.

Corsaro, W. (1985). *Friendship and peer culture in the early years.* Norwood, NJ: Ablex.

Cunningham, C. M., & Kelly, G. J. (2017). Epistemic practices of engineering for education. *Science Education 101*, 486–505. doi.org/10.1002/sce.21271.

Ellen, R. F. (1984). *Ethnographic research: A guide to feneral conduct.* New York: Academic.

Emerson, R. M., Fretz, R. I., & Shaw, L. L. (1995). *Writing ethnographic fieldnotes.* Chicago, IL: University of Chicago Press.

Fairclough, N. (1992). *Discourse and social change.* Boston, MA: Blackwell Publishing.

Fairclough, N. (2010). General introduction. In *Critical discourse analysis. 2nd edition* (pp.1–21). New York: Routledge.

Frank, C., Dixon, C. N., & Green, J. L. (Eds.). (1999). Classrooms as cultures: Understanding the constructed nature of life in classrooms. *Primary Voices*, 7(3).

Garfinkel, H., Lynch, M., & Livingston, E. (1981). The work of discovering science construed with materials from the optically discovered pulsar. *Philosophy of the Social Sciences, 11*, 131–158.

Gee, J. P., & Green, J. L. (1998). Discourse analysis, learning, and social practice: A methodological study. *Review of Research in Education, 23*, 119–169.

Goodwin, C. (1994). Professional vision. *American Anthropologist, 96*(3), 606–663.

Green, J. L. (1983). Research on teaching as a linguistic process: A state of the art. *Review of Research in Education, 10*, 151–252.

Green, J. L., & Bloome, D. (2004). Ethnography and ethnographers of and in education: A situated perspective. In J. Flood, S. Brice Heath, & D. Lapp (Eds.), *Handbook of research on teaching literacy through the communicative and visual arts* (pp. 181–202). New York: Macmillan.

Green, J. L., & Bridges, S. M. (2018). Interactional ethnography. In F. Fischer, C. E. Hmelo-Silver, S. R. Goldman, & P. Reimann (Eds.), *International handbook of the learning sciences* (pp. 475–488). New York: Routledge.

Green, J. L., & Castanheira, M. L. (2012). Exploring classroom life and student learning: An interactional ethnographic approach. In B. Kaur (Ed.), *Understanding teaching and learning: Classroom research revisited* (pp. 53–65). Rotterdam, NL: Sense.

Green, J. L., Dai, Y., Joo, J., Williams, E., Liu, A., & Lu, S. C. Y. (2015). Interdisciplinary dialogues as a site for reflexive exploration of conceptual understandings of teaching–learning relationships. *Pedagogies: An International Journal, 10*(1), 86–103.

Green, J. L., & Dixon, C. (Eds.). (1993). Santa Barbara Classroom Discourse Group [Special issue]. *Linguistics & Education, 5*(3&4).

Green, J. L., & Joo, J. (Ji Eun). (2016). Classroom interaction and situated learning. In S. Wortham, D. Kim, & S. May (Eds.), *Discourse and education, Encyclopedia of language and education. 3rd edition* (pp. 55–70). Switzerland: Springer International Publishing.

Green, J. L., Skukauskaite, A., & Baker, W. D. (2012). Ethnography as epistemology: An introduction to educational ethnography. In J. Arthur, M. Waring, R. Coe, & L. V. Hedges (Eds.), *Research methodologies and methods in education* (pp. 309–321). London: Sage Publications.

Green, J. L., & Wallat, C. (1979). What is an instructional context? An exploratory analysis of conversational shifts over time. In O. Garnica & M. King (Eds.), *Language, children and society*. New York: Pergamon.

Green, J. L., & Wallat, C. (1981). Mapping instructional conversations: A sociolinguistic ethnography. In J. L. Green & C. Wallat (Eds.), *Ethnography and language in educational settings* (pp. 161–205). Norwood, NJ: Ablex.

Green, J. L., Weade, R., & Graham, K. (1988). Lesson construction and student participation: A sociolinguistic analysis. In J. L. Green & J. O. Harker (Eds.), *Multiple perspective analyses of classroom discourse* (pp. 11–47). Norwood, NJ: Ablex.

Gumperz, J. J. (1982). *Discourse strategies*. Cambridge, UK: Cambridge University Press.

Gumperz, J. J. (2001). Interactional sociolinguistics: A personal perspective. In D. Schiffrin, D. Tannen, & H. E. Hamilton (Eds.), *Handbook of discourse analysis* (pp. 215–228). Malden, MA: Blackwell.

Gumperz, J. J., & Hymes, D. (Eds.). (1986). *Directions in sociolinguistics: The ethnography of communication*. New York: Blackwell.

Heap, J. L. (1995). The status of claims in "qualitative" educational research. *Curriculum Inquiry, 25*(3), 271–292.

Heath, S. (1982). Ethnography in education: Defining the essential. In P. Gilmore & A. Glatthorn (Eds.), *Children in and out of school* (pp. 33–58). Washington, DC: Center for Applied Linguistics.

Heath, S. B., & Street, B. V. (2008). *On ethnography: Approaches to language and literacy research. Language & literacy (NCRLL)*. New York: Teachers College Press.

Hymes, D. (1974). *Foundations of sociolinguistics: An ethnographic approach*. Philadelphia, PA: University of Pennsylvania.

Jaworski, A., & Coupland, N. (Eds.). (1999). *The discourse reader*. New York: Routledge.

Kelly, G. J. (2006) Epistemology and educational research. In J. L. Green, G. Camilli, & P. Elmore (Eds.), *Handbook of complementary methods in education research* (pp. 33–55). Mahwah, NJ: Lawrence Erlbaum Associates.

Kelly, G. J. (2008). Inquiry, activity, and epistemic practice. In R. Duschl & R. Grandy (Eds.), *Teaching scientific inquiry: Recommendations for research and implementation* (pp. 99–117; 288–291). Rotterdam: Sense Publishers.

Kelly, G. J. (2014a). Discourse practices in science learning and teaching. In N. G. Lederman, & S. K. Abell (Eds.), *Handbook of research on science education, Vol. 2* (pp. 321–336). Mahwah, NJ: Lawrence Erlbaum Associates.

Kelly, G. J. (2014b). Analysing classroom activities: Theoretical and methodological considerations. In C. Bruguière, A. Tiberghien, & P. Clément (Eds.), *Topics and trends in current science education: 9th ESERA conference selected contributions* (pp. 353–368). Dordrecht: Springer.

Kelly, G. J. (2016a). Learning science: Discourse practices. In S. Wortham, D. Kim, & S. May (Eds.), *Encyclopedia of language and education, Vol. 3: Discourse and education* (pp. 1–15). New York: Springer.
Kelly, G. J. (2016b). Methodological considerations for the study of epistemic cognition in practice. In J. A. Greene, W. A. Sandoval, & I. Braten (Eds.), *Handbook of epistemic cognition* (pp. 393–408). New York: Routledge.
Kelly, G. J., & Brown, C. M. (2003). Communicative demands of learning science through technological design: Third grade students' construction of solar energy devices. *Linguistics & Education, 13*(4), 483–532.
Kelly, G. J., Carlsen, W. S., & Cunningham, C. M. (1993). Science education in sociocultural context: Perspectives from the sociology of science. *Science Education, 77*, 207–220.
Kelly, G. J., & Chen, C. (1999). The sound of music: Constructing science as sociocultural practices through oral and written discourse. *Journal of Research in Science Teaching, 36*(8), 883–915.
Kelly, G. J., & Crawford, T. (1996). Students' interaction with computer representations: Analysis of discourse in laboratory groups. *Journal of Research in Science Teaching, 33*(7), 693–707.
Kelly, G. J., Crawford, T., & Green, J. L. (2001). Common tasks and uncommon knowledge: Dissenting voices in the discursive construction of physics across small laboratory groups. *Linguistics & Education, 12*(2), 135–174.
Kelly, G. J., & Green, J. L. (1998). The social nature of knowing: Toward a sociocultural perspective on conceptual change and knowledge construction. In B. Guzzetti & C. Hynd (Eds.), *Perspectives on conceptual change: Multiple ways to understand knowing and learning in a complex world* (pp. 145–181). Mahwah, NJ: Lawrence Erlbaum Associates.
Knorr-Cetina, K. (1995). Laboratory studies: The cultural approach to the study of science. In S. Jasanoff, G. E. Markle, J. C. Peterson, & T. Pinch (Eds.), *Handbook of science and technology studies* (pp. 140–166). Thousand Oaks, CA: Sage Publications.
Kress, G., Jewitt, C., Ogborn, J., & Charalampos, T. (2001). *Multimodal teaching and learning: The rhetorics of the science classroom.* New York: Continuum.
Lemke, J. L. (1990). *Talking science: Language, learning and values.* Norwood, NJ: Ablex.
Lewis, C. I. (1929). *Mind and the world-order: Outline of a theory of knowledge.* New York: Charles Scribner's Sons.
Lynch, M. (1992). Extending Wittgenstein: The pivotal move from epistemology to the sociology of science. In A. Pickering (Ed.), *Science as practice and culture* (pp. 215–265). Chicago, IL: University of Chicago Press.
NGSS Lead States (2013). *Next generation science standards: For states, by states.* Washington, DC: The National Academies Press.
Rogers, R., Schaenen, I., Schott, C., O'Brien, K., Trigos-Carrillo, L., Starkey, K., & Chasteen, C. C. (2016). Critical discourse analysis in education: A review of the literature, 2004 to 2012. *Review of Educational Research, 86*(4), 1192–1226.
Rorty, R. (1989). *Contingency, irony, and solidarity.* New York: Cambridge University Press.
Rorty, R. (1991). *Objectivity, relativism, and truth.* New York: Cambridge University Press.
Santa Barbara Classroom Discourse Group [Green, J. L., Dixon, C., Floriani, A., Bradley, M., Paxton, S., Mattern, C., & Bergamo, H.] (1992a). Constructing literacy in classrooms: Literate action as social accomplishment. In H. Marshall (Ed.), *Redefining student learning: Roots of educational change* (pp. 119–150). Norwood, NJ: Ablex.

Santa Barbara Classroom Discourse Group [Dixon, C., de la Cruz, E., Green, J. L., Lin, L., & Brandts, L.] (1992b). Do you see what I see? The referential and intertextual nature of classroom life. *Journal of Classroom Interaction, 27*(2), 29–36.

Santa Barbara Classroom Discourse Group [Floriani, A., Heras, A. I., Franquiz, M., Yeager, B., Jennings, L., Green, J. L., & Dixon, C.] (1995). Two languages, one community: An examination of educational opportunities. In R. F. Macias & R. G. Garcia Ramos (Eds.), *Changing schools for changing students: An anthology of research on language minorities, schools & society* (pp. 63–106). Berkeley, CA: UC Linguistic Minority Research Institute.

Smith, D. (1996). Telling the truth after postmodernism. *Symbolic Interaction, 19*(3), 171–202.

Strauss, S., & Feiz, P. (2014). *Discourse analysis: Putting our worlds into words.* New York: Routledge.

Toulmin, S. (1972). *Human understanding, Vol. 1: The collective use and evolution of concepts.* Princeton, NJ: Princeton University Press.

Toulmin, S. (1999). Knowledge as shared procedures. In Y. Engeström, R. Miettinen, & R.-L. Punamaki (Eds.), *Perspectives on activity theory* (pp. 53–69). Cambridge, UK: Cambridge University Press.

Vygotsky, L. (1978). *Mind in society: The development of higher psychological processes.* Cambridge, MA: Harvard.

Wittgenstein, L. (1958). *Philosophical investigations. 3rd edition.* (G. E. M. Anscombe, Trans.). New York: Macmillan Publishing.

2

MAKING SCIENCE AND GENDER IN KINDERGARTEN

Alicia M. McDyre

Positioning of Young Girls in Science

As we watch television or scroll through news stories we are more likely to see advertisements connecting women or girls to STEM related images now than in the past. We hear more about women's accomplishments than we have in the past, in part due to our changing political society, but also in part because women are developing a louder voice and are demanding to be heard. Historically women and girls were not the universal image brought to mind when picturing a scientist or engineer. Women and girls have been marginalized within the space of science (e.g., Brickhouse, Lowery, & Schultz, 2000; Longino, 1993; Sadker & Sadker, 1995), traditionally positioned with less power and intellect within the science classroom (Sadker & Sadker, 1995). Researchers suggest that girls learn that their scientific identity may be antagonistic to their gendered identity, which may be enforced by how they are positioned in the curriculum and classroom (Sadker & Sadker, 1995). Even with an increase of portrayals of woman scientists and engineers gender gaps are still present and more work needs to be done in order to increase our understanding of how women are positioned in science and engineering. Typically, most gender research in this area has been performed while girls are in their middle school years/adolescence (Carlone, 2004), but I would argue that in order for us to understand why girls are not doing as well in science or are not interested in science in middle school and high school, we need to look at how they have historically been positioned throughout their formative years of schooling beginning in kindergarten. Therefore, my study focused on a community of young learners and their positioning and identity within that kindergarten classroom community during science instruction.

Science Reform, Practices, and Positioning

The newest science reform documents focus on the integration of core disciplinary ideas, scientific and engineering practices, and cross-cutting concepts (NRC, 2012). Each of these areas is important to learning science; however, the study presented in this chapter focused primarily on scientific and engineering practices. As students participate in classroom science, sharing evidence from an investigation or their ideas about a claim, they are taking a brave step into the practices of science. They are trying out new words, patterns of speech, and ways of making sense within their classroom science community. They may be asserting new ideas or disagreeing with a classmate and it is within this space that girls may be faced with challenges of positioning and authoring.

The science classroom as a whole consists of a community of learners, each with their own thoughts, comfort levels, and ways of doing science, including the teachers. Lave and Wenger (1991) called this community, a community-of-practice, where the learners are learning from the environment and their interactions with others. The kindergarten classroom is socially constructed by the ways the inhabitants are doing science associated with the disciplinary-based practices of science (Kelly & Chen, 1999; Reveles, Cordova, & Kelly, 2004). These practices are connected to not only content, but also to context (Reveles *et al.*, 2004; Tobin, Elmesky, Seiler, Cox, & Carpenter, 2005). When thinking about the context of the kindergarten classroom, situated within the practices of science (NRC, 2012), I view identity work as an essential element of how the practices of science are taken up or not taken up within the community. I align myself with the construct of identity as a fluid entity that is constructed socially within community, and therefore termed identities-in-practice (Lave & Wenger, 1991). This entity is affected by the positioning of oneself or how one is positioned within the community. Specifically, how students' discursive identities are formed based upon the scientific literacy practices that students are surrounded with in the classroom (Brown, Reveles, & Kelly, 2005). Therefore, my work represents the ways members of the science community in the kindergarten classroom are positioned at different times throughout the day, the week, the year, and how the identities-in-practice move fluidly as a result of the positioning. This is not a new model, in fact Barton, Tan, and Rivet (2008) used a similar model when looking at hybrid spaces for identity development among middle school girls in science, but it is a new model with respect to looking at kindergarten girls' access to science instruction with a focus on the scientific practice of constructing explanations with evidence.

The orienting theory which I used to examine the fluidity of identity consisted of a grounded sociolinguistic approach and the analysis was informed by educational ethnography. This chapter is situated within the context of a study that showed the ways in which kindergarteners participated in science. This was shown by the ways in which norms were established in the classroom, and by analyzing how girls were positioned or not positioned as science learners. Within this context, the use of ethnographic methods was essential as learning, in this study, was defined as changing, iterative, and situated in context and environment around the learner (Brown, Reveles, & Kelly, 2005; Lave & Wenger, 1991; NRC, 2012).

Methods and Flexibility

Due to the ways that identities-in-practice are constructed through cultural practices, I chose to utilize an ethnographic approach in order to capture what the group proposed, communicated, and interactionally accomplished. In order to justly serve this theoretical approach to the relevant phenomena, the research methods should be used to accurately depict the interpretive, iterative, and dynamic actions of interpretation. In this way, the researcher is situated as a participant observer within the cultural system, as noted by Denzin and Lincoln (2005): "Qualitative research is a situated activity that locates the observer in the world" (p. 3). Researchers drawing from an ethnographic perspective do not seek to understand variables in isolation, but instead examine the variables in their natural context without manipulating them. Therefore, ethnographers will interpret phenomena from the vantage point of the participant (Glesne, 2006) and let patterns emerge from the data. Due to my orienting frame, I view learning and identity as fluid and dynamic; what counts as science to one community is an empirical question, as is the performance of identity.

Due to the use of ethnographic methods the following approaches to data collection were chosen for my study: video recording of student discourse, student interviews, ethnographic field notes, photographs of student science notebooks and additional artifacts, teacher informal interviews, and a parent/guardian questionnaire. Using ethnographic methods required longitudinal observations and, at its best, participant observation techniques to report on the shared culture between the researcher and participants (Geertz, 2000).

In order to begin such a study, a researcher needs to find a site that allows for the intrusion of a participant observer over time, as well as a willing community of participants that demonstrate a connection to the focal point of the study. My entry into my study site occurred over a two-year period of time. In the beginning, I was a participant in a video study group where members learned about building content storylines while using methods for building explanations from evidence. Members of this study group volunteered to record each other's teaching and came together to analyze the video. While I was working in this group I had the privilege of working with a kindergarten teacher who was trying to implement some of the strategies discussed in our meetings. She had previously worked with another university researcher in her classroom as she was trying to implement the four strands of proficiency – to know, use, and interpret scientific explanations, to generate and evaluate scientific evidence and explanations, to understand the nature and development of scientific knowledge, and to participate productively in scientific practices and discourse – in science (Duschl, Schweingruber, & Shouse, 2007) in her classroom and was asking questions about delivery and student voice. The kindergarten teacher, Caroline, asked me to help her with an investigation and as I began to see her inquisitive nature and desire to try new things I began to think that this kindergarten classroom would be an ideal site for my research study. After the study group disbanded, I asked Caroline if she would be willing to consider taking part in another research project. She agreed and we met a few times before the next school year to discuss her kindergarten science curriculum, lesson planning, what the term participant observer meant, where I would sit in the classroom, where I could plug in my recording devices, how I would introduce the study to the students and parents and obtain their consent, and how frequently I would be in her classroom. After seeking and obtaining research, participant, and school board approval, Caroline and I felt ready to begin the study.

Gaining access into the actual classroom community was something that I knew had to be negotiated with the students and other teachers in the space. On this and many following occasions, I paused or took some time to check-in with Caroline, asking her if I was in her way, or if she needed me to sit somewhere else or change the way I helped the students. Each time we had a chance to talk, Caroline was excited to have me there and expressed her appreciation for my help. Gaining access with the students did not take as long as I had expected but did fluctuate in authenticity over time. The best way that I can explain the changes that occurred is to begin with defining my role as a participant observer in the kindergarten classroom. A participant observer (Spradley, 1980; Geertz, 1973, 2000) "learns" the culture by being ensconced in the culture, i.e., looking for meanings of science and practices associated with science in the setting and girls' participation within and against these meanings. As Spradley (1980) explained, a participant observer may learn from cultural behavior, cultural artifacts, and speech messages used by the participants within the community throughout their daily activities. The goal of participant observation is to observe with direction, while allowing for new patterns and practices to unfold and to be able to zoom in and zoom out throughout the process in order to achieve a more complete analysis of the culture. During participant observation, I was involved in the context of the classroom in different roles. One role was as researcher, which included observing what was taking place, taking ethnographic notes, asking follow-up questions, and recording classroom discourse. The other was as participant, which involved observing, working with, and being a part of the culture that was being studied. As these are two separately challenging roles, my involvement in the class as a participant varied throughout the year. At the beginning of the academic year, I was introduced by Caroline as a student at the neighboring university, as a science teacher, and as a researcher. When I was present for class, I participated as a member of the class, sitting near the students, either on the carpet or on a chair nearby. When I was not able to make it to class, Caroline asked the students to retell me what happened in my absence to fill me in on the work that they had discussed. If students asked questions during whole group discussions, I would defer to Caroline, but if she needed my help with answering their questions I would help. If a student asked me a direct question, I would answer them. At first, I was very involved in participating, but over time, as my study progressed, I pulled back my participation, as I was having a difficult time operating my research tools, recording my observations, and hoping to maintain an emic stance (Kottak, 2006). I began to observe from the periphery, not sitting on the carpet but sitting a few feet back at a table. I held my ethnographic notebook in my lap and my camera was positioned nearby. I still participated in whole class science talks, small group explorations, and individual science notebook sessions, and I walked throughout the room asking questions of students about their work, but my physical presence was stationed at the periphery of the classroom most of the time.

Reflexivity: Examining Perspective

Because this study examines the practices and knowledge building associated with science instruction that is focused on explanation building with evidence, the "practices, roles, and positions do not come to students automatically as they might in the prototypical figured world of school science learning" (Carlone *et al.*, 2011, p. 482). Rather, students are asked to wonder, investigate, develop their own claims, and communicate their thinking to their peers and teachers. Therefore, I needed to be vigilant, maintain consistency, persistence, and endurance when I observed and participated within this environment in order to analyze patterns and interactions among the participants. I needed to unlearn what was the norm in my mind and find value in asking, "What counts as science and science identity *in this setting*?" (Kelly, Chen, & Crawford, 1998). My perspective is grounded in my own experiences, my identity, and my desire to see young girls have access to classroom science instruction focused on explanation building with evidence. My perspective for what counted as science could have overshadowed or filtered what I observed and recorded, unintentionally, because of my experiences in various classrooms, or with my own children. This was a difficult hurdle to face, as I struggled with allowing the study to be ethnographic and not limited by my views, while succumbing to the needs of the teachers. Caroline would frequently ask me if she "did something correctly" or "should I have X, Y, Z instead of A, B, C," seeing me as an expert because of my involvement in the previous video study group, being a university researcher and teacher, and having instructed students in science for ten years previous to this study. Taking on the "expert" role, however unintentional, still created a power dynamic that existed in this space.

Seeing me as an expert may have supported the instructional context within the classroom, as Caroline asked for help with content and connection to instructional techniques associated with the argumentation model labeled "CER" – claims, evidence, reasoning. I was able to co-plan with her and discuss and reflect with her after she taught a lesson or two, so even the lesson designs may have included my contributions. However, she did not ask me about the identities of the girls, or whom she should call on, or where she should have the students sit in the classroom. Other than speaking with her about ideas within my notes, our conversations were predominately about the science instruction in the classroom.

Another area of concern was the presence of the video camera in the classroom. I introduced the camera as a way to collect information about what the students were saying, and as a way for me to go back to the classroom activities of the day so that I could remember what we did in class, but it did have its own presence in the classroom and may have affected the participation and interactions of the participants. In the same vein, my pulling certain students into the hallway to talk with them and show them video throughout the year may have affected their participation in the class, as well as others' participation and interactions when they were not chosen to go out into the hallway with me. I tried to combat this situation by adding additional videotaping sessions with all students and compiling an end-of-the-year video for each child showcasing their learning in science.

Analysis and Flexibility

By being in the science classroom throughout the year, taking field notes, interviewing participants, and conducting initial analyses, I had a better sense of the language, interactions, behaviors, and practices among the kindergarteners and the teachers within the culture of the classroom. Wolcott described in his book, *Ethnography: A Way of Seeing* (1999), that a study with ethnographic perspectives "provides a rich database for further research and results in a contribution to knowledge" (p. 61), and that was what I hoped to gain by choosing this perspective. Studying science learning and practices requires an understanding of what it means to learn and practice science. Becoming a member of a scientific field requires knowledge of the practices, and meanings associated with these practices, when becoming scientifically literate. Members within this community construct cultural meanings that identify them as such. Latour and Woolgar (1986) denoted "science in the making" is defined by the developing and evolving social processes of its members. In consideration of ways that science has been shown to be constructed through cultural practices (Knorr-Cetina, 1999) and ways that the classroom culture (Green & Harker, 1988) was constructed by participants, it was imperative to be able to uncover patterns when viewing reform-based science practices in order to situate the new phenomena among the participants in the classroom. By researching the practices associated with evidence-based science explanations in the classroom, I was able to distinguish among the positioning of the girls amid these practices, as well as their authoring within these practices. Employing ethnographic methods makes these local interpretations central to the analysis. As Bucholtz commented, "Gender does not have the same meanings across space and time, but is instead a local production, realized differently by different members of a community; thus, an ethnographic orientation yields particularly fruitful results for language and gender research" (1999, p. 210). As I studied the interactions and discourse in this kindergarten classroom I was able to locate patterns among participants and use these patterns to study the girls' identities-in-practice.

Due to the rich context, data, and interactions in the science instruction in the kindergarten classroom, I utilized an ethnographic case study design to showcase the product of the telling case (Mitchell, 1984). Mitchell (1984) defines a telling case as one that makes visible what has not been previously known and is theoretically important. The size of the unit is not the defining factor – the holistic nature of it is central.

> Case studies [telling cases] are the detailed presentations of ethnographic data relating to some sequence of events from which the analysis it seeks to make theoretical inference. The events themselves may relate to any level of social organizations: a whole society, some section of a community, a family or an individual. What distinguishes case studies from more general ethnographic reportage is the detail and particularity of the account. Each case study is a description of a specific configuration of events in which some distinctive set of actors have been involved in some defined situation at some particular point of time.
>
> *(Mitchell, 1984, p. 222)*

Drawing from sociocultural perspectives, the central theoretical constructs of the study are identities-in-practice and positioning. It would have been difficult to provide clearly delineated findings based on only one of the constructs due to the connectivity that they have with each other and the telling case approach supports this type of openess. The telling case study approach was also chosen to collectively narrate the story of four girls within classroom science instruction. Using sociolinguistic analysis helped to illuminate the case studies of the girls as I investigated the co-construction of norms in the classroom focused on explanation building with evidence and how the girls' authoring and being positioned as learners within the normative view of the classroom either supported or conflicted with their developing identities-in-practice; therefore, the students' discourse and interactions in the classroom provided primary sources of data for my study. The actions, dialogue, interactions, and interpretations of the students in the classroom were captured on video and provided me with a rich data source for examining authoring, positioning, and norms of participation within the classroom science instruction of explanation building with evidence. Video was the most abundant source of primary data collected and was used as one source of triangulation during analysis (Kelly *et al.*, 1998). While I was in the classroom I also took 176 pages of field notes over 55 days (Emerson, Fretz, & Shaw, 1995).

Analyzing the copious amounts of data took different forms throughout the study. Initially, I made "grand tour" observations (Spradley, 1980) while I viewed the classroom for the first few days. I used this time to become familiar with the environment and the people in the environment. I began to look for features that Spradley referred to as the major dimensions of every social situation (1980, p. 78). These dimensions include space, actor, activity, object, act, event, time, goal, and feeling. I used my journal as a place for reflexive practice, as well as a place for field notation. My field notes (Emerson *et al.*, 1995) accompanied my observations and were expanded upon in response to what Geertz denotes as "thick description" or "cooking the notes" (1973). This allowed me to include audience and stance within my renderings of what occurred in the classroom during the day. While jotting down notes in a stream of consciousness writing method during the taking of the notes, I was only able to include a minimal amount of detail and writing, even though I knew I should be taking the time to write the field note with as much detail and description as possible. At times, I was involved in the events of the classroom and could not take extensive notes. I wrote all of my field notes in a notebook, using the margins as a place for recording the time and memos. At times, my notes included diagrams, listings, and charts that I made to record the classroom setting if I wanted to take specific notes about student placement, daily agendas, and actions. While I was cooking the field notes, I typed them into a dissertation notebook section, which I created on my computer. Many of the notes I took were observational and I tried to use as much verbatim language as I could (e.g., "good fit books," "star paper," "word compare"). When I typed the field notes, at a later date, I added my personal thoughts and connections to theory, asked questions, included thoughts to bring up with Caroline and gave more specific titles to sections within the notes, such as searching for evidence, planting seeds, etc. As my time in the classroom progressed, my field notes began to change as a result of the ethnographic process. I began to take more focused notes, concentrating on words and actions used during science talks and note booking. As I selected four girls to observe more closely for my case studies, my notes became more refined and focused. An example of my refined field notes may be found in Figure 2.1.

During phase one analysis I developed initial observations and looked for patterns of science discourse. Throughout this process I continued to ask questions of my data, created representations of my data, and interpreted my representations. While doing this, my interpretations and the data led to new questions and new insights, which showed how the process was iterative and allowed me the

* Wed., 1/11/'12- "Discussing living and nonliving things"
• 8:45 am Starting the day with science because it is too cold to go outside for recess in the morning, so the students will be going out in the afternoon and science was moved from the afternoon to the morning.
• New star papers are being introduced for discipline. They include sections on them for the students to check. Each morning the students come in and complete their lunch count, review their good fit books, sign I on name sheet and get their star paper for the day, out their name on it and decorate it. If they finish all of this then they come to the carpet and wait or talk to each other. If they don't finish it, Caroline tells them they can finish later. 8:47 am This morning Caroline wakes them up by having them bump elbows with each other and say good morning.
• 8:49 am Caroline began science discussion today with the word compare. She introduced the word to the students and told them it was like the math word compare.
• 8:53 am She paired the students together and asked them to talk with each other about whether they agree or disagree with each other about the living and nonliving things they put into their notebook. Daphne and B, Mary and Mimi, Lucy and JP, Olive and Bruce, Molly and A, Lara and Jim, Josie and Hayden, and Job and Adam. Caroline reminded the students about the rules of a science conference. She asked them to listen to each other, agree, or disagree, kindly with each other • 8:56 am Many students talked with each other and this is all written in my notebook and on video.

FIGURE 2.1 Example of ethnographic field notes, cooked.

opportunity to zoom in and out of the scope of analysis (Castanheira, Crawford, Dixon, & Green, 2001). I zoomed in to look at specific interactions and zoomed out to look at the structures surrounding those interactions. I began to create event maps in my computerized data log informed by classroom observations, video files of classroom discourse, and my ethnographic notes. An event map is constructed by examining and categorizing the discourse that occurs in a space and noting the patterns of discourse as events. These event maps depicted the time of the event, the interaction units that constructed the event in sequences, and the overall cycle which comprised the events. From these event maps, I was able to see patterns emerging from the data. Without using event maps my data would have been developed, but I would not have been able to see the pattern of when certain statements were being made or how students were positioned in the classroom.

During the next phase of analysis, I listened to the recorded videos and transcribed the utterances from video data, created more detailed event maps, and coded data. By looking at my initial event maps and my field notes and video record log I was able to pick out the hours of video recording that I wanted to transcribe through a process of theoretical sampling. For instance, as I was focused on which girls were talking or not talking, and when, and what was being said based on my observation data, I chose to transcribe particular utterances when the four girls from my telling cases appeared. It was also important to me to be the one to transcribe the discourse. While I was doing so I was able to re-look at the event situated in time, re-think about the situated context of the event in comparison to other events, and watch for subtleties in the video that I may have missed while taking notes in the classroom. My transcripts were organized by line, time, speaker, message unit, and nonverbal actions. An example of a transcript can be seen in Figure 2.2. Message units were delineated by boundaries of utterances or social actions, and are the smallest linguistic unit represented in my transcripts (Green & Wallat, 1981; Kelly & Crawford, 1997). These message units were denoted by pitch, stress, fluctuation in speech, pauses, and intonation (Gumperz, 1982).

After I prepared the transcripts with message units, I printed the documents and analyzed the transcripts for action units by hand. Again, this was due to my need to have a physical representation of what I had heard and how the units were connecting. See Figure 2.3 for an example of what the analyzed transcripts looked like. Action units show a relationship between message units and represent an observed intended act by the speaker (Green & Meyer, 1991; Kelly & Crawford, 1997). I then looked at the relationship between action units of

Line	Time segment	Speaker	Discourse	Nonverbal
1	00:00:00	JC	We see this lightbulb	pointing to lightbulb in KLEW chart
2		JC	that's where we wrote down	
3		JC	the things that we	
4		JC	learned	
5		JC	that lightbulb went off	
6		JC	and we said	
7		JC	oh	
8		JC	I just really learned this	
9		JC	and I know for sure that that's what happened	
10		JC	scientists call that a claim	
11		JC	we can claim that something happened	
12	00:00:20	JC	then these eyes	
13		JC	were what?	

FIGURE 2.2 Example of a transcript with message units.

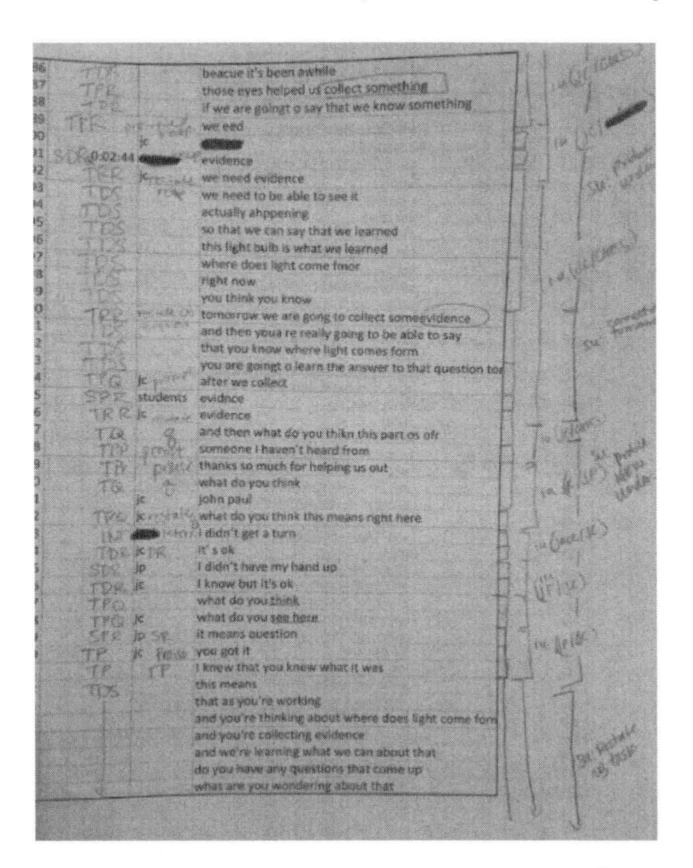

beacue it's been awhile
those eyes helped us collect something
if we are goingt o say that we know something
we eed
jc
0:02:44 evidence
jc we need evidence
we need to be able to see it
actually ahppening
so that we can say that we learned
this light bulb is what we learned
where does light come fmor
right now
you think you know
tomorrow we are gong to collect someevidence
and then youa re really going to be able to say
that you know where light comes form
you are goingt o learn the answer to that question to
jc after we collect
students evidnce
jc evidence
and then what do you thikn this part os ofr
someone I haven't heard from
thanks so much for helping us out
what do you think
jc john paul
jc what do you think this means right here
I didn't get a turn
jc it's ok
jp I didn't have my hand up
jc I know but it's ok
what do you think
jc what do you see here
jp it means question
jc you got it
I knew that you knew what it was
this means
that as you're working
and you're thinking about where does light come form
and you're collecting evidence
and we're learning what we can about that
do you have any questions that come up
what are you wondering about that

FIGURE 2.3 Analyzed transcript with action units.

connected speakers, which I labeled interaction units. These interaction units showed the interactions between speakers and were used to show how the interactions in the space connected to show sequence units and ultimately events and cycles within this kindergarten classroom.

After I was finished typing the transcripts, I put together more detailed event maps that included sequences and interaction units. An example of an event map can be found in Figure 2.4.

Within this event map, the sequences of actions are delineated and times are associated with each event. Looking at the event maps helped me to re-analyze the norms of practice within the science classroom by looking for specific phrases and events that happened in patterns. After specific phrases were identified, I made a table to calculate the different pedagogical and scientific practices that were occurring in each curricular unit, so that I could compare the practices being used in each of the units where Caroline was co-constructing the norms in the science classroom with the students.

Cycle: Exploring the construction of different shadows using a block and discussing findings (1/26/12)

1. Event: Preparing students with directions, object NB set-up for independent work with block and tracing shadows (6 min 35 sec)

Sequences:
Introduction of task of placing block on hand to observe
Interruption behavior redirect
Giving directions for task of holding block
Interruption behavior redirect
Looking for shadow of block in hand while students observe and look for theirs
Giving directions for the next task; NB directions
Clarifying directions for those who are unsure
Checking in with student's as they work

2. Event; Teachers walking around and discussing observations with students in small groups/independent work time with blocks and shadows (1 min 45 sec)

Sequences:
Discussing observations with small group of students
Revise directions for NB to include writing and not just drawing

3. Event: Discussion of observations of block and shadows and manipulating the block to see different shadows (2 min 20 sec)

Sequence:
Discussing observations of different shadows

FIGURE 2.4 Example of an event map from the Light and Shadows unit.

In phase 3 I performed a deeper analysis of the interactions and discourse patterns among the data. Studies using identities-in-practice (Barton & Tan, 2010; Brickhouse & Potter, 2001; Carlone *et al.*, 2011; Carlone, 2004; Carlone & Johnson, 2007; Tan & Barton, 2008a, 2008b) suggest the need for close examination of the discourse processes and contextual activity within the classroom to help identify the positioning and participation reflected by the girls in the study. Within this context, I examined the nature of and responses to the girls' bids for recognition (e.g., when they did so, for what reasons, from whom they bid) so as to draw inferences from evidence about how the structures surrounding the girls helped or hindered their positions during science instruction, what they deemed important enough in order to get recognition, whose recognition mattered to them, and the ways their teachers and peers responded (Carlone *et al.*, 2011). Specifically using the Light and Shadows curricular unit, I examined the four case study girls' participation with whole group science talks and individual science notebook work. I chose to analyze the girls in these contexts because of what I had learned from my previous analysis of the event maps. Some participants were showing heightened participation during times of independent work, i.e., science notebook time, and others were showing signs of full participation during whole class discussions. I began analyzing the interactions among the girls, Caroline, and the class by looking at transcription notes. It is from there that I developed tables to visualize the interactions occurring between the members in the school classroom science community. I began by listing daily interactions on a chart marked by the day of the science lesson time. Each participant that began the interaction was listed first followed by a / and then I listed who that person interacted with next. I color-coded the interactions that included the four girls in my study giving each of the four girls a different color, e.g., Caroline/Molly could be read as Caroline began the interaction and she interacted with Molly. Molly's interaction was marked with a red highlight. From this data I developed graphs to depict interactions for the entire Light and Shadows unit and the interactions of the four girls from the Light and Shadows unit (Figure 2.5) so that I could compare the number of interactions among the girls to the number of interactions from the entire consented class.

I distinguished between random actions and the development of identities by locating the repetitive patterns of the spaces in which participants author identities. This pattern would not be present in random acts, which would not contribute to the authoring of these identities within the community of the science classroom (Barton *et al.*, 2008). The choices girls make when they are participating within the scientific community reflect the ownership or lack of ownership of their scientific identity (Barton *et al.*, 2008). After I looked at the interactions occurring within the unit, I needed to take another pass at the transcriptions from

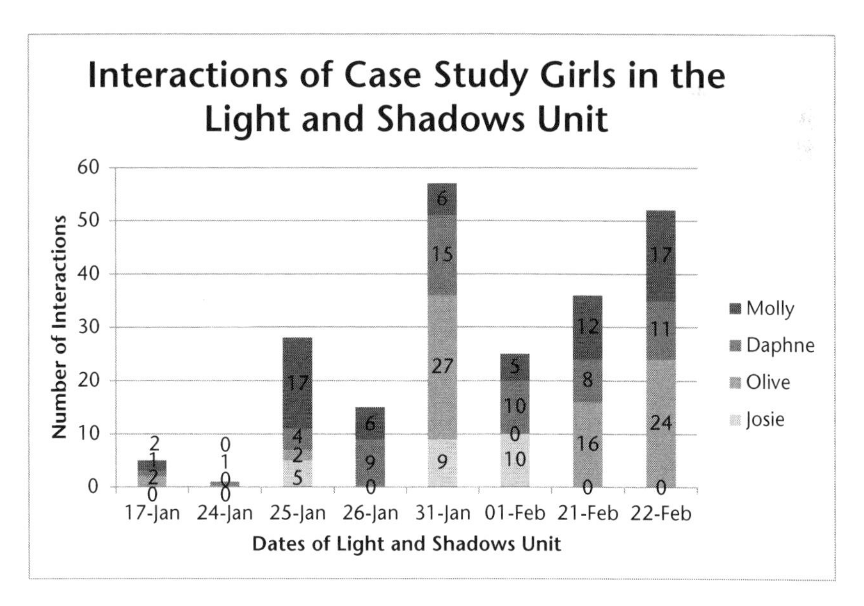

FIGURE 2.5 Graph of the interactions of case study girls throughout the Light and Shadows unit.

the Light and Shadows unit to open code for scientific practices among the case study girls. As I open coded for practices of science, I also used Gee's "Identities Building Tool" (2011). The "Identities Building Tool" helped me to:

> ask what socially recognizable identity or identities the speaker is trying to enact or to get others to recognize and ask how the speaker's language treats other people's identities, and what sorts of identities the speaker recognizes for others in relationship to his or her own. Also, reminds me to ask how the speaker is positioning others, and what identities the speaker is inviting others to take up.
>
> *(Gee, 2011, p. 110)*

I chose to use this tool as I coded the transcripts and my ethnographic notes for scientific literacy practices and participation markers.

During the next stage of analysis, I used the coded transcripts and notes that I took from the margins of the transcripts to code for phrases and actions by hand.

Speaker	*Talk*	*Notes*
JC-teacher	"Can you help him out because you noticed the same thing?"	Question to prompt talk, offering a space of authoring
Molly-case study girl	"When you standed (sic) it up it had shadows all around it and I found a triangle shadow right there (pointing to her paper), cause a shadow was a different shape because it was turned up"	Stating what she observed, authoring her own explanation for position of shadows
JC-teacher	"So, Molly's saying when she laid her block in a different direction on the paper she noticed that the shadow looked a bit different which is what you did too"	Rephrasing what Molly stated and using her example for comparison to a peer

At this point during science instruction the class was having a science talk about an investigation they completed with a block, a piece of white paper, and a light source. The teacher was speaking with one of the girls in the study and I noted on the right column of the table the types of pedagogical talk moves associated with the science talk and the authoring and/or positioning that occurred during the science talk. When I reviewed my transcripts, I circled the lines of teacher talk and boxed the lines of student talk for ease of noticing patterns. In this example, I labeled the left column with the speaker. On my transcripts I used pink highlighting when a student was authoring an idea and blue highlighting when the teacher was offering a space for authoring from a student. In this example excerpt, I added the text to the right column in the chart for ease of reading. I also underlined certain words in my transcripts due to their significance to the meaning making within the unit of study e.g., Light and Shadow.

After I coded the transcripts for positioning and authoring identities-in-practice, and reviewed the practices associated with science that each girl was exhibiting, I made individual webs for each case study girl (Figure 2.6). Each web had the girl's name in the middle and connected to her name were statements about the girl that developed from patterns I uncovered while analyzing the discourse. Some of the statements were quotes made by the girl and others were examples of her written work. I made the webs to inform my analysis so that I could describe and visualize how the authoring of identities-in-practice and positioning for each girl was surrounding them.

Cross-case analysis was the final step I took in completing the analysis for this study. I reviewed all data and created a table to record examples of my cross-case

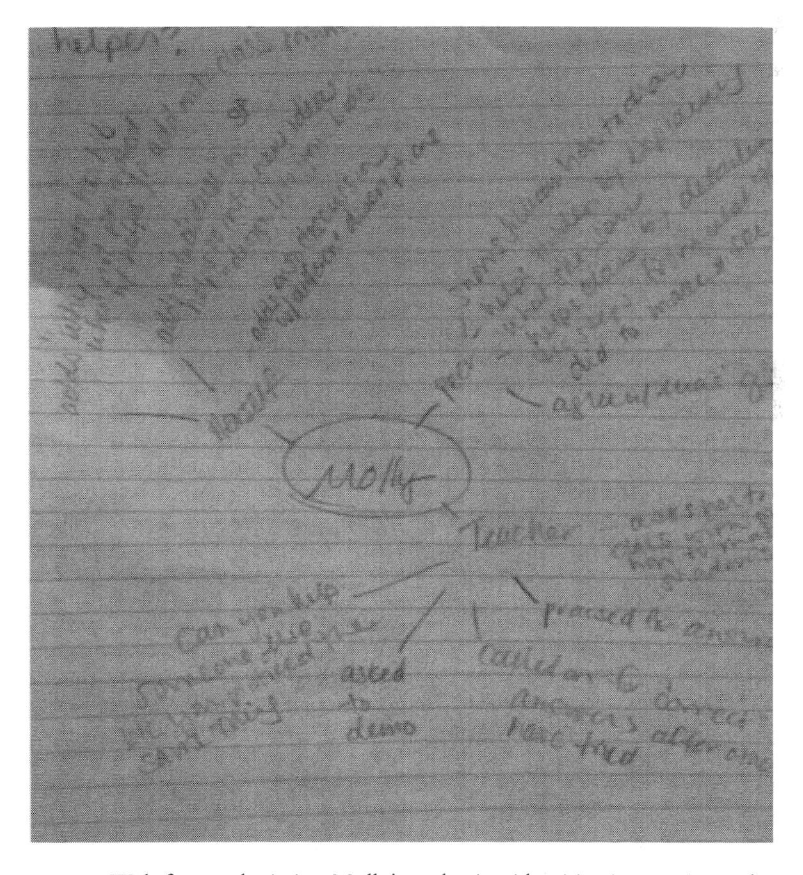

FIGURE 2.6 Web format depicting Molly's authoring identities-in-practice and positioning as a science learner.

analysis findings. Using the theoretical lenses of identities-in-practice and positioning, I used my analysis of the cases to craft three assertions that became evident to me as I compared the four girls' case studies.

Results Informed by Ethnographic Methods

By using sociolinguistic analysis, I was able to note ideas of student understanding, find patterns across contexts, and examine teaching practice. The girls in this study authored a variety of identities-in-practice for science learning through classroom science instruction focused on explanation building with evidence. They were able to participate in the norms of the science classroom, and while doing so gained exposure to science practices. These girls were also able to work on their identities-in-practice as they wrote in their science notebooks, participated in whole group science talks, and became part of the science learning community. One of the findings I ascertained by using interactional sociolinguistics as a theoretical approach (Green & Meyer, 1991; Gumperz, 1982; Ochs, 1979) in this study was that identities-in-practice manifest differently in different literacy practices (whole group discussion, written work) and show how students choose to be science students across time and activities. A focus on one literacy practice alone is insufficient to understand identity. Notable were the scientific identities-in-practice that emerged as the young girls were called upon and how those differed from the participation offered in their written work. For example, one girl drew in her science notebook and wrote questions by her drawings but when the class was asked questions by the teacher relating to the work in their notebooks this girl did not raise her hand to contribute. When the teacher directly asked her a question she responded by using what she had written in her science notebook which allowed her classmates to ask additional questions. By looking at my ethnographic notes, coded transcripts, and detailed event maps I was able to see patterns emerge among the participants. These patterns prompted further analysis and findings.

The ways in which the teacher positioned girls, especially "quiet girls," was essential for engaging them in productive participation in science discourse and learning. This can contribute to shaping identities-in-practice. The teacher in the study used talk moves and scientific discourse to engage students with the phenomenon. She would not let the girls answer "I don't know" without prompting them and giving them wait time in order to think about their ideas. This was integral for the developing identities-in-practice the girls were enacting. Positioning girls as science learners helped the "quiet" girls find a space to participate, and, in turn, they asked questions and demonstrated their knowledge in the learning community.

This study, informed by situated learning theory and sociocultural perspectives on learning (Greeno, 1998; Lave & Wenger, 1991) provides the science community with research to warrant the claim that using a socially constructed scientific practice, constructing explanations from evidence, helped students to find a place to author themselves in the science learning community. By providing all learners with unique opportunities to construct their own or co-construct their explanations with evidence gives students an opportunity to participate in the practices of science in ways that work for them and the classroom community (Lave & Wenger, 1991). Students were surrounded in the community of science learners, and how the expert, or teacher, chose to proceed in that community had a direct connection to how the students will be able to practice their own developing scientific identities, even with young learners who can do science.

By utilizing an ethnographic study approach patterns of discourse were made visible to me within a socially constructed environment. In understanding that the context of the kindergarten classroom was situated and socially constructed through coordinated interactions over time it was imperative to choose methods that would be attentive to the details of the discourse of positioning, able to depict changes in interactions over time, and offer the flexibility to adjust the foci of analysis throughout the research process. A survey of student feelings may not have captured this phenomenon, nor would a pre- or post-test assessment. Using an interactional sociolinguistic theoretical approach allowed me to note where identities-in-practice were constructed, and thus, was the locus for my analysis which made the findings more rich and contextual.

Discussion for Science Teacher Education and Research

These assertions have important implications for ways in which science is taught in elementary school, the science education community, science education research, and education communities. This study used evidence informed by educational ethnographic methods to illustrate the learning, practices, and burgeoning identities-in-practice of kindergarten girls as science learners, and in so doing adds to the body of research regarding identity. It is important for teachers, policy makers, and researchers to consider the positioning and authoring of young students as they create curricula, create and support new laws, and develop professional learning opportunities because it is essential to create these new or revised artifacts and practices with a focus on sociocultural learning. This study also provided insight on how examining the positioning and authoring of girls as science learners by analyzing discourse highlighted their identities-in-practice as different types of science learners. This continues to be an important area of contribution as it helps us understand how gender and science are affected by different learning environments, discourse moves, and positioning of students by others in the classroom. Using sociolinguistics helps to identify nuanced ways of doing and learning science, as well as the different barriers to learning science, as one has access to look critically at discourse while examining the culture in the space.

References

Barton, A. C., & Tan, E. (2010). We be burnin'! Agency, identity, and science learning. *The Journal of the Learning Sciences, 19*(2), 187–229.

Barton, A. C., Tan, E., & Rivet, A. (2008). Creating hybrid spaces for engaging school science among urban middle school girls. *American Educational Research Journal, 45*(1), 68–103.

Brickhouse, N., Lowery, P., & Schultz, K. (2000). What kind of a girl does science? The construction of school science identities. *Journal of Research in Science Teaching, 37*(5), 441–458.

Brickhouse, N. W., & Potter, J. T. (2001). Young women's scientific identity formation in an urban context. *Journal of Research in Science Teaching, 38*(8), 965–980.

Brown, B. A., Reveles, J. M., & Kelly, G. J. (2005). Scientific literacy and discursive identity: A theoretical framework for understanding science learning. *Science Education, 89*(5), 779–802.

Bucholtz, M. (1999). "Why be normal?": Language and identity practices in a community of nerd girls. *Language in Society, 28*, 203–223.

Carlone, H. (2004). The cultural production of science in reform-based physics: Girls' access, participation, and resistance. *Journal of Research in Science Teaching, 41*(4), 392–414.

Carlone, H., Haun-Frank, J., & Webb, A. (2011). Assessing equity beyond knowledge/ and skills-based outcomes: A comparative ethnography of two fourth-grade reform-based science classrooms. *Journal of Research in Science Teaching, 48*(5), 459–485.

Carlone, H., & Johnson, A. (2007). Understanding the science experiences of success-ful women of color: Science identity as an analytic lens. *Journal of Research in Science Teaching, 44*(8), 1187–1218.

Castanheira, M. L., Crawford, T., Dixon, C. N., & Green, J. L. (2001). Interactional ethnography: An approach to studying the social construction of literate practices. *Linguistics and Education, 11*(4), 353–400.

Denzin, N. K., & Lincoln, Y. S. (Eds.). (2005). *The Sage handbook of qualitative research*. Thousand Oaks, CA: Sage.

Duschl, R. A., Schweingruber, H. A., & Shouse, A. W. (Eds.). (2007). *Taking science to school: Learning and teaching science in grades K-8*. Washington, DC: The National Academies Press.

Emerson, R. M., Fretz, R. I., & Shaw, L. L. (1995). *Writing ethnographic fieldnotes*. Chicago, IL: University of Chicago Press.

Gee, J. P. (2011). *How to do discourse analysis: A toolkit*. London: Routledge.

Geertz, C. (1973/2000). *The interpretation of cultures*. New York: Basic Books.

Glesne, C. (2006). Making words fly: Developing understanding through interviewing. *Becoming qualitative researchers: An introduction* (pp. 79–107). Boston, MA: Pearson.

Green, J. L., & Harker, J. O. (1988). *Multiple perspective analysis of classroom discourse*. Norwood, NJ: Ablex.

Green, J. L., & Meyer, L. A. (1991). The embeddedness of reading in classroom life: Reading as a situated process. In C. A. Baker & A. Luke (Eds.), *Towards critical sociology of reading pedagogy* (pp. 141–160). Philadelphia, PA: John Benjamin Publishing Company.

Green, J. L., & Wallat, C. (1981). Mapping instructional Conversations: A sociolinguistic ethnography. In J. L. Green & C. Wallat (Eds.), *Ethnography and language in educational settings* (pp. 161–208). Norwood, NJ: Ablex.

Greeno, J. G. (1998). The situativity of knowing, learning, and research. *American Psychologist, 53*(1), 5.

Gumperz, J. J. (1982). *Discourse strategies* (Vol. 1). Cambridge, UK: Cambridge University Press.

Kelly, G. J., & Chen, C. (1999). The sound of music: Constructing science as sociocultural practices through oral and written discourse. *Journal of Research in Science Teaching, 36*(8), 883–915.

Kelly, G. J., Chen, C., & Crawford, T. (1998). Methodological considerations for studying science-in-the-making in educational settings. *Research in Science Education, 28*(1), 23–49.

Kelly, G. J., & Crawford, T. (1997). An ethnographic investigation of the discourse processes of school science. *Science Education, 81*(5), 533–559.

Knorr-Cetina, K. (1999). *Epistemic communitites.* Harvard, MA: Harvard Educational.

Kottak, C. P. (2006). *Mirror for Humanity.* New York: McGraw-Hill.

Latour, B., & Woolgar, S. (1986). *Laboratory life: The construction of scientific facts.* Princeton, NJ: Princeton University Press.

Lave, J., & Wenger, E. (1991). *Situated learning: Legitimate peripheral participation.* Cambridge, UK: Cambridge University Press.

Longino, H. (1993). Subject, power, and knowledge: Description and Prescription in feminist philosophies of science. In L. Alcoff & E. Potter (Eds.), *Feminist epistemologies.* New York: Routledge.

Mitchell, J. (1984). Typicality and the case study. In R. F. Ellen (Ed.), *Ethnographic research: A guide to conduct.* New York: Academic Press.

National Research Council. (2012). *A framework for K-12 science education: Practices, crosscutting concepts, and core ideas.* Committee on a Conceptual Framework for New K-12 Science Education Standards. Board on Science Education, Division of Behavioral and Social Sciences and Education. Washington, DC: The National Academies Press.

Ochs, E. (1979). Transcription as theory. In E. Ochs & B. B. Schieffelin (Eds.), *Developmental pragmatics* (pp. 43–72). New York: Academic Press.

Reveles, J. M., Cordova, R., & Kelly, G. J. (2004). Science literacy and academic identity formulation. *Journal of Research in Science Teaching, 41*(10), 1111–1144.

Sadker, D., & Sadker, M. (1995). *Failing at fairness: How our schools cheat girls.* New York: Touchstone.

Spradley, J. P. (1980). *Participant observation.* Orlando, FL: Harcourt Brace Jovanovich College Publishers.

Tan, E., & Barton, A. C. (2008a). From peripheral to central, the story of Melanie's metamorphosis in an urban middle school science class. *Science Education, 92*(4), 567–590.

Tan, E., & Barton, A. C. (2008b). Unpacking science for all through the lens of identities-in-practice: The stories of Amelia and Ginny. *Cultural Studies of Science Education, 3*(1), 43–71.

Tobin, K. G., Elmesky, R., Seiler, G., Cox, C. A., & Carpenter, J. R. (2005). Improving attitudes toward teaching science and reducing science anxiety through increasing confidence in science ability in inservice elementary school teachers. *Journal of Elementary Science Education, 1*(2), 14–34.

Wolcott, H. (1999). *Ethnography: A way of seeing.* London: Rowman Altamaria.

3

MULTIMODAL ANALYSIS OF DECISION MAKING IN ELEMENTARY ENGINEERING

Carmen M. Vanderhoof

Introduction

Recent reform movements in science education call for integration of multiple STEM (Science, Technology, Engineering, and Mathematics) disciplines with a new focus on engineering education. The *Next Generation Science Standards* (NGSS Lead States, 2013) highlight the overlap between engineering and science practices and specify learning progressions starting with kindergarten. Previously, engineering education mainly took place at the college level and began upon completion of a solid base of science and math prerequisites (Cunningham & Carlsen, 2014). There is limited research on engineering education at the elementary level specifying what opportunities and challenges this move towards curriculum integration presents.

In K-12 engineering education students may be asked to participate in collaborative design planning, hands-on building, testing, and improvement of a product or process, which requires different skillsets and knowledge compared to planning and conducting a controlled science experiment. When engineering challenges are embedded in STEM-integrated curriculum units, there is potential for overlap between disciplines. For example, if students need to draw on science concepts to solve engineering problems, they can learn science while working on engineering projects (Cunningham, 2018). The science classroom has been described as full of complex semiotic resources students need to navigate, use, and transform to make meaning (Kress, Jewitt, Ogborn, & Tsatsarelis, 2001). Social semiotics theory emphasizes how sign-making is a motivated and transformative process and how different modes shape knowledge. This framework is especially applicable to the engineering context, where materiality plays an even more salient role and where design principles are based on making informed choices from an array of possible design pathways.

In this chapter, I will focus on how the social, process, and materials-oriented engineering education context necessitates that researchers consider which methodological approaches are best suited for gaining the most insight from this type of rich interactional data (Green & Harker, 1988; Kelly, 2006). For example, if the focus of the research question deals with students' co-construction of explanations to fill a knowledge gap, the analysis tools would be different from a research question dealing with how student groups engage in an iterative design process involving material and semiotic resources to solve a problem. When the study context features interactions with materials and design thinking, a multimodal lens combined with an ethnographic approach would enable a researcher to take an open-ended exploratory orientation (Hammersley & Atkinson, 1995) to different types and layers of data – drawings, construction materials, gestures, body positioning, speech (as illustrated in the subsequent transcript). In this manner, researchers can compile evidence through an inductive non-linear process using a descriptive stance that reaches beyond the surface layer, allowing for emerging patterns over multiple iterations instead of imposing *a priori* theoretical constructs or coding schemes.

Working with extensive video and audio records presents many rich opportunities to examine educational phenomena. Educational ethnographers applied and developed discourse analysis in conjunction with complimentary methods across disciplines to create approaches to systematically explore human and material interactions within the local and wider contexts of the classroom space (Green & Harker, 1988). Through these multiple perspectives, researchers have been able to look across different layers of classroom activity to examine the typicality of events, establish how classroom processes are constructed by the participants in the moment and across timescales, and notice "what difference a difference make[s]" (Green & Harker, 1988, p. 5). There is extensive literature using these methods investigating academic literacy across disciplines, as situated in social practice within the classroom and beyond (Castanheira, Crawford, Dixon, & Green, 2001; Bloome, Carter, Christian, Otto, & Shuart-Faris, 2005; Kelly & Chen, 1999; Kelly, Crawford, & Green, 2001).

In contrast to educational ethnography, multimodal analysis has historically been used with textual artifacts like magazines and other periodicals, but it has much broader applications currently, including examining classroom interactions, computer software design and use, and even touch and feel responses in horseback riding lessons (Norris, 2012). More recently, a special issue of *Linguistics and Education* featured detailed multimodal analysis of interactions in different contexts to show how participants drew on and assembled semiotic resources for meaning-making in the moment, where many actions co-occur (Erickson, 2017). Thus, a focus on multimodality may manifest differently across research areas, but an agreed starting point is "extend[ing] the social interpretation of language and its meanings to the whole range of representational and communicational modes or semiotic resources for making meaning that are employed in a culture – such as image, writing, gesture, gaze, speech, posture" (Jewitt, 2009, p. 1). The tools I will be describing come from very different theoretical and methodological orientations that have changed and evolved over time – ethnography from nineteenth-century anthropology (Hammersley & Atkinson, 1995) and multimodal social semiotics analysis from Critical Discourse Analysis (CDA) (Fairclough, 2013), which has its roots in Systemic Functional Linguistics (SFL) from the late 1970s (Jewitt, Bezemer, & O'Halloran, 2016). Further complicating these already diverse fields, linguists like Saussure (1857–1913) were conducting multimodal research before the term was coined, and currently the term is so popular that it has been adopted by many other disciplines, including education, sociology, and psychology. Needless to say, there are many theoretical boundary overlaps and an extensive history of each research method that is beyond the scope of this chapter (for further reading, see Hammersley & Atkinson, 1995; Erickson, 1992; Jewitt, 2009).

This chapter will focus on an example of an inductive, iterative, and recursive multimodal approach, uniquely suited for collaborative elementary engineering design challenges, but also applicable to a wide range of study contexts involving student–student interactions and a heavy focus on materials, tools, and student-produced artifacts. Rather than using *a priori* coding schemes, the interactional ethnography perspective allows for patterns to emerge from the records through a non-linear process based on multiple iterations from different angles and timescales ranging from microanalysis of moment-to-moment interactions to macroanalysis of the patterned ways sociocultural groups affiliate and construct social norms and meanings. The multimodal lens will complement the interactional ethnographic approach by highlighting the variety of semiotic resources the participants draw on and the affordances and constraints of each mode. Therefore, the aim of this chapter is to establish the groundwork for a robust, context-dependent, multilayered approach for analyzing social discourse processes rich with artifacts and other materials from a descriptive stance, rather than an evaluative one.

Overview and Relevance of Study

This chapter will make visible how and what different analytical perspectives supported my exploration of small group interactions during an elementary design challenge. Analytic tools from interactional sociolinguistics, microethnography, and multimodal social semiotics analysis will be introduced. To illustrate these different types of analyses and raise methodological questions, data from a dissertation pilot study on elementary engineering group dynamics will be presented. The purpose of the dissertation research is to closely examine how students engage in different aspects of the engineering design process in order to draw implications for curriculum design, professional development, and structuring the learning environment to facilitate collaboration and optimize learning opportunities.

To focus on small group interactions of third graders engaged in a bridge design unit from the *Engineering is Elementary* (EiE) project (Cunningham, 2009), I posed the following research questions after an initial exploratory phase:

(1) *How do students negotiate moments of uncertainty among the group members?*
(2) *How does student positioning (of self and others) affect the group's decision-making process?*

To explore what each epistemological perspective made possible to investigate, I examined episodes of uncertainty (moments of doubt or disagreements about ideas), which I viewed as rich points for analysis (Agar, 1994), given that they are instances where students present and evaluate different ideas and ways to proceed. In such episodes, research has shown that students must resolve these instances in order to continue progress towards the end goal (Metz, 2004; Jordan & McDaniel, 2014). Framing problem-solving in terms of uncertainty management, Jordan and McDaniel (2014) described this process as a social phenomenon dependent on peer interactions, as opposed to something that only happens at the individual level. At such points, they argue, different types of uncertainties and management strategies can be identified in an effort to determine the factors associated with productive vs. unproductive strategies (for example, peer support is associated with productive uncertainty management). By employing the methodological approach introduced in this chapter, patterns emerged that were not present in the literature. Thus, through analysis of the video records of small group interactions in a third-grade class engaged in an EiE civil engineering unit (Cunningham, 2009), I explored how students' management of uncertainty was nuanced – there was no clear productive/unproductive dichotomy. The variety of negotiations among students in these moments of uncertainty presented changing social dynamics, different types of persuasive arguments, and overlap between scientific, engineering, and literacy practices.

Roots of the Multiple Perspective Study

My initial researcher comments considered the value of these uncertainty encounters that stalled the work or created a detour into a design direction that did not work or was intentionally abandoned for other reasons. A more linear uninterrupted design path may produce results faster and may be perceived initially to be more productive, but considering multiple ideas is part of the creative process associated with the improvement cycle of engineering design. In my analyses that follow I will demonstrate how different epistemological and methodological tools enabled me to explore the argument that there is value in exploring competing ideas, even if they lead to divergences in the work and may not end up being incorporated in the final engineering product or process. Through the analyses that follow, I will make visible the importance of drawing on multiple perspectives and methodological tools to explore this complex and developing process.

The design of the present study, therefore, involved exploration of emerging patterns by tracing the interactional processes at uncertainty episodes across the whole dataset. The pilot study, (Vanderhoof, 2017), made visible that potential design paths were articulated by students, and through persuasion and other peer interaction, some were taken up and others were left unexplored through material means. After a design plan was agreed upon and there were issues with the execution, students would sometimes disagree how to resolve the problem. During this process of managing uncertainty, students took up different roles to make a case for their ideas and comment on their teammates' contributions. Drawing on positioning theory (van Langenhove & Harré, 1999) and multimodal social semiotics analysis tools (Kress, 2011), I focused on episodes of uncertainty to examine how the different research perspectives supported my analysis of how students positioned themselves and others while they made a case for why their idea was worth pursuing. By following the evolution of ideas at these uncertainty checkpoints, I aimed to describe both the decision-making processes that students undertook in more detail in the pilot study, and to highlight how the different research tools and perspectives enabled me to explore and identify the social processes and resources students used during these interactions. For example, from an interactional ethnographic perspective, student interactions during moments of uncertainty are embedded in the communicative and social context of the classroom space across multiple lessons (Green & Harker, 1988). This local context instantiated in the moment is based on shared understanding, group participation structure, and rules established by the teacher-led classroom community over time, which is why it's important to analyze multiple layers and types of discourse. Conceptualizing discourse in multiple layers is also compatible with multimodal social semiotics perspective which treats meaning-making and communication as inherently made up of different modes or sign systems accessed and refigured by users/makers within social contexts (Jewitt *et al.*, 2016). Combining these perspectives allows for context-specific microanalysis beyond the surface level. Thus, through an iterative inductive process employing a descriptive rather than an evaluative stance I engaged in microanalysis without coding according to an *a priori* theoretical framework; this way patterns could emerge from the data, rather than be shaped to fit into pre-established categories.

Context and Data Analysis: A Developing Logic-of-Inquiry

The multi-view video records, audio records, and journal artifacts for this project were part of a larger NSF-sponsored experimental curriculum project from the Museum of Science, Boston (Cunningham, 2009; 2018). The analysis for this chapter focused on two third-grade classrooms engaging in the EiE civil engineering unit (approximatively twenty hours of video). The initial plan was to get familiar with the records from one unit, find and develop appropriate methods for analysis, and then apply it to a larger dataset looking across multiple units. Starting with an interest in group dynamics, I closely examined the video records and artifacts while making notes of anything that stood out along with a timestamp from the video or student journal page. I was especially interested in the conditions leading up to a student-proposed challenge and how group members responded, but I did not want to commit to a pre-determined theoretical model for analyzing student talk, such as argumentation frameworks like those based on Toulmin's model (1958) or the Exploratory Talk component of Wegerif and Mercer's (1997) dialogical framework. I observed instances of "competition between ideas" (Wegerif & Mercer, 1997, p. 57), but they unfolded very differently in this dataset and across groups. In many cases students were using science to figure out design decisions and persuade their group members to take up their ideas, rather than engaging in collective sense-making to fill a knowledge gap.

Since the initial orienting phase, I encountered methodological and theoretical challenges, changed and refocused my research questions from more general to more specific, tried out different discourse analysis tools, and experimented with different transcript formats. I will endeavor to re-create my journey as a beginning researcher to illustrate the progression of methodological decisions, but also to acknowledge the identity work involved in this process.

The body of pre-collected records I planned to analyze provided me with both advantages and methodological challenges. The sound was high quality and there were three camera views for each unit in addition to observation logs and student journals. On the other hand, I was unable to go back and interview the participants or resume data collection with the same participants. Even though I was not present at the research site to write fieldnotes, I realized that I could still rely on an ethnographic perspective to closely observe the social processes, discourse, and the interactions with materials, which played a prominent role in the engineering context. Coming up with a starting point was a challenge because the EiE team collected an extensive amount of records over the span of a few years and there were many to choose from. On page 54 there is a list of available EiE records (Figure 3.1) from a large-scale efficacy study (Lachapelle, Cunningham, & Oh, 2017) comparing EiE with a test curriculum, E4C (the list does not include a number of the quantitative instruments that were used in the larger efficacy study).

Record	Description
20 EiE curriculum units	hardcopy binders, each containing a book and 4 lessons per unit (5 of these had corresponding video from multiple classrooms)
1,582 hours of video	multiple views recordings (one camera at the front of the room and one or two cameras at the table group) of 605 classrooms across the country implementing the EiE curriculum and the test curriculum (E4C)
1,582 + hours of audio	teacher's mic and table mics recordings corresponding to video files
578 observation logs	Excel documents with extensive notes about the curriculum implementation completed by an EiE team member at the research site
18,057 student journals	estimated number of scanned pdf copies of de-identified student work corresponding to each video unit
80 student interviews	video recordings of group interviews with select students
62 teacher interviews	video recordings of interviews with select teachers

FIGURE 3.1 Engineering is Elementary (EiE) list of records for qualitative analysis.

In addition to wandering through the available project records and exploring different units, I ended up creating event maps for two units that a colleague (see Matthew Johnson's research in Chapter 5) was also analyzing so we could discuss the data and subsequent analysis. Being part of a research group (in our case, a group focused on discourse analysis) with varying levels of expertise and having shared data sessions was a valuable learning experience. This is how a pilot project emerged that will serve as a starting point for a larger dissertation study. Working with one unit at a time was beneficial because it was bounded in four sequential lessons and was a more manageable amount of video for microanalysis. For this chapter, I will present transcripts and preliminary findings from the initial analysis of two classrooms implementing the EiE civil engineering unit titled *To Get to the Other Side: Designing Bridges* (Engineering is Elementary, 2011).

The next challenge was determining how best to represent the student and material interactions on a transcript. The children in the data often engaged in overlapping excited talk, but also in long periods of non-verbal interactions while building and rebuilding the developing product, in this case, a model bridge. My previous experience with data analysis of high school student discussions was very different – there was less overlapping talk, more thematic coherence, and very little non-textual material interaction. In the section "Representing the Classroom Discourse" I will explain how I arrived at a transcription format informed by theory, but also by practical considerations.

I wrote analytical memos to keep track of questions I posed of the data and to document methodological decisions. Starting with the general questions such as *what is happening here?* and *what patterns of interaction are emerging?* led to more specific questions about the subject matter and about methodology. Researcher memos included the following: *where to focus the analytical lens* (how to get familiar with the large body of potential data and how to choose a portion to focus on); *how does the engineering context affect the group dynamics; how to make sense of science and engineering practices that sometimes overlap; how to represent participants that I have never met* (treating the data as a still or "stuck in time" event or considering the big picture – time passed since the original records were collected, other units were created, the teachers taught other units while students moved up to middle school); *what does the literature say about elementary engineering education; what are the structural and historical forces impacting students' participation and is that something I can realistically focus on without collecting more data*; and most importantly, *what is the story I want to tell with the evidence from the data*. I was unable to fully answer all of these questions, but they served as a starting point for a pilot study that I could then build on for my dissertation.

Using a microethnographic perspective, I closely examined the action, discourse, materials, and artifacts from student journals within the context of the elementary engineering units (Kelly, Crawford, & Green, 2001). Iterative cycles of analysis followed, starting with the macro level and then zooming in at the micro level. Each layer of analysis added extra background knowledge about the participants, their changing group roles, and the multiple iterations of the engineering design process that led to the final project.

Because classroom lessons have a regular structure, I was able to represent what was taking place in each lesson by constructing event maps using Matthew Johnson's Excel format as a starting point (see Chapter 5 for a detailed event map description and a sample in Table 5.3, page 110). I matched up the *phases* (coordinated action of participants around a common content focus) from the EiE observation logs (completed by an EiE staff member through direct observations in the classroom) with *sequences* that I determined based on contextualization cues and thematic shifts while closely reviewing the video data (Kelly & Crawford, 1997; Kelly, Crawford, & Green, 2001). Next to each sequence, I added comments that included direct quotations, observations, and other researcher comments. For each map, I summarized the action and analytical comments, while noting video segments to be investigated further.

After I isolated the areas of interest (moments of uncertainty within the group) using the event maps, I transcribed those segments using Transana 3.00 (video and audio analysis software that enables work with transcripts, coding, and creating collections). I noted the talk and action by speaker turn using select Jeffersonian notation symbols (Atkinson & Heritage, 1984), and included a summary of the relevant body language and gestures. I also used this software to take screen shots throughout the transcript to represent the action of the group members as they engaged with the bridge building and testing. Thus, the transcription processes were theoretical decisions that have consequences for what can be presented, referenced, and interpreted from the videotaped records (Skukauskaite, 2012).

Theoretical Framework: Building an Interactive Ethnographic Perspective

The field of Interactional Sociolinguistics (IS) provides the theoretical constructs that inform the research methods of my program of research in engineering education (Gumperz, 1982; 2001). This approach to understanding the construction of everyday life is a context-dependent view of communication as a social practice that is intentional, often goal-oriented, and based upon inferences and implicit background knowledge. During moments of miscommunication, the significant role of shared background knowledge in achieving understanding may become apparent to the participants and analysts alike. The unit of analysis is the *speech event*, which can be analyzed through empirical means that derive meaning from the data, rather than imposing meaning from theory. This inductive approach was key for my analysis of student–student interactions because it reminded me to push assumptions aside and focus closely on the speech, gestures, and materials within a speech event, while considering the greater context using the event maps. Nevertheless, all analysts form mental models based on experience, literature, and theories informing interpretation of cultural practices. Thus, being self-reflexive and transparent about methodological choices is essential to a well-informed research study.

The interactional sociolinguistic theory is complementary to other microethnographic methods. Historically, microethnography was influenced by many areas of study, including ethnography of communication, which is credited to both Dell Hymes and John Gumperz (1964, 1972). Ethnography and microethnography are related and distinct, yet often confounded. Erickson (1992) sorted this out by pointing out how the two methods are complimentary and that microethnography is defined as: "The close study of interaction through ethnographically oriented analysis of audiovisual records is a potentially useful component of an ethnographic study of education. It is not an alternative to more general ethnography but, rather, a complement to it" (p. 202). The second theoretical framework that influenced my work draws attention to a variety of features of communication and interaction, which was well suited for a multilayered microanalysis of children engaging in an engineering design challenge. The elementary engineering context provided an intersection of student-produced drawings, informational diagrams and symbols, written text, manipulation and reshaping of materials, hand and whole-body gestures, and a variety of speech patterns (overlapping excited talk, fragmented utterances, and extended explanations). Navigating these records with a multimodal lens does not mean just shifting focus from speech or text to image or other modes; it means considering all modes as part of a larger whole.

Multimodality can be thought of as a theory, a methodological approach, and a growing field of study (Jewitt, 2009). This work spans disciplinary boundaries and has a large variety of applications. I will specifically focus on one branch of study that stemmed from Systemic Functional Linguistics (SFL), semiotics theory, and Critical Discourse Analysis (CDA) (Jewitt *et al.*, 2016). In multimodal social semiotics analysis, the focus of the analysis is on the meaning-making potential of different modes. Kress *et al.* (2001) make a distinction between medium and mode: the medium or media (plural) is/are "the material substance which is worked on or shaped over time by culture into an organized, regular, socially specific means of representation, i.e. a meaning-making resource or a mode" (p. 15). Thus, the medium of sound may shape into the mode of language-as-speech. The materiality properties of each mode determine affordances and constraints for meaning-making. Using this approach added an extra layer to my analysis – keying in on the affordances of different modes and the specific resources students use to leverage ideas within small group discourse. Through this lens, a student-produced drawing is not just something that is referenced during talk, but it is also a design tool that gives concrete shape to a developing idea, enabling students to make an epistemological commitment (Kress, 2011).

Representing the Classroom Discourse

The process of creating transcriptions is a tricky part of data analysis – choices about what to include and how to make visible different aspects of interaction may limit or enhance what is made available to be seen and what meaning may be derived from the data (Ochs, 1979; Skukauskaite, 2012). In an age where transcription may be outsourced or automated by technological advancements, it's important to consider what counts as data and how it arrived in that format. Social science data is not found or collected, but actively constructed by the researcher from the available "raw records and artifacts" (Castanheira *et al.*, 2001, p. 358). It may seem that formats are arbitrary or inconsequential, but how data is represented may be as important as the content itself. Generally, transcripts contain line numbers, timestamps, speaker names/pseudonyms, speech turns, and sometimes features like pauses, prosody, gestures, etc. (for an example of an often-used system, see Jeffersonian notation in Atkinson & Heritage, 1984). Some transcripts include hesitations, filler words, and other variabilities/irregularities of speech, while others are "cleaned up" for various reasons, including clarity, ease of use, readability, or based on parsimony principles (O'Connell & Kowal, 1994). Thus, there is room for variation in format, order, content, and length, which needs to be based on a rationale that is in line with the methods of the study.

In addition to being a methodological choice, transcription can also be viewed as a situated and political act where the researcher makes impactful decisions about what to focus on and how to represent the participants and their discourse practices. The transcription text is not equivalent to the event within the data; instead, it's a "re"- presentation of an event (Green, Franquiz, & Dixon, 1997). This translation process is reductive, as researchers take parts of a fast-moving video and reshape it to a static representation on a page. In line with the analytical stance portrayed in this chapter, Mary Bucholtz (1999) recommends that researchers take a reflexive approach to transcription and realize the impact of transcription choices along with their limitations, and consider the underlying politics of interpretation and representation.

Researchers and scholars have known for a long time that transcription formats matter and that there is no set standard. In 1979, Elinor Ochs described transcription as "a selective process reflecting theoretical goals and definitions" and challenged researchers to really consider the type of format used and make deliberate choices based on the type of records available (p. 44). Thus, analyzing video of elementary student–student interactions requires a different transcript format than a sit-down interview with one adult participant. While constructing event maps, I noticed that the third graders moved a substantial amount even while sitting; there were many instances of excited overlapping talk; there were also long periods of time where students managed to communicate and coordinate efforts without talking. The challenge was to figure out how to represent what was happening without losing contextual cues that could aid in the analysis. Going back to my research questions, I considered what to highlight during the moments of uncertainty – verbal exchanges, body postures, eye gaze, manipulation of materials, prosody, etc. Which combination of these elements best illustrated positioning acts? I started with a transcript format based on Jeffersonian notation (see transcription conventions at end of chapter) that accounted for overlapping speech (Atkinson & Heritage, 1984). In sample transcript 1, I used a linear format that emphasized the verbal communication, but it was difficult to read and significant information was missing – the students adjusted their physical orientation as they talked and the materials moved back and forth between the students and the table space. After reading this transcript from the perspective of someone who did not see the video, I realized it was unclear what was happening and I needed to significantly change the format and content. For example, the students often relied on the use of pronouns instead of referencing the full name of each bridge prototype; this was in addition to using pronouns to refer to other participants. To draw attention to this, I bolded all instances of ambiguous indexical pronouns in sample transcript 1 where students make predictions while building and testing bridge prototypes (see Figure 3.2 on p. 59).

The transcript excerpt represents students' building and testing of three bridge prototypes from index cards and wood blocks: (a) beam, (b) deep beam, and (c) arch. The beam bridge (or "normal beam bridge" in line 20) features straight index cards, while the deep beam (referred to as a "double beam" in line 13) has an accordion fold in between index cards. The third bridge has a curved or arch design. Up until line 10, the students referred to the prototypes and the design features using pronouns. In line 10, Annie makes a prediction about which bridge will be the strongest and uses the term "deep beam bridge" twice. Up until then, it was unclear what the students were discussing. The other ambiguity is about how the group is structured. The students working at a pod of four desks are split up into two pairs that are simultaneously building and testing prototypes – Annie and Dan on the left side and Ellen and Chris on the right side.

In order to address the limitations of transcript 1, I considered representing the talk in side by side columns with different colors for each speaker, separating

Line #	Speaker	Utterance
01	Annie:	Okay, no, I got **it**. Do you want to do the **other one**?
02	Dan:	Sure, **which one**? Oh, yeah, **this one**.
03	Ellen:	Can we ( )?
04	Annie:	You fold **it** in half.
05	Dan:	Oh, yeah, I know how to do **it**.
06	Annie:	Are we supposed to do the accordion fold, but
07	Dan:	You have to do **this** first to make **it** straight
08	Annie:	Yeah, your ( )
09	Dan:	**This** isn't <perfect>, but **it**'s close enough
10	Annie:	I think that the ah now comes for my prediction. I think that the deep beam bridge would be the <strongest>. I think [the deep beam bridge would be the strongest.]
11	Ellen:	[I agree with you. °I agree with the deep beam bridge°]
12	Annie:	What?↑
13	Ellen:	I think the double beam bridge is going to be the strongest.=
14	Annie:	=**It**'s the <u>deep</u> beam bridge.
15	Chris:	Oh, we already wrote arch bridge.
16	Annie:	You wrote arch bridge?
17	Ellen:	No, I didn't.
18	Annie:	Yeah, she did.
19	Dan:	Oh, arch, what?
20	Annie:	She wrote <u>normal</u> beam bridge.
21	Chris:	She did?
22	Annie:	She did!
23	Dan:	((sings))
24	Ellen:	How do <u>you</u> know?
25	Annie:	Because I <u>saw</u> **it**.
26	Ellen:	Okay, can you just fold **this**?
27	Dan:	Are you done yet? Are you done yet?
28	Annie:	( ) Uh
29	Dan:	I think the uh double beam and the arch bridge are [about the same]
30	Ellen:	[Now what do we do?]
31	Annie:	< I don't>
32	Ellen:	Wait, how do you make **it** like **that**? (save me!)

FIGURE 3.2 Sample transcript 1.

out the participants based on their position at the tables (left vs. right) and aligning the overlapping speech side by side (see sample transcript 2 in Figure 3.3). Next, I constructed a representation of the desks and materials along with student postures and eye gaze direction adapted from figure 5 in Kelly *et al.* (2001). This second iteration of the format highlighted the differences in the number of turns per table group and provided a visual representation of the body postures, eye gaze (arrows), and the location of the bridge materials (small square).

The multiple column format was especially helpful for this collaborative setting where two student dyads worked simultaneously side by side. It was easier to track who said what and their relative location. There was a combination of talk among each pair, crosstalk, and overlapping speech. The students on the left articulated what they were doing more so than the students on the right, even

Left Group

Line #	Speaker	Utterance
01	Annie:	Okay, no, I got it. Do you want to do the other one?
02	Dan:	Sure, which one? Oh, yeah, this one.
04	Annie:	You fold it in half.
05	Dan:	Oh, yeah, I know how to do it.
06	Annie:	Are we supposed to do the accordion fold, but
07	Dan:	You have to do this first to make it straight
08	Annie:	Yeah, your ( )
09	Dan:	This isn't <perfect>, but it's close enough
10	Annie:	I think that the ah now comes for my prediction. I think that the deep beam bridge would be the <strongest>. I think the deep beam bridge would be the strongest.
12	Annie:	What?↑
14	Annie:	It's the deep beam bridge.
16	Annie:	You wrote arch bridge?
18	Annie:	Yeah, she did.
19	Dan:	Oh, arch, what?
20	Annie:	She wrote normal beam bridge.
22	Annie:	She did!
23	Dan:	((sings))
25	Annie:	Because I saw it.
27	Dan:	Are you done yet? Are you done yet?
28	Annie:	( ) Uh
29	Dan:	I think the uh double beam and the arch bridge are about the same.
31	Annie:	< I don't>

Right Group

Line #	Speaker	Utterance
03	Ellen:	Can we ( )?
11	Ellen:	I agree with you. °I agree with the deep beam bridge°
13	Ellen:	I think the double beam bridge is going to be the strongest.
15	Chris:	Oh, we already wrote arch bridge.
17	Ellen:	No, I didn't.
21	Chris:	She did?
24	Ellen:	How do you know?
26	Ellen:	Okay, can you just fold this?
30	Ellen:	Now what do we do?
32	Ellen:	Wait, how do you make it like that? Save me!

Physical Orientation

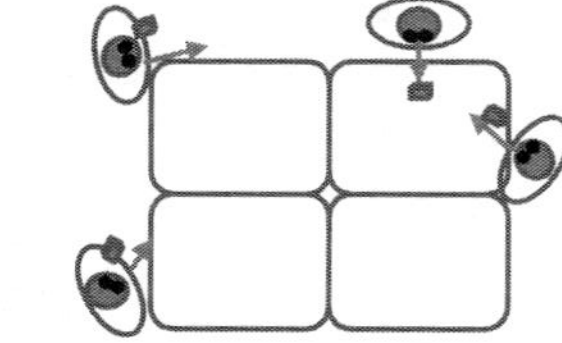

FIGURE 3.3 Sample transcript 2.

though they were all actively building and testing. The significant event in this episode is the prediction in line 10 and the whispered agreement in line 11. Ellen declares her agreement with Annie's prediction, but her teammate Chris points out that their written prediction was different – "**we** already wrote arch bridge" (line 15). When Ellen denies this other prediction, she speaks only for herself instead of the team – "No, **I** didn't." (line 17). In line 18 there is another pronoun shift. Annie had addressed Ellen in second person in line 16, but in lines 18, 20, and 22 the pronoun changes to third person. This disagreement over Ellen's prediction contains instances of positioning that reflect group dynamics that were already unfolding with the correction in line 14. Annie takes on a position of authority over Ellen's journal prediction because she claims that she "saw it" (line 25). Ellen does not deny it further and the group resumes building and testing. The takeaway here is that each student has a different written prediction in their engineering journal (Annie predicted deep beam, Chris predicted arch, Ellen predicted beam, and Dan predicted a tie between deep beam and arch), but in speech mode the prediction is influenced by previous discourse, social relationships, and other factors in addition to scientific and engineering principles. Some students might feel compelled to agree with a student in a leadership position rather than take ownership over their own prediction or they may change their mind after discussions with their group. In this case, establishing a consensus about predictions appeared to be more critical in speech mode compared to written mode. The classroom culture and norms also influence students' choices. In this case, the teacher did not provide explicit instructions to students to establish consensus for predictions in their notebook. This is in contrast with another class where the students were expected to report the same values in their journal tables.

Even though the transcript 2 format provided more information (eye gaze, body posture, and location of materials) compared to transcript 1, there were still other issues to resolve – *what did the materials look like as they're being manipulated? How can a diagram be designed to represent a student who is touching or grabbing materials from across the table?* To address this issue, my third iteration of transcription format incorporates screen shots featuring the materials and any prominent gestures. Since it wasn't feasible to include all of the video frames, I aimed to strike a balance between the frequency of screen shots and a written summary of activity.

The third transcript format was adapted from multimodal social semiotics analysis (Kress, 2011; Jewitt *et al.*, 2016) and featured: (a) extended descriptions of gestures, body positioning, and other discourse elements; (b) screen captures of significant gestures; and (c) excerpts from the students' journal that were explicitly or indirectly invoked in talk (see Figure 3.4 on pp. 63–66). Rather than using different colors to represent each student's contributions, I bolded the verbal utterances to set them apart from the non-verbal descriptions. This episode features a different group of four students (with pseudonyms Alex, Ryan, Tim, and Kara) from another classroom who are collectively building and testing the bridge prototypes (same lesson as transcripts 1 and 2). In this case, there was less of a need to separate the utterances into multiple columns because all group members are building and testing with the same set of materials. One transcript draft not shown here used columns to separate the text from the images, but was not as effective in embedding the different components of the transcript into one cohesive narrative. The format featured in transcript 3 (Figure 3.4 on pp. 63–66) is better suited for multimodal analysis because there is not as much separation between the screen shots, utterances, and the description of the activity.

The transcript 3 sample also featured disagreement, instances of positioning, and changing group dynamics. The students conduct multiple rounds of testing of their bridge prototypes and when the results are inconsistent the group has to resolve the uncertainty about which result should be reported in the journal (they were instructed to reach group consensus). In line 1 Alex counts out loud the number of weights the arch bridge can hold before it collapses. Ryan repeats the last count – "it was fifteen" (line 2), using past tense to indicate that was the last value before the bridge gave out. The critical moment in this episode is when Tim disagrees with the result (line 3) not because he observed something different or counted a different amount of weights, but because the group had already recorded a value of eighteen in their journals (line 15). During the rest of the episode the students negotiate whether to conduct additional trials and what value to ultimately report in their journals, which serve as the official group record.

The first act of positioning in this episode is when Kara stands up and strengthens Tim's value of eighteen through an overlapped excited utterance – "It was eighteen!" (line 4). In this case, this overlap was less of an interruption and more evidence of alignment with Tim's claim. In line 5 Tim extends and emphasizes "yeah," indicating his recognition of Kara's support. Meanwhile, Alex starts to articulate a thought (line 6) while manipulating testing materials but is interrupted by Kara who tells him "No, but **we** did it the first time. **You** don't do it again!" (line 7). Positioning also unfolds in the speech grammar, which is why I bolded the pronouns used to refer to group members. The second sentence structure resembling a command combined with the extra emphasis on the word "again" positions Kara as a group leader and authority over the reporting of results. Soon after there is a shift from "you" to the collective "we," which pushes for a group consensus with the repeated line "**We**'re not doing it again!" (lines 10, 14, 16, and 19). Kara's vocal persistence strongly contrasts Ryan's silence and Alex's soft-spoken line 8 and hesitation in line 11 where he tries to articulate his position, but lacks a reason why – "**I**'m looking at it right." Analyzing the gestures and material manipulation reveals a tug of war over the testing supplies that mirrors the back and forth speech turns. In conjunction with line 10, Kara takes an index card from the bridge prototype to attempt preventing Alex from re-testing. She holds the paper out even further, limiting Alex's access to the materials. Alex displays resourcefulness by finding another index card to rebuild the bridge.

Alex places bolts on top of an arch bridge prototype. The bridge collapses under the weight.

1 Alex: **Thirteen, fourteen, fifteen.**
2 Ryan: **It was fifteen!**

Alex erases his former result and writes down something else in his journal.

3 Tim: **No, it wasn't. It was eighteen the [highest.]**

Kara stands up at her desk.

4 Kara: **[It was eighteen!]**

5 Tim: **Y:eah!**
6 Alex: **I thought you were-**

Alex gathers up the bolts from the table and holds up a large index card.

7 Kara: **No, but we did it the first time. You don't do it <u>again</u>!**

FIGURE 3.4 Sample transcript 3.

(continued)

Alex bends the index card and places it between the wooden blocks serving as abutments (the first step in making an arch bridge prototype).

8 Alex: **No I-**
9 Tim: **The firs- wait-**
10 Kara: **We're not doing it again. We only did it the <u>last</u> time.**

Kara takes the top index card from Alex.

11 Alex: **I'm looking. I'm looking (at it right).**
12 Kara: **It was fifteen.**

Kara holds the index card even further away from Alex. He takes a different large index card and starts to fold it.

13 Tim: **I thought it was eighteen.**

Tim looks at Kara.

14 Kara: **It was eighteen. We're not we're not doing it again!**

Alex added another large index card on top of the arch.

15 Tim: **Because we already wrote it down.**
16 Kara: **We already wrote it [down]. We're not doing it again.**

Kara reaches for the other index card and starts to pull; Alex does not let go.

17 Alex: **[Stop!]**
18 Tim: **Yeah and I wrote it down.**
19 Kara: **We already wrote it down. We're not doing it again.**

Alex starts to add bolts on top of the arch bridge. Ryan stands.

FIGURE 3.4 *(continued)*

(continued)

Tim points to Alex's bridge and addresses Kara.

20 Tim: **Okay, how about if he does it but we won't write it down again?**
21 Kara: **Okay.**

Alex continues to add bolts on his beam bridge.

Alex gets thirteen bolts. Kara reminds him that it was eighteen. The teacher walks by and tells them "Keep going; you're doing a great job." Alex keeps the eighteen value in his journal.

In this case, Kara's vocal persistence with repeated statements is matched by Alex's determination with maintaining control over materials and the physical act of re-testing.

Along with line 16, Kara tries to take the new card away, but Alex holds onto it and tells her to "Stop!" In line 18 Tim takes Kara's side and points out "Yeah, and **I** wrote it down." In spite of the strong resistance to re-testing, Alex starts another round of testing while Ryan stands to watch (after line 19). Tim proposes a compromise (line 20) that resolves the tension, but not the uncertainty over the results. In an effort to shorten the transcript, I summarized the utterances that followed because the outcome was already decided (re-testing would be done but would not influence the final results). Alex tested again with a result of thirteen, which is 28% lower than the original eighteen value that remained in the journal; this inconsistency was not discussed. The students did not explore the issue of multiple trials further and the teacher did not notice the negotiation of results. Ultimately, Alex was able to explore the issue of multiple trials in material, gesture, and speech modes, but not in the written mode. Because the written mode is associated with the permanent record of the event, Kara and Tim's act of blocking access to alter the original text is equivalent to ignoring Alex's contribution. There are many potential reasons why this event unfolded the way it did, but without additional records there is no way of knowing why the group did not write down multiple results, averaged their trials, or picked the mode or median instead of the first value. These students are third graders who may not be familiar with mathematics and science concepts that could help them make sense of multiple trials and their significance.

The reason why I featured the two interactive speech events in this chapter was to discuss the many factors that go into deciding on a transcript format and what to include. In these episodes students were building and testing bridge prototypes, coordinating tasks, making predictions, and writing in their journals. Which features of these interactions and activity are relevant and need to be represented in the transcript and in what level of detail? If Kara's fourth repetition of a command is as significant as her gesture of grabbing the index card, and just as much as the final value in the journal, then all these elements need to be featured in the transcript for a more complete narrative or re-presentation of the original event.

Another challenge with transcripts was where to set the "episode" boundary for analysis. It was important to be firmly grounded in the data at the macro level before zooming in for microanalysis. In addition, conducting multiple rounds of systematic analysis allowed for patterns to emerge from the data and to strategically select evidence to construct a coherent argument. The other inherent challenge is "showing" vs. "telling" when reporting transcript evidence in publications that put a limit on how much to include. For the purpose of analysis, there is no such limit and transcripts may look very different than those constructed for publication. Most importantly, transcripts need to be useful for analysis and be matched up with the research questions. Formats, layout, contents, and episode boundaries need to be strategically chosen and in line with the research methods.

Initial Findings: Making Visible Rich Points for Opportunities for Learning

While using interactional ethnography-informed methods in conjunction with a multimodal approach, I described how students position themselves and each other while pushing for their ideas during moments of uncertainty. These uncertainty episodes represent *rich points* (Agar, 1994) for multimodal analysis where students consider, evaluate, and align multiple ideas or viewpoints. Reaching consensus in a group can be messy and issues of access and equity could be considered. Working through instances of uncertainty and disagreement also provides space for redefining positions and authentic opportunities for students to explain their ideas and position on an issue. Such opportunities provide students access to the social practices and relevant knowledge of science and engineering contextualized in organized activity. The educational value of the processes of working through uncertainty can be made visible through the multimodal, interactional ethnographic perspective.

The short excerpts presented in this chapter from the larger dataset point to some initial results of the analyses. The positioning within the groups was fluid and leadership roles changed over time (van Langenhove & Harré, 1999). Students employed a variety of resources and strategies to reposition themselves and others while making a case for their idea or their viewpoint. These included: persistence with alternative ideas (reintroducing the same idea repeatedly or rephrasing it and then reintroducing it), seeking agreement from the group leader, taking possessions over the materials, using evidence, or calling for a vote. The process of managing uncertainties was used as a checkpoint for aligning ideas, redefining positions, and as a potential space for identity exploration, in addition to engaging with and trying important disciplinary knowledge and practices of science and engineering. The complex social and cognitive processes of attempting to resolve uncertainty are part of the work of engineering. These findings make visible the ways that engaging in epistemic practices of engineering entail both cognitive and identity work (Kelly, Cunningham, & Ricketts, 2017).

Discussion and Implications for Future Research

The context of engineering-integrated units is unique and new to many classrooms. The advantages and challenges of integrating engineering design into curricula need to be researched in more detail using systematic, multidimensional research methods. In my experience, multiple passes through the records with different lenses helped accomplish multiple goals: (a) first, to get a broad overview of the group dynamics and activities using event maps, (b) then, to focus in closely on the speech events related to decision making and the array of semiotic resources students drew on to leverage their ideas, (c) to consider which theoretical constructs were compatible with the social processes observed, and (d) finally to refocus and address my research questions using multiple layers of evidence. Because of the shifting analytical lens, I purposely adjusted the transcripts to highlight different aspects of the group interactions. Transcript 1 focused on speech accuracy and overlapping speech. Transcript 2 shifted the talk into columns to indicate the relative body positioning of the participants in order to draw attention to the talk between partners compared to talk across groups. Transcript 3 incorporated multimodal principles to highlight the variety of semiotic resources students drew on to communicate and push for their ideas. Through these iterations of data analysis, the transcripts I constructed evolved in both content and form, which made visible the differences in my understanding of the relevant educational phenomena pertaining to science and engineering education.

Collaborative group work that incorporates the engineering design process allows students with varying skillsets to be successful at different components. When students work together to solve an engineering design challenge, there is a variety of tasks to be delegated among the team members and opportunities to learn from each other. In the EiE civil engineering unit, students engage in activities within and across visual, written, speech, gesture, and other modes associated with tools and materials. Depending on their strengths, students can contribute to their teams in different ways, such as interpreting diagrams, generating design ideas through drawings, calculating projected cost of design plan, exploring, manipulating, or tinkering with materials, recording and calculating testing results, constructing evidence-based explanations, and identifying ways to improve. For example, a student just beginning to learn the language of instruction may be most comfortable with design drawings and manipulating materials. In this way, the student may be able to participate in all aspects of the design challenge as a group member by communicating their knowledge and contribution through multiple modes. There are opportunities for all students to take responsibility for their own learning, especially when they are invested in their design ideas (Cunningham, 2018). Thus, through collaboration, students can develop ownership over their design ideas and be recognized for their diverse contributions to the group, their leadership, and ability to facilitate group goals.

Teacher professional development could address specific ways teachers can facilitate small group collaboration to allow students to work through moments of uncertainty and how to decide when to step in to help and when to allow the group to work through disagreements and doubt. Teachers may have to overcome their instinct to step in and resolve the uncertainty the students are grappling with; instead, they could observe from afar or join the group as a co-participant, not as a leader or evaluator. After a period of observation, teachers may pose open-ended questions to allow students to problem-solve collectively. Video analysis of lessons could help teachers learn to identify how groups strategize and work through uncertainties. There is value in recognizing that certain types of discourses may appear to be off task at first glance, but upon closer examination, they could be purposeful and offer opportunities for students to engage in science and engineering practices.

Working through uncertainty may take up extra time that is worth spending to allow students to practice using different strategies for listening and presenting ideas in a safe space. Thus, curriculum designers may want to build intentional choices that will create opportunities for students to stop and weigh different options. A balance needs to be struck between a design task that is too restrictive and offers few design choices and one that is too open and difficult for students to navigate.

Further research is needed to determine how teachers construct collaborative classroom environments where students' voices can be heard. The teachers from the EiE units helped create norms for group collaboration well before the start of this particular study. At the beginning of the year, teachers set expectations and establish ground rules for class and group work participation. Students' notion of group leadership may be based on the modeling the teacher puts forth.

Asking questions, managing tasks, listening, comparing, and critiquing ideas may seem common sense, but these are skills that are modeled and taught over time. Articulating specific strategies for inter-group communication could be beneficial. Nevertheless, there are many questions still lingering regarding group dynamics: (a) *How can equity be promoted within groups?* (b) *How can teachers facilitate group work before, during, and after the design challenge?* (c) *What are the implications for students' affinity towards science and engineering careers?* Using multiple perspectives and research methods grounded at multiple levels of context will begin to elucidate the complex social and cognitive processes involved in these types of classroom interactions.

References

Agar, M. (1994). *Language shock: Understanding the culture of conversation.* New York: William Morrow and Company.

Atkinson, J. M., & Heritage, J. (Eds.). (1984). *Structures of social action: Studies in conversation analysis.* Cambridge: Cambridge University Press.

Bloome, D., Carter, S. P., Christian, B. M., Otto, S., & Shuart-Faris, N. (2005). *Discourse analysis and the study of classroom language and literacy events: A microethnographic perspective.* New York: Routledge.

Bucholtz, M. (1999). The politics of transcription. *Journal of Pragmatics, 32*(10), 1439–1465.

Castanheira, M. L., Crawford, T., Dixon, C. N., & Green, J. L. (2001). Interactional ethnography: An approach to studying the social construction of literate practices. *Linguistics and Education, 11*(4), 353–400.

Cunningham, C. M. (2009). Engineering is elementary. *The Bridge, 30*(3), 11–17.

Cunningham, C. M. (2018). *Engineering in elementary STEM education: Curriculum design, instruction, learning, and assessment.* New York: Teachers College Press.

Cunningham, C. M., & Carlsen, W. S. (2014). Precollege engineering education. *Handbook of research on science education.* Mahwah, NJ: Lawrence Erlbaum Associates.

Engineering is Elementary. (2011). *To get to the other side: Designing bridges.* Boston, MA: Museum of Science, Boston.

Erickson, F. (1992). Ethnographic microanalysis of interaction. In M. D. LeCompte, W. L. Milroy, & J. Preissle (Eds.), *The handbook of qualitative research in education* (pp. 201–225). San Deigo, CA: Academic Press.

Erickson, F. (2017). Conceiving, noticing, and transcribing multi-modality in the study of social interaction as a learning environment. *Linguistics and Education, 41*(October), 59–61.

Fairclough, N. (2013). *Critical discourse analysis: The critical study of language* (2nd ed.). New York: Routledge.

Green, J. L., Franquiz, M., & Dixon, C. (1997). The myth of the objective transcript: Transcribing as a situated act. *Tesol Quarterly, 31*(1), 172–176.

Green, J. L., & Harker, J. O. (Eds.). (1988). *Multiple perspective analyses of classroom discourse.* Norwood, NJ: Ablex.

Gumperz, J. J. (1982). *Discourse strategies* (Vol. 1). Cambridge: Cambridge University Press.

Gumperz, J. J. (2001). Interactional sociolinguistics: A personal perspective. In D. Schiffrin, D. Tannen, & H. E. Hamilton (Eds.), *Handbook of discourse analysis.* Malden, MA: Blackwell.

Gumperz, J. J., & Hymes, D. (1964). The ethnography of communication: Special issue. *American Anthropologist, 66*(6), 137–154.

Hammersley, M., & Atkinson, P. (1995). *Ethnography: Principles in practice.* New York: Routledge.

Hymes, D. H., & Gumperz, J. J. (Eds.). (1972). *Directions in sociolinguistics: The ethnography of communication.* New York: Holt, Rinehart and Winston.

Jewitt, C. (Ed.). (2009). *The Routledge handbook of multimodal analysis.* New York: Routledge.

Jewitt, C., Bezemer, J., & O'Halloran, K. (2016). *Introducing multimodality.* New York: Routledge.

Jordan, M. E., & McDaniel Jr, R. R. (2014). Managing uncertainty during collaborative problem solving in elementary school teams: The role of peer influence in robotics engineering activity. *Journal of the Learning Sciences, 23*(4), 490–536.

Kelly, G. J. (2006). Epistemology and educational research. In J. L. Green, G. Camilli, & P. B. Elmore (Eds.), *Handbook of complementary methods in education research* (pp. 33–56). New York: Routledge.

Kelly, G. J., & Chen, C. (1999). The sound of music: Constructing science as sociocultural practices through oral and written discourse. *Journal of Research in Science Teaching, 36*(8), 883–915.

Kelly, G. J., & Crawford, T. (1997). An ethnographic investigation of the discourse processes of school science. *Science Education, 81*(5), 533–559.

Kelly, G. J., Crawford, T., & Green, J. L. (2001). Common task and uncommon knowledge: Dissenting voices in the discursive construction of physics across small laboratory groups. *Linguistics and Education, 12*(2), 135–174.

Kelly, G. J., Cunningham, C. M., & Ricketts, A. (2017). Engaging in identity work through engineering practices in elementary classrooms. *Linguistics and Education, 39*(June), 48–59.

Kress, G. (2011). Discourse analysis and education: A multimodal social semiotic approach. In R. Rogers (Ed.), *An introduction to critical discourse analysis in education.* New York: Routledge.

Kress, G., Jewitt, C., Ogborn, J., & Tsatsarelis, C. (2001). *Multimodal teaching and learning: The rhetorics of the science classroom.* New York: Continuum.

Lachapelle, C. P., Cunningham, C. M., & Oh, Y. (2017, April). *An efficacy study of Engineering is Elementary: Quantitative modeling of outcomes.* Paper presented at the NARST Annual International Conference, San Antonio, TX.

Metz, K. E. (2004). Children's understanding of scientific inquiry: Their conceptualization of uncertainty in investigations of their own design. *Cognition and Instruction, 22*(2), 219–290.

NGSS Lead States. (2013). *Next generation science standards: For states, by states.* Washington, DC: National Academies Press.

Norris, S. (Ed.). (2012). *Multimodality in practice: Investigating theory-in-practice-through-methodology* (Vol. 4). New York: Routledge.

Ochs, E. (1979). Transcription as theory. *Developmental Pragmatics, 10*(1), 43–72.

O'Connell, D. C., & Kowal, S. (1994). Some current transcription systems for spoken discourse: A critical analysis. *Pragmatics: Quarterly Publication of the International Pragmatics Association (IPrA), 4*(1), 81–107.

Skukauskaite, A. (2012). Transparency in transcribing: Making visible theoretical bases impacting knowledge construction from open-ended interview records. *Forum Qualitative Sozialforschung/Forum: Qualitative Social Research, 13*(1).

Toulmin, S. (1958). *The uses of argument.* Cambridge: Cambridge University Press.
Vanderhoof, C. (2017, April). *Managing uncertainty within elementary engineering groups.* Paper presented at the NARST Annual International Conference, San Antonio, TX.
van Langenhove, L., & Harré, R. (1999). Introducing positioning theory. In R. Harré. & L. van Langenhove (Eds.), *Positioning theory: Moral contexts of intentional action* (pp. 14–31). Oxford: Blackwell Publishing.
Wegerif, R., & Mercer, N. (1997). A dialogical framework for investigating talk. In R. Wegerif & P. Scrimshaw (Eds.), *Computers and talk in the primary classroom* (pp. 49–65). Clevedon: Multilingual Matters.

Transcription Conventions

Transcription symbols adopted from Jeffersonian notation (Atkinson & Heritage, 1984)

( ) unsure speech; either left blank or best transcription guess in between parentheses

(( )) description of non-verbal communication or activity

[ ] overlapping speech; turns are aligned to show overlap

< > slower rate of speech (compared to the speaker's previous utterances)

° whisper or lower volume speech

↑ increased pitch

= latched speech (one utterance closely follows another)

- interrupted utterance

:: prolongation of a word

______ extra emphasis

4

TRANSLANGUAGING ABOUT SOCIOSCIENTIFIC ISSUES IN MIDDLE SCHOOL SCIENCE

Peter R. Licona

Introduction

Our constantly changing public elementary and secondary science classrooms provide both opportunities and challenges for providing authentic, relevant, and responsive science education for all students. Recent calls for science education reform with greater foci on discourse and practices (National Research Council, 2012) occur at a time of increasing cultural and linguistic diversification of our public schools. Taken together, the confluence of these two factors challenges researchers to investigate how major science education reform impacts the science learning of the growing population of culturally and linguistically diverse (CLD) students. The purpose of this chapter is to describe the methodological decisions made while planning and implementing a research study investigating a reform-based science curriculum intervention in an English/Spanish dual language middle school science classroom. I will first situate the study in its contemporary importance, then describe various phases of the research study in depth, and finally discuss results and implications of the study related to bilingual education, science education, and ethnography of education.

Calls for science education reform, such as *A Framework for K-12 Science Education* (NRC, 2012) and subsequent *Next Generation Science Standards* (NGSS Lead States, 2013), recommend a three-dimensional approach to science education that promotes an intertwining of disciplinary core ideas, crosscutting concepts, and scientific and engineering practices to engage students in science learning that mirrors the work done by career scientists. Explicit attention to scientific and engineering practices is an attempt to engage students with the diverse practices that constitute scientific inquiry. The inclusion of scientific and engineering practices, many of which require the extensive use of discourse, both written and verbal, is anticipated to place significant language demands on all students, but these demands will be greatest for CLD students, such as English Learners (EL) and emergent bilinguals. Lee, Quinn, and Valdés (2013) note that engaging in discourse-intensive scientific and engineering practices, such as scientific argumentation, will require discipline-specific and demanding uses of language for English Learners. These authors further note that research is needed to examine the language demands presented by the inclusion of these practices in K-12 science education.

In addition to the curricular and pedagogical changes precipitated by recent science education reform, schools in the United States are continuing to shift demographically, particularly with an increase in CLD students, the majority represented by Latina/o students. CLD students are often underserved and underrepresented in science education and related fields, and include English Learners and emergent bilinguals. CLD takes into account cultural and linguistic diversity and represents myriad ethnicities, languages, and cultures. The difference between the use of English Learners and emergent bilingual is subtle, but important; emergent bilingual indicates that students are actively in the process of learning two (or more) languages, such as students in dual language settings, whereas English Learner often denotes that a student has a home language other than English and through formal assessment is at less than fluent levels of English proficiency as compared to peers. By far, the largest group of CLD students is represented by Latina/o, or Hispanic, students. Excelencia in Education (2015) reported that from 2004 to 2015 Hispanic students increased from 19% to 24% of all students in US schools. This shift in student demographics has resulted in communities and schools that are increasingly CLD. Cultural and linguistic diversity in our schools is not a new phenomenon and offers unique opportunities to create inclusive science programs. A perennial concern of many educators, researchers, and policy makers is how to plan science learning environments that are relevant and responsive to the educational needs of CLD students, such as emergent bilingual Latina/o students.

Past research indicates that traditional science education pedagogy and curriculum have often resulted in the inaccessibility of science to CLD students. This inaccessibility has resulted in student underperformance in traditional school science outcomes (Lee & Luykx, 2006), lack of representation in the science workforce (Landivar, 2013), and underrepresentation in STEM teaching (U.S. Department of Education, 2016). While traditional measures of participation and success in science are indeed important, it is also critical to realize that exclusion from science can impact CLD students' ability to engage in meaningful ways with persistent socioscientific issues (SSI) outside of schooling that necessitate an understanding of scientific principles and engagement in scientific practices. As science and science education have been historically criticized for being less accessible for students from diverse cultural and linguistic backgrounds, it is important that the research community implement effective and innovative research methodologies that are able to investigate how science education reform efforts impact

CLD students' access to the practices and content of the science classroom. One avenue is for researchers to investigate pedagogy that renders science education more accessible to CLD students.

Science Pedagogy and Scientific Practices

To examine some of the substantive and methodological issues facing emergent bilingual students, this study reports on the implementation of a socioscientific issues approach to science education, coupled with a scientific argumentation framework in an English/Spanish dual language middle school science classroom. A socioscientific issues approach to science education is a problems-based approach that focuses on controversial social issues with conceptual and/or procedural ties to science (Sadler, 2004). The loss of biodiversity, pollution, and human-driven energy demands are but a few examples of socioscientific issues. In order to develop students' ability to engage with these types of issues outside of the classroom, a socioscientific issues approach has been recommended as a pedagogical approach; an approach which embodies many of the recent science education reform recommendations, such as presenting science education as relevant to students' out of classroom lives and engaging students with the practices of science. Research on this approach demonstrates that it is effective in addressing multiple educational goals such as learning the Nature of Science (Kolstø, 2001), content learning (Sadler & Zeidler, 2005), moral and ethical development (Sadler, 2004), and scientific argumentation (Zohar & Nemet, 2002).

Argumentation, as a scientific practice, has been and continues to be a focal point within the science education research community. Many researchers have advocated for the inclusion of argumentation in the K-12 science classroom (Duschl & Osborne, 2002; Jiménez-Aleixandre & Erduran, 2007; Tiberghien, 2007). Arguing about socioscientific issues, or socioscientific argumentation, is a fairly specific form of scientific argumentation in which students engage as they attempt to reason through an ill-structured problem or respond to an open-ended question. Socioscientific argumentation often includes a decision-making component that is designed to mirror authentic decision making outside of the classroom. As opposed to scientific argumentation in which students marshal scientific evidence to support a scientific claim, socioscientific argumentation opens the argumentative task to allow multiple arguments that originate from alternative, and often, competing vantage points. Thus, socioscientific argumentation affords students the opportunity to argue from scientific, moral or ethical, economic, and/or personal perspectives. Both scientific argumentation and socioscientific argumentation are discourse-intensive practices that afford students opportunities to talk science in authentic and meaningful ways. A unique feature of the socioscientific issues approach is that it expands the range of language demands required of participating students.

Dual Language Education and Translanguaging

In addition to the relevance of this research to science pedagogy, curriculum, and scientific practices, this study examines how a reform-based curriculum intervention was constructed and implemented in an English/Spanish dual language classroom. Dual language education is a model of bilingual education in which students receive instruction in two languages, such as English and Spanish. This model of education is currently gaining support from educators and policy makers for its ability to promote bilingualism and address the educational needs of our growing population of emergent bilinguals. Dual language education is one form of bilingual education characterized as offering instruction through the use of two languages, each of which can be framed as either the native and/or the target language.

Two models of dual language education programs are generally described in the literature: the 50-50 model, characterized by equal instructional time devoted to both native and target languages, and the 90-10 model, characterized by 90% of the instruction being conducted in the target language and 10% being conducted in the native language. Both models generally operate under a language separation or language-bracketing paradigm in which the use of each language is separate from the other with little to no translation or repetition in the other language (Collier & Thomas, 2004). In general, language bracketing can be achieved by teaching different content subjects in different languages (e.g., science in Spanish and social studies in English). The rationale for a language-bracketing model is that this creates an environment which involves students in a second language learning experience, without allowing them to fall back upon the familiarity of their home language. The bracketing of languages suggests an additive bilingualism approach to the learning of two languages, in which one language is added to another language. While language bracketing is generally one of the hallmarks of current dual language education models, it is inevitable that there will be a mixing of languages, similar to the mixing of languages in bilingual communities.

Translanguaging, or the fluid and dynamic language practices bilinguals employ to make sense of their bilingual communities (García, Kleifgen, & Falchi, 2008), has garnered much interest in the bilingual education research community for its use in meaning making by students and as a pedagogical strategy. While not a new linguistic practice, it has also gained the attention of particular research communities due to its potential for providing emergent bilinguals access to the content and practices in formal learning environments. García, Ibarra Johnson, and Seltzer (2017) note four purposes of a translanguaging pedagogy: supporting learners as they engage with and comprehend complex content and texts; providing opportunities for learners to develop linguistic practices for academic contexts; making space for learner bilingualisms and ways of knowing; and supporting learner bilingual identities and socioemotional development. Translanguaging, as a pedagogical strategy, embodies both the orientations and pedagogical knowledge and the skills of linguistically responsive teachers as proposed by Lucas and Villegas (2013) as the educational needs of emergent bilinguals are addressed in bilingual educational settings. In addition, translanguaging as pedagogy is supportive of a linguistically relevant approach to teaching, as the linguistic practices of emergent bilinguals' out-of-school environments are congruent to those inside the classroom.

The changing linguistic landscape of the K-12 science classroom combined with the recent calls for science education reform offer important and timely opportunities for investigating how science education reform can be successfully implemented in linguistically diverse classrooms. With this as the research focus, I began planning a study guided by the following research questions: What are the challenges and opportunities in implementing an argumentation-based, socioscientific issues approach in an English/Spanish dual language science classroom? What are the language demands for emergent bilingual students engaging in socioscientific argumentation in an English/Spanish dual language science classroom? What are the demands for bilingual science teachers engaging in socioscientific argumentation in an English/Spanish dual language classroom? These research questions provided me with a basis for my study but, as will be seen later, through my initial phases of the ethnographic study, I revised my research questions. The sections that follow will describe in detail the various research methods employed to investigate the complex learning environment that characterized this study.

Logic of Inquiry for the Study of Translanguaging in Middle School Science

Complex cultural and linguistic settings, such as dual language science classrooms, require research methodologies that allow researchers to fully capture, describe, and analyze such complexity. Taking into account this complexity and considering an appropriate research methodology, this study drew on the work of Castanheira, Crawford, Dixon, and Green (2001), Gumperz (2001) and Kelly (2014). While not a traditional ethnography, this study made use of ethnographic logic of inquiry in order to make sense of the complex cultural and linguistic interactions. Castanheira *et al.* (2001) refer to this approach as interactional ethnography, an epistemological perspective that guides theoretical and methodological decisions about data collection and analysis. Interactional ethnography is one tradition of qualitative research. While not an algorithmic approach, the tradition itself is purposefully malleable to the dynamic research setting and research questions. As such, my approach was dictated by my specific research questions that could only be answered in a very specific learning environment. My approach also drew from an interactional sociolinguistic approach, as described by Gumperz (2001), which is characterized by two stages: an initial stage of ethnographic research designed to provide insight into the norms and expectations of the communicative setting and a second stage in which findings from stage one allow the researcher to select events for further analysis. In addressing the theoretical and methodological considerations of analyzing classroom activities, Kelly (2014) notes five themes for analyzing classroom activities: discourse practices are situated in social practice, there are different ways of representing social action and practices, the need to make analyses systematic, research can drive pedagogical change, and research frameworks are bound by certain limitations. Each of these themes was taken into account in formulating and implementing the described research methodology used to investigate the complexity of a dual language science classroom implementing reform-based science education. The following sections will discuss the chronology of this research study.

Negotiating Access

One of the first steps of this research study was to identify an appropriate school to conduct this research. While dual language education has been gaining support in recent years, this type of educational setting is not prevalent in all geographical areas of the United States. Finding and negotiating access to a bilingual/dual language school was necessary to my research agenda. Fortunately, in my 15+ years of working with various educators in formal and informal settings in a large and diverse metropolitan area, I had collaborated with many professionals concerned with the education of bilingual/bicultural Latina/o youth. I had an existing connection to administrators and teachers at a charter school, at which I was previously employed as a middle and high school science teacher, which provided education to a mostly Latina/o student population. The former principal, Mr. Lucero (a pseudonym), and a former classroom teacher, Ms. Pagoda (a pseudonym), of the school, in conjunction with other community members, decided to found a dual language school that would serve the educational needs of the growing bilingual student population in the area.

The AB Language School (a pseudonym) was founded and began providing education for students and families desiring formal education in English and Spanish in 2010. This charter school serves students from a large metropolitan area that has a significant and growing Latina/o/Hispanic population. The majority of the students educated by the school are classified as Hispanic, with a small percentage consisting of Black, non-Hispanic, White, non-Hispanic, or students from two or more races. According to the school's charter application, starting in kindergarten, 50% of the daily instruction at the school will be in Spanish and 50% will be in English. The school strives to employ teachers who are fluent in both English and Spanish, in order to support the bilingual focus of the school's mission.

I reached out, via e-mail communication, to both Mr. Lucero and Ms. Pagoda regarding the school. Mr. Lucero was now a member of the AB Language School board and Ms. Pagoda, who earned a principal's certificate, was now the school's principal. Through a face-to-face discussion with Mr. Lucero, I learned of the school's history, mission, and vision and was provided with a copy of the school's original charter. I then contacted Ms. Pagoda to visit the school and conduct an informal observation of a dual language learning environment. My initial visit to the school consisted of observing both an elementary level and middle level classroom. During the visit Ms. Pagoda and I discussed the potential of using the school as a future research site. I contacted Ms. Pagoda a second time to meet with her and determine the school's suitability as a research site and to explain my initial research ideas. Ms. Pagoda agreed to allow the school to be used as a research site and then suggested that I work with the 7th grade teacher. I mention this process in detail as gaining access to very specific and unique research settings with particular student and teacher populations requires a significant amount of time and effort.

After the initial visits with the school's principal and determining the suitability of the site, I began planning the research proposal in anticipation of collaborating with the 7th grade science teacher. As I was in the initial stages of researching and writing the curriculum intervention, Ms. Pagoda took my research proposal to the school's board where it was approved and I then moved forward with securing IRB (institutional review board) approval from my home institution. As the research was to be conducted in a bilingual community, I had to also consider that materials for parents should be in both English and Spanish. I originally penned the informed consent form, which informed the parents of the research and sought permission, in English and then translated it to Spanish. I am a Spanish speaker, but sought an external review of the translation for accuracy. The informed consent form was verified for accuracy by a native Spanish speaker with Spanish teaching and tutoring experience. Again, conducting research in unique settings with particular populations requires a researcher to engage in specific activities necessitated by the research.

Construction of an Archive of Records

Four main phases of constructing an archive of records and analysis characterize the research methodology of this study. I use the term archive of records, as these records did not actually become data until they were analyzed and applied to the research questions. While these phases appear to be discrete, in fact many analytical activities appear throughout the phases. For example, the video records were reviewed while the archive was being constructed. Nonetheless, phase one consisted of initial classroom observations and construction of the curriculum intervention, phase two consisted of classroom observation and video recording of the curriculum implementation, phase three consisted of the analysis of video records, and phase four consisted of identifying, transcribing, and coding instances of teacher translanguaging. Table 4.1 demonstrates the four main phases of constructing an archive of records and the corresponding dates for each phase.

TABLE 4.1 Phases of constructing an archive of records

Phase	*Activity*	*Dates/Timeframe*
Phase One	Classroom Observations and Collection of Field Notes.	September 13, 16, October 4, 7, November 14, 15, and December 16, 2013; and January 6, 2014.
	Construction of Curriculum Intervention.	September 2013 to January 2014.
Phase Two	Implementation of Curriculum Intervention.	January 30 to March 12, 2014.
Phase Three	Analysis of Video Records: Pass One – Initial Coding Pass Two – Classroom Activities and Scientific Practice.	March 12, 2014 to May 2015.
Phase Four	Identification, Transcription, and Coding of Teacher Translanguage.	December 2015 to May 2015.

Phase One: Classroom Observations and Collection of Field Notes

The first phase consisted of eight full days of classroom observation, over the course of five months, prior to the implementation of the curricular intervention. I visited the classroom twice in September, twice in October, twice in November, once in December, and once in January. The purpose of the classroom observations was multifold:

- to learn the norms and expectations of the school as a whole;
- to come to know the students and teacher on academic and personal levels;
- to understand the established and developing classroom culture;
- to observe the implemented curriculum and pedagogy;
- to understand the languaging practices of the teacher and students; and
- to develop an insider, or emic, perspective of the learning environment.

On the first observation date, I met with the 7th grade teacher, Ms. Ramirez (a pseudonym), to fully discuss my research program, my teaching background, and my research proposal. Ms. Ramirez and I also briefly discussed her educational background, most particularly her formal coursework in science education. During the meeting, a *co-expertise* model was discussed in order to construct a curriculum intervention that drew from both my and Ms. Ramirez's areas of expertise. My upcoming presence in the classroom was also framed as professional development for Ms. Ramirez, who expressed interest in my assistance with improving her classroom science curriculum and pedagogy.

Throughout the observations, ethnographic field notes (Emerson, Fretz, & Shaw, 1995) were collected in order to characterize the norms and expectations, the curriculum and pedagogy, and the linguistic practices of the classroom. Field notes (see Table 4.2) were recorded using paper and pencil and later wordprocessed for ease of reading, storage, and retrieval. As indicated in Table 4.2, the format consisted of date/time, observations, reflective comments, and additional details.

The observations recorded ranged from describing the classroom's physical environment, describing my discussions with the teacher and/or students, to describing the use of English and Spanish by both the teacher and students. I often wrote analytical memos of ideas or questions that arose during classroom observations. These memos guided my ideas regarding the research questions, the construction of the curriculum intervention, and future data collection and

TABLE 4.2 Field notes example

Date/Time	*Observations*	*Reflective comments*	*Additional Details*
9.13.13 7:30-8:15	Meeting with classroom teacher • Discussed my research (SSI, CLD, Discourse) • Teacher set up science lab on fats for the 6th grade classes • Students enter close to 8:00, some speaking English, some speaking Spanish • Talkative, friendly, open, inviting classroom • Classroom hangings are in both English and Spanish • Directions on bulletin board are in Spanish, "*como la humanidad cambia los lugares*" "warm up" is in English and this is what students have to do first thing • Discussed her education (K-6 cert.), mentions her affinity for science, has had 3 science-related courses in college: 2 content classes, one sci method class • Traditional classroom set up – not a science laboratory, no lab area • Teacher mentions that some students are new to school in that they are in upper grades, but not familiar with bilingual learning environment	I greet students • One in English • One, initially in English, then I switch to Spanish • Some students greet me and introduce themselves to me	Room somewhat warm upon arrival, T turns on fans and portable AC unit

analysis. For example, at the end of the first classroom observation, I wrote various questions to myself regarding this research. Questions that I later considered during future activities, include the following:

- Do I want the trifold (species information packets) in English and Spanish?
- How many officially classified ELLs in the class?
- How many students have English as the primary home language? How does the teacher address answers in "Spanglish"?

In maintaining transparency in my work as an ethnographic researcher, I announced and described the reason for my presence in the classroom to the students. I gave a brief presentation to both 7th grade classes, and both 6th grade classes, even though the 6th grade classes were not part of my future research program. During these presentations, I discussed my professional and personal background, my research goals, and allowed students to ask questions of me. Throughout my research, I allowed students to view my field notes and any video recordings made. Most students were uninterested in my field notes, and focused mostly on how to set up and operate the video cameras. In little time, I found that the students welcomed my presence in the classroom and soon accepted me as a common feature of the class.

On Roles and Relations as an Observer: From Passive to Full Participation

Throughout this observation phase, and during all my time in the classroom, my role fluctuated between observer and participant; in each instance I was a participant observer with more or less active participation based on the situated contexts of activity and my strategic decisions about when and how to engage (Spradley, 1980/2016). Throughout this phase of the research, I observed the classroom events and recorded field notes; in my role, I was often drawn into or led the class discussions or activities, as I was framed as an expert in science education by the classroom teacher. There was considerable personal tension in my mind due to my fluctuating roles in the classroom as I, a former teacher, found it somewhat challenging to be in a classroom and only assume the role of observer and researcher. Regardless of the tensions I experienced, the classroom observations proved to be extremely important in assisting me plan future research activities and reflect on my observations.

During this first phase, I also had extensive conversations with the classroom teacher throughout the school day, building on what Spradley (1979) frames as informal ethnographic interview conversations. Our discussions ranged from her undergraduate studies, her curriculum and pedagogy, my research agenda and teaching background, the upcoming curriculum intervention, to discussions related to my evaluation of her classroom pedagogy.

Drawing on informal conversations with the classroom teacher, observations of the classroom pedagogy and curriculum, review of literature on science curriculum and pedagogy, and review of field notes the curriculum intervention was constructed throughout this first phase. A description of the curriculum writing process follows this section.

Construction of the Curriculum Intervention

The ongoing process of negotiating access to and observing a suitable research setting required the co-construction of a reform-based science curriculum intervention designed to engage students (and the teacher) in discourse-intensive scientific practices. The curriculum intervention, focusing on biodiversity, was informed based on my experience with planning and implementing a pilot curriculum during a summer supplemental science course. The pilot curriculum was implemented with an entirely different population of students and, in the case of this study, served only to guide my construction and implementation of the research program. The biodiversity curriculum intervention implemented during this research program was also constructed by drawing on a review of *A Framework for K-12 Science Education* (NRC, 2012) and literature on teaching sequences (Leach, Ametller, Hind, Lewis, & Scott, 2005; Leach & Scott, 2002). Teaching sequences are generally short and innovative approaches to classroom instruction. In constructing a teaching sequence, Leach *et al.* (2005) recommend six steps: (a) content analysis with attention to grade level and official curriculum; (b) review of literature on teaching and learning content; (c) identification of learning demands; (d) explicit teaching goals; (e) design of teaching activities; and (f) pre- and post-curricular assessment. The curriculum intervention focused on biodiversity-related socioscientific issues, particularly endangered species and the factors responsible for the decrease in a particular organism's population. The curriculum was formulated with explicit input from the classroom teacher who was involved with the co-implementation of the curriculum. Based on my collaboration with the classroom teacher, the decision was made to make all materials (assessments, assignments, resources) available in both English and Spanish. Table 4.3 provides an overview of the construction of the curriculum intervention based on the approach proposed by Leach *et al.* (2005).

In addition to using teaching sequences literature to guide the construction of the curriculum intervention, I drew on my classroom observations to assist with making the curriculum relevant to the students. In considering the relevance of the curriculum, I decided to choose three iconic animals species (the green turtle, the Puerto Rican coqui, and the timber rattlesnake) to be featured in the curriculum. The first species, the green turtle, is a culturally iconic species featured in the movie *Finding Nemo*, which was an enormously successful and popular movie among middle school students. The Puerto Rican coqui, a culturally iconic species in Puerto Rico, was chosen as many of the students were of Puerto Rican

TABLE 4.3 Overview of construction of curriculum intervention

Step of Teaching Sequence	*Description*
Content analysis with attention to grade level and official curriculum	Review of the Pennsylvania Department of Education (PDE) *Academic Standards for Environment and Ecology* (2009) at the 7th grade level and the *Next Generation Science Standards: For States, By States* (NGSS Lead States, 2013) life sciences disciplinary core ideas at the middle school level.
Review of literature on teaching and learning content	Review of literature on socioscientific issues approach, teaching and learning of ecosystems, systems thinking, endangered species, invasive species, and scientific argumentation.
Identification of learning demands	Review of literature on the difficulties students have with learning to engage in scientific argumentation and the increased language demands of reform-based science education on English Learners. Discussions with classroom teacher.
Explicit teaching goals	Identification of teaching goals related to: • student learning of content, as found in the PDE *Academic Standards* and *NGSS*; • student engagement in the suite of practices comprising scientific argumentation, utilization of the Claims, Evidence, Reasoning (CER) framework; • student engagement in systems thinking within an ecosystems context; and • student ability to recognize and address various perspectives of a socioscientific issue.
Design of teaching activities	Construction of intended curriculum: • Lesson One: Pre-Assessment • Lesson Two: Endangered Species • Lesson Three: Setting the Problem • Lesson Four: Ecosystems • Lesson Five: The Case of the Green Turtle • Lesson Six: Scientific Explanations/Argumentation (CER Framework) • Lesson Seven: The Case of the Puerto Rican Coqui • Lesson Eight: The Case of the Timber Rattlesnake • Lesson Nine: Post-assessment.
Pre- and post-curricular assessment	Construction, implementation, and evaluation of pre- and post-curricular assessment of students' ability to formulate an argument in response to open-ended, ill-structured socioscientific issues.

descent and either migrated from or had friends and family living in Puerto Rico. The coqui, as a collective species, is a very unique frog species often featured in Puerto Rican literature, art, and music. The timber rattlesnake is a culturally iconic species in the Mid-Atlantic states (location of the research site), but is also a very recognizable species in the United States and throughout the world. The green turtle is an endangered species and both the Puerto Rican coqui and timber rattlesnake are species of concern in the herpetological research community. While considering the use of these species in the curriculum intervention, I met with three herpetologists to assist me with further understanding of the species – one expert on timber rattlesnakes working in Pennsylvania and two experts on the coqui working in Puerto Rico. While the formation of this curriculum was for research purposes, I chose implementing a curriculum focusing on endangered species, because of my professional background as a biologist and biology teacher, my personal background as a naturalist and herpetologist, and the importance of promoting understanding of issues of biodiversity.

Initial participant observations led to the identification of particular linguistic practices of both the teacher and students that served as anchor for how these practices influenced curricular and pedagogical decisions. These practices involved dynamic and fluid mixing of Spanish and English in both the classroom and the community surrounding the school. During these observations, it was common to hear a conversation conducted solely in English, solely in Spanish, or through a combination of both English and Spanish. Based on a combination of classroom observations and informal conversations with the classroom teacher these conversations served as what Agar (2006) called a rich point, a point where culture happens and the researcher begins to explore the pathways leading to and from this point. These observations and conversations also led to a decision by the design team (researcher and co-teacher), through the co-expertise model, to construct all curriculum materials.

Phase Two: Implementation of Curriculum Intervention

Phase two consisted of an extended period (19 consecutive days) of time during which the curriculum was implemented. During this phase, classroom interactions were video recorded and field notes were collected. As with the first phase, I positioned myself in the front of the classroom, and continued my role as participant observer (Spradley, 1980/2016), although most of my actions during this phase were focused on actively engaging with students. This process provided both opportunities to observe how students were engaging with the curriculum and to identify challenges and opportunities related to the pedagogical approach. During this phase of the research, two cameras were employed: one camera was placed in the far back corner of the classroom and captured the board, students, and teacher; the second camera placed in the front of the classroom captured the discourse of pairs and small groups of students. The front camera was also paired with a lavalier microphone which was able to capture finer details of small group and paired discourse. In response to my desire to capture pairs of small-group student interactions, the classroom teacher experimented with strategic student grouping that would be captured by the front camera. The classroom teacher, drawing on her knowledge of her students, attempted to form pairs of students based on English proficiency or bilingualism (e.g., pairing a student with higher levels of proficiency in both English and Spanish with a student considered an English Learner who was more proficient in Spanish). This attempt at pairing was unsuccessful as the students were frequently absent, would shift their pairs or small groups, or grouping decisions were made by the teacher due to classroom management challenges. The challenge of student absences and its impact on learning is beyond the scope of this chapter.

Curriculum Implementation

The curriculum intervention originally consisted of nine lessons designed to introduce new science content knowledge and scientific practices, while promoting the use of discourse in the learning of science. Three additional lessons were added to the intervention based on inclement weather and the classroom teacher's responsiveness to the learning needs of the students. All written curriculum materials (assessments, homework assignments, in-class assignments, posters, and PowerPoint presentations) were provided in both English and Spanish.

After the completion of the curriculum intervention and final collection of video records, I entered phase three which involved various passes through the corpus of video records. The entire corpus of video records consisted of approximately 84 hours – 21 days × 2 cameras (one whole class angle, one student pair angle) × 2, 50-minute class periods. The video records were transferred from the digital cameras to an external hard drive for storage and retrieval. I used Windows Media player in conjunction with a pair of headphones to review the video records. The use of Windows Media Player allowed me the flexibility of viewing the video records and I was able to pause, rewind, and review the video records various times. Each pass through the video records allowed me to narrow my focus until it became clear that my analysis would center on the use of translanguaging in the classroom.

Pass One: Initial Coding of the Video Records

The first pass of video records consisted of reviewing all whole class video records. The whole camera view captured teacher discourse, so the majority of the analysis is based on these video records. A total of 21 days, and roughly 40 hours, of video were analyzed during phase one. During phase one, I constructed time-stamped event maps (Brown & Spang, 2008), in Microsoft Word, which allowed me to simultaneously identify: the major events of the classroom; interactional space; language used; and researcher notes. This phase of analysis allowed me to further develop my conceptions of the classroom culture and the practices of both the teacher and students. Furthermore, this phase allowed me to develop a big picture of the classroom and identify areas for more detailed analyses.

My format is displayed in Table 4.4 and demonstrates how I recorded my observations of the video records. The format included the following: date/time stamp, event (topic), interactional space, language, and researcher notes. The event category allowed me to record my observations of the major classroom events. Interactional space referred to how the members of the class – teacher, students, researcher – were configured among each other and relevant artifacts (Green, 2009; Heras, 1993). These interactional spaces constructed orientations and each afforded particular discourse practices (Kelly & Crawford, 1997), with a focus on the teacher. In general, the interactional space fell into the following categories: teacher–whole class; teacher–small group; teacher–student; teacher–researcher, students–students; researcher–whole class; researcher–students; and researcher–student. Language refers to the use of English, Spanish, or both by the members of the classroom community. Researcher notes referred to analytical notes or comments that I produced while viewing the video records. These notes were meant to mark instances in the video records that I felt were interesting or warranted further analysis. The notes were varied and ranged from instances of humor in the classroom to questions that I asked of myself related to my analysis. For example, I made notes related to the teacher's choice of words (i.e. opinion) in framing the new practices in the classroom. I also made notes related to the language practices in the classroom.

TABLE 4.4 Portion of event map format

Date 02.28.2014 Time Stamp (in minutes and seconds)	Event T – Teacher R – Researcher S – Student Eng. – English Span. – Spanish	Interactional Space T – Teacher Ss – Students WC – whole class	Language T – Teacher S – Student E – English Sp – Spanish B – Both	Researcher Notes
500	T and R work with small groups (in Eng. and Span.).			
600	T working with small group. Starts conversation in Eng. and moves to Span.	T – Ss	T – B S – Sp	Translanguaging here.
1743	T asks S which language is better for communication.		T – Sp	Translanguaging here?
2411	T announces class discussion of Puerto Rican Coqui CER case. T speaks in Eng. and Span.	T – WC		

During this first pass of the video records, I identified and time stamped the major and minor events of the classroom and any time there was a change in activity. Major types of events of the class included, but were not limited to: the beginning and ending of the class; teacher providing directions for in-class activities; individual student work; paired work; whole class work; and PowerPoint presentations. Minor events of the class included, but were not limited to: students passing out folders; teacher setting up computer; English as a Second Language (ESL) teacher takes students out of class; and teacher passing out materials for the lesson. These activities were demarcated by the discourse and actions of the classroom participants. The researcher notes included not only the types of events, but also a short description of the substantive content of the respective events.

Pass Two: Coding for Classroom Activities and Scientific Practices

The second pass of video records consisted of reviewing all whole class video records and adding to the initial event map coding from the first pass of video records. As with the first pass, a total of 21 days, and roughly 40 hours, of video were analyzed. During phase two, I coded for classroom activities and scientific practices following the constant comparative method (Glaser, 1965). The purpose of this pass was to identify the larger classroom activities in which the class engaged prior to, during, and after the curriculum intervention. Additionally, this pass allowed me to identify the scientific practices – broadly defined – in which the students were engaged prior to, during, and after the curriculum intervention. These were both added to the event maps constructed during phase one.

Classroom activities were coded into broader, yet more specific, categories that took into account the varied activities in which the teacher and students engaged. These larger scale activities were a summary of the major and minor events of the classroom. For example, classroom activities included but were not limited to: review of homework; introduction of new content; whole class discussion; teacher-led discussion; small-group work; and individual work. These allowed me to return to my event maps in order to find specific events or activities when engaging in my analyses.

Scientific practices were defined codes that developed as I reviewed the video records. These codes were developed through open coding: I did not base these codes on any existing frameworks on scientific practices in middle school science classrooms. Rather, these codes were informed by studies of scientific practices (Kelly & Licona, 2018) and close attention to the patterned activities constructed by the participants. These codes represented a mix of in-vivo codes (emergent from classroom activity as defined by participants) and sociologically constructed codes (as defined from the literature in science studies and science education, see Strauss, 1987). For example, the following represented scientific practices that I identified throughout the curriculum: asking questions; discussing questions; discussing answers; discussing claims; challenging evidence; and constructing scientific arguments. Coding for scientific practices allowed me to see how these practices changed throughout the curriculum and to compare and contrast pre-curriculum practices with those practices brought about by the curriculum intervention.

Pass Three: Coding for Language Practices

The third pass of video records consisted of reviewing a portion of the whole class video records. A total of 11 days, and roughly 22 hours, of video were analyzed. These 11 days were purposefully selected based on the introduction and implementation of the scientific argumentation framework in the classroom. It was during this phase of analysis that I had a very important interaction with language scholar and future member of my dissertation committee, Dr. Megan Hopkins. After an extensive conversation between Dr. Hopkins and myself I decided to draw on literature about translanguaging – this conversation brought into focus language practices that I was beginning to recognize as salient. This changed my research dramatically and represented a pivot point at which my analytical focus changed. While I did find challenges and opportunities in implementing science reform-based curriculum in a dual language science classroom, my focus was now on the dynamic and fluid use of both English and Spanish, translanguaging, in the classroom. As such, the following new research questions emerged: How does translanguaging as a pedagogical strategy facilitate teacher framing of scientific argumentation about socioscientific issues? How does translanguaging as a pedagogical strategy facilitate student uptake of scientific argumentation about socioscientific issues?

During the third pass, I coded for the classroom language practices of the teacher and students. The purpose of this pass was to identify instances and patterns of the use of English and/or Spanish by both the teacher and students concerning the substantive concepts regarding the socioscientific issues. For example, I coded for when the teacher and students were speaking in English, speaking in Spanish, or speaking a mix of both English and Spanish. Additionally, this pass allowed me to identify instances of translanguaging in which the teacher and/or students moved fluidly between English and Spanish during classroom activities. In addition, I took notes regarding any interesting language practices or interactions for further analysis. For example, one instance that I identified for further analysis consisted of an interaction in which the teacher began to construct a scientific argument on the board in conjunction with input by students. This interaction between the teacher and a particular student was interesting as the teacher was asking questions in Spanish and the student was responding in English. In other words, the teacher and student were communicating with each other, each using a different language. This coding was added to the event maps constructed during phases one and two.

Pass Four: Identifying, Transcribing, and Coding Instances of Teacher Translanguaging

The fourth pass of video records consisted of strategic viewing and transcribing of the discursive work done by the teacher and students through translanguaging. I transcribed all instances of translanguaging initiated by the teacher and the surrounding discourse of the students with whom she was communicating. I defined translanguaging as any instance in which there was an interaction with the teacher, and students and the teacher in a dynamic, fluid, and responsive manner used both English and Spanish in a communicative situation. While I use the phrase "teacher translanguaging" it is important that I remind the reader that translanguaging is an interactional activity. As such, I focused on the teacher-initiated social activity as she engaged in translanguaging with students in the class. All students were identified in the translanguaging clips.

Transcripts were constructed in Microsoft Excel, using both English and Spanish, with English translation or rephrasing of Spanish discourse. As an English and Spanish speaker, I conducted all transcription and translation of classroom discourse events. I note this, as my proficiency across two languages afforded me the ability to accurately transcribe English and Spanish discourse, which also afforded me the ability to become intimately familiar with the classroom interactions. Of all phases of video analysis, this phase was the most energy-intensive and I spent much time transcribing the English and Spanish

TABLE 4.5 Sample transcript

Speaker	*Turn/Line*	*Talk*	*Translation*
Ms. Ramirez	1.1	Evidence. Excellent. What?	
	1.2	Okay. So let's think of the	
	1.3	yes first. What evidence	
	1.4	helped you come up with	
	1.5	what you, to say that yes.	
Duane	2.1	Um, the, they have a lot of	
	2.2	threats.	
Ms. Ramirez	3.1	Okay, have a lot of threats.	
Duane	4.1	Yeah.	
Ms. Ramirez	5.1	*¿So, tienen mucho peligro, verdad?*	So, they have much danger
	5.2		(threats), correct?
Duane	6.1	Yep.	
Ms. Ramirez	7.1	*So, tienen mucho peligro.*	So, they have much danger (threats).
Duane	8.1	Uh huh.	
Ms. Ramirez	9.1	*¿Qué más?* That's it? Do you	What else?
	9.2	think that's enough to	
	9.3	convince someone else?	

discourse of the students and teacher. An example of a transcript is provided in Table 4.5, which demonstrates a brief instance of teacher translanguaging.

As with the scientific practices of the classroom, I utilized open coding when analyzing the instances of teacher translanguaging. These open codes were fairly descriptive of the interaction in which the translanguaging occurred. For example, I coded an interaction as "Teacher requesting claim and evidence from student." This open code was then further described with the following note:

> Teacher requesting claim and evidence from student. Teacher, in Spanish, describes what is needed to have a good claim. Teacher then restates the original question, in Spanish. Teacher then gives examples of claims that answer the question. Teacher then asks if students understood, in Spanish. Teacher then asks student in English to state his claim.

This translanguaging occurred as the teacher and students, as a whole class, were collectively constructing a scientific argument on the white board using student responses. The note describing the code allowed me to more fully describe the interaction as well as compare and contrast it to other codes. These codes represented sociologically constructed codes (Strauss, 1987) in which I provided a label for these codes. Open coding allowed me to provide a lengthy descriptive account of each instance of teacher translanguaging. I combined similar codes, collapsed others, until I identified three major themes of translanguaging: maintaining classroom culture; facilitating the academic task; and framing epistemic practices. The results of this analysis will be further discussed in the results section. I will now discuss methodological results implications from the use of interactional ethnography.

Results

As mentioned earlier, interactional ethnography is an appropriate approach for researching complex social and linguistic cultural groups. This approach offers insight into the complexity of everyday life in classrooms. The approach is what I would deem "responsive" in that the research questions and even the methods may shift in fluid and dynamic ways according to the shifting nature of the research settings. While my original research questions were framed around opportunities and challenges of implementing reform-based science education in a dual language setting, the flexibility of this approach allowed me to reframe my research questions around teacher translanguaging. This followed the ethnographic research cycle and considered emerging descriptions of the cultural phenomena as relevant to subsequent research decisions.

Before discussing the results of classroom discourse, particularly teacher translanguaging, it is necessary to describe the initial results of my observations of the classroom, and school as a whole, in order to situate how these observations impacted my research program. In this section I will describe the established and developing norms and expectations of the classroom, the implemented curriculum, the classroom teachers' pedagogy, and the established linguistic practices of the classroom community.

Review of field notes and classroom observations yielded a fairly in-depth description of the norms and expectations, implemented curriculum, pedagogy, and linguistic practices of the learning environment prior to the implementation of the curriculum intervention. The classroom was arranged in a traditional manner, with desks singly or doubly in long rows or in groups of four facing each other; while this was a science classroom, there was no laboratory area or standard scientific apparatuses (e.g., lab tables, sink, etc.). The atmosphere was very talkative, friendly, open, and caring. The teacher and students were often engaged in conversations with each other during free or transition times. The established norms and expectations of the classroom included requiring students to raise their hands in order to participate in class discussion or ask questions, work independently on most academic tasks, and to remain in their seats at all times. Interesting to note is that there was a classroom rule that explicitly forbade "arguing"; I note this as the curriculum intervention was designed to engage students in scientific argumentation, bringing into focus the differences between arguing as a fight and constructing an argument by formulating evidence for a particular audience.

The school did not follow an established 7th grade science curriculum. As such, the teacher was responsible for constructing and implementing the science curriculum. Through an informal conversation, the teacher told me she was attempting to make the science course relevant to what she perceived were her students' interests. The implemented science curriculum can be best characterized as a mix of curricular materials collected from various sources. One source of curriculum was the books from a FOSS kit that focused on ecosystems. Another source of curriculum was the internet. Prior to my engagement with the classroom, it appeared as if the curriculum was pieced together according to topics that the teacher thought would be interesting and engaging for the students, in combination with the books provided by the FOSS curriculum. The students were studying diverse and marginally connected science topics that included food webs/food chains, ecosystems, motion, rate/distance/time, and the biology of the milkweed bug.

The teacher's pedagogy could generally be described as teacher-centric, although there were activities that could be considered student-centric, such as engaging in measurement and calculation of velocity of moving bodies (e.g., cars and ramps). For the most part, a traditional approach was implemented, in which the teacher would present content material in English or Spanish and the students would copy the material into their notebooks. Student in-class activities were generally limited to note-taking, translating notes, completing worksheets, conducting internet searches, and engaging in individual assessments. Students engaged in other activities, such as building dioramas and calculating velocity of toy cars moving down ramps, but these were limited. As related to classroom discourse patterns, the most common discourse pattern was a traditional initiate, response, evaluate (IRE) interaction. The rationale for describing the curriculum and pedagogy is not to be overly critical of the classroom teacher, as Ms. Ramirez took her teaching responsibilities seriously. Rather, it is to describe the established science learning environment to indicate that the curriculum intervention brought about a change in both curriculum and pedagogy.

Perhaps the most fascinating finding of this research, from a linguistic standpoint, was the language practices in the science classroom and throughout the school. Upon entering the school, I was immediately impressed by the mix of English and Spanish, both written and spoken. As the school is considered a dual language school, one would expect to hear both languages, but I was surprised by the extent of how teachers, administrators, staff, and students were all communicating through a mix of English and Spanish. This was also evident in the 7th grade classroom. Ms. Ramirez was aware of her students' linguistic needs and often engaged each student based on their comfort and fluency in either Spanish or English. Ms. Ramirez also engaged in this linguistically responsive approach (Lucas & Villegas, 2013) with visitors, such as parents, administrators, etc., to the classroom. In addition to communicating in English or Spanish, based on the needs of her interlocutor, Ms. Ramirez often exhibited fluid and dynamic languaging practices while engaging with either Spanish-speaking or English-speaking students. García, Kleifgen, and Falchi (2008) describe this language practice as translanguaging. The above results are a general descriptive account of the practices, culture, curriculum, and pedagogy of the classroom. The following section will discuss the three major functions of teacher translanguaging that emerged from the analysis of video records.

Functions of Teacher Translanguaging

The following results are based on the ways teacher translanguaging emerged during the presentation and utilization of the scientific argumentation framework. Three major functions of teacher translanguaging were identified: (1) maintaining classroom culture, (2) facilitating the academic task, and (3) framing epistemic practices. Each of these functions, of equal importance in this dual language classroom, will be briefly defined and discussed in the following section.

Classroom culture refers to the norms and expectations, rights and obligations, and roles and relationships that are constructed by both the teacher and student as related to what it means to be a member of the class. Green and Castanheira (2012, p. 54) refer to this as "what members of a particular class or group need to know, understand, produce, and predict to engage in the social and academic life in culturally relevant and socially significant ways." The culture of the classroom can also be thought of in terms of a community of practice (Lave, 1991) in which activity, learning, and doing are all part of the culture that was and is being constructed, negotiated, and maintained by the participants in a particular setting; in this case, the bilingual 7th grade science class. Therefore, in this study, classroom culture was related to questions such as "What are the established language practices of the class?," "What are the established academic practices of the class?," and "What does it mean to do science class?" Constructing and maintaining classroom culture refers to ways that teacher translanguaging provided communicative processes to identify and negotiate norms and expectations, role and responsibilities, and rights and obligations. Based on field observations (see Table 4.2 for examples of classroom culture) and review of the video records, the classroom culture could be characterized as one in which: English and Spanish were both freely used, separately and together; a caring environment was established; a valuing of participation by all; and both teacher and students learned from each other. As directly related to the teacher's use of translanguaging in order to maintain the classroom culture, practices included, but were not limited to: responding to non-academic matters; talking informally with students; redirecting student behavior; affirming student identity; supporting a caring classroom culture; promoting bilingualism/biliteracy/biculturalism; and positioning all members of the classroom as both teachers and learners.

Facilitating the academic task refers to teacher translanguaging in order to assist students engaging in and completing academic tasks. Academic tasks were defined as: receiving directions for an in-class assignment, exam, or homework assignment; being oriented to new expectations; and learning new vocabulary. In simpler terms, academic tasks could be framed as students "doing" school. Therefore, teacher translanguaging associated with explaining directions, reorienting students to questions or tasks, assigning homework, clarifying in-class assignments, providing materials for in-class assignments, and defining vocabulary would all fall under this function. Additionally, this refers to the new academic tasks such as learning how to engage with socioscientific issues, differentiating the difference between scientific argumentation and colloquial definitions of arguing, and engaging in peer review of assignments.

Framing epistemic practices refers to teacher translanguaging in order to support members of the community learning to propose, justify, and evaluate knowledge claims related to scientific argumentation (Kelly, 2008). Of all categories of teacher translanguaging, framing epistemic practices was most pertinent to science class, given the need to interpret knowledge claims around the socioscientific issues. Epistemic practices, in this study, center on scientific argumentation and the construction of scientific explanations. These include practices such as the generation and evaluation of CER; the evaluation of the appropriateness of a scientific explanation; or the purpose of the scientific argumentation framework. As scientific argumentation and explanation building were new classroom practices, teacher translanguaging provided a very important scaffold for the emergent bilinguals. Examples of this scaffolding include, but were not limited to: translanguaging to construct an oral scientific explanation with the whole class; translanguaging to elicit a claim, evidence, or reasoning from students; and translanguaging to critique the claim, evidence, or reasoning of a scientific explanation.

The use of interactional ethnography resulted in an in-depth understanding of how translanguage as pedagogy performed many functions. While the engagement with the content and practices of science was accomplished through translanguaging, in fact translanguaging allowed the teacher to construct a translanguaging classroom characterized by the free, fluid, and dynamic use of English and Spanish to conduct all classroom activities.

Discussion

While this study resulted in numerous findings related to the translanguaging as pedagogy and the functions of translanguaging in framing and engaging in scientific argumentation about socioscientific issues, the discussion will briefly address the implications of this research to science education and bilingual education, but attention will be placed on the various implications on the methodological implications of this study.

Translanguaging and Science Education

While translanguaging is a general pedagogical strategy, in fact there are implications related to science education. Translanguaging emerged as a key pedagogical strategy leading to teachers framing and students engaging in epistemic practices of scientific argumentation. While my research questions were specific to scientific argumentation, the use of translanguaging as pedagogy has implications beyond this one scientific practice. As science education reform recommendations place attention on the increased use of discourse, translanguaging may prove beneficial in framing other language-intensive scientific practices. I am not suggesting that translanguaging only has the potential to assist students to engage in language-intensive scientific practices, rather I am suggesting that one of the benefits of using authentic linguistic practices found outside the classroom is assisting students to engage in language-intensive scientific practices inside the classroom. In this way, translanguaging draws from the extent linguistic repertoire of the students and teacher, and through its use in science class, may render the practice of science more accessible and relevant to the participants.

This research also has implications for science education scholars who call for curriculum and pedagogy that offer relevant experiences for students. In this case, translanguaging can be considered linguistically relevant. Relevance of science education is not solely conceptual, but also linguistic as it relates to students' discursive practices outside of school. Much like students who are engaged by curricular materials that are relevant to their conceptual world outside of the classroom, translanguaging could be used to engage students in science through linguistically relevant practices. By drawing on the same linguistic practices found outside of the science classroom, translanguaging inside the science classroom can be leveraged to promote the learning of science. Studies exist that demonstrate the value of providing linguistically relevant science learning environments. Brown and Spang (2008) noted how out-of-school discourse practices can be synthesized with science discourse practices as students make sense in the science classroom. Mazak and Herbas-Donoso (2014), described the tension between the everyday language practices (e.g., Spanish) and the language of the university science class (e.g., English) in Puerto Rico and how translanguaging provided a linguistically relevant classroom in which both English and Spanish were used to learn science. By removing language barriers or redefining the accepted languaging practices, translanguaging can position students as competent members of a particular scientific discourse community.

Implications for Bilingual Education

In considering the impact of this work for educating emergent bilinguals, the most salient implication of translanguaging as pedagogy for bilingual education relates to the dual language education paradigms supporting language bracketing. If we consider that the main models of dual language education suggest language bracketing, then we see that translanguaging as a pedagogical strategy or classroom practice does not fit very well into current dual language paradigms. Translanguaging seems to suggest that dual language education paradigms could be informed by the free and dynamic language integration and how these practices can and should be leveraged for teaching and learning purposes. It is beyond the scope of this chapter to discuss in depth the opportunities and challenges of translanguaging as pedagogy in dual language learning environments. It is anticipated that other researchers will investigate the potential of translanguaging as pedagogy and how pre-service and in-service teacher preparation programs can benefit from exploring this potential.

Implications of Interactive Ethnography

As this chapter is about an approach to researching classroom culture, I will close by discussing a few key lessons I have learned as a researcher before noting some implications of this research as it relates to the use of interactional ethnography to investigate complex cultural and linguistic settings. While many lessons were learned, a few warrant special attention. One lesson learned early in the research process was the value of a co-expertise model. While my experience in science classrooms and working with Latina/o students was an asset that assisted me in conducting research in a dual language classroom, in fact, my research study would have taken a different turn had it not been for the explicit input of the classroom teacher. Ms. Ramirez had extensive knowledge of her students' cultural and linguistic backgrounds and this proved essential in planning and implementing the research study. Her assistance allowed the study to respond to the educational, cultural, and linguistic needs of her students. While this was a research study, in fact it was also about student learning. Initially, I planned to investigate the implementation of a reform-based science curriculum intervention in a CLD dual language classroom. As the study progressed, it became clear that the co-expertise model that was emerging necessitated my role shifting between participant and observer (Spradley, 1980/2016). This co-expertise model resulted in all participants (the teacher, students, and researcher) learning. The students learned from both the teacher and researcher, the teacher learned from both the researcher and students, and I learned from both the teacher and students. Perhaps the most interesting learning I gained relates to the teacher's fluid and dynamic use of English and Spanish, or translanguaging. Ms. Ramirez's translanguaging was not prompted by me and was a natural response to her student's linguistic abilities. As mentioned earlier, Ms. Ramirez framed the co-expertise model and my presence in the classroom as a professional development opportunity. The co-expertise model resulted in a change of pedagogy and curriculum for Ms. Ramirez. In fact, this model resulted in my study becoming one of *research with the teacher* and not *research on the teacher.*

A second lesson learned, and closely related to the co-expertise model, was the value of ongoing negotiation. From the initial contact with the school, this research study was characterized by on-going negotiation. From negotiating access to the school, to negotiating the flow and design of the curriculum, to negotiating access to the students' and teacher's trust, the importance of negotiation cannot be underestimated. Negotiating access to a very unique learning environment, such as a dual language school, could have been very difficult had I not had existing contacts with school administration. Nonetheless, I had to negotiate access and permission to conduct research in this setting. In addition, at a more theoretical level, there was significant negotiation with the records collected and which records would transform into data used to tell the story of this study. As I did collect various records, such as images of the classroom, classroom and homework assignments, interviews with the students and teacher, field notes, and video recordings, only certain records were used to make a case for the functions of teacher translanguaging. Additionally, and as mentioned earlier, I negotiated the addition of a new faculty member to my dissertation committee. This resulted in further negotiation of my research questions and consequent dissertation focus.

A final point resulting from the planning, implementation, and evaluation of this interactional ethnographic research study, was the importance of the ethnographer as learner. Interactional ethnography is not a hard and fast process for conducting research, rather it is dynamic and responsive to the complex setting and complex research questions. As an ethnographer, I learned, from this approach, that research questions often change as the interactional ethnographic approach progresses. My research questions did, in fact, change. I also learned that ethnographers must exhibit reflexivity. The deeper I became involved with the research, the more reflexivity I demonstrated. This reflexivity led me to examine not only my role in the study, but the purposes of ethnographic research and what can be learned through the study of cultural practices. This reflexivity occurred through the everyday research work such as generation of analytical memos, passes through the field notes, multiple views and angles of vision of the video records, and an eventual reformulation of research questions resulting in a final analytical focus. In addition, I learned the value of developing a systematic approach to the collection, maintenance, and review of field notes and video records.

In closing, interactional ethnography is an effective and appropriate approach to investigating complex and dynamic cultural and linguistic settings, such as dual language science classrooms. The malleability, flexibility, and responsiveness of the approach afforded me a general framework for exploring and describing how reform based science curriculum unfolded in an English/Spanish dual language science classroom. Additionally, this approach facilitated a research process that eventually resulted in a focus on the linguistic practice of translanguaging. Furthermore, this approach yielded many more research questions that I hope to address in future iterations based on this initial study.

References

Agar, M. (2006, September). An ethnography by any other name . . . *Forum Qualitative Sozialforschung/Forum: Qualitative Social Research*, 7(4).

Brown, B. A., & Spang, E. (2008). Double talk: Synthesizing everyday and science language in the classroom. *Science Education*, 92(4), 708–732.

Castanheira, M. L., Crawford, T., Dixon, C. N., & Green, J. L. (2001). Interactional ethnography: An approach to studying the social construction of literate practices. *Linguistics and Education*, 11(4), 353–400.

Collier, V. P., & Thomas, W. P. (2004). The astounding effectiveness of dual language education for all. *NABE Journal of Research and Practice*, 2(1), 1–20.

Duschl, R. A., & Osborne, J. (2002). Supporting and promoting argumentation discourse in science education. *Studies in Science Education*, 38, 39–72.

Emerson, R. M., Fretz, R. I., & Shaw, L. L. (1995). *Writing Ethnographic Fieldnotes* (p. 254). Chicago, IL: University of Chicago Press.

Excelencia in Education. (2015). *The Condition of Latinos in Education: 2015 Factbook*. Washington, DC: Excelencia in Education.

García, O., Ibarra Johnson, S., & Seltzer, K. (2017). *The Translanguaging Classroom: Leveraging Student Bilingualism for Learning*. Philadelphia, PA: Caslon.

García, O., Kleifgen, J. A., & Falchi, L. (2008). From English language learners to emergent bilinguals. *Equity Matters: Research Review No. 1*.

Glaser, B. G. (1965). The constant comparative method of qualitative analysis. *Social Problems*, 12, 436–445.

Green, J. L. (2009). *A Guidebook for Exploring Discourse in Classrooms: Developing a Transparent Logic of Inquiry Uncovering Opportunities for Learning in Classrooms*. Santa Barbara, CA: University of California.

Green, J. L., & Castanheira, M. L. (2012). Exploring classroom life and student learning. In B. Kaur (Ed.), *Understanding Teaching and Learning* (pp. 53–65). Rotterdam: Sense Publishers.

Gumperz, J. (2001). Interactional sociolinguistics: A personal perspective. In D. Schiffrin, D. Tannen, & H. E. Hamilton (Eds.), *The Handbook of Discourse Analysis* (pp. 215–228). Malden, MA: Blackwell Publishing.

Heras, A. I. (1993). The construction of understanding in a sixth-grade bilingual classroom. *Linguistics and Education*, 5(3), 275–299.

Jiménez-Aleixandre, M. P., & Erduran, S. (2007). Argumentation in science education: An overview. In S. Erduran & M. P. Jiménez-Aleixandre (Eds.), *Argumentation in Science Education* (pp. 3–27). Netherlands: Springer.

Kelly, G. J. (2008). Inquiry, activity, and epistemic practice. In R. Duschl & R. Grandy (Eds.), *Teaching Scientific Inquiry: Recommendations for Research and Implementation* (pp. 99–117; 288–291). Rotterdam: Sense Publishers.

Kelly, G. J. (2014). Analyzing classroom activities: Theoretical and methodological considerations. In *Topics and Trends in Current Science Education* (pp. 353–368). Netherlands: Springer.

Kelly, G. J., & Crawford, T. (1997). An ethnographic investigation of the discourse processes of school science. *Science Education*, 81(5), 533–559.

Kelly, G. J., & Licona, P. (2018). Epistemic practices and science education. In *History, Philosophy and Science Teaching* (pp. 139–165). Switzerland: Springer.

Kolstø, S. D. (2001). Scientific literacy for citizenship: Tools for dealing with the science dimension of controversial socioscientific issues. *Science Education*, 85(3), 291–310.

Landivar, L. C. (2013). Disparities in STEM employment by sex, race, and Hispanic origin. *Education Review*, 29(6), 911–922.

Lave, J. (1991). Situating learning in communities of practice. In L. B. Resnick, J. M. Levine, & S. D. Teasley (Eds.), *Perspectives on Socially Shared Cognition* (pp. 63–82). Washington, DC: American Psychological Association.

Leach, J., Ametller, J., Hind, A., Lewis, J., & Scott, P. (2005). Designing and evaluating short science teaching sequences: Improving student learning. In K. Boersma, M. Goedhart, O. de Jong, & H. Eijkelhof (Eds.), *Research and the Quality of Science Education* (pp. 209–220). Netherlands: Springer.

Leach, J., & Scott, P. (2002). Designing and evaluating science teaching sequences: An approach drawing upon the concept of learning demand and a social constructivist perspective on learning. *Studies in Science Education*, 38, 115–142.

Lee, O., & Luykx, A. (2006). *Science Education and Student Diversity: Synthesis and Research Agenda*. Cambridge: Cambridge University Press.

Lee, O., Quinn, H., & Valdés, G. (2013). Science and language for English language learners in relation to next generation science standards and with implications for common core standards for English language arts and mathematics. *Educational Researcher*, 20(10), 1–11.

Lucas, T., & Villegas, A. M. (2013). Preparing linguistically responsive teachers: Laying the foundation in preservice teacher education. *Theory into Practice*, 52(2), 98–109.

Mazak, C. M., & Herbas-Donoso, C. (2014). Translanguaging practices and language ideologies in Puerto Rican university science education. *Critical Inquiry in Language Studies*, 11(1), 27–49.

National Research Council. (2012). *A Framework for K–12 Science Education: Practices, Cross-cutting Concepts and Core Ideas*. Washington, DC: National Academies Press.

NGSS Lead States. (2013). *Next Generation Science Standards: For States, By States.* Washington, DC: National Academies Press.

Pennsylvania Department of Education (2009). *Academic Standards for Environment and Ecology*. Retrieved January 1, 2011 from http://static.pdesas.org/content/ documents/ academic_standards_for_environment_and_ecology.pdf.

Sadler, T. D. (2004). Informal reasoning regarding socioscientific issues: A critical review of research. *Journal of Research in Science Teaching*, 41(5), 513–536.

Sadler, T. D., & Zeidler, D. L. (2005). The significance of content knowledge for informal reasoning regarding socioscientific issues: Applying genetics knowledge to genetic engineering issues. *Science Education*, 89(1), 71–93.

Spradley, J. P. (1979). *The Ethnographic Interview*. Fort Worth, TX: Harcourt Brace Jovanovich.

Spradley, J. P. (2016). *Participant Observation*. Long Grove, IL: Waveland Press. (Original work published in 1980.)

Strauss, A. (1987). *Qualitative Analysis for Social Scientists*. Cambridge: Cambridge University Press.

Tiberghien, A. (2007). Foreword. In S. Erduran & M. P. Jiménez-Aleixandre (Eds.), *Argumentation in Science Education* (pp. ix–xv). Netherlands: Springer.

U.S. Department of Education, Office of Planning, Evaluation and Policy Development, Policy and Program Studies Service. (2016). *The State of Racial Diversity in the Educator Workforce*. Washington, DC.

Zohar, A., & Nemet, F. (2002). Fostering students' knowledge and argumentation skills through dilemmas in human genetics. *Journal of Research in Science Teaching*, 39(1), 35–62.

5

LEARNING THROUGH IMPROVEMENT FROM FAILURE IN ELEMENTARY ENGINEERING DESIGN PROJECTS

Matthew M. Johnson

Introduction

The purpose of this chapter is to illustrate the theory and research methods leading to decisions made while using a large video archive to investigate students and teachers socially constructing the phenomena of failure and improvement in elementary engineering design projects. I will also describe the development of an analytic rubric as a way to investigate socioculturally constructed phenomena *in situ*, including the comparison of the student discourse from the video and journal writings as a way of establishing validity for the analysis of student artifacts as complementary to video analysis. The chapter is organized using the research method framework described in Chapter 1 (Kelly & Green, this volume).

The inclusion of engineering in the *Next Generation Science Standards* (NGSS) marked a shift in the thinking about science education in the US (NGSS Lead States, 2013). This move challenges teachers and teacher educators who often lack experience with engineering. As these teachers now need engineering curricula, it also created opportunities for those of us interested in curriculum development, teacher education, and student learning. One of these opportunities is in studying students and teachers as they engage in the practices of engineering.

The framers of NGSS identified ten practices of scientists/engineers that students should use to learn disciplinary ideas (NRC, 2012; NGSS Lead States, 2013). They chose to concentrate on the similarities between science and engineering; however, some have suggested that the field should recognize and capitalize on the opportunities for learning those differences in the disciplinary practices provide. For example, Cunningham and Carlsen (2014) suggest that science and engineering are distinct *because* of differences in the ways they socially derive solutions or explanations, and Cunningham and Kelly (2017) synthesized from the literature 16 *epistemic practices* (Kelly, 2008, 2011) of engineers, including *persisting and learning from failure*.

Failure occurs in most aspects of our lives, even prompting some academics to post their "curriculum vitae of failures" (Haushofer, 2016). In science, there are books romanticizing failure (see Firestein, 2015) or mythical stories of serendipitous mistakes leading to discoveries (Allchin, 2003, 2012). In school settings, failure has a negative connotation related to academic failure. But failure is thought of and used differently in engineering. Scientists rarely report on false starts (Zaringhalam, 2016). However, in engineering, forensic analysis of catastrophic failure like the Tacoma Narrows Bridge collapse is used as a teaching tool, and journals exist for articles aimed at helping other engineers avoid similar failures. It is also used to allow for comparison between different materials (e.g., fishing line is rated for the weight it can hold) or for verifying the composition of materials like concrete (e.g., destructive testing). It is also used as a measure of reliability (e.g., mean time between failure), and as a way to improve designs quickly (Matson, 1996). As a result, not all failures in engineering are intended, but many are productive.

Engineering curricula are being developed to respond to the recent educational reforms, but the lack in understanding of how students engineer and the support teachers need have led to a wide range of curricula with varying quality. This chapter describes the method used to better understand the productive use of failure, a practice that is distinct between science and engineering, to inform curriculum and instruction. The analysis of classroom video and student engineering journals led to some initial frameworks about types and causes of failure, teacher reactions to students' failed designs, and conditions necessary for improvement (Johnson, 2016). This chapter will focus more on the methods that were used to construct a set of findings regarding the usefulness of failure for learning engineering.

Asking Ethnographic Questions

The theoretical framework that guides this work is sociocultural. It is informed by "engineering studies," the empirical study of engineering practice across settings, and it considers the materials used in the engineering design process to be contributors to the interactions that should be considered. The theoretical framework guides the types of questions, methodology for investigation, and analytic decisions; and because the discourse is contextually dependent, interactional sociolinguistics was used as a way to improve our understanding of the language use of the cultures that make up the classrooms studied.

Engineering studies give us a basis for considering epistemic practices of engineers, like persisting and learning from failure, and the ways in which precollege students engage in them (Cunningham & Kelly, 2017). Kelly and Licona (2018) describe epistemic practices as being socially constructed among people through concerted activity, situated within social practice and cultural norms, reliant on references to prior discourses or artifacts, and consequential for what and whose knowledge counts. Studies of practices then should focus on the ways participants interact to accomplish their goals (Johri, 2011). Common engineering practices are developed by engineers collectively enacting their interpretation of good engineering work, with meanings related to their histories and perceived futures (Suchman, 2000), and the technologies they develop are manifestations of these beliefs and assumptions (Styhre, 2011). Pickering (1993) describes the practices he argues are involved in sequentially improving the design of a bubble chamber for detecting ions as a series of accommodations to resistances, which he calls the *mangle of practice*. But the development of technologies through this process involves both material and human actors that should be viewed as "mutually and emergently productive of one another" (Pickering, 1993, p. 567).

This view of both material and social components to engineering practices has been called a sociomaterial perspective (Styhre, Wikmalm, Ollila, & Roth, 2012) in which the social and material aspects are inseparable and should be studied in this way (Orlikowski & Scott, 2008). Styre and his colleagues (2012) assert that engineering accomplishment always derives from the capacity to identify and overcome failure, and relies on the *feedback* and *backtalk* from the artifacts, where feedback is intentionally derived, and backtalk is unexpected (Yanow & Tsoukas, 2009). In addition, the practices of engineers, particularly precollege engineers, should be understood as sociomaterial bricolage (Johri, 2011), because they are constrained by the available materials and as bricoleurs make do with what they have (Levi-Strauss, 1962). My analyses focus on this collective series of practices that rely on interactions among and between the actors and materials.

Although I do not aim to investigate the individuals' mental activities, I am interested in the ways their thinking manifests itself through interactions with classmates, teachers, and the materials (Bjørn & Østerlund, 2014; Frederiksen & Donin, 2015). The field of sociolinguistics studies language usage in cultural groups (Gumperz, 1982; Gumperz & Hymes, 1972). The elementary students in this study are developing and refining ways of thinking, talking, and interacting as a part of their cultural groups (class and small group) and their participation in other cultural groups in their daily lives gives them unique perspectives that come to bear on the classroom discourse (Kelly & Green, 1998; Green & Dixon, 1993). Interactional sociolinguistics is an approach in which the researcher initially uses an ethnographic perspective to gain insights into the norms and the context in which the study is conducted before looking more closely at events or interactions (Gumperz, 2001). This approach allows for an iterative and systematic analysis of a particular phenomenon within a large video archive, provides a basis for analytic decision making and theoretical sampling, and informs discourse analysis within the broader context (Kelly, 2014).

This theoretical framework guided the research questions, methods, and analytic decisions. Since classroom engineering projects are usually completed in small groups of students and involve collective thinking, negotiating, and problem solving, an interactional sociolinguistic approach (Gumperz, 2001) was chosen to investigate the following research questions:

1. What is the nature of failure in elementary engineering design projects?
    a. How do failures happen?
    b. Why do failures happen?
2. How do the collective actions of students and teacher support or constrain the process of improvement from engineering design failure?

Expanding on the methods of Kelly and colleagues over past the two decades (1998, 1999, 2001, 2014), I completed an extensive video analysis and developed an analytic rubric to analyze student journals as artifacts to answer the questions. Since the *process* of improvement is important to answering these questions, instruments that measure changes pre and post are inappropriate. Others have approached similar research questions regarding failure using interviews with students and teachers (Lottero-Perdue & Parry, 2017), but found that concepts related to engineering failure can be conflated with academic failure. For these reasons, I took an ethnographic perspective similar to the co-authors of this book as a way to investigate the phenomena of failure and improvement *in situ*.

Identifying Site for Knowledge Construction and Negotiating Access

The video archive and student journals were collected by researchers at *Engineering is Elementary* (EiE). EiE is a commercially available engineering curriculum series intended for elementary students that is produced by a team at the Museum of Science in Boston. Data were constructed from these archives as part of a large-scale efficacy project investigating the relative benefits of their curriculum and a comparison curriculum. In total, there were over 1,500 hours of recorded classroom activity and 18,057 scanned student journals. Therefore, my process of negotiating access to the study participants was different than it is for many researchers using this approach. Rather than struggling to collect enough usable data, the primary challenge I faced was to both learn the educational contexts from observation and isolate in a principled way a subset of data from the archive to study. In essence, there was *too much* data from which to conduct my research—so much, that it was impossible to study all the available records.

Recognizing the Relevant Data Sources for Interactional Ethnography

The curricular units comprising the full corpus of data included projects in electrical, package, landscape, or environmental engineering. Half of the teachers in the archive taught a civil engineering unit prior to teaching one of these units in order to test for a dosage effect. I chose to focus my research project on civil engineering for two reasons. First, failures seemed be more easily recognizable—a broken structure (bridge model) is easier to identify than a poorly performed oil spill cleanup (an environmental engineering task). Easy identification of failures was important because this was the first study of its kind specifically studying engineering design failure in elementary schools, so there were no protocols for identifying failure. Second, the civil engineering units were always the teachers' first time teaching engineering. This was also a key consideration because I am interested in understanding the students' and teachers' needs when initially doing an engineering unit and this choice eliminated classes with prior experience.

The larger efficacy study conducted by EiE staff was focused on quantitative comparisons of science learning, awareness of engineering, and interest levels and contrasted student outcomes in classes using EiE with those from classes using a comparison curriculum called *Engineering 4 Children* (E4C). It is important to note that the comparison curriculum, E4C, which was created by EiE staff, was not designed to be used outside of this study. For this reason, I chose not to compare learning outcomes from them directly—E4C intentionally leaves out the components that EiE designers consider critical to engineering design projects, like the opportunity to improve designs. But by including the comparison curriculum it offered the opportunity to view more failures in design. Using a theoretical sampling approach (Patton, 1990), I identified 139 hours of digital video recordings to analyze from eight classrooms (four EiE and four E4C) engaged in civil engineering. The classrooms were from both Northeast and Mid-Atlantic states; some had racial and/or socioeconomic diversity and others were homogeneous.

In each classroom, three cameras recorded classroom activity; one was a wide view of the class and captured overall movement and whole-group settings. Two additional cameras were trained on individual groups of three or four students and their work was audio recorded using portable recorders set on their desks, which were later synched to the video using Transana multiuser 3.0 software. This data collection strategy affords the opportunity to analyze classroom discourse when a teacher (or participant observer) is not present. It also avoids the mistake of a researcher recording only charismatic groups or limiting recording to only isolated events (like formal testing of a design). This increases the potential for exploring commonalities and differences within experiences.

Collecting video data of students presents challenges to maintaining privacy. Student groups that were recorded had all received parental content and care was taken to avoid recording those students who did not. For example, students without consent wore lanyards to signal this fact to researchers in charge of recording. When students without permission appeared on camera inadvertently, their faces were digitally scrubbed. EiE staff de-identified the teachers and students by assigning numbers to the classes and to the student engineering journals prior to granting me access. In cases where individuals were called by name on video, pseudonyms were assigned for transcripts and written representations or analyses.

These decisions were used to defend a manageable sampling of a large video data archive. The decisions were guided by a theoretical framework that considers engineering learning and failure to be a phenomenon that is socially constructed by students and teachers trying to accomplish their daily lives by engaging in classroom engineering practices. Then I defined research questions that could be investigated through a systematic analysis of classroom discourse.

Discourse and Sociocultural Practices in Everyday Life, in Time and Space

Failure is a phenomenon that most humans experience. Phenomenology attempts to understand human experience by exposing aspects that are taken for granted (Starks & Trinidad, 2007) and illuminating details that may be considered trivial (Laverty, 2003). Van Manen (1990) opines that a study using this method should elicit the "phenomenological nod" from the readers as an outward recognition of experiences they have had. But phenomenology is both a philosophy and a methodology that needs to be further explicated to justify the alignment with my theoretical framework. Views that have formed about phenomenology and the many versions of it vary greatly in both the philosophy and methods of using it.

Husserl is credited with the origins of phenomenology, and thought experience was the primary source of knowledge building (Racher & Robinson, 2003). But he thought avoiding researcher bias was key and that description of the phenomenon should be free from interpretation and cultural context (Husserl, 1970). Heidegger disagreed, and suggested the researcher's role is to point toward essential understanding that could not be mutually exclusive from his previous experience and culture (Laverty, 2003). In his view, analysis should consider parts of the experience as well as the broader context, which was later called the *hermeneutic circle* by Polkinghorne (1983). Further, Gadamer (1989) argued that our linguistic experience is what makes understanding possible (Dowling, 2007).

The version of phenomenology used in this study views the phenomenon of failure and improvement to be culturally embedded and inseparable from the sociomaterial contexts in which they are co-constructed. Thus, the goal of interpretive phenomenology should be to find culturally grounded commonalities (Benner, 2000) as the suspension of researcher bias is implausible (Gadamer, 1989). However, acknowledgment of the possibility of bias places a greater responsibility on the researcher to establish trustworthiness of the interpretive narrative (Fleming, Gaidys, & Robb, 2003).

To increase trustworthiness, suggestions of Creswell and Miller (2000) were followed. First, they suggest *collaboration* and *peer review*. This study was done as a doctoral dissertation, so I collaborated with my advisor and participated in a research group focused on classroom discourse. Both served to question and challenge assertions and assumptions made in this work. Trustworthiness is also enhanced by maintaining an *audit trail* (Creswell & Miller, 2000). The goal of an audit trail is to be able to justify decisions and analyses to a "friendly skeptic." Frequent and ongoing analytic notes were created to maintain an ongoing record of the progress of the research, and all event maps, transcripts, and other work products were maintained. Last, a *thick description* (Geertz, 1994) is suggested to guide the reader in interpreting the analyses. This style of reporting is important to orient the reader, particularly in describing an interaction in a way that the salient points are evident.

The engineering units in this study were designed to take several class periods, culminating in an engineering design challenge that involved designing

TABLE 5.1 A description and comparison of the activities in the experimental curriculum (EiE) and the comparison curriculum (E4C)

E4C	*EiE*
1. Critical load—Students read about the work of civil engineers and build a tower with playing cards that should be as tall as possible and hold as much weight as possible.	1. Students read the storybook *Javier Builds a Bridge*. After falling off an unstable bridge leading to his fort, Javi helps design a new bridge with the help of his stepfather, Joe. Civil engineers and their work are highlighted in this story, and the characters use the engineering design process throughout the process. Several types of bridges are also introduced.
2. Leaning tower of pasta—Students build a tall, strong structure using spaghetti and marshmallows, test their structures and discuss observations.	2. Pushes and pulls—Students examine several different structures and consider how they are affected by force. They also evaluate some solutions aimed to prevent forces from causing structures to fall. A discussion of civil engineers and their work to counteract unbalanced forces and increase stability and strength concludes this lesson.
3. Tall tower challenge—Students read about famous strong, stable structures and design towers out of pipe cleaners and drinking straws.	3. Bridging understanding—Students create and test three bridge types (beam, arch, deep beam) and evaluate the amount of weight each can support. Students also examine the materials available to them to consider ways in which they can be used to increase the strength and stability of a bridge.
4. Popsicle bridge—Students read about different bridge types and parts of bridges and design and build a bridge out of popsicle sticks and masking tape to support a 5-pound weight over a 14-inch span.	4. Designing a bridge—Students apply the Engineering Design Process as they work in small groups to design, build, and test a bridge that is able to cross a 15-inch span, will support toy cars crossing, and is able to allow a "barge" to roll under it without touching the bridge or the abutments. Students are then given the opportunity to improve their design.

TABLE 5.2 Descriptive statistics of the classrooms studied. *Mr. Tanner and Ms. Houseman taught in the same school; ★Ms. Maddux and Ms. Clay taught in the same school

	Pseudonym	*Grade*	*% Free/reduced lunch prices*	*Demographics (% underrepresented minority)*	*S:T ratio*
E4C	Ms. Lyle	4th	15%	16%	15:1
	Ms. Flemming	5th	35%	97%	18:1
	Mr. Tanner*	5th	60%	30%	15:1
	Ms. Houseman*	5th			
EiE	Ms. Thomas	3rd	2.7%	19%	18:1
	Ms. James	4th	6.6%	22.6%	16:1
	Ms. Maddux★	3rd	19%	16%	19:1
	Ms. Clay★	3rd			

and constructing structures meant to hold a weight without collapsing. Both the E4C and EiE units spent time introducing students to civil engineering as a discipline and defined specific criteria and constraints for the designs. However, E4C purposefully left out critical components viewed to be important to the developers of EiE. In EiE, problems are contextualized, investigations of relevant science concepts are done to inform designs, opportunities to improve original prototypes are provided, and evaluations of designs are based on multiple criteria to avoid "pass/fail" results. Table 5.1 compares the unit designs.

One key difference is the number of structures designed by the students in the respective treatment groups. EiE spends the first two lessons contextualizing the problem, the role of civil engineers, and engaging students in investigations about balanced forces. It would be less time consuming to analyze only lessons where design and construction occur in EiE; however, Kelly (2014) emphasizes the importance of analyzing text that zooms in and out, from parts of the experience to the whole, similar to Polkinghorne (1983) and his description of the hermeneutic circle. By analyzing the classroom discourse in the lessons leading up to the design, I could better interpret language usage and referents used by the actors in their interactions. The depth in which EiE teachers taught the unit led to a total of 97 hours of video compared with 42 hours in E4C classes. Table 5.2 describes the class characteristics of the eight teachers.

Data Representation and Units of Analysis, in and over Time

In this section, two types of data representations of discourse events are presented as ways to make sense of the data. The first is called an event map (Kelly & Crawford, 1997; Brown & Sprang, 2008). Interactional sociolinguistics typically begins with a period of ethnographic research to understand the general communicative routines (Gumperz, 2001), so videos were watched and notes were taken to describe the activities, interactions, and potentially interesting events. Event maps were generated in a spreadsheet in which each row represents one minute of time and time stamps were made in order to easily find later the relevant episodes for further investigation and micro-level analysis. At the end of the first viewing, analytic notes were compiled on a separate document to keep a record of initial impressions, and to serve as part of the audit trail (Creswell & Miller, 2000) to maintain a history of the development and rationale behind codes and other decisions.

The definitions of sociolinguistic units used come from Green and Wallat (1981) and Kelly (2004). Observation logs from EiE research staff were used to classify coordinated activity of the class, called *phases* (e.g., designing bridges). Next, *sequences* were identified through semantic and context clues, and included activities like "testing the span." The phases and sequences were added as separate columns on the spreadsheet by merging rows, providing a visual representation of the amount of time spent on each. *Action units*, comprised of utterances or action identified through context clues that represented an observed intention of the speakers (Kelly & Crawford, 1997; Kelly & Chen, 1999), were also developed. These action units also considered the physical artifacts as relevant to the discourse. The combination of time stamps, sequences, and action units enabled future rounds of analysis, including coding of failure types, failure causes, and teacher reactions. An additional column was used for open coding potentially interesting aspects.

Event maps (Baker & Green, 2007; Kelly, Crawford, & Green, 2001) also served in the place of participant observation, considered by some to be a hallmark of ethnographic research (Spradley, 1980). A participant observer learns firsthand about the communicative ecology of the research site; however, field notes are limited in space and time to only those interactions or conditions available to the researcher. Event maps generated from video of three concurrent events enable a researcher to take more field notes, although they are limited only to events that are recorded. See Table 5.3 for an excerpt of an event map.

The second data representation is a transcript of talk and action. In order to illustrate an interaction between students or between students and teachers, a transcript is a word-by-word account of the discourse. The interactions transcribed were between five seconds and two minutes in duration of bounded activity, and recorded in a table format. Time stamps mark the beginning and end of the interaction, and lines are numbered to easily reference specific parts of the transcript in the description. Participants are arranged in columns according to their position on the video (i.e., the person on the left side of the video screen occupies the leftmost column in the transcript). Each student and teacher were assigned a pseudonym. Teachers were named Mr./Ms. and a last name; students were assigned only a first name. This enables the reader to easily identify the teacher in the discourse event. A column on the right is labeled, "context clues," and provides a place for the analyst to provide relevant commentary on the

TABLE 5.3 An excerpt from an event map demonstrating the features and how they are used to organize activity, note times, and code for failure cause, type, and teacher reaction

Phase	*Sequence*	*Time*	*Action Units*	*Cause*	*Type*	*RXN*
Improve step	Install piers	16:33	The boy adds a pier of rolled up paper. Girl asks T if they have to count the tape toward the cost			
		17:45	Boy and small girl cut and match a second pier			
		18:18	They are planning to add supports just like T2. They have also added straws as curbs on the decking.			
		19:15	Accusal of copying by T2. Girl says they aren't copying—just doing something "similar." Another boy comes in and comments that "everyone is doing the same thing." Girl is amazed at how strong the bridge is.			
		20:15	Group seems satisfied. Tough to see if and what kind of support is under the bridge. Will have to check the journals.			
		21:50	Girl installs piers. Cuts a few times to get the right height.			
		22:40	G wants to add another pier—group suggests she measure before she cuts.			
		23:16	T tells Ss to wrap up so they can test. They test using the barge, then add another pier.			

	24:45 G—It's good enough, Ava, right? The final design looks like it has 5 piers, a straw-reinforced deck, and lined with straws to keep the car on. Public testing has begun.			
Public testing begins				
T1 Public testing	27:10 T1 start their public test. Barge passes. The car does not fall off the side, but doesn't pass—so they get another car.			
	28:12 Car finally makes it, Girl says she wants to add another pier. T says that's fine, she'll come back later—group collectively decides they just want to test now. Car passes all four times. They begin weight test.			
	30:05 Bridge breaks at 46. T—oh, 46. G—that's the most we've got. T gets interrupted by another group, says, "Great job" and leaves. Only 2 of the Ss use their journal. They tear down the bridge.	KST	HIO	M
Clean up	31:38 T calls for Ss to clean up if they have tested.			

actions accompanying the talk and frequently refers to the materials or artifacts with which the students are working. In cases where intonation or emphasis was determined to be important, Jeffersonian transcription symbols were used; however, they were used sparingly and context clues were used to enhance the readability.

Table 5.4 is an example of a transcript of turn-by-turn talk and action. In this interaction, the teacher's reaction to the student's bridge failure is classified as *manager* (Johnson, 2016). The students are adding weights to the deck until it collapses to determine a strength score for their design. Their words are drawn out (denoted by enclosing the words in angle brackets). The context clues include notations for each weight they add, when the bridge collapses, and that Leah refers to her journal to find the score on a rubric in the journal. Using the event map and considering the events leading up to this interaction allow for the analysis that the teacher is concerned with the time left in class and her reaction is a result of managing class time rather than engaging them in a discussion about the cause of the failure and ways to improve.

These data displays were used both in analysis and in reporting results of the research. Event maps were useful in initial stages for classifying and quantifying time spent on the different activities. They were also used to locate events for further analysis and for referencing antecedents to failure and improvement. This process of theoretical sampling based on the event maps identified interactions around failure. From these interactions, transcripts were generated that required in-depth analysis, and focused attention on both how the participants (students, teachers) interacted with each other and with the materials. Transcripts were also useful in demonstrating salient concepts generated from analysis, and scores from the rubrics represent complex interactions that were useful in considering the use of journals in evaluating improvement.

TABLE 5.4 An example of a transcript using Jeffersonian symbols. Ms. Maddux is the teacher, and context clues refer to materials and how they are used in the interaction

Transcript – From event map T14143BrL42d1T1B

Time	*Line*	*Ms. Maddux*	*Leah*	*Farrah*	*Rory*	*Context Clues*
9:37	1	<Three>		<Three>		Places a weight
	2	<Four>	<Four>			Places a weight
	3	<Five>		<Five>		Places a weight
	4	<Six> Wow↑			<Six>	Places a weight
	5	<Seven>	<Seven>			Places a weight
	6	Eight		Eight		Bridge collapses
9:55	7	Good job! That's				Leah checks her journal
	8	great. Ok, all				for a score as
	9	right, record all your scores				Ms. Maddux leaves

Building Representations of Practice, Finding Patterns, Reaching Conclusions

The analysis of classroom discourse on video also led to the development of an analytic rubric to study both the video and the journals as student go through the process of improvement. Through multiple rounds of viewing the video, developing event maps, and microanalysis of transcripts, a rubric was developed based on the necessary elements of *systematic improvement* (Johnson, 2016). Improvement could occur through luck or by copying another design, but *systematic* improvement relies on: (a) acknowledgment of failure; (b) an attribution of the failure cause; (c) a criterion chosen for improvement that aligns with the acknowledgment of failure (i.e., aiming to improve strength when the design scores poorly in that criteria); (d) a strategy for improvement employed that is specifically aligned with the attribution of failure; and (e) a result in the criteria the group sought to improve that is better than the previous prototype (Table 5.5).

Using journals to ascertain scores from this rubric is dependent on alignment between what students say and do on video and what they write in their journals. Journals were de-identified, and were grouped only by class when I received them. I cross-referenced the journals with the event maps based on unique characteristics (e.g., the number of weights their bridge prototypes held in lesson three) to find the journals that belonged to the 16 student groups that were recorded. Both event maps and journals were scored using the rubric and scores were compared. Paired t-tests revealed no significant differences in the scores. This suggests that engineering journals can be used to score improvement using this rubric to enhance the video data analysis, which is both costly to acquire and collect and is time-intensive.

The rubric was then tested for interrater reliability. After training sessions with three colleagues, the rubric was used on a subset of the journals and the rubric was modified based on feedback. One of those colleagues used the rubric to analyze a larger subset of the journals and scores were compared. In addition, two researchers untrained in the use of the rubric also analyzed the larger subset. Cohen's kappa measurement of interrater reliability showed moderate to significant agreement (Viera & Garrett, 2005) with each of the three scorers.

The Hawthorne effect describes potentially misleading outcomes resulting from research subjects being aware they are being studied (Brown, 1992). To address this concern, journals from students not on video were compared with those that were. Average scores of groups on camera differed with those off camera, but were mixed—in two classes off-camera students scored higher and in two classes they scored lower. This evidence and in-depth analysis of the behavior of students over 139 hours suggested the Hawthone effect was not relevant in this case. The students did not appear to remember they were being recorded shortly after the beginning of the unit!

Figure 5.1 shows the journal scores from the four classes in the EiE treatment. Each column in the graph shows the average improvement scores earned by the

TABLE 5.5 The rubric developed for assessing systematic improvement including journal page references and examples

Page number	*Question*	*Example of a "Yes"*	*Example of a "No"*
32/33 & 37/38	Did the design fail? Yes+1 No—DO NOT SCORE	"It collapsed when we added weight" or Scores of **<4** for stability or <5 for strength	"We got the highest score **you** can get"
32/33 & 37/38	Was there evidence of an attribution of failure? Yes+1 No+0	". . . because we didn't have enough supports" or "because the deck was too flimsy"	"[it was our lowest score] because it only got a **2**." "We got a **2** because it collapsed when we added weight"
34 & 39	Was the criterion for improvement (cost, strength, or stability) aligned with a failure they identified? Yes+1 No+0	The design only earned a "1" for strength, so they aimed to improve strength	The design earned a 1 for strength but they aimed to improve cost
34 & 39	Was there evidence of a strategy for improvement aligned with their stated goals? Yes+1 No+0	"We will add more supports" (if improved strength is the goal) "We will add another layer to the deck to make it more rigid" (if improved stability is the goal)	"We will make it stronger"
37, 42, & 46	Was there evidence that the design improved due to that strategy? Yes+1 No+0	"We went from holding **2** weights to **24**," Documented scores from the chart on **46** (as long as improved score was aligned with their goal (tried to improve strength and strength score increased—not necessarily total design score))	"It held the same" "It got worse"

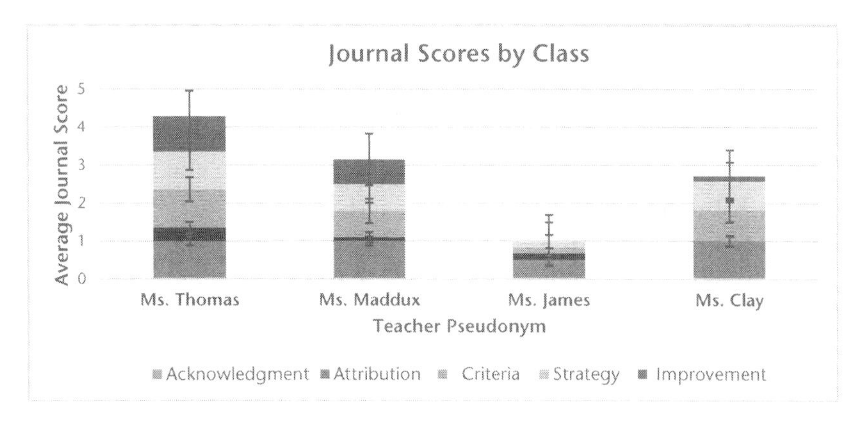

FIGURE 5.1 Average improvement scores per attempt at improvement by the groups' video recorded.

groups in each class whose journals were scored and are broken down into the five components from the rubric. This display demonstrates differences noted between the classes. The journal scores reflected the groups' attempts at improving their design, and contributed to the model of improvement described in Johnson (2016). In the cases when student groups did not achieve a score of five, the reasons map onto either the three obstacles to improvement (a lack of opportunity, a lack of a fair comparison, or a lack of productive strategies) (Johnson, 2016), or in some cases, the students did not even acknowledge there was a failure. For example, one of the groups from Mrs. James' class did not have the opportunity to improve because they misinterpreted her directions, so the group did not earn an improvement score. In Ms. Thomas' class, one group failed to demonstrate improvement because their strategy of stabilizing the bridge deck was not productive. Analysis of student and teacher discourse on video and student artifacts with an analytic rubric allowed me to gain a clearer understanding of how the groups attempted to improve their designs. In some instances, the co-construction of talk and action did not need to be written down. For example, efforts to improve a collapsed bridge signaled an acknowledgment of failure, but did not require them writing it down in the journal. In other cases, their actions were not easily observed in talk and action, but were clarified in written form when prompted by the journal instructions. Additionally, patterns in these scores could be used to identify areas in which teachers could add interventions. In these four classes, students were often unable to attribute a cause of failure, which is important in devising a productive strategy. This could be a target for the teachers' next iteration of the unit.

Interpreting Results

The use of interactional sociolinguistics (Gumperz, 2001; Green & Meyer, 1991) to investigate the types of failure, the causes of failure, and the collective actions of students and teachers' contributions toward improvement *in situ* was instrumental in developing a model of improvement described in detail in a dissertation thesis (Johnson, 2016). I will first give a summary of the model of improvement and then describe in greater depth the ways these methods were used to classify three types of reactions teachers have when student designs fail.

Research Question 1: How Do Failures Happen in Engineering Design?

Through analysis, three continua of failures were generated. First, failures are either done intentionally or they happen unintentionally. *Intended* failures occurred either to compare prototypes to inform the final design or in acquiring a final score for strength. *Unintended* failures occur when a design does not achieve the required criteria within the given constraints. The second continuum refers to the stakes under which the failure occurs. *Low stakes* failures occur in early prototyping in which students have sufficient time and opportunity in which to improve. They may be either intended or unintended. *High stakes* failures occur in formal tests, often done in front of the class. Depending on the situation, they may have the opportunity to redesign. The third continuum is based on what the performance of the design is being compared with. *Objective* failure occurs when it does not meet given criteria within constraints understood by the class. *Subjective* failure occurs when a design is deemed to be inferior compared with a different set of criteria, such as another group's design. Each of the 270 failure events were categorized as intended or unintended and low stakes or high stakes; the referent axis (objective, subjective) was determined to be less important for this work. The unspecified word "failure" encompasses too many situations, and it is important to understand the nature of the failure to better interpret the reactions to it.

Research Question 2: Why Do Failures Happen in Elementary Engineering Design?

Just as the type of failure will affect the reactions, the causes of the failures will affect the strategies engineers must use to improve. Event maps were used to identify failed designs. Four codes were developed through inductive analysis in order to classify each failure cause, and each failure was classified into one of four groups (Table 5.6)

Without knowledge of the class activities prior to the design, failures would be difficult to code or would be coded incorrectly. One group in an EiE classroom tried to use an arch to support the deck because they had tested smaller prototypes of three bridge designs and arch was the strongest. However, the bridge design required a wider span, and index cards used for the arch were

TABLE 5.6 A description of characteristics and examples of the four identified causes of failure (Johnson, 2016)

Cause	*Characteristics of Causes*	*Specific Examples*
Lack of knowledge of science/ technology	The students do not understand a key science or technology concept	Lesson 1—Cards need to support the area where the load is applied. Lesson 4—Piers or rigid deck are necessary to support the 5-pound load
Lack of knowledge of materials	The students do not understand the characteristics of materials they are using	Students thinking masking tape makes paper rigid enough to hold a weight
Poor craftsmanship	The reaction seems to be aimed at helping the students think about improving or to consider what went wrong and why	Designing a bridge that is uneven so the load falls off
Limitations of materials	Eventually, even a well-designed solution fails due to constraints within the material or the activity	Lesson 1—even a tower that is designed using software to optimize its strength will eventually break if the goal is testing until failure

too short, so they used two arches. The load was placed in between the arches, limiting the benefit of that style of bridge. The failure could have been attributed to misunderstanding the material (paper) used for the deck and arches; however, they chose the arch bridge based on their experience in small-scale testing. Their misunderstanding of the mechanism of an arch's ability (a lack of knowledge of science/technology) to transfer a downward load into the abutments led to their weak bridge, but this interpretation relied on understanding the group's activity leading to the design.

Research Question 3: How Do the Collective Actions of Students and Teachers Support or Constrain the Process of Improvement from Engineering Design Failure?

Among the collective actions of students and teachers, I was particularly interested in the reactions teachers had to failure. As I argued earlier, improvement requires an attribution of failure and a strategy aimed at overcoming the design flaw; so, I was interested in teachers' ability to support students in learning from the failure and improving in the next iteration. Also, through inductive coding and a series of expanding and collapsing (and re-naming) categories, three were named: the *manager*, the *cheerleader*, and the *strategic partner*. The three reaction types are directly related to the multiple responsibilities of teachers. They protect the students from unnecessary disappointment (the cheerleader), they help students learn (the strategic partner), and they must be aware of class and time management (the manager).

In this first example, Ms. Clay's class is testing their second bridge for strength. They add weights until it collapses.

Time	*Line*	*Ms. Clay*	*Researcher*	*Lacey*	*Rena*	*Context Clues*
46:53	1				Thirteen	Places a weight
	2			Fourteen		Places a weight
	3				Fifteen	Places a weight,
	4					some
	5					weights fall off the side
	6	That's it, right? That's it.	Oop. Good job			
	7		Fifteen↑			
	8	Fifteen			Fifteen? That	Puzzled look
	9				was worse	on Rena's
	10				than the first one	face
	11	Oh, dear, you'll				
	12	have to figure				
	13	out what				
	14	went wrong. That's part of your job				
	15			We need		Quietly to
	16			more tape right here		Rena, points to bridge deck
	16	But we had fun,				
	17	didn't we?				
	18			Yeah		Grabs roll of tape
47:18	19	And you did a				
	20	good job, didn't you. Yes, you did				

In this example, Lacey and Rena are trying to find an attribution for the fact their bridge scored lower after redesigning (lines 15–18). Ms. Clay focuses her comments on praise, feedback likely aimed at lessening their disappointment, but ineffective in helping the students learn (Mueller & Dweck, 1998).

The second example is of Lara, Madden, and Reggie's group after frequent low stakes failures. Ms. James sits down with them to help them respond to their latest failure.

Time	*Line*	*Madden*	*Reggie*	*Ms. James*	*Context Clues*
46:32	1 2				Lara, Madden, and Reggie are looking at the bridge
	3		We have so many ideas		Ms. James sits down
	4 5 6			Ok, so you're shooting and brainstorming ideas with each other?	Reggie replies inaudibly
	7 8 9			Ok, so you need counter forces because you have a weakness in the center	
	10		Yes		
	11 12 13 14 15			All right, failure in the center. What are some options that you can have, even looking around to see what other are doing	
	16 17 18	We were trying to put a popsicle stick (across but it didn't work)			Madden demonstrates to Ms. James
	19 20			Ok, so did you think about doing a deep beam?	
	21	Uh, no (inaudible)			
	22 23 24 25 26 27 28 29 30 31 32 33 34 35			Ok, so you may have to make an improvement. You may have to go open your wallet and buy something else because you do need to make it stable and strong, so . . . we do know that the deep beam is stronger than the beam. And it may be an adjustment you can make, especially since you have to get the barge through and you already have piers built, ok?	Madden nods All three students stare at bridge

(continued)

(continued)

Time	*Line*	*Madden*	*Reggie*	*Ms. James*	*Context Clues*
	36			Uh, what other ideas are	Students look
	37			people doing?	around at
	38				other groups.
	39				Madden points at one but his words are inaudible
47:58	40			Ok (pause of 6 seconds).	Mrs. James
	41			All right	gets up and leaves. Lara sighs

Ms. James takes a direct approach to help the students develop a new strategy rather than asking leading questions. This is likely due to the lack of time the group has to enact their new plan. She first helps them with attributing the failure to a lack of a pier (lines 7–9), she then suggests they consider features from other students' designs (lines 13–14), suggests a design for them (lines 19–20), and uses evidence from an earlier lesson to suggest they use a deep beam design (lines 28–29). This feedback is considerably different than the example with Ms. Clay, because it is focused on helping them learn and use more effective strategies. This is called the *strategic partner* reaction.

The last example is from Ms. Flemming's class. The class period is almost over, but they are testing the strength of their structures with weights.

Time	*Line*	*Class (in unison)*	*Ms. Flemming*	*Context Clues*
45:55	1	<ele:ven>,		Students add nuts one at
	2	<twe:lve>,		a time
	3	<thir:teen>		
	4			Structure collapses, class
	5			reacts with surprise and disappointment
46:02	6		>Ok, quickly, quickly	Class runs to the next
	7		let's go to the last	group to test
	8		group<	

In this example, Ms. Flemming's reaction is primarily focused on being efficient with time management. The class is running out of time, and as soon as the group gets a score, she moves on to the next group. But this reaction does little to help students in improving future structures.

Elementary teachers are tasked with wearing many hats in the classroom. And these reaction types are aligned with three of the roles teachers must play.

These archetypical reactions are not aimed to be judgmental; but, as an impartial observer the effect of the feedback on student learning and progress toward improvement is salient. The group in Ms. James' class went on to build an improved design. The other two groups did not. Further, only 35 reactions were coded out of 137 failures in the EiE group, primarily because teachers were busy with managing the materials. I argue that the reactions to failure of the students are much more important than that of the teacher, and teaching the students about failure analysis prior to designing might be a productive activity to prepare students to improve their prototypes.

Conclusion

In this chapter, I used a study of failure and improvement in elementary engineering design to illustrate a methodology and some of the key decisions made in carrying out this investigation of classroom activity. A sociomaterial perspective of engineering emphasizes the inseparable nature of the cultural aspects of learning and the materials they use to accomplish their classwork. Thus, the discourse is situated in the classroom context that must be made clear to the reader through data representations. Event maps were used to organize and represent several hours of talk and activity with a broad view. Transcripts of instances of talk and action were used to look closely at specific interactions, and were analyzed using discourse and context cues dependent on classroom culture and specific events leading to them. Analysis of a large video record like the one described must be systematic and puts the responsibility of developing trustworthiness on the researcher.

I argue that understanding the type and cause of failure by both the students and teachers is important in attributing the failure to specific and controllable aspects that can be improved through productive strategies. Teachers can support the practice of improvement in their feedback and through discussions and examples of how engineers accomplish their work, especially when they recognize these failures as an opportunity for learning. I also argue that through the development of analytic rubrics, student engineering journals can be used as a proxy for what students say and do in their group work and can be used to evaluate the process they use in design—in this case, improvement.

Engineering research of this type is timely due to the recent reforms in science education. The emphasis on engaging students in engineering practices to learn science and engineering concepts (NRC, 2012) is a shift from prior efforts, and challenges most teachers with little experience with engineering. Therefore, research in curriculum and instruction are necessary to support teachers in this endeavor. Research of classroom discourse in engineering projects will bolster other investigations and help lead to improvements in curriculum and in engineering teaching and learning.

References

Allchin, D. (2003). Scientific myth-conceptions. *Science Education*, 87(3), 329–351.

Allchin, D. (2012). Teaching the nature of science through scientific errors. *Science Education*, 96(5), 904–926.

Baker, W. D., & Green, J. L. (2007). Limits to certainty in interpreting video data: Interactional ethnography and disciplinary knowledge. *Pedagogies: An International Journal*, 2(3), 191–204.

Benner, P. (2000). The tradition and skill of interpretive phenomenology in studying health, illness, and caring practices. In P. Benner (Ed.), *Interpretive Phenomenology: Embodiment, Caring, and Ethics in Health and Illness* (pp. 99–127). Thousand Oaks, CA: Sage

Bjørn, P., & Østerlund, C. (2014). *Sociomaterial-Design: Bounding Technologies in Practice*. London: Springer.

Brown, A. L. (1992). Design experiments: Theoretical and methodological challenges in creating complex interventions in classroom settings. *The Journal of the Learning Sciences*, 2(2), 141–178.

Brown, B. A., & Sprang, E. (2008). Double talk: Synthesizing every day and science language in the classroom. *Science Education*, 89(4), 770–802.

Creswell, J. W., & Miller, D. L. (2000). Determining validity in qualitative inquiry. *Theory into Practice*, 39(3), 124–130.

Cunningham, C. M., & Carlsen W. S. (2014). Precollege engineering education. In N. G. Lederman & S. K. Abell (Eds.), *Handbook of Research on Science Education, Vol. II*. New York: Routledge.

Cunningham, C. M., & Kelly, G. J. (2017). Epistemic practices of engineering for education. *Science Education*, 101(3), 486–505.

Dowling, M. (2007). From Husserl to van Manen: A review of different phenomenological approaches. *International Journal of Nursing Studies*, 44(1), 131–142.

Firestein, S. (2015). *Failure: Why Science Is So Successful*. New York: Oxford University Press.

Fleming, V., Gaidys, U., & Robb, Y. (2003). Hermeneutic research in nursing: Developing a Gadamerian-based research method. *Nursing Inquiry*, 10(2), 113–120.

Frederiksen, C. H., & Donin, J. (2015). Discourse and learning in contexts of educational interaction. In N. Markee (Ed.), *The Handbook of Classroom Discourse and Interaction* (pp. 96–114). West Sussex: John Wiley & Sons, Inc.

Gadamer, G. H. (1989). *Truth and Method*, second ed. London: Sheed and Ward, [translation revised by Weinsheimer J. and Marshall D. G.].

Geertz, C. (1994). Thick description: Toward an interpretive theory of culture. In M. Martin & L. C. McIntyre (Eds.), *Readings in the Philosophy of Social Science* (pp. 213–231). Cambridge, MA: MIT Press.

Green, J. L., & Dixon, C. (1993). Santa Barbara classroom discourse group [Special issue]. *Linguistics and Education*, 5(3).

Green, J. L., & Meyer, L. (1991). The embeddedness of reading in classroom life: Reading as a situated process. In C. Baker & A. Luke (Eds.), *Toward a Critical Sociology of Reading Pedagogy* (pp. 141–160). Amsterdam: John Benjamins.

Green, J. L., & Wallat, C. (1981). Mapping instructional conversations: A sociolinguistic ethnography. *Ethnography and Language in Educational Settings, Vol. 5* (pp. 161–195). Cambridge, MA: MIT Press.

Gumperz, J. J. (1982). *Discourse Strategies, Vol. 1*. Cambridge: Cambridge University Press.

Gumperz, J. J. (2001). Interactional sociolinguistics: A personal perspective. In D. Schiffrin, D. Tannen, & H. E. Hamilton (Eds.), *Handbook of Discourse Analysis*. Malden: Blackwell.

Gumperz, J. J., & Hymes, D. (Eds.). (1972). *Directions in Sociolinguistics: The Ethnography of Communication*. New York: Blackwell.

Haushofer, J. (2016). CV of Failures, www.princeton.edu/~joha/Johannes_Haushofer_CV_of_Failures.pdf, retrieved 11/18/2017.

Husserl, E. (1970). *The Crisis of European Sciences and Transcendental Phenomenology: An Introduction to Phenomenological Philosophy*. Evanston, IL: Northwestern University Press.

Johnson, M. M. (2016). Failure is an option: Reactions to failure in elementary school engineering design projects. (Doctoral dissertation). Retrieved from Penn State Electronic Theses and Dissertations for Graduate School database. Catalogue number 28775.

Johri, A. (2011). The socio-materiality of learning practices and implications for the field of learning technology. *Research in Learning Technology*, 19(3).

Kelly, G. J. (2004). Discourse, description, and science education. In R. K. Yerrick & W. M. Roth (Eds.), *Establishing Scientific Classroom Discourse Communities* (pp. 85–114). Mahwah, NJ: Routledge.

Kelly, G. J. (2008). Inquiry, activity, and epistemic practice. In R. A. Duschl & R. E. Grandy (Eds.), *Teaching Scientific Inquiry: Recommendations for Research and Implementation* (pp. 99–117; 288–291). Rotterdam, Netherlands: Sense Publishers.

Kelly, G. J. (2011). Scientific literacy, discourse, and epistemic practices. In C. Linder, L. Ostman, D. A. Roberts, P.-O. Wickman, G. Erickson, & A. MacKinnon (Eds.), *Exploring the Landscape of Scientific Literacy* (pp. 61–73). New York: Routledge.

Kelly, G. J. (2014). Analyzing classroom activities: Theoretical and methodological considerations. In C. Brugière, A. Tiberghien, & P. Clément (Eds.), *Topics and Trends in Current Science Education* (pp. 353–368). Netherlands: Springer.

Kelly, G. J., & Chen, C. (1999). The sound of music: Constructing science as sociocultural practices through oral and written discourse. *Journal of Research in Science Teaching*, 36, 883–915.

Kelly, G. J., & Crawford, T. (1997). An ethnographic investigation of the discourse processes of school science. *Science Education*, 81(5), 533–559.

Kelly, G. J., Crawford, T., & Green, J. L. (2001). Common tasks and uncommon knowledge: Dissenting voices in the discursive construction of physics across small laboratory groups. *Linguistics and Education*, 12(2), 135–174.

Kelly, G. J., & Green, J. L. (1998). The social nature of knowing: Toward a sociocultural perspective on conceptual change and knowledge construction. In B. Guzzetti & C. Hynd (Eds.), *Perspectives on Conceptual Change: Multiple Ways to Understand Knowing and Learning in a Complex World* (pp. 145–181). Mahwah, NJ: Lawrence Erlbaum Associates.

Kelly, G. J., & Licona, P. (2018). Epistemic practices and science education. In M. Matthews (Ed.), *History, Philosophy and Science Teaching: New Research Perspectives* (pp. 139–165). Netherlands: Springer.

Laverty, S. M. (2003). Hermeneutic phenomenology and phenomenology: A comparison of historical and methodological considerations. *International Journal of Qualitative Methods*, 2(3), 21–35.

Levi-Strauss, C. (1962). *The Savage Mind (La Persee Sauvage)*. London: Weidenfeld & Nicolson.

Lottero-Perdue, P. S., & Parry, E. A. (2017). Elementary teachers' reflections on design failures and use of fail words after teaching engineering for two years. *Journal of Pre-College Engineering Education Research (J-PEER)*, 7(1), 1.

Matson, J. V. (1996). *Innovate or Die: A Personal Perspective on the Art of Innovation*. Monroe, WI: Paradigm Press.

Mueller, C. M., & Dweck, C. S. (1998). Praise for intelligence can undermine children's motivation and performance. *Journal of Personality and Social Psychology*, 75(1), 33.

National Research Council, Schweingruber, H., Keller, T., & Quinn, H. (Eds.). (2012). *A Framework for K-12 Science Education: Practices, Crosscutting Concepts, and Core Ideas*. Washington, DC: National Academies Press.

NGSS Lead States. (2013). *Next Generation Science Standards: For States, By States*. Washington, DC: National Academies Press.

Orlikowski, W. J., & Scott, S. V. (2008). Sociomateriality: Challenging the separation of technology, work and organization. *Academy of Management Annals*, 2(1), 433–474.

Patton, M. (1990). *Qualitative Evaluation and Research Methods* (pp. 169–186). Beverly Hills, CA: Sage.

Pickering, A. (1993). The mangle of practice: Agency and emergence in the sociology of science. *American Journal of Sociology*, 99(3), 559–589.

Polkinghorne, D. (1983). *Methodology for the Human Sciences: Systems of Inquiry*. Albany, NY: State University of New York Press.

Racher, F., & Robinson, S. (2003). Are phenomenology and postpostivism strange bedfellows? *Western Journal of Nursing Research*, 25(5), 464–481.

Spradley, J. P. (1980). *Participant Observation*. Fort Worth, TX: Holt, Rinehart, and Winston.

Starks, H., & Trinidad, S. B. (2007). Choose your method: A comparison of phenomenology, discourse analysis, and grounded theory. *Qualitative Health Research*, 17(10), 1372–1380.

Styhre, A. (2011). Sociomaterial practice and the constitutive entanglement of social and material resources: The case of construction work. *Vine*, 41(4), 384–400.

Styhre, A., Wikmalm, L., Ollila, S., & Roth, J. (2012). Sociomaterial practices in engineering work: The backtalk of materials and the tinkering of resources. *Journal of Engineering, Design and Technology*, 10(2), 151–167.

Suchman, L. (2000). Embodied practices of engineering work. *Mind, Culture, and Activity*, 7(1–2), 4–18.

Van Manen, M. (1990). *Researching Lived Experience: Human Science for an Action Sensitive Pedagogy*. Albany, NY: State University of New York Press.

Viera, A. J., & Garrett, J. M. (2005). Understanding interobserver agreement: The kappa statistic. *Family Medicine*, 37(5), 360–363.

Yanow, D., & Tsoukas, H. (2009). What is reflection-in-action? A phenomenological account. *Journal of Management Studies*, 46(8), 1339–1364.

Zaringhalam, Maryam. (2016). Failure in Science Is Frequent and Inevitable—and We Should Talk More about It. *Scientific American*. https://blogs.scientificamerican.com/guest-blog/failure-in-science-is-frequent-and-inevitable-and-we-should-talk-more-about-it/?WT.mc_id=send-to-friend, retrieved 11/18/2017.

6

AN INTERACTIONAL ETHNOGRAPHY PERSPECTIVE TO ANALYZE INFORMAL FORMATIVE ASSESSMENTS (IFAS) TO BUILD EPISTEMIC AND CONCEPTUAL COHERENCE IN SCIENCE LEARNING

Asli Sezen-Barrie and Rachel Mulvaney

This work was supported by National Science Foundation [grant number 1239758]. This material is based upon work supported by the National Science Foundation under Grant #1239758. Any opinions, findings, and conclusions or recommendations expressed in this material are those of the author(s) and do not necessarily react the views of the National Science Foundation.

> Scientific papers are written as if their authors knew from the start where they were heading and saw all along where the data were leading. The false starts, the misinterpretations, the wasted efforts, the failed experiments – these are almost always expunged from published reports Because rational reconstruction is the norm for scientific reporting, many scientists follow this pattern even when speaking off the record, perpetuating the image of scientists as coldly rational, even robotic.
>
> *(Oreskes, 2001, p. xii)*

Scientific research involves more than the perfect world created in the published reports and is inseparable from feelings, personalities, and experiences of the people involved. That was why Oreskes (2001) invited 17 scientists to contribute to the development of Plate Tectonic Theory and write a chapter for the book *Plate Tectonics: An Insider's History of the Modern Theory of the Earth*. An important goal of the chapters in their book was to bring a "multiplicity of perspectives," i.e., to understand the difference in the ways scientists approached their work, made different contributions, and used essential means and tools.

Similarly, in this chapter, we aim to look at the multiplicity of perspectives in the interactions between people: an educational researcher (Dr. Asli Sezen-Barrie – first author of the chapter), a scientist (Dr. Amy Foster), and a math education college instructor (Dr. Winnie Lee), who together develop the tools and means for the climate unit used in the study. Dr. Lee, who is a college level instructor in the math education department, is assigned to teach a new course titled "Perspectives in Science and Math Education" to preservice teachers who are majoring in secondary science and math education departments. This new course required Dr. Lee to integrate scientific principles with mathematical practices. While she was working on developing the course, Dr. Sezen-Barrie, who is an assistant professor of science education, and Dr. Foster, who is a full professor of environmental sciences, were working on a project on supporting university faculty's integration of climate change into their college level courses. This was part of a larger two-state wide project both Drs. Foster and Sezen-Barrie were involved in as institutional PI (Principal Investigator) and CoPI (Co-Principal Investigator) respectively. Dr. Lee contacted Drs. Foster and Sezen-Barrie to work on integrating climate change into her new course "Perspectives in Science and Math Education."

In this chapter, we utilize interactional ethnography (Crawford, Castanheira, Dixon, & Green, 2001) to "tell a case" (Mitchell, 1984) where a scientist, a mathematics instructor, and an educational researcher worked together to develop a unit on climate change as a part of a junior level (university 3rd year) course for secondary science and math education majors. We choose Mitchell's "telling cases" approach while recognizing the difference between "searching for a typical case" which concerns to be statistically representative of a larger population and "the search for a 'telling' case" which signifies the particular circumstances, distinct social relationships between the actors and the tools (Mitchell, 1984, p. 239). The work we present here has a distinct context which makes using the telling cases approach meaningful.

The interdisciplinary nature of our project team connecting different backgrounds has unique affordances that manifest in the discourse processes across cultures and disciplines. The limited knowledge and our assumptions about each other's field of study led to puzzlements in the interactions between the project members. Our work towards solving these puzzlements shaped the instructional agenda and relevant assessment practices. As an ethnographer, we want to look at the role of these relevant assessments for learning constructed through oral, written, and visual discourses across a timescale (Crawford, 2005). The methodological challenge here is not only to report what we found out about the role of assessments in coherence building for learning, but also to recognize the epistemic differences across disciplines. In describing the research perspective, we also aim to unpack how the members of the design team from different disciplines made decisions in developing and implementing a unit on climate change (Baker & Green, 2015).

The decisions made before by the design team or during the instruction by the instructor and students are not independent for the norms and rules that govern the interactions in the classroom (Engeström, 1999). As science classrooms are informed by practices of scientists (Crawford, 2005; Sezen-Barrie, Tran,

McDonald, & Kelly, 2014), we see epistemic practices of scientists, particularly those of climate scientists, providing norms for both the complex interactions between the interdisciplinary design team and the classroom community. In the unique case of our study, these communities were trying to reach instructional goals on a complex, interdisciplinary, and (assumed) controversial topic of modern climate change. We will therefore first start with a background on the importance of epistemic practices in coherence building in science classrooms. We will particularly look at contextualized epistemic practices of climate scientists to understand how these distinct practices of an interdisciplinary field might shape the classroom interactions. Second, we will provide a background on formative assessments, i.e., the assessment for learning. Since curriculum, instruction, and assessment are linked (Duschl, Maeng, & Sezen, 2011), the decisions on what count as core ideas, epistemic practices, and students' learning in science classrooms might have influenced how, when, and where assessments are used.

Building Coherence through Participation into Epistemic Practices

Epistemic Practices of Scientists and Implications for Science Learning

Two recent policy documents in science education, *A Framework for K-12 Science Education: Practices, Crosscutting Concepts, and Core Ideas* (NRC, 2012) and *Next Generation Science Standards* (2013) are both calling for shifts in focus on what teachers need to know in preparation to teach science. One of these areas is to understand science learning as a coherent progression, which will connect related concepts and scientific practices around core ideas in a meaningful sequence that will build on students' background and experiences (Reiser, 2013; Roth *et al.*, 2011). This idea was not new but rather inspired by the previous work on epistemic practices in science education (Duschl, 2008; Kelly, 2008). Influenced by this work, we see the need for intertwined conceptual and epistemic goals so as to accomplish the desired instructional outcomes for coherence building.

Despite the focus on coherence for meaningful learning of science, teachers often give more importance to putting together engaging activities. Such activities too often get students busy with completing tasks but fail to connect to the core concepts and practices of the disciplines. Several studies showed that teachers could learn to construct coherent storylines for their lessons through effective professional development (e.g., Hanuscin *et al.*, 2016; Roth *et al.*, 2011), but the dynamic nature of classroom discourse requires further in-the-moment decisions by teachers (Janssen, Westbroek, & Van Driel, 2013).

In science education, recent studies suggest engaging students in epistemic practices to effectively connect related scientific ideas to anchoring phenomena and the driving question (Reiser, 2013). Epistemic practices are the social practices through which knowledge is constructed, and claims are evaluated or justified within communities (Kelly, 2005). Further, within various disciplines of science, scientific knowledge is constructed culturally. Knorr Cetina (1999) uses the concept of "epistemic cultures" to explain the processes involved in creating and warranting knowledge in various specializations and activities of science. This conceptual framework helps us understand differences between specializations beyond the conceptual knowledge. Epistemic cultures are "sets of practices, arrangements, and mechanisms bound together by necessity, and historical coincidence that, in a given area of professional expertise, make up how we know what we know" (Knorr Cetina, 1999, p. 67). The variations in the practices, arrangements, and mechanisms of scientific specialties or disciplines create cultural diversity and make it impossible for a unity in scientific methods to respond to all the scientific questions (Knorr Cetina, 1999).

Epistemic Culture of Climate Science and Implications for Science Learning

The case we tell in this chapter examines how teachers, instructors, and students draw from the interdisciplinary area of climate science to make sense of human-caused, modern climate change with particular attention to uses of alternative energy sources. Due to its interdisciplinary nature, the climate science field has developed through research in a variety of disciplines including meteorology, oceanography, geography, hydrology, geology, glaciology, and plant ecology (Hadorn *et al.*, 2008). Thus, to understand the principles of the Earth's climate system and communicate that knowledge productively requires a background in different disciplines of natural and social sciences (Weart, 2013). As an example, in sensemaking of how changing climate impacts oceans, one needs to understand the chemistry of oceans such as their salinity and acidity levels, biodiversity in oceans, and the economics of fish markets (Galaz *et al.*, 2012).

This interdisciplinary complexity made it easier for fossil fuel industries, who are blamed for the human-caused, modern climatic changes, to promote doubt around humans' role in the modern climate change (Gelbspan, 1997). The denial theories were further accentuated by think-tanks, politicians, and even some scientists (Dunlap & McCright, 2011). One of such denial theories claims the Sun as being responsible for the climatic changes rather than humans, which taps into people's misconception or lack of knowledge on solar cycles. This denial theory presents a view that the 11-year-long recent solar cycle has increased the sunspots on Earth which lead to warming temperatures. However, global data models comparing temperatures to the number of sunspots could not find a significant correlation (GISS Surface Temperature Analysis, NASA, 2015; Hansen *et al.*, 2010). Although major scientific organizations continue to refute these claims with strong scientific evidence and reasoning, the denial theories create "assumed" controversy among many science classrooms (Plutzer *et al.*, 2016).

Due to the importance given to factual scientific information in isolated chemistry, physics, and biology courses at high school and college level courses in many traditional science classrooms (Zeidler, 2016; Kurland *et al.*, 2010), teachers and students often struggle with coherent and integrated sensemaking of scientific concepts (such as solar cycles and climate change) and related epistemic practices (interpreting global temperature anomaly data). Interrelationships between these concepts and epistemic practices are significant for supporting claims that human impact is the most contributing factor for modern climatic changes (Intergovernmental Panel on Climate Change, 2013). Not recognizing such interrelationships creates great potential for instruction that can lead to confusion among students and fail to provide a basis for re-examining pseudoscientific ideas (Plutzer *et al.*, 2016; Sezen-Barrie, Shea, & Borman, 2017). Attending to these pseudoscientific ideas in classroom discourse is further challenged with teachers' unfamiliarity with contextualized epistemic practices of climate scientists such as historical interpretation (Sezen-Barrie, 2018). One study done with 1,500 public middle- and high-school science teachers from all 50 US states showed that despite many available lessons and activities on weather and climate, the difference and similarities between these concepts are still confusing to students. The confusions create obstacles in understanding nature of evidence in climate science (Plutzer *et al.*, 2016). In response, researchers call attention to improve students' sensemaking of contextualized practices of climate scientists such as "thinking about time on geological time scales, understanding the Earth as a complex system, and spatial thinking as applied to geoscience" (Kastens *et al.*, 2009, p. 265).

We discussed here that sensemaking of epistemic practices of science and engineering and also recognizing how such practices are embedded in, and constitute, epistemic cultures (i.e., contextualized in scientific fields) have implications for science learning. The uses of epistemic practices becomes especially important for sensemaking if we want students to construct scientific explanations or figure out solutions (NGSS, 2013) as part of constructing knowledge of core ideas. We use the term core ideas here to refer to the scientific ideas which anchor related interdisciplinary scientific concepts and epistemic practices. These core ideas then provide the basis for reasoning for a more significant scientific claim such as humans are the primary drivers of the recent climatic changes (Intergovernmental Panel on Climate Change, 2013). We argue here that an ethnographic understanding of the discourse processes of formative assessments can aid in examining how knowledge is construed around core ideas to help a classroom community to build more extensive claims about climate change.

On the Role of Formative Assessments in Coherence Building

Formative assessments are assessments for learning which aim to provide feedback to both the instructors and students in order to make instructional decisions (Black & Wiliam, 1998). These assessments support moving towards instructional goals while building coherence among concepts (Furtak, 2017). Formative assessments can either be "Formal Formative Assessments (FFAs)" that are pre-planned and often used at predetermined times or "Informal Formative Assessments (IFAs)" which are in-the-moment assessments. IFAs frequently happen during everyday classroom talk, and do not require official record keeping such as in FFAs (Leahy, Lyon, Thompson, & Wiliam, 2005). Early studies on these in-the-moment assessments observed a common cycle of interaction in classroom discourse: Initiation – Response – Evaluation/Feedback (Mehan, 1979; Sinclair & Coulthard, 1975). In these cycles, the teacher initiates the cycles, students respond, and then the teacher evaluates or gives feedback. More recent research sought to determine what a more contextualized, complex cycle looks like across a range of classrooms discourses. Mortimer and Scott (2003) suggested that these cycles sometimes might not be closed after one student's response and teachers might refer to other students' responses for productive thinking in the classrooms (Initiate – Response – Feedback – Response – Feedback –). Ruiz-Primo and Furtak (2007) see a similar pattern with the IFA cycle that they defined as Elicits, Student Responds, Recognizes, Uses (ESRU) and revised this cycle as ESR – ERS – ERS – ERS – ESRU. More recent studies showed that teachers who are effectively using IFAs have even more complex and at times more extensive IFA cycles (Minstrell, Li, & Anderson, 2009; Sezen-Barrie & Kelly, 2017).

Previous studies suggest IFAs, as dialogic, scaffolding tools to help teachers make students' reasoning explicit and guide teachers in planning the next activity (Ruiz-Primo *et al.*, 2011). IFAs are constructed through in-the-moment instructional dialogues among the members of the community. As ethnographers, we suggest that telling contextual uses of IFAs can help teachers and teacher educators to respond to the challenges of building coherence across concepts and epistemic practices utilized to justify the claim that humans are the main cause of the modern climate change (Intergovernmental Panel on Climate Change, 2013; NASA, 2015). We are further interested in how decisions about the use of IFAs can be shaped by FFAs and instructional decisions such as those made by the design team members.

In this chapter, we will show a methodological approach which first presents how and where IFA cycles are used to support the instruction to connect concepts and epistemic practices to the core ideas (ideas that anchor various concepts) and establish a coherent instructional agenda. Second, to understand what shaped how and why the IFA cycles are constructed, we searched for intertextualities (Fairclough, 1992) in students' written and visual discourses in response to pre-planned FFA probes. Third, we searched for intertextualities (Fairclough, 1992) between these assessments and design team decisions. While doing so, our goal is to illustrate a methodology that responds to the following overarching research question of *What is the relationship between the designed team decisions, students' produced written artifacts, and the Informal Formative Assessments (IFAs)?* We operationalized this broad question through the two following research questions:

1. How do Informal Formative Assessments (IFAs) constructed through classroom discourse shape conceptual and epistemic coherence within the climate science interdisciplinary unit?
2. How do discourses in FFA probes and the interactions among project team members (the educational researcher, scientists, and math education instructor) lead to the decisions on what, where, and when IFAs are used in the classroom?

Research Approach

Driven from the social and cultural construction of meaning (Gee & Green, 1998), we use an interactional ethnography perspective (Castanheira, Crawford, Dixon, & Green, 2001) to look at the assessment practices at a college course for preservice teachers. In this regard, we focused on the role of IFAs, constructed through discursive moves, to examine ways that the curriculum, instruction, and assessment aims to build conceptual and epistemic coherence. We look at IFAs as the part of the whole assessment system that is aligned with instructional and curricular goals of teaching (Erickson, 1979).

Educational Setting

The data of this study came from Dr. Lee's course, "Perspectives in Science and Math Education" taught during fall 2016 when 12 female and seven male secondary-school science and math majors were enrolled in the class. The members of the design team, Drs. Foster, Sezen-Barrie, and Lee developed a unit, entitled "Catch the Wind: How Can Wind Power Provide a Solution to the Climate Change Problem?" This unit was revised after comments from the course instructor. The researcher took an *emic* (insiders) perspective and actively participated in the development of the unit, teaching at various times, and participating in group discussions (Spradley, 2016). The core ideas which related to modern climate change included: energy sources, CO_2 and global temperatures, alternative energy sources, and designing solutions to increasing use of energy sources.

The overarching goal of the unit was to engage future teachers into the practices of analysis and interpretation of authentic data and designing solutions while using mathematical and computational skills. Climate science, whose major claims rely on vast amounts of data and meaningful modeling (Edwards, 2010), provided a context for the students to engage in these practices. To achieve this goal, students were guided through activities like jigsaw readings, guided data interpretation group activities, carbon footprint calculators, poster presentations, and designing wind turbine blades. The conceptual and epistemic coherence throughout the unit is established with the roadmap shown in Figure 6.1 which was constructed by the design team. This roadmap shows the negotiated meaning of coherence building among multidisciplinary design team members towards understanding modern climate change. Students were first engaged through a

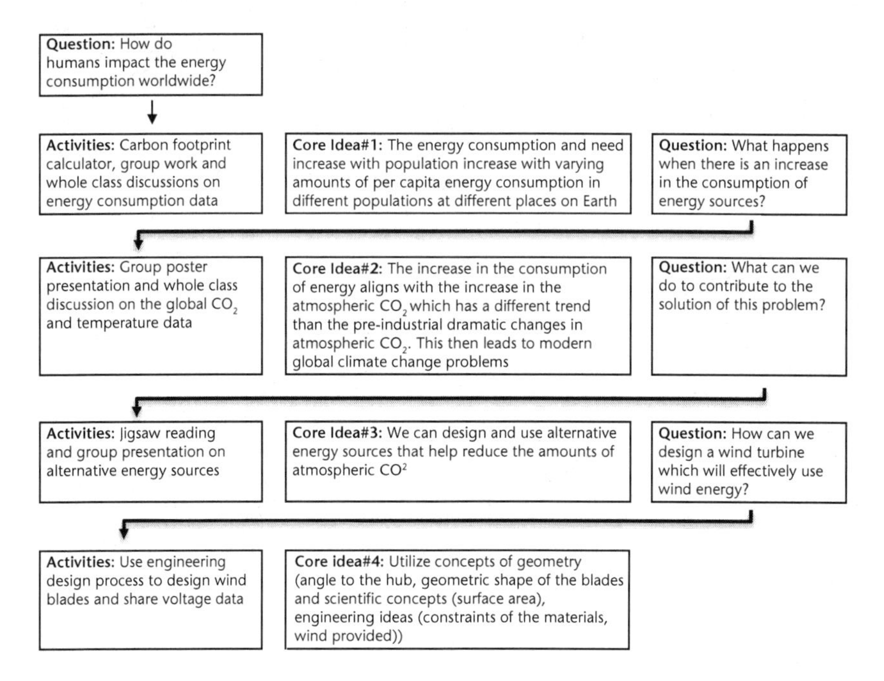

FIGURE 6.1 Driving questions, activities and core ideas.

question on "How do the humans impact the energy consumption worldwide?" Then, they were engaged in activities to build the first core idea on the impact of increasing populations on the energy consumptions. Through discussions, the students were guided to the next step question on "What happens when there is an increase in the consumption of energy sources?" This led to other sets of activities that helped us reach the second core idea. The core ideas were linked with ending wonderment questions from the previous idea.

Data Sources

The data of the study comes from a variety of sources (Figure 6.2). One set of data comes from the classroom implementation. This set includes video and audio records of five, 90-minute classes, instructional tools (e.g., jigsaw readings, guides for activities) and formal formative assessment probes, students' written artifacts (e.g., group posters, reflections on wind blade design), and field notes. The second data set comes from the records of interactions between the project members developing the unit on climate change. This data set includes written reflections, written feedback, and email exchanges between an educational researcher, math education instructor, and the scientist. The variety in the data sets helped us in the multi level (micro, meso, sociocultural level) analysis of how IFAs are constructed through discursive moves in the classroom and what

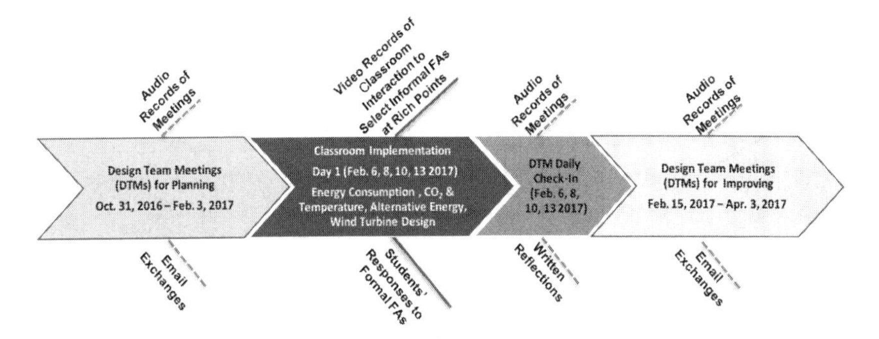

FIGURE 6.2 Sources of data and timeline of data collection.

sociohistorical aspects of climate science knowledge shaped, and when and how IFAs are used. We use these sources to examine systematically the assessment practices both at the micro level to identify the visible moves that the instructor undertook to achieve the goals of the lesson and at the macro level as a part of the whole unit coherence framed by the experts from different disciplines.

Analysis and Findings

We see discourse as a crucial tool to accomplish desired instructional outcomes in science classroom settings (Kelly, 2011; Sezen-Barrie, Tran, McDonald, & Kelly, 2014). Therefore, our analysis will consider multiple discourses of oral (in-the-moment IFAs), written (students' explanations in response to FFA prompts), and visual (students' inscriptions in response to FFA prompts). Due to the contextual nature of epistemic practice (Kelly, 2016), such discursive interaction between the members of the classroom and the broader communities (e.g., the unit design team interactions in this study) should be analyzed across time and settings embedded in *situ* (Kelly, Chen, & Crawford, 1998). For our study, to have an in-depth understanding of students' sensemaking and also to tell the broader context of the case as both the classroom community and the design team community, we mapped our data backward in time (Green, Skukauskaite, & Baker, 2012), which will be elaborated below.

Steps of Backward Mapping

Step 1: Analysis of Classroom Interactions

To explore the question of how IFAs are shaped by classroom interactions, we examined the discursive moves throughout four 90-minute instruction sessions. By exploring these discursive moves, we identified *rich points*, which are "those surprises, those departures from an outsider's expectations" and therefore make visible the divergences "between the languaculture [local and cultural language of a community] of the insiders that gives direction to subsequent learning" (Agar, 2006, p. 2). In this study, we adapt this concept of rich points in order to identify times where a challenging, confusing, or surprising idea emerged in the classroom. Then this idea was followed by the instructor's use of IFA cycles of interaction around frame clashes for an extended period of time. The frame clash is an observed difference in understanding between the instructor and students (Gee & Green, 1998). Through this process, we sought to explore how these frame clashes constructed socially as rich points. We were specifically interested in rich points at IFA cycles due to our initial conjecture that these cycles help to keep the agenda for the conceptual and epistemic coherence that was decided by the design team.

For each cycle of interaction or rich point, we involved the context and the interaction between the instructor and the students through sociolinguistics tools of event maps (Green & Wallat, 1981; Green & Meyer, 1991; Kelly & Chen, 1999), and transcripts, building on Green and Wallat (1981), which provided a textual (re)presentation of the phases of the interactions. The event maps were constructed as macro level representations of the cycles of activity (Table 6.1). To identify phase units, we marked shifts in the topic of the instructional conversation by identifying the discourse markers used on the participants. These phase units were then linked together through the developing idea (topic) and/or objective of the teacher for the chain of activity. Each phase unit was also divided into sequential units that identified the thematically connected discursive turns (Kelly & Chen, 1999; Baker, Green, & Skukauskaite, 2008). Once the phase units were identified for each event, transcripts of talk and action were constructed to represent the discursive moves at the rich points (Table 6.1). Each turn was identified by actions (Spradley, 2016) to describe the moves of the participant during the IFA rich point to construct a telling case (Mitchell, 1984) and to make theoretical inferences about what each chain of interactions was accomplishing. Once the transcripts were constructed, we then read them to identify codes that were drawn from previous studies on classroom discourse, questioning, assessment conversations, and informal formative assessments (Christie, 2002; Duschl, 2003; Furtak & Ruiz-Primo, 2008; Wells, 1993). The conceptual coherence decided by the team and interdisciplinary practices of climate science (Edwards, 2010) supported the refinement of the codes (Figure 6.1). As indicated in Figure 6.3, analyzing the identifying rich points and analyzing the turn taking process represented in the transcript constituted the first step in mapping the cycles of interaction/activity that the teacher undertook with the students.

Step 2: Exploring Intertextualities in Students' Responses to FFA Probes

In order to explore the intertextual relationship (Fairclough, 1992) between the IFA cases that led constructed rich points, we looked at students' written and visual discourses in the prior FFA prompts. We went backward in our data timescale for understanding how students' written discourse or visual inscriptions or their lack of informed the instructor's decision about how to use IFA cycles. Particularly, we searched for alignment of the topic at rich points at IFAs and students' responses.

Step 3: Searching Intertextualities at the Records of Design Team Meetings (DTMs)

As a third step, analysts look at records of information kept during project meetings, emails, and written reflections by the project members. As analysts, we went to the records of information to determine how it's related to the highlighted rich point and the use of FFA in classrooms. This process involved backward mapping (Green, Skukauskaite, & Baker, 2012) to identify curriculum goals of the project. This phase of analysis involved exploring project meetings and/or impromptu meetings that were held before the students were asked to respond to the FFA being examined. This phase also examined reflections that were written about previous lessons by team members for the design process. This analysis showed that the IFAs, where rich points were highlighted, occurred after the discussions among projects members and the analysis of students' responses to FFAs.

In our analysis of the three transcript episodes presented subsequently, we will adapt the order of analysis rather than the order of actual occurrences to make our process of analysis procedures explicit. Under each episode, we will first present "classroom interactions" where we noticed rich points on the transcripts of discursive interaction within classrooms. We will use examples from the transcripts to show how IFAs are shaped through the interaction between Dr. Lee and her students to clarify challenging or problematic concepts and anchor these two core ideas. We will then move to "Response to Formal Formative Assessment Probe" where we highlighted intertextual relationships with the IFA observed in the classroom interaction. Finally, we will describe the intertextualities we

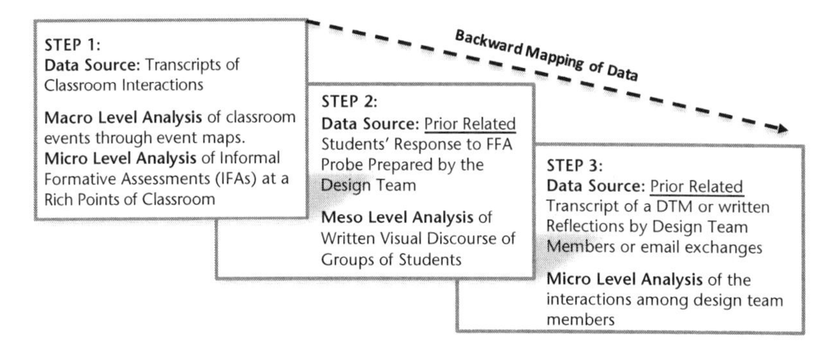

FIGURE 6.3 Order of analysis from classroom interactions back to prior FAs and DTM decisions.

noticed in the records of information from project team members' meetings or reflection under "Project Group Interaction." The intertextual analysis between IFAs and students' responses to FFA probes can help us understand in what ways the instructor's decisions on extending time on some IFAs are influenced by the excluded or misrepresented ideas in students' written and visual discourses in FFAs. In this manner, the rich point put emphasis on the IFA event which then led to the examination of the formal assessment, and an analysis of the planning phase pre-dating the event.

The episodes below will describe how the multi-layer discursive events shaped the clarification of each core idea determined by the design team when there were rich points, i.e., moments of confusion or instances of lack of clarity. These episodes below highlight how more scientific or mathematical concepts (such as carbon emissions, heat-trapping gasses, and change in rate), or epistemic understanding (such as spatial and temporal interpretation of data, designing solutions) helped the classroom community to reach to a shared understanding of the core idea and be able to move forward with the next step questions.

Analysis of IFA Episode 1: Tapping into Spatial Reasoning of Energy Consumption Data

In this episode, we will first provide a case from the discursive interaction on comparing local and global energy consumption which led to series of IFAs shaped at the moment that students struggled to make sense of data. The sensemaking occurred as the instructor highlighted epistemic features that are critical for the learning outcome. For Episode 1, the instructor aimed for students to understand that both increases in population and change in lifestyles have an impact on the change in climate that connects to the overarching claim about modern climate change. The epistemic practice of using multiple lines of evidence that helped students was climate scientists' use of spatial reasoning (such as looking at different locations on Earth) in their interpretation of data. This interaction is from the second day of the unit. Table 6.1 outlines the phase and sequence units on day two. We choose two episodes (one starts at the time of 0:01:52.0 and the second starts at 0:37:27.0) from the event maps because these episodes include rich points. The example transcript was from the beginning of the day where students were working in groups to calculate how much energy a family is consuming via heating and cooling in the US and how this relates to CO_2 produced per kilowatt hour when generating electricity with fossil fuels. Then students compared their findings to the data on global carbon dioxide emissions between the years 1860 and 2011. While working on data, one group of students got confused while "recognizing a mathematical relationship between population increase, energy consumption and CO_2 levels" (0:09:56.0). Therefore, the instructor used IFA to guide students. It is important to note that this sequence was right after students responded to a related formal formative assessment probe on their worksheet.

TABLE 6.1 Event map of day 2 presenting phase and sequence units

	Time Stamp	*Phase Unit*	*Time Stamp*	*Sequential Units*
Episode 1	0:01:52.0	Group work on energy consumption data	0:01:52.0	Making calculations and reducing data to simplified, connected version
			0:05:36.0	Interpreting data by constructing graphs (formal formative assessment probe on worksheet)
			0:09:56.0	Recognizing mathematical relationship between population increase, energy consumption, and CO_2 levels
			0:15:05.0	Driving conclusions (formal formative assessment probe on worksheet)
	0:16:12.0	Group work on preparing posters (while responding to formal formative assessment probes)		.
				.
				Sequence units not shown for these phases
	0:23:06.0	Instructor's overviews presentation guidelines		
	0:25:14.0	Presentation on greenhouse gases		
Episode 2	0:37:27.0	Whole class discussion on greenhouse gases	0:37:27.0	Summarizing the important greenhouse gases and their role
			0:39:38.0	Comparing two CO_2 data from different time periods
			0:50:12.0	Whole class discussion on various sources of data representations
	0:52:16.0	Instructor is summarizing the main ideas from the day's lesson		

Classroom Interaction

The case below was from the audio record on day 2 while students were engaged in group work called "Energy Consumption Data." We noticed a rich point while students were "Recognizing mathematical relationship between population increase, energy consumption, and CO_2 levels" (Table 1, 0:09:56.0). In the transcript below, the instructor wanted students to interpret data not only describing the trends that students see, but also to notice the nature of data representation which is constructed with global averages of energy consumption. Such data representation then assumes no matter where you live on Earth, you have the same average energy consumption. During the first part of the interaction, the instructor initiated the IFA while bringing students' attention to the numbers calculated for different locations, i.e., countries. This was followed by interactions between students and the instructor on common understanding of the instructor's question. When Abby (464) noticed that the data is showing an increase, the instructor asked for further elaboration of the interpretation (465). Later, the instructor wanted students to think about the assumptions in their calculations of energy consumptions in comparing the carbon dioxide produced over the years (468, 472).

Line#	*Speaker*	*Talk*	*Action*
464	Abby	We've really gone up that much in five years?	Student 3 is responding and asking for confirmation
465	Instructor	Well, but what is the information that you included in here?	Instructor is highlighting to further interpretation of the data
466	Donna	We're dead. *Laughs*	Student 2 is expressing emotion
467	Abby	I don't think I understand your question. Apart from it increasing significantly in the last five years	Student 3 is asking for clarification
468	Instructor	So the data we put in here though was assuming that everybody on the planet has an average usage or every household	Instructor is clarifying and highlighting the assumption in the graph
469	Abby	Oh right right	Student 3 is confirming her understanding
470	Instructor	has an average use . . . hold of 550-kilowatt hours —	Instructor is highlighting the taking of averages in data interpretation process
471	Abby	kilowatt hours	
472	Instructor	Per month right? So, that's just an assumption though like that's assuming —	Instructor is highlighting the assumption in the graph by connecting to student's
473	Sam	Ohhhhhhhh	Student 1 is recognizing instructor's point

Once Sam attended to Dr. Lee's comment by saying "Ohhhhhhhh" (473), the instructor highlighted the context of the data again (476), Sam then came up with a response "There's no yeah there's no way" (477). Another group member Abby attended to Sam's response by saying "I'm just still sad though." Dr. Lee then repeated the question by describing Maryland as the location of the data on energy usage. Then, Sam's explanation starting with "So you want us to realize . . ." brings him to the same point as the instructor Dr. Lee (482). The other students in the group, Donna and Abby, also join this common understanding (483–485).

Line#	*Speaker*	*Talk*	*Action*
476	Instructor	Nigeria or you're here, you all use the same amount?	Instructor is highlighting the context of data
477	Sam	There's no yeah there's no way	Student 3 is commenting
478	Abby	I'm just still sad though	Student is expressing emotions
479	Instructor	So if we all use the same amount, as you know, people in Maryland use then we would be producing the globe would be producing so many more	Instructor is highlighting the context of data
480	Sam	Ugh okay so —	
481	Instructor	Using yeah —	
482	Sam	So you want us to realize is that not everyone in the world is using 550-kilowatt hours a month because there are people who don't even have electricity	Student 1 makes sense
483	Donna	Or use way too much	Student 2 makes sense
484	Sam	And of course, there are people who use more than that, it's just an average	Student 1 elaborates
485	Abby	You know what we should have done was do this for the United States and not the entire world	Student 3 elaborates

The interaction at this rich point allowed students to be able to compare the use of energy in Maryland vs. other places on Earth. We see that students conclude about variations in the use of energy in different spaces. Such spatial understanding of energy use data is important to build coherence to the local impact of human choices on the modern climate change problem. Moreover, paying attention to such local causes to increased carbon emissions establishes a background on why people in economically developed countries should be creative about using alternative energy sources, which is another core concept of the unit.

Response to Formal Formative Assessment Probe

Intertextual references and uses of artifacts were important for the engagement in the epistemic practices. Following our ethnographic point of view, we, then, looked at students' worksheets on which they formulated a response to the FFA probe. The worksheet (Figure 6.4) highlights two important interpretations. One is the increasing trend in emissions per person over the years (see the far right column of the table and graph). Second is the difference between energy consumption when Dr. Lee used lignite coal vs. natural gas in her calculation (seen below the graph). The intertextual analysis of students' responses to an FFA probe, shows that students do not show a contextual comparison on energy consumption as with Dr. Lee's neighborhood vs. global averages. Thus, while the students engaged in the epistemic practices of graphing data over time and making calculations based on recorded data, they missed the opportunity to use spatial reasoning to make sense of the local variances while taking a global average.

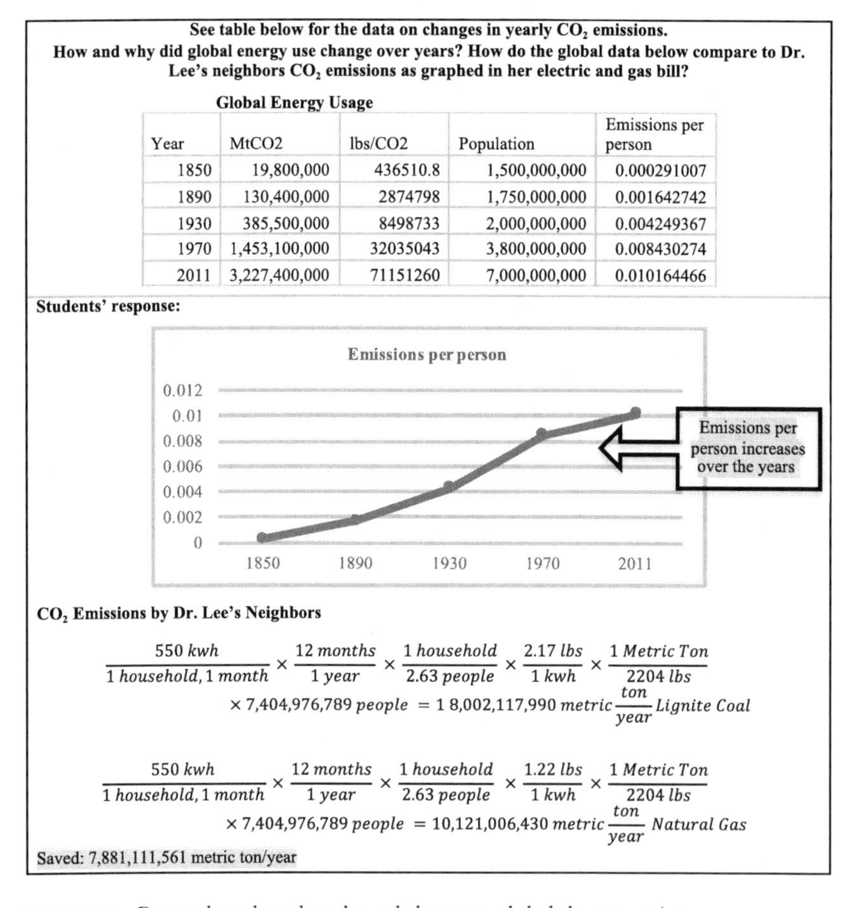

See table below for the data on changes in yearly CO_2 emissions.
How and why did global energy use change over years? How do the global data below compare to Dr. Lee's neighbors CO_2 emissions as graphed in her electric and gas bill?

Global Energy Usage

Year	MtCO2	lbs/CO2	Population	Emissions per person
1850	19,800,000	436510.8	1,500,000,000	0.000291007
1890	130,400,000	2874798	1,750,000,000	0.001642742
1930	385,500,000	8498733	2,000,000,000	0.004249367
1970	1,453,100,000	32035043	3,800,000,000	0.008430274
2011	3,227,400,000	71151260	7,000,000,000	0.010164466

Students' response:

CO_2 Emissions by Dr. Lee's Neighbors

$$\frac{550\ kwh}{1\ household, 1\ month} \times \frac{12\ months}{1\ year} \times \frac{1\ household}{2.63\ people} \times \frac{2.17\ lbs}{1\ kwh} \times \frac{1\ Metric\ Ton}{2204\ lbs} \times 7{,}404{,}976{,}789\ people = 1\ 8{,}002{,}117{,}990\ metric \frac{ton}{year}\ Lignite\ Coal$$

$$\frac{550\ kwh}{1\ household, 1\ month} \times \frac{12\ months}{1\ year} \times \frac{1\ household}{2.63\ people} \times \frac{1.22\ lbs}{1\ kwh} \times \frac{1\ Metric\ Ton}{2204\ lbs} \times 7{,}404{,}976{,}789\ people = 10{,}121{,}006{,}430\ metric \frac{ton}{year}\ Natural\ Gas$$

Saved: 7,881,111,561 metric ton/year

FIGURE 6.4 Reproduced students' worksheet on global data exercise.

Design Team Interactions

The idea of understanding global measures of climate data was shaped by the discussions of the importance of the epistemic practice of spatial reasoning in making sense of climate science data. This idea was brought to our attention as the scientists in our group pointed out the lack of crucial details on the students' data interpretation poster prepared prior to this interaction (Personal Communication, 10/17/2016). An impromptu meeting at the end of the first day of the unit highlighted the suggestion regarding the collection of data from many countries of the world, assessing the impact of changes in data all over the world (Intergovernmental Panel on Climate Change, 2013). This idea was also apparent in the scientist's written reflection at the beginning of the first lesson where the math education instructor guided students through a carbon footprint activity. She noted in her reflection to the design team that, "I think more discussion time on what contributes to a high footprint and what happens when you change it would have been helpful. Similarly, exploring the difference between the non-USA footprints and theirs could have been discussed more." In response, the math instructor said:

> I can give students local energy data and have them compare that to global energy use. Students can see the "big picture" behind the data exercise, which was that everyone on the globe uses as much energy as "my neighbors" do in the form of ignite coal. The global energy figures would be much higher.
>
> *(10/15/2016)*

Episode 1 presented how the interaction between Dr. Lee and students in one group shaped IFAs. This was due to students' lack of attention on the spatial reasoning on interpreting energy consumption data as is seen in their responses to the FFA (Figure 6.4). Students failed to represent that yearly average energy consumption is higher than in other countries in the world such as Nigeria. When we traced backward (to one day prior) to the reflection written by project members, we saw that the scientists and the math instructor Dr. Lee highlighted the importance of spatial interpretation of data. The tracing backward to the preparation discussions identified that design team discussions shape the instructor's in-the-moment decision about focusing on spatial reasoning for an extensive amount of time that constructs a rich point.

Episode 2: Challenges on Comparing Long-Term and Short-Term Climate Data

The second episode presented in this chapter also occurred on the second day of the unit (Table 6.1, under sequence units, time stamped at 39:38.0) while the whole class was discussing how CO_2 concentrations have been changing over the course of history. Prior to this sequence of the unit, students discussed how high usage of energy results in more CO_2 and developed an understanding of CO_2 as a heat-trapping greenhouse gas. The data exercise in this sequence was designed to help students recognize how long-term data tells climate scientists the relationship between warming global temperatures and increasing amount of atmospheric CO_2. The classroom instruction below shows how a rich point is constructed while students are challenged by the difference in scales on two data graphs (one on long-term increase in atmospheric CO_2 and the other on long-term changes in average global temperatures). This classroom interaction was right after a group presented their jigsaw reading on greenhouse gases. We then traced the long-term comparisons of data on different scales at students' FFA responses and to the records of information from project members' meetings.

Classroom Interaction

A rich point occurred when the instructor recognized the pedagogical challenge due to an artifact of the data graphs – the same numerical values didnot correspond to the same time frame on the x-axes of two graphs on CO_2 concentrations. For a very long time, the class had a disagreement about whether they could compare pre-human and long-term CO_2 trend data sets. Then, the instructor guided students' attention to the spike in one of the graphs and then asked students the time frame that CO_2 concentrations took to have the rapid change (712). Once one of the students, Cara, started aligning the values on the X-axis (715), the instructor called for interpretation of the rate of change (716). This then help students to see the comparison and make a conclusion that the last 200 years of CO_2 concentrations are increasing at a much higher rate.

Line#	*Speaker*	*Talk*	*Action*
712	Instructor	Okay, so 10,000 years and then in my second graph let's take a look at how long it took to make that same amount of difference? Do you guys notice a spike here because I think I do? Can you see that? Okay, so there is this huge spike here going on So how long did it take us to go from down here to about 100 more than that?	Instructor is highlighting the spike in the CO_2 concentrations Instructor is asking a question
713	Cara	5 years at least —	Student is responding
714	Instructor	So this is 1,000 years, 1,000, 3,000, so this is between 0 to 1,000	Instructor is asking student for an exact value
715	Cara	Like 2, 000 – oh, sorry 200	Student is responding – sensemaking of X-axis values

716	Instructor	200 years? So what is this telling us?	Instructor is recognizing revised response and **asking for interpretation**
717	Cody	The amount it took for the carbon dioxide to kind of naturally increase by 100 parts per million was 10,000 years so you would expect that if time went on it would take another 10,000 years for it to increase from the 275-ish to 375 if humans didn't mess things up, or contribute a lot more. But then back let's say 200 years ago we decided to start burning fossil fuels as our source of energy and that caused so much more carbon dioxide release going on	Student is responding – interpreting based on a new orientation of the X-axis
718	Instructor	And so within that 200 years, we caused it to raise by 100 parts per million and normally it would've taken about 10,000 years to do that	Instructor recognizes student's response by rephrasing student's response
		Do you guys see that from the graphs? I notice that your group wrote that you didn't really see a relationship between the two graphs so could you explain what you meant by that?	Instructor is connecting back to the student's initial question
719	Ilene	It's just because it was hard for us to tell like since the X-axis on both the graphs is different like timewise, it was hard to find where that one, like the little chunk of the right one came from the left one because it doesn't look similar at all because it seems like it's changing so much and on the right it's very stiff	Student is responding – explaining the reasons for confusion

In this transcript, the math instructor Dr. Lee has aimed to support students to visualize the relationship between the rapid CO_2 and temperature changes during the last 200 years when industrial revolution happened. The goal here is also to compare the rate of change during the last 200 years to the changes prior to the 1800s. However, students had a challenge in comparing these graphs which then shaped the rich point at the IFA cycle in the transcript.

Response to Formal Formative Assessment Probe

The related FFA (Figure 6.5) asked students to compare two CO_2 graphs that were received from the EPA's (Environmental Protection Agency) online educational resources. The second point in students' responses states that these are different graphs instead of comparing the two. This might be why

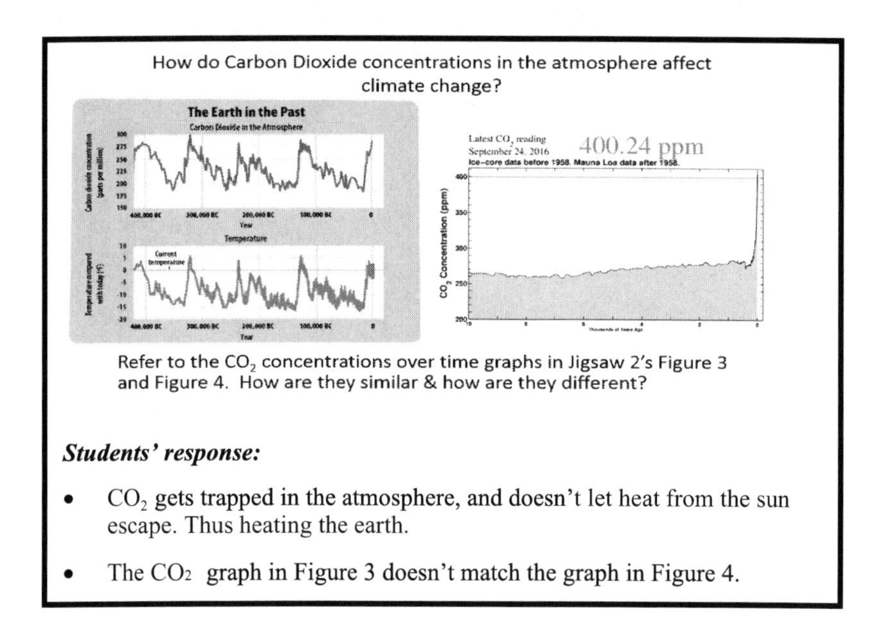

FIGURE 6.5 Reproduced students' poster on CO_2 data comparisons.

the instructor attended to the problem of the different meaning of values in X-axes of both graphs.

The intention is comparing two CO_2 concentration graphs which entail two different time periods. The students' figure 4 (in Figure 6.5) on the left represents a section of prehistoric times whereas the students' figure 3 on the right includes post-prehistoric and current CO_2 measures. However, the challenge students had in comparing different scales created the rich point discussed in the classroom interaction. The confusion at the rich point was made clear when student Ilene said:

> It's just because it was hard for us to tell like since the X-axis on both the graphs is different like time wise, it was hard to find where that one, like the little chunk of the right one came from the left one because it doesn't look similar at all because it seems like it's changing so much and on the right it's very stiff.
>
> *(line 719)*

In this instance, we see that the student is trying to use an epistemic practice of interpreting graphs, but also highlighting the confusion in regards to temporal representation, which is an epistemic practice heavily used in climate science. Therefore, the students are having a hard time in constructing an explanation on CO_2 concentration differences during natural climatic changes that occurred during preindustrial revolution and modern climatic changes that we have observed since the 1950s.

Design Team Interaction

The idea of focusing on the difference in long-term CO_2 concentrations and pre-human changes was one of the themes of a project group discussion by the team of instructors on August 27, 2016. In this discussion, the instructor wanted students to understand how scientists graph CO_2 concentrations and she wanted to use a regression analysis activity.

Math instructor	I can have students do a regression analysis on the rate of change in CO_2
Scientist	Yeah but more importantly students should be able to understand how recent climatic changes are different than the past climatic changes
Educational researcher	One of the most common denials is the idea that climate has changed before. Deniers focus on both climatic changes have similar ups and down and then claim that it is the same, the climatic changes are all natural
Math instructor	They can compare the slopes of a graph showing past climatic changes and one that shows the current changes
Scientist	What if they can't understand the regression analysis? This data is complicated. Why don't we just tell them?
Educational researcher	If we just tell them, we are not modeling effective teaching. They should be engaged in the scientific practice of data interpretation

In this episode, the interdisciplinary team considered one of the cognitive goals of graphical analysis (regression) and also how such analysis makes visible the anomalous features of the current CO_2 production in the context of the Earth's history. This shows attention to the historical interpretation that is a critical epistemic practice in Earth Sciences. This has significance for the unit as it helps to clarify the distinction between pre- and post-industrial climatic changes.

Episode 3: Reasoning behind Decisions on Engineering Design

The third episode chosen for detailed presentation in this chapter is from the third day when the class started working on alternative energy sources as a solution to the climate change problem. At 0:27:54.0 (Table 6.2), students started working on their wind blade designs. While students are working on drawing and explaining their plans, the instructor asked one group to explain the reasons behind their design choices. The instructor then asked all the groups to do the same and explain their reasoning for their design choices.

Classroom Interaction

The interaction below is from a rich point when Dr. Lee wanted to make students design choices explicit while students were planning their design by drawings of

TABLE 6.2 Event map of day 3 presenting phase and sequence units

	Time Stamp	*Phase Unit*	*Time Stamp*	*Sequential Units*
	0:02:13.0	Presentation on alternative renewable energy		
	0:18:14.0	Instructor's overview of the history of wind turbines and their use as alternative energy source		
	0:24:03.0	Instructor's introduction to building the wind blades		
Episode 3	0:27:54.0	Students are working in groups for the initial design of their wind blades	0:27:54.0	Students' reviewing design debrief on goals and constraints
			0:29:53.0	Students are brainstorming and making decisions around which design to choose
			0:32:38.0	Students are planning their design by drawings of the turbine blades
			0:51:14.0	Students are creating their wind blade design
			1:22:32.0	Students are testing their wind blades at one of the two stations
	1:29:11.0	Instructor is explaining how they will continue revising and testing in the next class		

the turbine blades (Table 6.2, sequence unit at 0:32:38.0). The transcript is when the first group share their reasoning. We chose this group because the instructor decided to ask students about their reasoning when she went to this table and looked at their planning sheet. In the IFA cycle below, when the instructor asked about students' reasoning on the number of blades (1099), one student responds by using his previous experience with wind turbines. Then, the instructor asks why the shape of the blade is not like a wind turbine (1101). Another student responds by using the scientific idea of "surface area" and previous experience on ceiling fans.

Line#	*Speaker*	*Talk*	*Action*
1096	Instructor	Why did you choose the number of blades you did? How many do you have?	Instructor is asking a question
1097	Meghan	We have three	Student is responding
1098	Emily	We have three	Another student is responding
1099	Instructor	Three? Okay, how did you pick that?	Instructor is recognizing the response and asking for elaboration on design choice
1100	Aeron	Most wind turbines we've seen have three, so we went with three	Student is responding – using **previous knowledge on turbines**
1101	Instructor	Hmm but the shape is not like actual turbine. So, how did you pick this design?	Instructor is asking for elaboration on design choice
1102	Aeron	Well, we figured we wanted it to catch a lot of wind. Something with a high surface area would be favorable. So we decided to go with an oblong fan shape, so hopefully, that works. We just have to test it	Student is responding – using previous knowledge on ceiling fans
1103	Emily	If you look at most . . . ceiling fans. They are in the shape of a pentagon. Fanning out like this	Student is responding – using previous knowledge on ceiling fans
1104	Instructor	Okay! Good	Instructor is recognizing – giving evaluative feedback

The classroom interaction here makes explicit why students choose to model the number of blades on the wind turbine, but not the geometric shape of the blades. The idea that, up to a point, increased surface area leads to increased energy transfer is essential in building a core idea that wind can be an efficient alternative energy source as humans need to consume energy escalates.

Response to Formal Formative Assessment Probe

The related FFA from one group of students was drawing and explaining of their wind blade design. The goal here was to engage students to a possible engineering solution to a climate change problem and to encourage students to think of ways humans who have the biggest role in this problem can also be agents of solution through engineering design. It is important to note that the unit or the course did not prepare students for scientific concepts that will help to reason on their design decisions. However, some students use their scientific understanding from other courses in their choices. Below is the plan drawing of the students

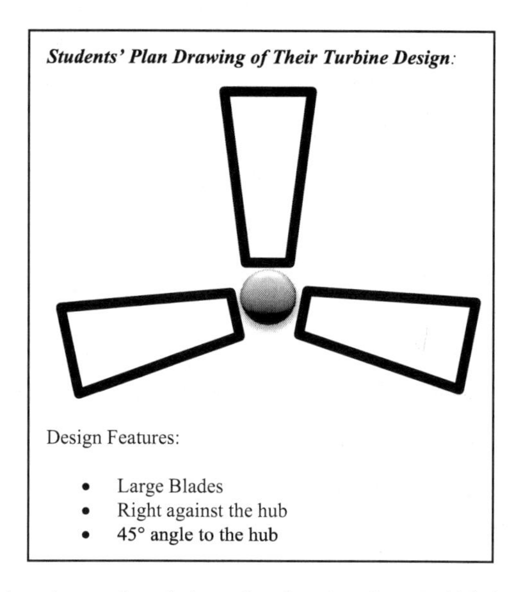

FIGURE 6.6 Students' reproduced sheet for planning the wind blades design.

who were involved in the classroom interaction in this episode (Figure 6.6). Although their plan includes the choice of the shape and the number of blades, it does not explain the reasons why students decided on large, oblong shape blades like in ceiling fans.

Design Team Interaction

Students' use of previous experiences for their engineering design came up in an email exchange while planning the engineering activity. The math instructor Dr. Lee wanted to set a competition between groups to encourage students to come up with creative designs and then be able to discuss what design worked and why. She was worried that all groups will come up with the same design, while the scientist was concerned that the students will rely on their previous experiences only to build their wind vanes with different materials for a different context.

Math Instructor on September 22, 2017: "Should we tell students to select certain design? They have all seen turbines. I think students will try to replicate the wind blade design." Scientist on September 23, 2017:

> But it is a totally different context. For a real turbine, direction and strength of the wind varies frequently. It's different materials. Also, students won't be able to construct a three-dimensional design. I will be curious to see if students will just rely on their previous experiences.

Both of these comments made during the email exchange have importance for thinking epistemic practices of engineering for education. Evaluating previous applications of the knowledge within the constraints of the new context is an engineer's practice. Moreover, the feasibility in classrooms also requires further constraints on the materials and experience brought in to the design process (Cunningham & Kelly, 2017). Thus, the experience provided access to some, but not all, of the relevant engineering design considerations. For the purposes of this lesson, the instructors sought to engage students in the design challenge as part of a larger educational goal of understanding how to address climate change. The ethnographic analysis was able to show that the students were drawing from their previous backgrounds to design their turbines. Backward tracing showed why the instructor paid particular attention to the question of students' choices of number and shapes of blades.

The analysis of the data revealed answers on how IFAs supported the construction of conceptual and epistemic coherence within a unit on climate change. In response, three central themes emerged in our analysis. The use of IFAs (a) highlighted disciplinary aspects of epistemic practices, (b) emphasized connections to core scientific ideas on students' written artifacts, and (c) made students' content background and personal experiences explicit. Because epistemic practice is intertextual (Kelly, 2016), we then described how IFAs were shaped by the norms of climate science discussed during the interactions between people from different disciplines, i.e., the project team.

Discussion

Studies suggest IFAs as critical elements of students' learning that are socially and culturally situated (Jordan & Putz, 2004; Moss, 2008). Moreover, researchers recently discussed how IFAs could be tools to respond to students' ideas and make in-the-moment changes in the nature of their explanations and activities (Furtak, 2012). In this chapter, we identified how IFAs shape the epistemic and conceptual coherence by using an interactional ethnography perspective. Although IFAs were frequently constructed during the unit, we choose IFA cycles which were during "rich points" (i.e., confusions and instances of lack of clarity among students). These discussions around rich points led to prolonged interaction within the sequence unit as relevant core ideas and epistemic practices were in question. Our backward tracing of students' work showed that the IFAs constructed during rich points made explicit conceptual and epistemic ideas which were needed to establish the core ideas of the unit. We then explained how the interactions between the educational researcher, math education instructor, and the scientist informed the way IFAs at rich points are constructed.

During the unit developed by the design team members, students engaged in classroom activity to make meaning around core ideas to reason the current climatic changes (Figure 6.1). Across three episodes, we highlighted the significance of contextualized practices such as long-term interpretation of data, also referred to as "deep time" in geosciences, the spatial reasoning of the data location (Kastens *et al.*, 2009), and contextual constraints to engineering design (Cunningham & Kelly, 2017). These unique features of epistemic practice can be explained by the epistemic cultures that focus on the specific processes involved in doing science within disciplines or sub-disciplines (Knorr Cetina, 2009).

Although NGSS (2013) explains eight epistemic practices, the epistemic cultures of every discipline (such as climate science) are not highlighted in the standards (Cunningham & Kelly, 2017). The transcripts here showed the instructor needed to highlight further distinctive features such as considering the context of the data and search for any assumptions in mathematical representations. These unique disciplinary features of epistemic practice have also been discussed at our meetings with scientists by using well-respected sources of climate science such as the Intergovernmental Panel on Climate Change report (2013) and the National Oceanic and Atmospheric Administration findings (2016). We, therefore, suggest that teacher education programs not only expect teachers to learn the scientific practices highlighted in the standards, but to recognize distinctive features of these practices for different activities. This is particularly important for educational contexts such as college mathematics and science courses focused on specific disciplinary core ideas.

In this chapter, we also showed how the interaction between project members from different disciplines created learning opportunities on the importance of disciplinary epistemic practices from geosciences or engineering to make meaning on the core ideas related to climate change. By taking an ethnographic perspective, we focused attention to particular epistemic practices evinced through interactional rich points that were traced back to records of information from the unit development such as meeting notes, written reflections, and email exchanges. By providing such transparency of the development of our project (American Educational Research Association, 2006), we wanted to build an understanding of how these prior interactions are related to knowledge construction in the science classroom (Kelly, 2006). This can then help other researchers, educators, and scientist from other contexts to make sense and interpret our research approach and the discourses constructed in our study (Baker & Green, 2015).

References

Agar, M. (2006). Culture: Can you take it anywhere? Invited lecture presented at the Gevirtz Graduate School of Education, University of California at Santa Barbara. *International Journal of Qualitative Methods*, 5(2), 1–16.

American Educational Research Association. (2006). Standards for reporting on empirical social science research in American Educational Research Association (AERA) publications. *Educational Researcher*, 35(6), 33–40. doi:10.3102/0013189X035006033.

Baker, W. D., Green, J. L., & Skukauskaite, A. (2008). Video-enabled ethnographic research: A micro-ethnographic perspective. In G. Walford (Ed.), *How to Do Educational Ethnography* (pp. 77–114). London: Tufnell.

Baker, W. D., & Green, J. L. (2015). Exploring challenges in designing and teaching (inter) disciplinary and (inter) cultural programmes in higher education. *Pedagogies: An International Journal*, 10(1), 1–4.

Black, P., & Wiliam, D. (1998). Assessment and classroom learning. *Assessment in Education*, 5(1), 7–74.

Castanheira, M. L., Crawford, T., Dixon, C. N., & Green, J. L. (2001). Interactional ethnography: An approach to studying the social construction of literate practices. *Linguistics and Education*, 11(4), 353–400.

Christie, F. (2002). *Classroom Discourse Analysis: A Functional Perspective*. London: Continuum.

Crawford, T., Castanheira, M., Dixon, C., & Green, J. L. (2001). What counts as literacy: An interactional ethnographic perspective. In J. Cumming, & C. Wyatt-Smith (Eds.), *Literacy and the Curriculum: Success in Senior Secondary Schooling* (pp. 32–43). Melbourne: Acer Press.

Crawford, T. (2005). What counts as knowing: Constructing a communicative repertoire for student demonstration of knowledge in science. *Journal of Research in Science Teaching*, 42(2), 139–165.

Cunningham, C. M., & Kelly, G. J. (2017). Epistemic practices of engineering for education. *Science Education*, 101(3), 486–505.

Dunlap, R. E., & McCright, A. M. (2011). Organized climate change denial. In D. Schlosberg, J. Dryzek, & R. Norgaard (Eds.), *The Oxford Handbook of Climate Change and Society* (pp. 144–160). Oxford: Oxford University Press.

Duschl, R. A. (2003). Assessment of inquiry. In M. Atkin & J. Coffey (Eds.), *Everyday Assessment in the Science Classroom* (pp. 41–59). Boston, MA: NSTA Press.

Duschl, R. A. (2008). Science education in three-part harmony: Balancing conceptual, epistemic, and social learning goals. *Review of Research in Education*, 32(1), 268–291.

Duschl, R., Maeng, S., & Sezen, A. (2011). Learning progressions and teaching sequences: A review and analysis. *Studies in Science Education*, 47(2), 123–182.

Edwards, P. N. (2010). *A Vast Machine: Computer models, Climate Data, and the Politics of Global Warming*. Cambridge, MA: MIT Press.

Engeström, Y. (1999). Activity theory and individual and social transformation. In Y. Engeström, R. Miettinen, & R. L. Punamaki (Eds.), *Perspectives on Activity Theory* (pp. 19–38). Cambridge, United Kingdom: Cambridge University Press.

Erickson, F. (1979). On Standards of Descriptive Validity in Studies of Classroom Activity. *Occasional Paper No.* 16.

Fairclough, N. (1992). Discourse and text: Linguistic and intertextual analysis within discourse analysis. *Discourse & Society*, 3(2), 193–217.

Furtak, E. M., & Ruiz-Primo, M. A. (2008). Making students' thinking explicit in writing and discussion: An analysis of formative assessment prompts. *Science Education*, 92(5), 799–824.

Furtak, E. M. (2012). Linking a learning progression for natural selection to teachers' enactment of formative assessment. *Journal of Research in Science Teaching*, 49(9), 1181–1210.

Furtak, E. M. (2017). Confronting dilemmas posed by three-dimensional classroom assessment: Introduction to a virtual issue of Science Education. *Science Education*, 101(5), 854–867.

Galaz, V., Crona, B., Österblom, H., Olsson, P., & Folke, C. (2012). Polycentric systems and interacting planetary boundaries: Emerging governance of climate change – ocean acidification – marine biodiversity. *Ecological Economics*, 81, 21–32.

Gee, J. P., & Green, J. L. (1998). Discourse analysis, learning, and social practice: A methodological study. *Review of Research in Education*, 23(1), 119–169.

Gelbspan, R. (1997). *The Heat Is On: The High Stakes Battle over Earth's Threatened Climate.* Reading, MA: Addison-Wesley.

Green, J. L., & Wallat, C. (1981). *Ethnography and Language in Educational Settings.* Norwood, NJ: Ablex Publishing.

Green, J. L., & Meyer, L. A. (1991). The embeddedness of reading in classroom life: Reading as a situated process. In C. Baker & A. Luke (Eds.), *Towards a Critical Sociology of Reading Pedagogy* (pp. 141–160). Amsterdan: John Benjamins.

Green, J. L., Skukauskaite, A., & Baker, W. D. (2012). Ethnography as epistemology: An introduction to educational ethnography. In J. Arthur, M. Waring, R. Coe, & L. V. Hedges (Eds.), *Research Methodologies and Methods in Education* (pp. 309–321). London: SAGE.

Hadorn, H. G., Hoffmann-Riem, H., Biber-Klemm, S., Grossenbacher, W., Joye, D., Pohl, C., . . . & Zemp, E. (2008). The emergence of transdisciplinarity as a form of research. In G. H. Hadorn, H. Hoffmann-Riem, S. Biber-Klemm *et al.* (Eds.), *Handbook of Transdisciplinary Research* (pp. 19–39). Heidelberg: Springer.

Hansen, J., Ruedy, R., Sato, M., & Lo, K. (2010). Global Surface Temperature Change. *Reviews of Geophysics*, 48(4).

Hanuscin, D., Lipsitz, K., Cisterna-Alburquerque, D., Arnone, K. A., van Garderen, D., de Araujo, Z., & Lee, E. J. (2016). Developing coherent conceptual storylines: Two elementary challenges. *Journal of Science Teacher Education*, 27(4), 393–414.

Intergovernmental Panel on Climate Change. (2013). *Climate Change* 2013: The Physical Science Basis. Contribution of Working Group I to the Fifth Assessment Report of the Intergovernmental Panel on Climate Change. Cambridge, United Kingdom and New York: Cambridge University Press.

Janssen, F., Westbroek, H., & Van Driel, J. (2013). How to make innovations practical. *Teachers College Record*, 115(7).

Jordan, B., & Putz, P. (2004). Assessment as practice: Notes on measures, tests, and targets. *Human Organization*, 63(3), 346–358.

Kastens, K. A., Manduca, C. A., Cervato, C., Frodeman, R., Goodwin, C., Liben, L. S., . . . & Titus, S. (2009). How geoscientists think and learn. *Eos* 90(31), 265–272.

Kelly, G. J., Chen, C., & Crawford, T. (1998). Methodological considerations for studying science-in-the-making in educational settings. *Research in Science Education*, 28(1), 23–49.

Kelly, G. J., & Chen, C. (1999). The sound of music: Constructing science as sociocultural practices through oral and written discourse. *Journal of Research in Science Teaching*, 36(8), 883–915.

Kelly, G. J. (2005). Meaning making in secondary science classrooms. *Science Education*, 89(5), 875–877.

Kelly, G. J. (2006). Epistemology and educational research. In J. L. Green, G. Camilli, & P. B. Elmore (Eds.), *Complementary Methods in Education Research* (pp. 31–53). Mahwah, NJ: Lawrence Earlbaum (for AERA).

Kelly, G. J. (2008). Inquiry, activity, and epistemic practice. In R. Duschl & R. Grandy (Eds.), *Teaching Scientific Inquiry: Recommendations for Research and Implementation* (pp. 99–117; 288–291). Rotterdam: Sense Publishers.

Kelly, G. J. (2011). Scientific literacy, discourse, and epistemic practices. In C. Linder, L. Östman, D. A. Roberts, P.-O. Wickman, G. Erickson, A. Mackinnon (Eds.), *Exploring the Landscape of Scientific Literacy* (pp. 62–73). New York: Routledge/Taylor & Francis Group.

Kelly, G. J. (2016). Methodological considerations for interactional perspectives on epistemic cognition. In J. A. Greene, W. A. Sandoval, & I. Bråten (Eds.), *Handbook of Epistemic Cognition* (pp. 393–408). New York: Routledge.

Knorr Cetina, K. (2009). *Epistemic Cultures: How the Sciences Make Knowledge*. Boston, MA: Harvard University Press.

Kurland, N. B., Michaud, K. E., Best, M., Wohldmann, E., Cox, H., Pontikis, K., & Vasishth, A. (2010). Overcoming silos: The role of an interdisciplinary course in shaping a sustainability network. *Academy of Management Learning & Education*, 9(3), 457–476.

Leahy, S., Lyon, C., Thompson, M., & Wiliam, D. (2005). Classroom assessment: Minute by minute, day by day. *Educational Leadership*, 63(3), 18–24.

Mehan, H. (1979). *Learning Lessons: Social Organization in the Classroom*. Cambridge, MA: Harvard University Press.

Minstrell, J., Li, M., & Anderson, R. (2009). Evaluating Science Teachers' Formative Assessment Competency. Technical report submitted to NSF.

Mitchell, J. (1984). Typicality and the case study. In R. Ellen (Ed.), *Ethnographic Research: A Guide to General Conduct* (pp. 237–241). London: Academic Press.

Mortimer, E. F., & Scott, P. H. (2003). *Meaning Making in Secondary Science Classrooms*. Maidenhead, UK: Open University Press.

Moss, P. A. (2008). Sociocultural implications for the practice of assessment I: Classroom assessment. In P. A. Moss, D. Pullin, J. P. Gee, E. H. Haertel, & L. J. Young (Eds.), *Assessment, Equity, and Opportunity to Learn*. New York: Cambridge University Press.

National Aeronautics and Space Administration. (2015). GISS Surface Temperature Analysis (GISTEMP). Accessed April 15, 2015, from http://data.giss.nasa.gov/gistemp/.

National Oceanic and Atmospheric Administration. (2016). *National Centers for Environmental Information: Regional*. Retrieved from www.ncdc.noaa.gov/climate-information/regional on August 10, 2016.

National Research Council. (2012). A Framework for K-12 Science Education: Practices, Crosscutting Concepts, and Core Ideas. Washington, DC: National Academies Press.

NGSS Lead States. (2013). *Next Generation Science Standards: For States, By States*. Washington, DC: National Academies Press.

Oreskes, N. (Ed.). (2001). *Plate Tectonics: An Insider's History of the Modern Theory of the Earth*. Boulder, CO: Westview Press.

Plutzer, E., McCaffrey, M., Hannah, A. L., Rosenau, J., Berbeco, M., & Reid, A. H. (2016). Climate confusion among US teachers. *Science*, 351(6274), 664–665.

Reiser, B. J. (2013, September). What professional development strategies are needed for successful implementation of the Next Generation Science Standards. Paper presented at the *Invitational Research Symposium on Science Assessment*. K-12 Center at ETS, Washington, DC.

Roth, K. J., Garnier, H. E., Chen, C., Lemmens, M., Schwille, K., & Wickler, N. I. (2011). Video based lesson analysis: Effective science PD for teacher and student learning. *Journal of Research in Science Teaching*, 48(2), 117–148.

Ruiz-Primo, M. A., & Furtak, E. M. (2007). Exploring teachers' informal formative assessment practices and students' understanding in the context of scientific inquiry. *Journal of Research in Science Teaching*, 44(1), 57–84.

Ruiz-Primo, M. A., Briggs, D., Iverson, H., Talbot, R., & Shepard, L. A. (2011). Impact of undergraduate science course innovations on learning. *Science*, 331(6022), 1269–1270.

Sezen-Barrie, A., Tran, M. D., McDonald, S. P., & Kelly, G. J. (2014). A cultural historical activity theory perspective to understand preservice science teachers' reflections on and tensions during a microteaching experience. *Cultural Studies of Science Education*, 9(3), 675–697.

Sezen-Barrie, A. (2018). Utilizing professional vision in supporting preservice teachers' learning about contextualized scientific practices. *Science & Education*, 27(1–2), 159–182.

Sezen-Barrie, A., & Kelly, G. J. (2017). From the teacher's eyes: Facilitating teachers noticings on informal formative assessments (IFAs) and exploring the challenges to effective implementation. *International Journal of Science Education*, 39(2), 181–212.

Sezen-Barrie, A., Shea, N., & Borman, J. H. (2017). Probing into the sources of ignorance: Science teachers' practices of constructing arguments or rebuttals to denialism of climate change. *Environmental Education Research*, doi: 10.1080/13504622.2017.1330949.

Sinclair, J. M., & Coulthard, M. (1975). *Towards an Analysis of Discourse: The English Used by Teachers and Pupils*. London, UK: Oxford University Press.

Spradley, J. P. (2016). *Participant Observation*. Long Grove, IL: Waveland Press.

Weart, S. (2013). Rise of interdisciplinary research on climate. *Proceedings of the National Academy of Sciences*, 110(1), 3657–3664.

Wells, G. (1993). Reevaluating the IRF sequence: A proposal for the articulation of theories of activity and discourse for the analysis of teaching and learning in the classroom. *Linguistics and Education*, 5(1), 1–37.

Zeidler, D. L. (2016). STEM education: A deficit framework for the twenty first century? A sociocultural socioscientific response. *Cultural Studies of Science Education*, 11(1), 11–26.

7

EMOTIONAL DISCOURSE AS CONSTRUCTED IN AN ENVIRONMENTAL SCIENCE COURSE

Elizabeth Hufnagel

Introduction to Researching Emotions in Learning Climate Change

Underlying this chapter is the importance of researching emotions in science education, particularly during the learning of climate change. Emotions are often dichotomized from cognition and science, despite evidence of the importance of emotion in both cognition and science (Immordino-Yang & Damasio, 2007; Jaber & Hammer, 2016a, 2016b; Zembylas, 2016). *If* emotions are examined in science learning settings they are often along this false binary, perpetuating the notion that emotions are separate from the learning and the doing of science.

Despite this orientation toward emotion research in science education settings, interdisciplinary scholarship relating to social psychology, sociology, natural resource management, and public health demonstrate that emotions are prevalent in making sense of climate change (e.g., Myers, Nisbet, Maibach, & Leiserowitz, 2012; Ojala, 2015; Swim & Bloodhart, 2015). Furthermore, empirical studies in these fields connect emotions and actions (i.e. Buijs & Lawrence, 2013; Thomas, McGarty, & Mavor, 2009; Vining, 1987). In particular, recent research suggests that emotions are entangled in more than just sense-making but also motivation (Hornsey & Fielding, 2016) and coping (Caillaud, Bonnot, Ratiu, & Krauth-Gruber, 2016) about environmental issues like climate change. Although many questions still remain about how emotions and aspects of emotions—such as the type and intensity—influence actions, emotional sense-making is part and parcel of understanding, coping with, and taking action on such issues like climate change (Gifford, 2011, 2014; Swim *et al.*, 2011).

While studies of emotions have expanded into numerous fields, the historical perceptions of emotions as separate from science and learning are pervasive.

Science often characterizes nature objectively, removing "emotional ties that bind us to each other and our world" (Broom, 2011, p. 124). Even recent science reform policy portrays nature and environmental issues, including climate change, in a distanced manner (Hufnagel, Kelly, & Henderson, 2018). Furthermore, due to the ways in which emotions have traditionally been studied—in laboratory settings and with data collection methods that remove the contextual features of the expression—ways to examine emotions in situ have been stunted. In this chapter I provide a justification for why I constructed a logic of inquiry for examining expressions of emotions about climate change in situ that was grounded in interactional ethnography (Castanheira, Crawford, Dixon, & Green, 2000) and interactional sociolinguistics (Gumperz, 2001; Kelly, 2016). I draw from a study of 30 elementary education undergraduate students' emotional sense-making during an environmental science course at a large public university in the United States to illustrate how I constructed a logic of inquiry to explore students' *emotional expressions* in situ about climate change.

The goal of this chapter is to describe the sets of decisions that I made throughout my research to provide systemacity to the analysis of a large data set of video recordings, ethnographic field notes, student artifacts from the course (i.e. students' written assignments, drawings, representations constructed for the class), and seven sets of participant interviews. In doing so, I compliment my previous work by describing how the broader logic of inquiry of examining *emotional expressions* in situ in a climate change course took shape. In the following sections, I explicate the theories of emotions as social and situated that undergird my program of research; my larger program of research; the challenges I encountered in constructing my logic of inquiry; and the logic of inquiry I used to examine students' *emotional expressions* in situ in a climate change science course.

Emotions as Social and Situated

I grounded my inquiry in conceptualizations of emotions from social psychology that emphasize relational theories of emotions (Boiger & Mesquita, 2012; Keltner & Gross, 1999) to guide my analysis of *emotional expressions* in social interactions. As fundamental biological mechanisms to make sense of the world, emotions indicate what people take most personally and why (Shields, 2002). Boiger and Mesquita (2012) describe the situatedness of emotions and their expressions as embedded in moment-to-moment interactions that are imbued with both a history and a future of the relationships. In this way, emotions are not internal entities but a relationship to a specific event, experience, idea, and so forth. This specificity of an emotion's object, or the *aboutness* (Hufnagel, 2015, 2017; Shields, 2002), makes salient what is deeply personal and urgent. In addition to this specificity, emotions are evaluative in that they encapsulate how events, experiences, and knowledge relate to personal goals. For instance, emotions such as happiness and excitement result when an experience or information maintains or enhances, respectively, one's goals. Emotions such as anger, sadness, and frustration occur when one's personal goals are impeded. Hence, examining emotions provides opportunities to understand what people find most relevant and why.

Emotional Expressions

While there are physiological aspects of emotions, emotions reflect and are represented by social practices (Hufnagel, 2015; Hufnagel & Kelly, 2017). Recent scholarship suggests that the line between experiencing an emotion privately and expressing an emotion is blurry (Gross & Barrett, 2011; Kappas, 2011, 2013). Hence, I focus on *emotional expressions* to attend to the ways emotions are conveyed in talk and text through contextualization cues (Gumperz, 1982) at the nexus between the individual-collective, or the individual-within-the-collective scale. Similar to other research approaches that rely on language, talk, or text to infer learning, reasoning, and so forth, discourse mediates communication and in doing so serves as an entry point into examining *emotional expressions*. Hence, analyzing the discourse in which emotions are shared and responded to provides a systematic approach to examining this area of learning.

A Program of Research on Emotional Sense-Making of Climate Change

The context in which I developed this logic of inquiry of *emotional expressions* in situ was in an environmental science course on climate change. The initial goal of the ongoing project was to examine *emotional expressions* in a science classroom setting to determine which aspects of the content elicited emotions. However, as I describe in this chapter, the logic of inquiry changed as I collected and analyzed data (Heap, 1995). In other words, the analytical work I did informed the methods I used as well as the theories guiding my work and the theoretical inferences that I was able to construct through particular levels and forms of analysis. I grounded my research in the Ethnographic Research Cycle (Spradley, 1980) so that I could make sense of the culture of the classroom as a participant observer through an abductive, iterative, and recursive process (Agar, 2006). In order to understand the classroom culture, I attended to the cultural behaviors, cultural knowledge, and cultural artifacts as a participant observer (Spradley, 1980) within the class community. I simultaneously asked questions and observed interactions within the community, including with tools, texts, and other people. I attended to the physical characteristics of the social situation as well as what it felt like to participate (Spradley, 1980, p. 33). In recording these observations and reflections, I constructed recordings of the data that served as the basis for continued analyses, new questions, and new ways to focus data analysis, which in turn raised other questions (Agar, 2006).

Due to the abductive, iterative, and recursive nature of ethnography (Agar, 2006; Green, Skukauskaite, & Baker, 2012), this project has continued to develop in the five years since I first started collecting data. Thus, while my dissertation could be considered the product of this approach to inquiry, the inquiry process continues. As I wrote manuscripts for publication from my dissertation, I shifted the analysis in different ways and in doing so constructed new data sets to answer further questions. My process took shape in this way in part to fit the genre of the educational research article and in part because in returning to the archives I made sense of them in new ways (Heap, 1995; Mitchell, 1984). As a result, I have added to and revised the logic of inquiry based on my developing understanding of the ethnographic research stance as I gained further experience in understanding how participants expressed emotions and engaged with more recent scholarship on emotions. Hence, the analyses presented in this chapter are captured in a static manner by their inscription from the point of time of writing although the inquiry is currently ongoing as archives of a phenomenon are continuously interpreted and re-interpreted (Agar, 2006; Mitchell, 1984; Spradley, 1980).

This chapter builds on these histories to illustrate a body of work that is part of an interconnected program of research (Green, Skukauskaite, & Baker, 2012) on emotional sense-making of climate change. In the rest of this section, I briefly describe four strands of the research project: a methodological approach and three sets of empirical findings about the emotional sense-making of the students as they learned about climate change.

In our description of the methodology, Gregory Kelly and I (Hufnagel & Kelly, 2017) described the interactional, contextual, intertextual, and consequential aspects of *emotional expressions*. Through this work we illustrated how *emotional expressions* were identified through analyses of semantic, contextualization, and linguistic features of discourse. By using these features of discourse, we demonstrated how four dimensions of *emotional expressions* were illuminated within and across discourse forms: aboutness, frequency, type, and ownership. These dimensions provided a nuanced view of *emotional expressions* that moves beyond the *emotion label*, or *type*, and *intensity*. However, while the methodological paper was important to understanding how to analyze *emotional expressions*, it was not comprehensive given that it did not make salient the analytical decisions made at various stages of the study's design, data collection, and analysis processes. Hence, this chapter provides the elucidation of those steps.

Another strand of the ongoing project constituted a study of micro-level analyses of the emotions the students expressed about different aspects of climate change. The study (Hufnagel, 2015) focused on examining statements of *aboutness*, or reference to the object of the emotion, and of *ownership* of *emotional expressions* to identify which aspects of environmental problems were most relevant to the members of the class. This micro-level analysis of the *emotional expressions* made visible how *ownership* of *emotional expression* represented the ways in which students distanced themselves from their *emotional expressions* through the use of linguistic features such as hedging, third person, and passive voice.

Through this fine-grain analysis, I identified nuances of *emotional expressions* that indicated emotional connections and disconnections to different aspects of climate change (e.g., they emotionally connected to the impacts of climate change but on other beings than themselves). This micro-level analysis was not performed in isolation. Rather, it required attending to the broader discourse in which the *emotional expressions* were constructed.

The meso-level analyses within the logic of inquiry, which is the focus of another segment of the project (Hufnagel, in press), provided insights into the ways in which participants expressed emotions across time and text throughout the course. The expectations for *emotional expressions* were interactionally accomplished within and across time-scales and forms of discourse (talk and text). As such there were patterned ways in which emotions were expressed, making salient how frames, or expectations, for emotional expressions were constructed.

While both the meso- and micro- level analyses of *emotional expressions* attended to the individual-within-the-collective, a third set of empirical findings explores the emotional sense-making of select individuals-within-the-collective. In particular, this segment of the project entails examining how a select group of the students from the larger study made sense emotionally of their agency in climate change and the tensions underlying their conceptualizations.

Challenges of Studying Emotions in Classroom Settings

Researching emotions, especially in educational contexts, presents a broad set of challenges relating to epistemological underpinnings of and methods to analyze emotions. Underlying my initial guiding questions was considering *how* to study emotions in classrooms, as I could neither consider what emotions revealed about sense-making nor how to respond to them without being able to examine them. In this section, I describe five tensions I experienced as I developed a logic of inquiry to identify and analyze *emotional expressions* in situ and the means by which I addressed the challenges.

As I dove into the educational research literature to learn more about emotions, I noticed trends in emotion theories and operationalization. Since I was initially focused on how emotions impacted learning the science of climate change, I sought resources in the science education literature that explored emotions and learning. Due to the limited number of studies of emotions in the learning of science (see Milne & Otieno, 2007; Olitsky, 2007; Sadler & Zeidler, 2004, 2005; Tomas & Ritchie, 2011; Watts, 2005; Zembylas, 2004a, 2004b, 2004c, 2005), I broadened my search to other fields of educational research, including (science) teacher education, educational studies, environmental education, mathematics education, and educational psychology. I also read extensively outside of educational research, particularly in social psychology (e.g., Campos, Walle, Dahl, & Main, 2011; Keltner & Gross, 1999; Mesquita & Albert, 2007; Shields, 2002, 2007; Warner & Shields, 2009), but also in the fields of sociology

(Barbalet, 2002; Denzin, 1984; Jasso, 2007), and philosophy (Solomon, 2007; Nussbaum, 2001). In reading these and other works I experienced five tensions of examining emotions that were based on the way they were conceptualized as (a) silenced, (b) internalized, (c) essentialized, and often researched (d) more with teachers than students, and (e) along a binary of positive/negative. Each of these aspects of emotions is separated for the sake of clarity but are inter-related as they promote a prioritization of the emotion type and an individualistic sense of emotions, rather than the messiness of emotions—range, type, and nuance—as discussed in this section. In the following sections I explicate both the challenges I encountered in learning to study emotions and the ways I addressed these challenges in my logic of inquiry.

Emotion as a Silenced Phenomenon

One of the first questions I had as I began my inquiry was how to examine emotions if they are often silenced or marginalized in science learning settings. The history of emotion's exclusion from science is long and embedded in Western traditions that continue to serve as structures of neglect today. Emotion has traditionally been excluded from science (Watts, 2005) and science education (Zembylas, 2005) because of the underlying assumption in Western thought that knowledge is rational and unbiased (e.g., Boler, 1999; Shields, 2002; Solomon, 2007). As Midgley argues, the dichotomy between "reason and emotion and the threat that emotion poses to emasculate reason are long-standing Western notions, even though dichotomizing these qualities is itself not logically based" (as cited in Shields, 2007, p. 93). Boler (1999) suggests that emotion is purposefully excluded from both science and education based on the historical dichotomy between truth/reason and subjectivity/emotion. Science, as well as by extension science education, has traditionally been replete with dualisms, including the emotion/reason dualism pervasive since the Enlightenment (Brickhouse, 2001). Yet emotions shape and define our experiences (Boler, 1999, p. 142), and the dualism that separates reason from emotion limits not only our ways of making sense of the world but also the ways in which we express ourselves.

While the tide seems to be shifting in education and other social sciences to attend to emotion in research (Zembylas, 2016), how does one capture *emotional expressions* if they are not typically part of the discourse? I addressed this challenge throughout my entire logic of inquiry by attending to the discourse and cultural knowledge in which the silences are constructed. As a participant observer (Spradley, 1980), I engaged in the classroom in a way to "fully learn the cultural rules for behavior" (p. 60), which included supporting students in their group work tasks, designing and teaching some lessons, and crafting questions on assignments.

I wrote field notes when I could and memos after the class meetings when I could not write field notes. I also talked with students informally before and after class to both get to know them better and informally ask about trends I was noticing as a participant observer. In addition, by attending to how *emotional expressions* were framed throughout the course by instructors, texts, and participants, I could identify how emotional sense-making was constructed throughout the course. Furthermore, since the interpretation of emotions is in the eye of the beholder (Shields, 2002) I also noted if and how emotional sense-making was privileged and when in the course by the instructors. Another way I addressed the challenge of examining a silenced phenomenon was by providing opportunities for students to express emotions in discussions and on artifacts. One way this took shape was to fold questions into class assignments (pre/post assessments, exit slips, reading frames, exams) to ask students about their emotions, indirectly and directly. For instance, a direct question was, "People have a lot of feelings or emotions about human-caused climate change. What are your feelings or emotions about climate change?" given on the pre/post. An indirect question was "Think about this idea of organisms not having some place to go because of climate change. With so much ice melting, what do you foresee happening to various organisms and how does that impact you personally?" given as an exit slip at the end of a class meeting. In this way, the ongoing regular activities of the classroom served to offer students opportunities to reflect on and share their emotions about climate change while generating data for my study.

Emotions Conceptualized as Internalized Entities

Historically, emotions have been conceptualized as internal entities. While the physiological experiences correlating to emotions are important for a variety of reasons, a challenge I faced was how to assess emotions based on this theoretical conception. However, early in my inquiry I interacted with social psychology researchers and other social scientists investigating emotions and learned about different theories of emotions that include performative, embodied, and gendered ways of doing emotions (Denzin, 1984; Hargreaves, 1998, 2000; Oatley, 1993; Reser & Swim, 2011; Shields, 2007; Zembylas, 2004b, 2004c). As my understanding of emotions became more sophisticated I felt more comfortable articulating how my research interests fit into the larger field of emotion research. A comprehensive view of emotions includes understandings of the internal processes that occur physiologically and neurologically as well as the external processes like action and communication. Being an educator, expressions of emotions resonated with me because in school settings I relied on discourse to make meanings with others. Furthermore, since the interpretation of emotions is subjective (Shields, 2002), I wanted to attend to the interactional nature of emotions.

I shifted my focus from emotions to *emotional expressions* to better encapsulate the aspects of emotional sense-making on which I focused. In doing so, I approached *emotional expressions* as interactional, contextual, intertextual, and consequential (Hufnagel & Kelly, 2017). Additionally, focusing on *emotional expressions* rather than emotions accounted for the norms that shape who expresses which emotions, how, and when (Hufnagel, in press; Shields, 2002). Within interactions, there is a constant negotiation of relayed messages in order to construct shared interpretations (Gumperz, 2001). Inherent in these negotiations are the "background assumptions that underlie the negotiations of interpretations" (Gumperz, 2001, p. 218). The ways in which *emotional expressions* take shape in an interaction include "background assumptions" about which emotions are acceptable to express, by whom, and to what intensity.

An abductive, iterative, and recursive ethnographic approach to *emotional expressions* in classroom settings compelled me to ask questions about insider knowledge (Green *et al.*, 2012). For instance, my approach to understand what counted as *emotional expressions* was based on considering emotions as a form of cultural knowledge, which is continually constructed by members of a group. Coupled with this question was the intersection between individuals' interactions and norms for *emotional expressions* that have been constructed in other learning settings, science spaces, and so forth. Therefore, I sought to understand the broader discourse in which *emotional expressions* were constructed, framed, and expressed through a large archive of data that included ethnographic field notes and memos, video recordings of each class meeting, participant interviews, and all student artifacts.

Emotions Theorized and Examined as Essentialized Entities

In addition to wondering how to approach a phenomenon that is undervalued or even silenced and construed as solely internal, I also encountered the challenge of how to research emotions in situ. I experienced a tension between historical methods to examining emotions and how I understood discourse and meaning-making to be interactionally accomplished, contextual (situated in time and space), intertextual, and consequential (Kelly, 2016). Ultimately, my goal was to capture contextual aspects of *emotional expressions* so as to understand the richness of students' relations to climate change. Even with a shift in conceptualization of emotions to be relational (Boiger & Mesquita, 2012), Likert-style surveys are largely used to investigate emotions. Typically these surveys seek to identify the *type* and *intensity* of a particular emotion. This approach makes sense based on the history of emotion research in psychology that relies on laboratory studies. However, depending exclusively on individualized emotion data did not align with my understandings of the ways in which people make sense of events and ideas socially. The approach also conflicted with my understanding of emotions as inherently contextual and relational. The essentializing, or decontextualizing of emotions, separates emotional discourse from social life (Abu-Lughod & Lutz, 1990), reinforcing the notion that emotions are personal or private and universal in terms of their meaning regardless of context (White, 2000). Compounding the complexity of examining *emotional expressions* is that multiple emotional meanings may be conveyed concurrently (Shields, 2002), and people articulate their emotions in varying degrees of precision when using words (Barrett, 2006).

Similar in some ways to the use of self-report on Likert-style surveys is the use of facial recognition of emotions (Ekman & Friesen, 1978). According to this approach each type of emotion is expressed vis-à-vis a specific orientation of facial features. This method extrapolates emotions to a set of facial expressions that can be identified using still images of the participants. Questions have been raised as to the universality of emotions in facial expressions (Russell, 1994); however, this approach to identifying emotions continues and has become more prevalent in educational research settings. While recent science education research utilizing facial recognition uses it in conjunction with other methods (King, Ritchie, Sandhu, Henderson, & Boland, 2017), the focus of the approach is essentializing emotions and prioritizing the emotion type. These approaches to emotion research provide answers to particular questions about which emotions are expressed. In contrast, my logic of inquiry involved not separating the *emotional expressions* from the discourse. I also struggled with reconciling this strictly etic approach to identifying emotions because it also seemed to remove the contextual and relational aspects of *emotional expressions*.

While etic perspectives are inherently part of ethnographic work because we cannot separate ourselves entirely from the research (Agar, 2011), I sought to recognize the interplay between the insider cultural knowledge of *emotional expressions* and my interpretation of them. As such, I addressed the situated nature of emotions by connecting the *emotional expressions* to the context in a variety of ways. I captured impressions of *emotional expressions* in field notes and memos as I experienced them in the moment in order to return to video recordings of those moments later. As I watched and rewatched those segments of the videos, I attended to micro-level features of discourse, such as contextualization cues, as well as physical orientation and tools. In doing so, I drew from my participant observation experience of understanding the cultural knowledge to consider emotions from the point of view of the participants, as relevant to the discursive context of the moment. I utilized a similar technique with the written artifacts by reading and rereading them and attending to micro-level features of discourse in the text. I tracked all *emotional expressions* across the entire semester in an event map (Kelly & Chen, 1999) so that I could zoom in and out to understand how the expressions of emotion were situated within the course and were about particular climate change ideas.

Scholarship in Education Focuses on Teachers' Emotions

While I grappled with epistemological and methodological questions about how to examine *emotional expressions* in context, I also faced a two-fold challenge of how to study *emotional expressions* in a classroom of 30 students that would likely have diverse emotional experiences. I had limited resources to draw from that examined a large number of people's emotions in situ, let alone studies that captured and organized varied *emotional expressions* in time and space in the classroom.

I found the vast majority of emotion studies in education, especially those that did not rely on Likert-style surveys, focused on teachers' emotions. While this work is important and relevant to students' emotions, the focus was squarely on teachers, as they navigated a variety of tensions arising from education reform and personal motivations to teach (e.g., Rivera Maulucci, 2013; van Veen, Sleegers, & van de Ven, 2005; Zembylas, 2004a; 2004b). Furthermore, the studies investigated one or a handful of teachers' emotional experiences, rather than a large group. Since I knew my logic of inquiry was dynamic I wanted to create archives of data in ways that would leave open the possibility of analyzing both individuals' and collectives' *emotional expressions* since I would have data archives for 30 students. In order to address the challenge of organizing and analyzing *emotional expressions* throughout a course with 30 students, I sought to be systematic, thorough, and comprehensive in my inquiry by analysis. I constructed and drew from my archives of ethnographic field notes and memos of students' *emotional expressions* in class, video recordings of each class meeting with two cameras located at different sides of the room, all student written artifacts, and participant interviews to construct an event map of *emotional expressions* throughout the course based on these data sources.

Positively Valenced Emotions Prioritized

In the science education literature, when students' emotions were examined, a focus was on their collective, largely "positively" valenced, emotional engagement during classroom activities (Bellocchi, Ritchie, Tobin, Sandhu, & Sandhu, 2013; Milne & Otieno, 2007; Olitsky, 2013). However, I was interested in students' emotions about the science ideas of climate change they were learning, regardless of the type or valence. Since emotions are indicative of deeply personal and urgent connections, *any* emotion constitutes sense-making. In this way, I conceptualized emotions as sense-making rather than a requirement for learning. Underlying the scholarship in science education as I began this inquiry was that positively valenced emotions (i.e. happiness, excitement) enhance learning and negatively valenced emotions (i.e. anger, frustration) inhibit learning (see Hufnagel, 2015, 2017). However, recent work highlights how various emotional experiences are integral to learning science (Jaber & Hammer, 2016a, 2016b; Sinatra, Broughton, & Lombardi, 2014; Wickman, 2006). Examining all emotions, regardless of valence, about climate change provides a means for understanding how students find climate change relevant to their lives. Indeed, emotions such as fear or frustration, for example, may motivate students to learn more, take particular actions regarding climate change, or communicate their feelings to others.

Broughton, Sinatra, and Nussbaum's (2013) distinction between academic emotions, which are about academic outcomes (i.e. test anxiety), and topic emotions, which are about specific topics in a classroom, was valuable to my inquiry. Their focus on students' emotions about particular science ideas helped guide me to consider the contextual features of their expressions. Hence, I sought to construct a logic of inquiry that would allow me to examine students' *emotional expressions* about climate change ideas in situ with an eye toward capturing all *emotional expressions* across time and space about climate change. As a result, I examined every *emotional expression* regardless of valence and down-selected *emotional expressions* that were about climate change rather than focusing on a particular type or emotion label.

Logic of Inquiry for Examining *Emotional Expressions*

My logic of inquiry entailed collecting large sets of data throughout the entire environmental science course. In Kelly's (2014) work of meta-methodological considerations of interactional sociolinguistics, he suggests how to provide systematic analyses of large sets of interactional data. Since classroom life is highly situated, balancing flexibility with structure is challenging but required (Kelly, 2014). Video recordings of each class meeting, ethnographic field notes and memos, all instructional and student artifacts, and sets of two roughly 30-minute interviews with seven students provided a means to examine *emotional expressions* over time and space at different levels of analysis.

The ongoing project started with the overarching question, "Which emotions did students express in an environmental science course and why?" as seen in the box at the top of Figure 7.1. However, as I sought to answer this overarching question, four sets of generative sub-questions, shown by shading and letter: A1, B1, C1, and D1. in Figure 7.1, constituted the abductive, iterative, and recursive approach (Agar, 2006; Spradley, 1980). While the use of these letters suggests sequence, the exploration of these questions was not linear but abductive, iterative, and recursive.

As I sought to make analytical decisions about what counted as *emotional expressions* (A1) I noticed nuances of *emotional expressions* (B1). Hence, a related question that informed my decisions about what counted as *emotional expressions* was understanding "How were *emotional expressions* nuanced throughout the course?" Underlying both (A1) and (B1) was an epistemological orientation of emotions as relational, deeply personal evaluations with an object (having aboutness) informed by theories of emotions in social psychology (Campos, Walle, Dahl, & Main, 2011; Keltner & Gross, 1999; Shields, 2002). What became evident was that participants expressed emotions differently across time and space, including text (see D1 in Figure 7.1), which I explored in conjunction with the other sub-questions. As I understood the different ways participants expressed emotions about climate change, I examined how the students made

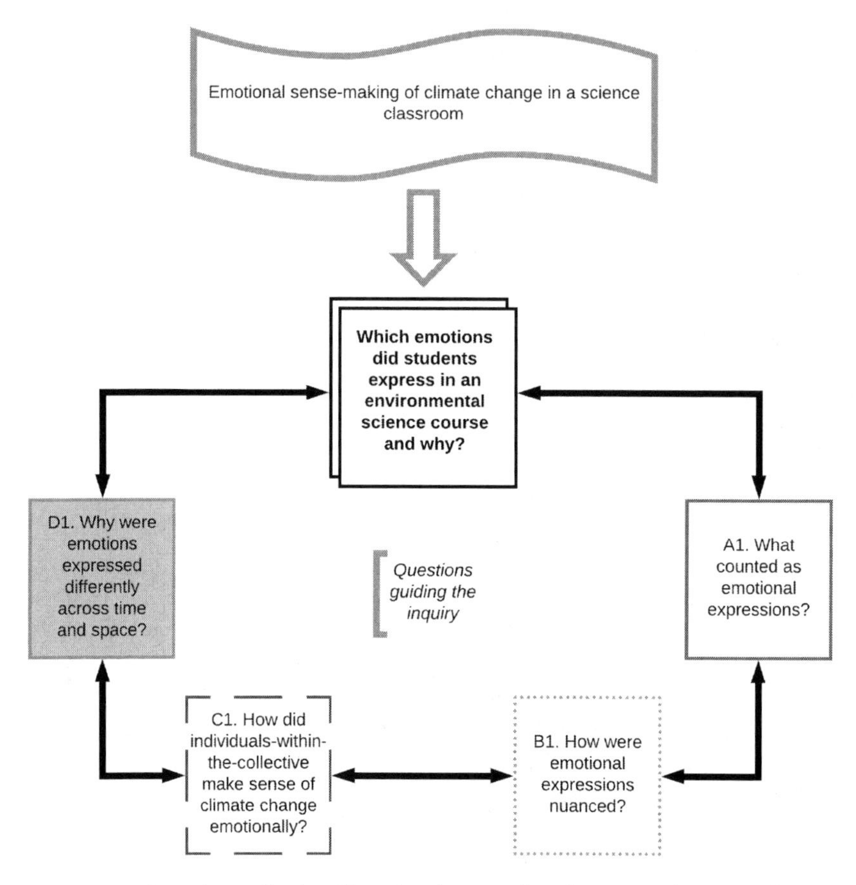

FIGURE 7.1 Overview of logic of inquiry about students' emotional sense-making of climate change in an environmental science course.

"sense of climate change emotionally" as individuals-within-a-collective (see C1 in Figure 7.1). In the following sections, I describe the records collected, analytic processes, and subsequent explorations that emanated from the four generative sub-questions in my logic of inquiry.

A1. What Counted as Emotional Expressions

In order to determine what counted as *emotional expressions*, I constructed an archive of records from which to make analytical decisions. These records were: ethnographic field notes and memos from each class meeting, two video recordings of each class meeting from different angles, and all student written artifacts. My ethnographic field notes and memos provided a foundation of the range of activities and discourses throughout the course. They also provided a means to capturing what others as well as myself as the analyst understood to be significant experiences (Emerson, Fretz, & Shaw, 1995) around emotions. Hence, my logic of inquiry quickly came to include four questions (A2, A3, A4, A5) related to "what counted as *emotional expressions*?" as seen in Figure 7.2.

From the three sets of archives (field notes, video recordings, written artifacts), I constructed data representations and then collected all potential *emotional expressions*, regardless of aboutness or ambiguity, unsure yet as to what counted as *emotional expressions*. *Emotional expressions* were interactional and therefore identifying them was not prescriptive. I examined my field notes for impressions of potential *emotional expressions* during class activities to identify which segments of the video recordings to transcribe. Drawing from Goodwin's (1994) framework for analyzing discursive practices, I highlighted the contents of discourse that conveyed emotions, making them more noticeable in both field notes and written artifacts. For instance, I highlighted direct quotes in my field notes that signaled potential *emotional expressions*, such as "not . . . extremely angry that people don't take action" and "I'm not extremely happy about it but I am not going

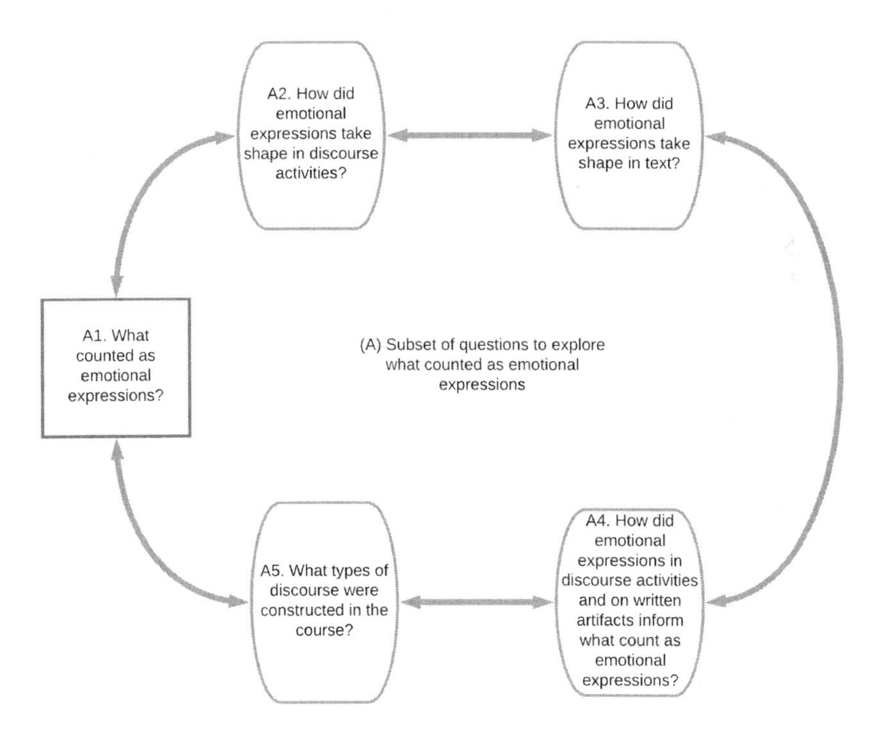

FIGURE 7.2 Subset of questions in the inquiry to explore what counted as emotional expressions.

to stop driving." I then went to the corresponding video recordings and watched and rewatched the segments. I drew on linguistic and paralinguistic features as well as gestures (see Hufnagel & Kelly, 2017) to inscribe these features in transcriptions to capture the expressions of emotions (A2 in Figure 7.2). As I made decisions about what counted as *emotional expressions* in discourse activities by utilizing my field notes and video recordings, I also concurrently examined how *emotional expressions* took shape in text (A3 in Figure 7.2). I highlighted potential *emotional expressions* on students' written artifacts, similarly to my approach for discourse events.

As I highlighted *emotional expressions* in each type of discourse, spoken and written, I referred to the initial potential markers of *emotional expressions* in each form of discourse to inform what may count as *emotional expressions* in the other type of discourse (A4 in Figure 7.2). I looked for instances of spoken discourse that had applicable features from the writing data set. For example, in my initial analysis of what counted as expressions of emotions, I highlighted instances of affect-type words to account for the range of ways people express emotions precisely (Barrett, 2006) as well as expressions of urgency in student writing. I then returned to the transcripts of spoken discourse to highlight instances of affect-type words and expressed urgency as potential instances of *emotional expressions.* While these words and phrases are not definitive markers of spoken emotions, they were instances I examined more closely to understand whether students were expressing emotions through contextualization cues. Hufnagel and Kelly (2017) explicate the micro-level analytical decisions of using semantics, contextualization, and linguistic features to determine what counted as *emotional expressions.* Semantics focused on coding for the content of expressions that included emotion words (i.e. scared, worried, guilty), affect words (i.e. bad, hurt), and personal value judgements (i.e. crazy, horrendous). Contextualization cues are verbal and nonverbal cues, such as prosody, gestures, intonation, pauses, outbreaths, and speed of speech, which convey particular situated meanings (Gumperz, 1982). Hufnagel and Kelly (2017) also identified linguistic features, including verb tense, point of view, and hedging, as integral to the nuanced ways participants expressed emotions.

Once I determined what counted as *emotional expressions* in discourse activities and written artifacts, I returned to my event map and coded the corresponding events and written artifacts as having emotional discourse. This process of demarcating emotional discourse led me to an interconnected analytic decision to consider what other types of discourse took shape during the course (A5 in Figure 7.2). While I was interested in the micro-level features of *emotional expressions* (A and B sub-questions), I also wondered how emotional discourse was part of the broader discourse of the entire course (A5 and D sub-questions). These other types of discourse, which were not mutually exclusive, were reflective (opinions, beliefs), science ideas and practices, teaching ideas and practices, and course logistics discourses.

B1. How Were Emotional Expressions Nuanced?

This question grew out of the generative (A) sub-questions about what counted as *emotional expressions*, as I noticed that *emotional expressions* took shape differently but with some consistent features. During the process of fine-grained analyses of potential *emotional expressions* (A1), particular dimensions of the expressions (B2 in Figure 7.3) became salient: aboutness, frequency, type, and ownership. Since these four dimensions are detailed in Hufnagel and Kelly (2017) in this section I describe the analytic decisions I made to explore the nuances of emotional expressions. I then elucidate how this piece of the inquiry led to new questions.

For this analysis, I focused on the archive I constructed in answering the subset of (A) questions: coded *emotional expressions* both in transcriptions from the classroom recordings and on the student written artifacts. I examined all the *emotional expressions* together, as an aggregate of the collective emotional sense-making, building upon my previous observations about different ways students expressed emotions. Through an abductive, iterative, and recursive process, I identified the four dimensions and codes within each dimension. However, as I began the process I started with different categorizations, as seen in Table 7.1. As I worked to determine what counted as explicit, implied, and ambiguous *emotional expressions*, I returned to the expressions to be systematic in my coding and noticed other nuances of the expressions, resulting in the identification of the four dimensions (B3 in Figure 7.3).

By attending to the nuances of the *emotional expressions*, I could analyze the dimensions to understand the nuances of *emotional expressions* in more depth (B4 in Figure 7.3). Exploring these dimensions required tallying, which is not out

TABLE 7.1 Emotional expression codes in the early stages of the logic of inquiry that would later evolve into four dimensions (aboutness, frequency, type, and ownership)

Type of emotional expression code	*Description*
Explicit	• Conveyed emotion through direct means like emotion words • Type of emotion discernable • About an aspect of climate change
Implied	• Conveyed emotion without emotion words • About an aspect of climate change
Ambiguous	• Conveyed emotion using ambiguous emotion words like "bad" or "upset" • About an aspect of climate change
Other	• Conveyed emotions with or without emotion words • About something other than climate change
None	• No communication of emotion

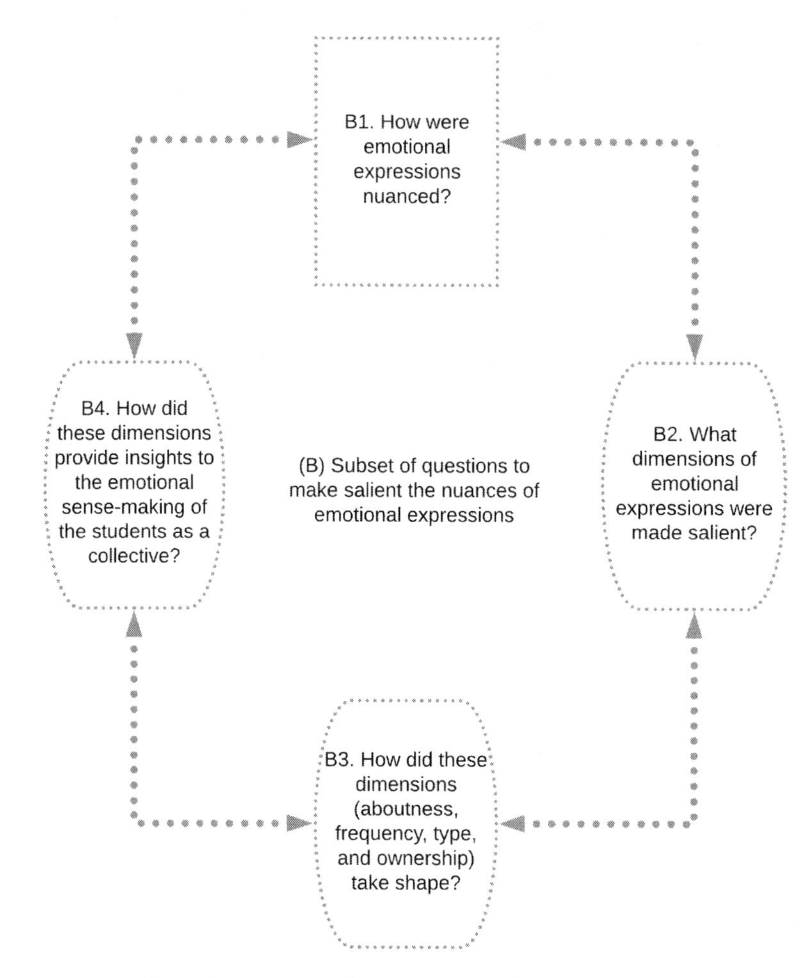

FIGURE 7.3 Subset of questions in the inquiry to make salient the nuances of emotional expressions.

of the realm of interactional ethnographic research (Heap, 1995). In doing so, I constructed different sets of archives using spreadsheet software to organize expressions by the dimensions (aboutness, frequency, type, and ownership), making salient aspects of the collective as well as individuals' emotional sense-making of climate change (C questions).

For the *aboutness* dimension, I developed a spreadsheet with every discourse activity and written assignment in which emotions about climate change were expressed. I tabulated how many *emotional expressions* were about each aspect of climate change (who/what causes it, who/what is impacted, who/what (should) address the problem, and severity/scale of the issue). I also included sub-codes within each aspect of climate change. For instance, *emotional expressions* about the impacts of climate change were about impacts on other people, themselves, and organisms other than humans (see Hufnagel, 2015).

I also accounted for the varied ways participants expressed *ownership* within their *emotional expressions* in the same spreadsheet. In addition to organizing the archives of *emotional expressions* by event and artifact, I also developed spreadsheets to track *emotional expressions* by aboutness and ownership by student. These spreadsheets proved useful for getting a sense of how individuals-within-the-collective emotionally made sense of different aspects of climate change (C questions).

For the *frequency* of *emotional expression* dimension, I returned to the event map to systematically represent this information both within the discourse activities and written artifacts. Including this code on the event map provided a zoomed-out view of the emotional discourse in the course, leading me to investigate why emotions were expressed differently across time and space (D questions).

Organizing a spreadsheet by the dimension of emotion *type* was also useful. First, it provided a way to get a sense of the range of emotion types expressed by the participants. Second, it illuminated "rich points" in the types of emotions expressed both within the study and compared to findings in previous educational research. For instance, guilt was a prominent emotion expressed (Hufnagel, 2015), which was unique in relation to the types of emotions previously researched in education. Furthermore, I drew from recent research about particular emotions in conjunction with the other dimensions to closely examine what those expressions indicated. Attending to the collective emotional sense-making to understand how *emotional expressions* are nuanced (B1), my logic unfolded to consider individual's emotional sense-making within-the-collective (C1).

C1. How Did Individuals-within-the-Collective Make Sense of Climate Change Emotionally?

While analyzing how the *emotional expressions* were nuanced (B questions) what became apparent in the archives were contrastive cases (Castanheira *et al.*, 2000; Kelly, 2014) of individuals' *emotional expressions* about climate change. Hence, I sought to examine how individual participants within a collective emotionally engaged with climate change.

The archived records I used for this analysis were spreadsheets I constructed in (B) to understand the dimensions of *emotional expressions*. I combined the four dimension spreadsheets (*aboutness*, emotion *frequency, type*, and *ownership*) into one and organized it by participant. I could then view which participants expressed which emotions (the *type*) about particular aspects of climate change (*aboutness*), how often in the course (*frequency*), and using which linguistic features to embrace or distance themselves from the expression (*ownership*). This compiled spreadsheet provided a landscape of the participants' emotional sense-making that I drew from when I returned to archives of participant interviews.

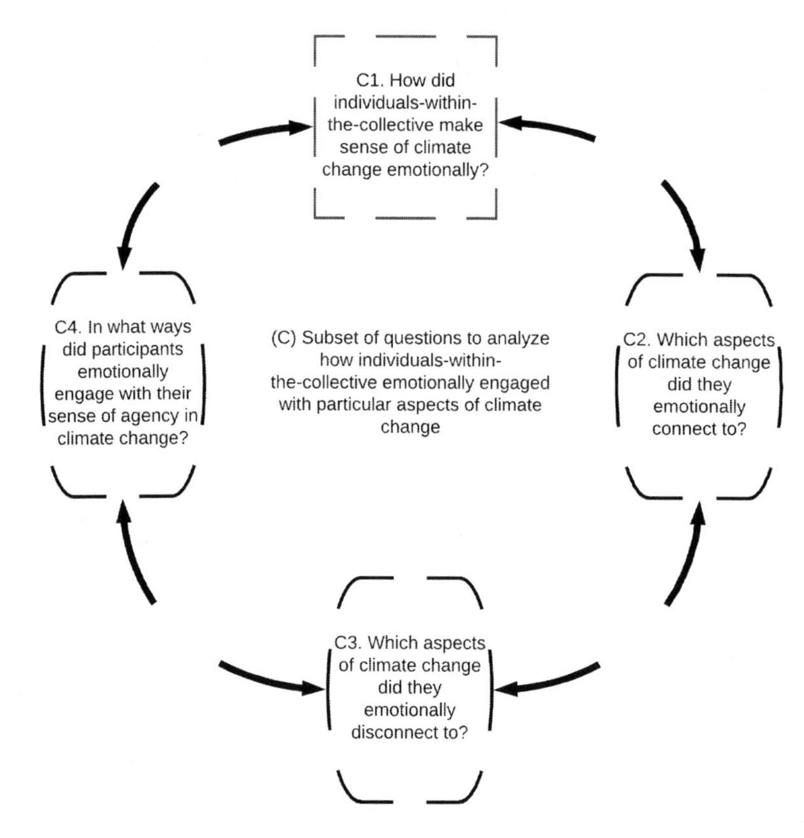

FIGURE 7.4 Subset of questions in the inquiry to analyze how individuals-within-the-collective emotionally engaged with particular aspects of climate change.

Due to the surprising number of the expressions of guilt (from question B4, Figure 7.3, and question C2, Figure 7.4), I was interested in learning more about the students' perceptions of their agency in climate change. The compilation of emotional expressions made salient tensions within overarching patterns about their collective sense of agency. I decided to explore these tensions on an individual level in more detail so I constructed another set of archives from which to do so (C4). While I had videos of interviews with numerous participants, seven students participated in both interviews (one in the first three weeks of the class and the second in the last two weeks of the class). These interviews were semi-structured and served to understand not only their emotional sense-making about climate change but their perceptions of the issue, nature more generally, and their role in ecosystem functioning. The second interview also provided me opportunities to ask clarifying questions about emotions they expressed throughout the course.

I rewatched the interview videos as I transcribed and coded the transcripts to examine how these seven participants perceived their agency in relation to their emotions. The analyses of these interviews were embedded in the ways I knew the culture of the course community (Spradley, 1980; Emerson *et al.*, 1995). Similar to my other coding processes, I used an abductive, iterative, and recursive approach to identifying codes about agency. Some of these codes captured their beliefs in the need for action and their perceptions of their own agency. I also coded for *emotional expressions*, utilizing the approach from the subset of (A) questions. As I coded the transcripts while watching the videos, I compared patterns about agency I was noticing to the participants' profiles of *emotional expressions* in the compiled spreadsheet. During this process, I noticed that the participants' *emotional expressions* during interviews were similar to those expressed during discourse activities and on written artifacts. In this way the emotions expressed in talk and text throughout the course were prevalent in the interviews as well, prompting me to wonder why emotions were expressed differently across time and space during the course (D questions).

D1. Why Were Emotions Expressed Differently Across Time and Space?

Throughout the inquiry, I experienced moments when my expectations for *emotional expressions* were different than the emotions expressed by members of the group. These "rich points" (Agar, 2006; Green *et al.*, 2012) made salient the cultural expectations for *emotional expressions* in the classroom, thereby serving as anchors to understand a phenomenon from an emic point of view. One such rich point involved my surprise during a particular discourse activity that seemed to have emotional undertones according to my field memo, but expressions on an exit slip immediately following were limited. Additionally, participants expressed emotions more often on written artifacts than in discourse activities, even when not specifically cued (Hufnagel, in press). These surprises led me to examine the framing of emotional discourse, as seen in the subset of questions in (D) of Figure 7.5.

These generative sub-questions gel around the question of "Why were emotions expressed differently across time and space?" (D1). In pursuit of answering this set of questions, I linked the analyses to the three other generative sub-questions (A1, B1, and C1) as their framing throughout the course were part and parcel of how they were expressed (A1, B1) and what the students found most relevant (C1).

This part of the inquiry involved constructing an archive of data that involved the event map, transcriptions of all events with *emotional expressions*, and all written artifacts with *emotional expressions*. Organizing the course activities into an event map provided a visual representation of how emotional discourse was patterned in the classroom. This part of the analysis painted a broad picture of the collective scale (Green, Skukauskaite, Dixon, & Córdova, 2007) whereby members jointly constructed meanings of emotional discourse. Hence, while the individual students were an integral part of the meaning-making of *emotional expressions*, the

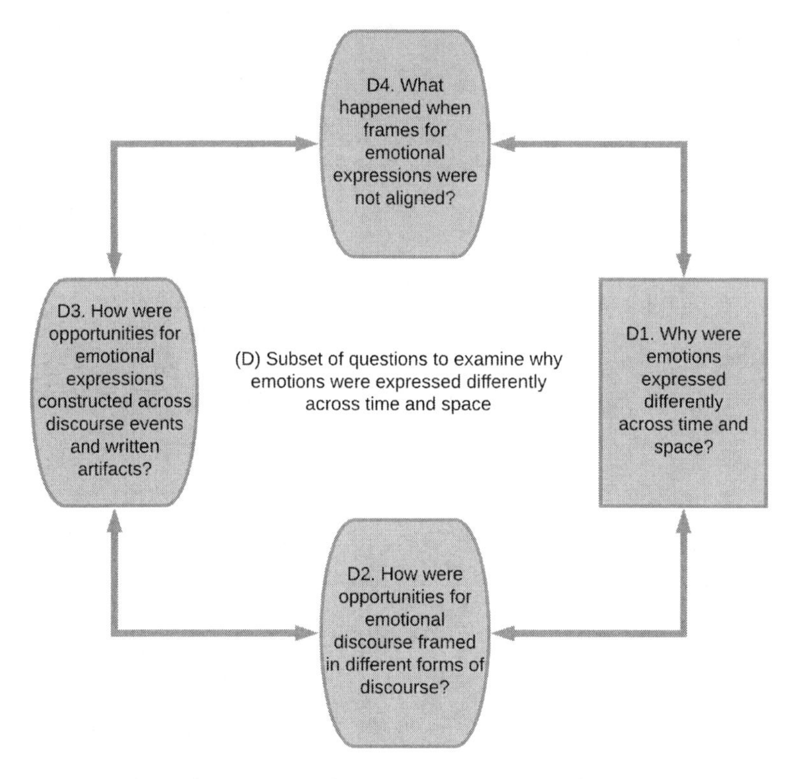

FIGURE 7.5 Subset of questions in the inquiry to examine why emotions were expressed differently across time and space.

patterned ways in which they constructed emotional discourse provided insight into what counted as *emotional expressions* (A1) within the collective actions and cultural norms of the group. In order to address this question, I performed analyses of separate sets of archived data (the event map, transcriptions of emotional expressions in discourse events, and written artifacts with emotional expressions) that I then used to build a case to identify reasons why emotions were expressed differently across time and space (D1).

The analytical process involved zooming-in to particular events with *emotional expressions* to understand the patterned ways in which emotions were expressed throughout the course. More specifically, I watched and rewatched the video recordings of events with different frequencies of *emotional expressions* to transcribe the full events in order to analyze them. An important piece of the transcription was capturing not only the linguistic, paralinguistic, and contextualization features of the members' communication but also their physical orientations. I continued to return to the video recordings to include more detail to transcripts as my inquiry progressed. This set of iterative and recursive coding of the archived data led me to explore how the members interactionally accomplished expectations, or frames (Green, 1983), for events with different frequencies of *emotional expressions*.

As I zoomed in and out of the archives to inquire about how emotions were expressed differently across time and space, I considered not only the framing of *emotional expressions* but any frame clashes that were constructed during events with *emotional expressions*. These frame clashes, or moments when members have differing expectations for the discussion (Green, 1983), prompted me to ask the question, (D4) "What happened when frames for *emotional expressions* were not aligned?" Frame clashes in discourse activities involved students expressing emotions without specific cues by the instructors and neither instructor nor another student picking up the expression in subsequent turns of talk. These events differed from those with multiple *emotional expressions* whereby specific sets of cues constituted through discursive moves and changing the physical orientation of members to not be seated in their usual table groups took shape in events with multiple *emotional expressions* (Hufnagel, in press). This sense of expectancy of emotions on the part of the instructor also indicated to me as a researcher that the students could still be emotionally making sense of climate change but not sharing it during class discussions. Hence, the analysis of written artifacts was also important in determining how participants emotionally connected to climate change outside of whole class discussions (B4 and C questions).

I performed a similar process with the written assignments, with an additional component. From being a participant observer, I knew the assignments were referenced in class, both leading up to their due dates and often following their submission. Hence, I returned to my field notes to identify when the assignments were referred to in class by member(s). I then watched and rewatched the video recordings of these moments to transcribe them, following a recursive transcription process as I did for identifying what counted as *emotional expressions* earlier. Coding these transcripts and the student assignments, I performed an intertextual analysis for how *emotional expressions* were framed across the semester (D2, D3) on written assignments.

Conclusion

Interactional ethnography and discourse analysis provided a framework to make analytical decisions about what counted as *emotional expressions* to examine the contextual nature of students' emotions about climate change across time and space during an environmental science course. In this chapter, I provided details of how my logic of inquiry took shape as I continued to collect and analyze data and understand what could be learned from *emotional expressions* about climate change. I focused on the four generative sub-questions that were part of my unfolding inquiry to illustrate the abductive, iterative, and recursive nature of this approach to *emotional expressions*. By approaching emotion research in this way, I addressed five specific challenges of researching emotions in situ in a classroom of 30 students with a wide range of emotional experiences about climate change throughout the entire course. In doing so, I explicated the systematic approaches I used in my logic of inquiry as transparency is critical for ethnographers engaging in constructions of social practices in the form of data archives or records (Green *et al.*, 2012). My hope is that this transparency will inform other scholars seeking to examine *emotional expressions* as interactional, contextual, intertextual, and consequential with a guide to many of my theoretical, methodological, and analytical decisions throughout the research project.

Despite decades of research demonstrating that models of deeply engaging with issues like climate change involve more than knowledge (see Chawla & Cushing, 2007; Hart & Nolan, 1999; Jensen & Schnack, 1997) the field of science education lags behind in exploring the intersection of learning and emotion. Research on emotions in science learning settings has provided a limited sense of the complexity and value of emotions in making sense of global issues due to both the historical dichotomization of emotion from reason and essentialized approaches to examining emotions. As public discourse about climate change becomes more contentious there is an urgency to understanding each other's emotions as expressed in the discourse in which they are constructed. Interactional ethnography and sociolinguistics together provides a means to analyze *emotional expressions* on a variety of levels to understand what is conveyed about a person's or a collective's emotions as well as how those expressions are shaped by interactionally accomplished norms. Attending to the richness and nuance of *emotional expressions* about climate change in research has implications for both the teaching and learning of climate change. A more comprehensive view of emotions can inform how science educators better support their own and their students' emotional sense-making of this burdensome issue, as teachers' emotions influence their instruction and views of climate change (e.g., Hufnagel, 2017; Lombardi & Sinatra, 2013).

References

Abu-Lughod, L., & Lutz, C. A. (1990). Introduction: Emotion, discourse, and the politics of everyday life. In C. A. Lutz & L. Abu-Lughod (Eds.), *Language and the politics of emotion* (pp. 1–23). Cambridge, UK: Cambridge University Press.

Agar, M. (2006). An ethnography by any other name . . . *Forum Qualitative Sozialforschung/ Forum: Qualitative Social Research*, 7, 271–292.

Agar, M. (2011). Making sense of one other for another: Ethnography as translation. *Language and Communication, 31*, 38–47. http://doi.org/10.1016/j.langcom.2010.05.001.

Barbalet, J. (2002). Science and emotions. In J. Barbalet (Ed.), *Emotions and sociology* (pp. 132–150). Malden, MA: Blackwell Publishing.

Barrett, L. F. (2006). Solving the emotional paradox: Categorization and the experience of emotion. *Personality and Social Psychology Review, 10*, 20–46.

Bellocchi, A., Ritchie, S. M., Tobin, K., Sandhu, M., & Sandhu, S. (2013). Exploring emotional climate in preservice science teacher education. *Cultural Studies of Science Education, 8*, 529–552. http://doi.org/10.1007/s11422-013-9526-3.

Boiger, M., & Mesquita, B. (2012). The construction of emotion in interactions, relationships, and cultures. *Emotion Review, 4*, 221–229.
Boler, M. (1999). *Feeling power: Emotions and education*. New York: Routledge.
Brickhouse, N. W. (2001). Embodying science: A feminist perspective on learning. *Journal of Research in Science Teaching, 38*, 282–295.
Broom, C. (2011). From tragedy to comedy: Reframing contemporary discourses. *International Journal of Environmental and Science Education, 6*, 123–138.
Broughton, S., Sinatra, G., & Nussbaum, E. (2013). "Pluto has been a planet my whole life!" Emotions, attitudes, and conceptual change in elementary students' learning about Pluto's reclassification. *Research in Science Education, 43*, 529–550.
Buijs, A., & Lawrence, A. (2013). Emotional conflicts in rational forestry: Towards a research agenda for understanding emotions in environmental conflicts. *Forest Policy and Economics, 33*, 104–111.
Caillaud, S., Bonnot, V., Ratiu, E., & Krauth-Gruber, S. (2016). How groups cope with collective responsibility for ecological problems: Symbolic coping and collective emotions. *British Journal of Social Psychology, 55*, 297–317. http://doi.org/10.1111/bjso.12126.
Campos, J. J., Walle, E. A., Dahl, A., & Main, A. (2011). Reconceptualizing emotion regulation. *Emotion Review, 3*, 26–35.
Castanheira, M. L., Crawford, T., Dixon, C. N., & Green, J. L. (2000). Interactional ethnography: An approach to studying the social construction of literate practices. *Linguistics and Education, 11*, 353–400.
Chawla, L., & Cushing, D. F. (2007). Education for strategic environmental behavior. *Environmental Education Research, 13*, 437–452.
Denzin, N. K. (1984). *On understanding emotion*. San Francisco, CA: Jossey-Bass Publishers.
Ekman, P., & Friesen, W. V. (1978). *Manual for the facial action coding system, part II*. Palo Alto, CA: Consulting Psychologists Press.
Emerson, R. M., Fretz, R. I., & Shaw, L. L. (1995). *Writing ethnographic fieldnotes*. Chicago, IL: University of Chicago Press.
Gifford, R. (2011). The dragons of inaction: Psychological barriers that limit climate change mitigation and adaptation. *American Psychologist, 66*, 290.
Gifford, R. (2014). Environmental psychology matters. *Annual Review of Psychology, 65*, 541-579.
Goodwin, C. (1994). Professional vision. *American Anthropologist, 96*, 606–633.
Green, J. L. (1983). Research on teaching as a linguistic process: A state of the art. *Review of Research in Education, 10*, 151–252.
Green, J. L., Skukauskaite, A., & Baker, W. D. (2012). Ethnography as epistemology: An introduction to educational ethnography. In J. Arthur, M. Waring, R. Coe, & L. V. Hedges (Eds.), *Research methodologies and methods in education* (pp. 309–321). London: Sage.
Green, J. L., Skukauskaite, A., Dixon, C., & Córdova, R. (2007). Epistemological issues in the analysis of video records: Interactional ethnography as a logic of inquiry. In R. Goldman, R. Pea, B. Barron, & S. Derry (Eds.), *Video research in the learning sciences* (pp. 115–132). Mahwah, NJ: Lawrence Erlbaum.
Gross, J. J., & Barrett, L. F. (2011). Emotion generation and emotion regulation: One or two depends on your point of view. *Emotion Review, 3*, 8–16.
Gumperz, J. (1982). *Discourse strategies*. Cambridge, UK: Cambridge University Press.
Gumperz, J. (2001). Interactional sociolingustics: A personal perspective. In D. Schiffrin, D. Tannen, & H. E. Hamilton (Eds.), *The handbook of discourse analysis* (pp. 215–228). Malden, MA: Blackwell Publishing.

Hargreaves, A. (1998). The emotional practice of teaching. *Teaching and Teacher Education, 14*, 835–854.

Hargreaves, A. (2000). Mixed emotions: Teachers' perceptions of their interactions with students. *Teaching and Teacher Education, 16*, 811–826.

Hart, P., & Nolan, K. (1999). A critical analysis of research in environmental education. *Studies in Science Education, 34*, 1–69.

Heap, J. L. (1995). The status of claims in "qualitative" educational research. *Curriculum Inquiry, 25*, 271–292.

Hornsey, M. J., & Fielding, K. S. (2016). A cautionary note about messages of hope: Focusing on progress in reducing carbon emissions weakens mitigation motivation. *Global Environmental Change, 39*, 26–34. http://doi.org/10.1016/j.gloenvcha.2016.04.003.

Hufnagel, E. (2015). Preservice elementary teachers' emotional connections and disconnections to climate change in a science course. *Journal of Research in Science Teaching, 52*, 1296–1324.

Hufnagel, E. (2017). Attending to emotional expressions about climate change: A framework for teaching and learning. In D. P. Shepardson, A. Roychoudhury, & A. Hirsch (Eds.), *Teaching and learning about climate change: A framework for educators* (pp. 43–55). New York: Routledge.

Hufnagel, E. (in press). Frames for emotional expressions across discourse in an ecology course. *International Journal of Science Education*. https://doi.org/10.1080/09500693.2018.1515512.

Hufnagel, E., & Kelly, G. J. (2017). Examining emotional expressions in discourse: Methodological considerations. *Cultural Studies of Science Education*. Advance online. http://doi.org/10.1007/s11422-017-9806-4.

Hufnagel, E., Kelly, G. J., & Henderson, J. A. (2018). How the environment is positioned in the Next Generation Science Standards: A critical discourse analysis. *Environmental Education Research, 24*, 731–753. http://doi.org/10.1080/13504622.2017.1334876.

Immordino-Yang, M., & Damasio, A. (2007). We feel, therefore we learn: The relevance of affective and social neuroscience to education. *Mind, Brain, and Education, 1*, 3–10.

Jaber, L. Z., & Hammer, D. (2016a). Engaging in science: A feeling for the discipline. *Journal of the Learning Sciences, 25*, 156–202. http://doi.org/10.1080/10508407.1015.1088441.

Jaber, L. Z., & Hammer, D. (2016b). Learning to feel like a scientist. *Science Education, 100*, 189–220. http://doi.org/10.1002/sce.21202.

Jasso, G. (2007). Emotion in justice processes. In J. E. Stets & J. H. Turner (Eds.), *Handbook of the sociology of emotions* (pp. 321–346). New York: Springer.

Jensen, B., & Schnack, K. (1997). The action competence approach in environmental education. *Environmental Education Research, 3*, 163–178.

Kappas, A. (2011). Emotion and regulation are one! *Emotion Review, 3*, 17–25. http://doi.org/10.1177/1754073910380971.

Kappas, A. (2013). Social regulation of emotion: Messy layers. *Frontiers in Psychology, 4*, 1–11. http://doi.org/10.3389/fpsyg.2013.00051.

Kelly, G. J. (2014). Analysing classroom activities: Theoretical and methodological considerations. In C. Bruguière, A. Tiberghien, & P. Clement (Eds.), *Topics and trends in current science education: 9th ESERA conference selected contributions* (pp. 353–368). Dordrecht, the Netherlands: Springer. http://doi.org/10.1007/978-94-007-7281-6.

Kelly, G. J. (2016). Methodological considerations for the study of epistemic cognition in practice. In J. A. Greene, W. A. Sandoval, & I. Braten (Eds.), *Handbook of epistemic cognition* (pp. 393–408). New York: Routledge.

Kelly, G. J., & Chen, C. (1999). The sound of music: Constructing science as sociocultural practices through oral and written discourse. *Journal of Research in Science Teaching, 36*, 883–915.

Keltner, D., & Gross, J. J. (1999). Functional accounts of emotions. *Cognition & Emotion, 13*, 467–480. http://doi.org/10.1080/026999399379140.

King, D., Ritchie, S. M., Sandhu, M., Henderson, S., & Boland, B. (2017). Temporality of emotion: Antecedent and successive variants of frustration when learning chemistry. *Science Education, 101*, 639–672. http://doi.org/10.1002/sce.21277.

Lombardi, D., & Sinatra, G. M. (2013). Emotions about teaching about human-induced climate change. *International Journal of Science Education, 35*, 167–191.

Mesquita, B., & Albert, D. (2007). The cultural regulation of emotions. In J. J. Gross (Ed.), *Handbook of emotion regulation* (pp. 486–503). New York: Guilford Press.

Milne, C., & Otieno, T. (2007). Understanding engagement: Science demonstrations and emotional energy. *Science Education, 91*, 523–553.

Mitchell, C. J. (1984). Typicality and the case study. In R. F. Ellens (Ed.), *Ethnographic research: A guide to general conduct* (pp. 238–241). New York: Academic Press.

Myers, T. A., Nisbet, M. C., Maibach, E. W., & Leiserowitz, A. A. (2012). A public health frame arouses hopeful emotions about climate change. *Climatic Change, 113*, 1105–1112. http://doi.org/10.1007/s10584-012-0513-6.

Nussbaum, M. (2001). *Upheavals of thought: The intelligence of emotions*. Cambridge, UK: Cambridge University Press.

Oatley, K. (1993). Social constructions of emotions. In M. Lewis & J. M. Haviland (Eds.), *Handbook of Emotions* (pp. 341–352). New York: Guilford Press.

Ojala, M. (2015). Hope in the face of climate change: Associations with environmental engagement and student perceptions of teachers' emotion communication style and future orientation. *The Journal of Environmental Education, 46*, 133–148. http://doi.org/10.1080/00958964.2015.1021662.

Olitsky, S. (2007). Promoting student engagement in science: Interaction rituals and the pursuit of a community of practice. *Journal of Research in Science Teaching, 44*, 33–56. http://doi.org/10.1002/tea.20128.

Olitsky, S. (2013). We teach as we are taught: Exploring the potential for emotional climate to enhance elementary science preservice teacher education. *Cultural Studies of Science Education, 8*, 561–570. http://doi.org/10.1007/s11422-013-9530-7.

Reser, J. P., & Swim, J. K. (2011). Adapting to and coping with the threat and impacts of climate change. *American Psychologist, 66*, 277–289.

Rivera Maulucci, M. S. (2013). Emotions and positional identity in becoming a social justice science teacher: Nicole's story. *Journal of Research in Science Teaching, 50*, 453–478. http://doi.org/10.1002/tea.21081.

Russell, J. A. (1994). Is there universal recognition of emotion from facial expression? A review of the cross-cultural studies. *Psychological Bulletin, 115*, 102–141. http://doi.org/10.1037/0033-2909.115.1.102.

Sadler, T. D., & Zeidler, D. L. (2004). The morality of socioscientific issues: Construal and resolution of genetic engineering dilemmas. *Science Education, 88*, 4–27. http://doi.org/10.1002/sce.10101.

Sadler, T. D., & Zeidler, D. L. (2005). Patterns of informal reasoning in the context of socioscientific decision making. *Journal of Research in Science Teaching, 42*, 112–138.

Shields, S. A. (2002). *Speaking from the heart*. Cambridge, UK: Cambridge University Press.

Shields, S. A. (2007). Passionate men, emotional women: Psychology constructs gender difference in the late 19th century. *History of Psychology, 10*, 92–110.

Sinatra, G. M., Broughton, S., & Lombardi, D. (2014). Emotions in science education. In R. Pekrun & L. Linnenbrink-Garcia (Eds.), *International handbook of emotions in education* (pp. 415–434). New York: Routledge.

Solomon, R. C. (2007). *True to our feelings: What our emotions are really telling us.* New York: Oxford University Press.

Spradley, J. P. (1980). *Participant observation.* Orlando, FL: Harcourt Brace Jovanovich College Publishers.

Swim, J. K., & Bloodhart, B. (2015). Portraying the peril to polar bears: The role of empathic and objective perspective taking toward animals in climate change communication. *Environmental Communication, 9*, 446–468. http://doi.org/0.1080/17524032.2014.987304.

Swim, J. K., Stern, P. C., Doherty, T. J., Clayton, S., Reser, J. P., Weber, E. U., . . . Howard, G. S. (2011). Psychology's contributions to understanding and addressing global climate change. *American Psychologist, 66*, 241–250.

Thomas, E. F., McGarty, C., & Mavor, K. I. (2009). Transforming "apathy into movement": The role of prosocial emotions in motivating action for social change. *Personality and Social Psychology Review, 13*, 310–333.

Tomas, L., & Ritchie, S. M. (2011). Positive emotional responses to hybridised writing about a socio-scientific issue. *Research in Science Education, 42*, 25–49.

van Veen, K., Sleegers, P., & van de Ven, P.-H. (2005). One teacher's identity, emotions, and commitment to change: A case study into the cognitive–affective processes of a secondary school teacher in the context of reforms. *Teaching and Teacher Education, 21*, 917–934.

Vining, J. (1987). Environmental decisions: The interaction of emotions, information, and decision context. *Journal of Environmental Psychology*, 7, 13–30.

Warner, L. R., & Shields, S. A. (2009). Status, gender, and the politics of emotional authenticity. In M. Salmela & V. Mayer (Eds.), *Emotions, ethics, and authenticity.* Philadelphia, PA: John Benjamins Publishing Company.

Watts, M. (2005). Science as poetry: Passion v. prescription in school science? In S. Aslop (Ed.), *Beyond Cartesian dualism: Encountering affect in the teaching and learning of science* (Vol. 23, pp. 197–208). Dordrecht, the Netherlands: Springer.

White, G. M. (2000). Representing emotional meaning: Category, metaphor, schema, discourse. In M. Lewis & J. M. Haviland-Jones (Eds.), *Handbook of emotions* (2nd ed., pp. 30–44). New York: Guilford Press.

Wickman, P.-O. (2006). *Aesthetic experience in science education: Learning and meaning-making as situated talk and action.* Mahwah, NJ: Lawrence Erlbaum.

Zembylas, M. (2004a). Emotional issues in teaching science: A case study of a teacher's views. *Research in Science Education, 34*, 343–364.

Zembylas, M. (2004b). Emotion metaphors and emotional labor in science teaching. *Science Education, 88*, 301–324.

Zembylas, M. (2004c). Young children's emotional practices while engaged in long-term science investigation. *Journal of Research in Science Teaching, 41*, 693–719. http://doi.org/10.1002/tea.20023.

Zembylas, M. (2005). Emotions and science teaching: Present research and future agendas. In S. Aslop (Ed.), *Beyond Cartesian dualism: Encountering affect in the teaching and learning of science* (Vol. 23, pp. 123–132). Dordrecht, the Netherlands: Springer.

Zembylas, M. (2016). Making sense of the complex entanglement between emotion and pedagogy: Contributions of the affective turn. *Cultural Studies of Science Education, 11*, 539–550. http://doi.org/10.1007/s11422-014-9623-y.

8

DISCOURSE OF PROFESSIONAL PEDAGOGICAL VISION IN TEACHER EDUCATION

Arzu Tanis Ozcelik and Scott P. McDonald

Learning Ambitious Practices

There has been an emphasis in science education reform documents on the practices of science for many years (NRC, 1996, 2000, 2007, 2012) and most recently, the *Next Generation Science Standards* (NGSS Lead States, 2013) framed participating in science practices and discourses of science as a critical part of students' science learning. Related research in science classrooms has demonstrated the importance of discourse (Kelly, 2011; Kelly & Crawford, 1997; Lemke, 1990; Roth, 2005), and how participating in authentic discourse forms a core part of participation in a disciplinary community (Lemke, 1990). The ways in which teachers engage students in *talking science* (Lemke, 1990; Moje, 1995; Roth, 1996) shape *what counts as* (Heap, 1991) science, as well as defining the epistemic knowledge students can develop through such discourses (Kelly, 2008, 2016). Thus, classroom science discourse constitutes a curriculum of science-in-the-making (Kelly, Chen, & Crawford, 1998).

The historic attention to the importance of authentic discourse in science education and its foundation in sociocultural perspectives on learning (e.g., Vygotsky, 2012; Brown, Collins, & Duguid, 1989) influenced reforms proposed in NGSS, in particular in terms of framing science learning in terms of science and engineering practices, which are accomplished through discourse. These new proficiency expectations and goals call for teachers to provide learning environments that promote engaging students discursively and interactively with disciplinary core ideas, scientific practices and discourses, and crosscutting concepts (e.g., systems thinking, scale, and function). Preservice teachers in the US, therefore, are expected to approach teaching through this reform-based orientation and to develop strategies for engaging students in productive discourse that develop understandings of the big ideas in science, as well as the processes and practices of science. Ambitious science teaching practices (Windschitl, Thompson, Braaten, & Stroupe, 2012) were characterized to provide guidance for preservice teachers (and practicing teachers) to organize classroom learning environments around productive discourses and practices of science. As these practices form the focus of our analysis, we will provide some detail about them before describing the details of our methodological approach.

Windschitl, Thompson, and Braaten (2011) suggested specific practices that could be tied to student thinking, and proposed high-leverage practices (HLPs) as the core repertoire of ambitious teaching: "ambitious teaching deliberately aims to get students of all racial, ethnic, class, and gender categories to understand science ideas, participate in the discourses of the discipline, and solve authentic problems" (p. 1315). They argue that this kind of pedagogy is both adaptive to students' needs and thinking and maintains high standards of achievement for all learners and identified four core teaching practices: planning for engagement with big ideas in science, eliciting student ideas, supporting ongoing changes in thinking, and pressing for evidence-based explanations (Windschitl et al., 2012).

By "big ideas" they refer to relationships between phenomena in the natural world and the scientific models that help students understand, explain, and predict various aspects of those phenomena. During planning for engagement with a big idea, teachers select complex natural phenomena or events representing the big ideas that students can relate to and that teachers can develop into the focus of a unit to help students develop explanatory models. The second practice of eliciting students' ideas, initiates the instruction and targets students' initial understandings of the phenomena and provides formative assessment to adapt instruction based on students' ideas. Supporting ongoing changes in thinking, focuses on laboratory work, readings, and other activities that build content knowledge and advance students' conceptual understanding of components of the phenomena of interest. Teachers are expected to engage students in material activity and discourse around the material activity to help students understand the science while participating in disciplinary practices. Finally, pressing students for evidence-based explanations aims to assist students in co-constructing a summative and evidence-based explanatory model for the phenomena. In this practice, students are expected to draw on all the investigations, readings, and experiences to finalize their explanatory models.

In the context of the student science practices advocated by the NGSS and ambitious science teaching designed to support them, this study examines how preservice science teachers develop professional pedagogical vision during a science teaching methods course. Using an ethnographic case study design and grounded theory analysis, we consider the ways that preservice teachers learn to see and negotiate ambitious science teaching (AST) practices. Both the novelty, as well as the richness and complexity, of ambitious science teaching as an approach to teaching requires significant negotiation and acculturation for preservice teachers. The teachers engaged in ambitious science teaching are essentially learning how to communicate in new ways that support their science students in acting and talking in new ways. A teacher education context focused on developing ambitious science teaching practices entails preservice teachers engaging in meta-level conversations about both teaching practices and student practices. This has the potential to create a wonderfully rich context for the investigation of the development of teaching expertise.

This study specifically examines, through analysis of the discourse among preservice teachers and their instructor, how preservice teachers co-construct this previously unfamiliar approach, and the practices they develop to undertake a new teaching model. In this chapter, we attempt to reflexively unpack our logic of use as we engaged in the analysis of a group of *preservice teachers* in the fourth year of their teacher education program in science education at a research-focused university in the Mid-Atlantic region of the US. Our research regarding preservice teachers developing professional vision for ambitious science teaching in science teaching methods course provides contribution and implications for the investigation of contexts where scholars are attempting to understand complex, inter-contextual, multilayered cultural construction through discourse.

Professional Pedagogical Vision

Learning to teach is complex and it has been studied in a variety of ways over the decades of teacher education. Understanding how beginning teachers develop their nascent expertise is particularly critical as initial teacher preparation is such a small window of time. Investigating the negotiation of preservice teachers' beginning expertise can help teacher educators to understand the process of preservice teachers' learning to identify, analyze, and create their own initial models of ambitious science teaching practices. This work is part of what in recent years has become a growing area of research that has focused on teachers' learning of core or high-leverage teaching practices (Ball & Forzani, 2009; McDonald, Kazemi, & Kavanagh, 2013). Teacher educators can better understand preservice teachers' sense making around high-leverage teaching practices through research around their engagement with (Lampert, Franke, Kazemi, Ghousseini, Turrou, Beasley, & Crowe, 2013), and analysis of, practice (McDonald, 2016). We conceptualize preservice teachers' expertise in terms of their professional vision, which Charles Goodwin (1994) defined as "socially organized ways of seeing and understanding events that are answerable to the distinctive interests of a particular social group" (p. 606).

In this study, teacher learning is considered as a sociocultural and situated activity in which preservice teachers negotiate understandings and practices of ambitious science teaching, as they interact in discourse communities over time (Lave & Wenger, 1991; Vygotsky, 2012). Sociocultural and situated lenses on teacher learning draw our attention to the nature of teachers' participation in activities (Putnam & Borko, 2000) as they participate in the course designed to support ambitious science teaching (in-the-making). As preservice teachers interact with other members of their discourse communities, we consider how they develop professional pedagogical vision for teaching and learning.

While preservice teachers will be building these practices in their local community, no community is independent. We consider the nature of communities of K-12 students nested in communities of preservice teachers and teachers, and communities of teachers and preservice teachers are then nested in communities of teacher educators, and finally, communities of teacher educators are nested within the larger community of researchers and policy makers in science education. All of these communities interact through discourses and these discourses are critical to the creation of professional pedagogical vision.

Charles Goodwin described professional vision through examples of the discursive practices of an archeologist in the field and police in courtroom testimony during the Rodney King trial. In the first example, Goodwin's (1994) study of archeologists' discourse and social practices demonstrated the ways archeologists study color, consistency, and texture of dirt through getting a sample with a trowel, highlight it by squirting it with water, and then hold the sample under holes cut into the Munsell color chart (which is used by archeologists all over the world as a standard for color descriptions). Through these processes, novice archeologists were able to learn to see dirt samples through professionally disciplined perception (Stevens & Hall, 1998) by participating with more knowledgable members of the relevant epistemic community.

Building on his perspective grounded in linguistic anthropology, Goodwin conceptualized professional vision in terms of the cultural production of disciplinary practices through discourse, broadly construed. Using his approach led us to consider cultural dimensions of learning how to teach and, in particular, the relevance of discourse analysis for understanding professional pedagogical vision in teacher education. Given the prominent role of discourse processes and practices in the ambitious science teaching practices, as well as in the conceptual framework of professional vision by Charles Goodwin (1994), our research methodologies needed to target these discourse-rich social practices. As preservice teachers interact with other members of the discourse communities, we consider how they develop professional pedagogical vision for teaching and learning. By looking at their discussions of teaching events and discourse around their analysis of teaching, this study makes claims regarding how beginning teachers develop professional pedagogical vision. This study follows preservice teachers in their early science teaching experiences when they are in the science teaching methods course as they make sense and build knowledge, practices, and commitments regarding teaching science.

Studying professional pedagogical vision in the teacher education context brings challenges for the researchers. The purpose of this chapter is to lay out in detail our "logic of inquiry" (Green, Dixon, & Zaharlick, 2003), to better characterize how complex learning contexts like these can be better understood. Teacher education contexts have a particular complexity in the form of interacting and meta-levels of practice (Windschitl & Stroupe, 2017), where there are students, preservice teachers, mentor teachers, and teacher educators in nested systems of discourse. In this chapter we make visible in detail the intricacies of doing empirical, discourse-focused work in these interlaced discourse communities. Later in the chapter, we describe the methodological challenges we faced, including: identified weaknesses in data collection, the challenge of untangling the constructs of highlighting and coding from Goodwin's framework, as well as the nature of Goodwin's (1994) material representations in this teacher education context. We also describe our approaches to managing these challenges.

Research Methods

In this section, we will detail the design decisions implicated in carrying out the data collection and analysis of our study. We begin by describing the general approach and context for the study, then present the research questions, followed by details about the phases of data analysis. All of this is an attempt to describe both our logic of inquiry and our logic of use as it evolved through the course of the project.

Design of the Study

The research design of this study is an ethnographic case study informed by ethnographic methods. This approach follows as a direct result of our theoretical framework and in particular an attention to the *in situ* construction of taken-as-shared understandings about the world through discourse. We examined a case of professional pedagogical visions of preservice science teachers who were enrolled in the second science teaching methods course in a teacher education program. We considered this study as a single embedded case study with multiple participants because the larger context of the study included the Science Teaching Methods II and the participants were bounded by the course. Even though there were multiple physical contexts when the preservice teachers went to the schools for field experiences, we considered the boundaries of the case to be students in the science teaching methods course with a field experience component. Thus, we examined how the professional pedagogical vision developed during the course and how preservice teachers negotiated the meaning of ambitious science teaching. This study was a representative or typical case of the science teaching methods course, which has a field placement component and includes peer-teaching rehearsals. However, it is also unique in the sense that it focuses on professional vision with ambitious science teaching practices. Including embedded subunits in the single case design allowed significant opportunities for extensive analysis and enhances the insights into the single case (Yin, 2009).

We used the case study to demarcate the boundaries of the inquiry, however, the study is ethnographic in nature because we made theoretical inferences through situated, detailed, and over-time analysis of the discussion of the preservice teachers with their instructor in the science teaching methods course. Through following preservice teachers in two consecutive science teaching methods courses as well as a seminar course, we wanted to capture how preservice teachers construct opportunities to develop professional pedagogical vision. Details of these courses will be provided in the next sections.

Context and the Participants of the Study

The context of this study included the secondary science teaching methods II course and the secondary education clinical application of instruction course, a seminar course the preservice teachers are concurrently enrolled in in a large Mid-Atlantic university's teacher education program as well as the four secondary schools in two districts where the preservice teachers were in their field placements. Preservice teachers were in the science teaching methods course for the first five weeks, then they went to field experience for six weeks and then they came back to the science teaching methods course for the last four weeks in a 15-week semester. They met for three hours two days a week. The course is the second science teaching methods course in the teacher preparation program. The science teaching methods course design draws on research on video analysis in teacher education (McDonald & Rook, 2014) as a form of deconstruction of practice (Grossman & McDonald, 2008), as well as rehearsals (Lampert *et al.*, 2013) as approximations of practice, and curricular planning in the form of a coherent content storyline (Roth, Garnier, Chen, Lemmens, Schwille, & Wickler, 2011).

The participants include six preservice teachers (four female and two male), their instructors, and the preservice teachers' mentor teachers. The details of their background are provided in Table 8.1. Four of the preservice teachers were certified in biology and one was certified in chemistry and one was certified in physics. Most of the preservice teachers' previous science teaching experience was limited to microteaching experiences in their previous science teaching methods course. The second author was the science education faculty in the study, and had ten years of experience as an education professor and six years' prior experience as a physics teacher. Their supervisor for their field placement and seminar course was a retired biology teacher with 40 years of experience. Debbie's and Erika's (see Table 8.1) mentor teachers were experienced chemistry and integrated science teachers in the same school district.

We wanted to follow preservice teachers from the first science teaching methods course to the second science teaching methods course to the field experience in order to understand how they develop ideas and practices about teaching. Two of the preservice teachers attended the previous science teaching methods course

TABLE 8.1 Participant background

Participants	*Major*	*Previous Teaching Experience*	*Field Experience Placement Grade/Subject*
Abby	Preservice teacher: Secondary Education Biology	Microteaching in the first science teaching course, previous field experience for one semester	9th Grade Biology class
Erika	Preservice teacher: Secondary Education Biology	Microteaching only in the first science teaching course	7th Grade Integrated Science and 8th Grade Physical Science
Debbie	Preservice teacher: Secondary Education Chemistry	Microteaching only in the first science teaching course	11th Grade Chemistry
Kayla	Preservice teacher: Secondary Education Biology	Microteaching only in the first science teaching course	9th Grade Biology class
Bryan	Preservice teacher: Secondary Education Physics	Microteaching only in the first science teaching course	No field experience
Mark	Preservice teacher: Secondary Education Biology	Microteaching in the first science teaching course, tutoring, a university course assistant	No field experience
Sean	Science Education Faculty	Six years K-12 science/physics teaching and ten years of science education faculty	Science teaching methods II course
Neal	Supervisor, Biology teacher	40 years of K-12 Science teaching, six years of college supervisor	Secondary education application of instruction course
Mr. Young (Debbie's mentor teacher)	Chemistry teacher	40 years of teaching experience	11th and 12th Grade honors and academic level Chemistry
Mr. Hersey (Erika's mentor teacher)	Integrated Science teacher	13 years of teaching experience	7th Grade Life Science and 8th Grade Physical Science

in the previous years. Four of the preservice teachers attended the first science teaching methods course together in the previous semester, so the first author was able to follow the four preservice teachers in the first science teaching methods course in the program. We have fieldnotes and course materials from that class as well. We had a low number of students in that semester in the program due to a range of different social, political, and academic factors. Since then the program has returned to the typical numbers of approximately 15–20 students.

Data Sources

We used ethnographic methods during the data collection and relied on multiple data sources including ethnographic fieldnotes (Emerson, Fretz, & Shaw, 2011); participant observation (Spradley, 1980) of the course; video recordings of the course; interviews with preservice teachers around their rehearsals, their field experience, and the course overall; interviews with instructors; and collected documents and the artifacts from the assignments and the course materials. The details of the data sources and their quantity were provided in Table 8.2 on page 189. This study was part of a dissertation study, so it includes a larger data set, but we analyzed only the video records of the science teaching methods II course, fieldnotes of the course, and 12 video analyses done by the preservice teachers of their own discourse 1 teaching (six) and ambitious science teaching exemplar videos of Bethany's teaching[1] (six) for all preservice teachers from the artifacts.

Researchers' Roles

In order to best understand how preservice teachers are co-constructing their professional vision through their shared experiences in the teacher education program, it was important for the researchers to be a legitimate participant in the social context. In this study, the first author was responsible for data collection and analysis, was a participant observer in the classroom, and also an interviewer. She attended all the meetings of the science teaching methods II course and the secondary education clinical application of instruction course with the preservice teachers. She video recorded all the interactions in the science teaching methods II course and collected any documents used in the courses to further her insights into answering the research questions. She also attended the first course in secondary science teaching methods during the semester when four of the participants were taking that course. She observed the class, took fieldnotes, and collected course materials. The purpose of that observation was to learn where preservice teachers were coming from in terms of their prior knowledge and experiences in teaching, and what course materials/readings they had before coming to the second science teaching methods course, and to make herself familiar to the participants.

TABLE 8.2 Research questions, data corpus, and analysis

Research Questions	*Data Sources*	*Duration (Quantity)*	*Data Analysis Undertaken*
How does the professional pedagogical vision (PPV) of science preservice teachers develop around ambitious science teaching practices in a semester-long secondary science teaching methods course?	Video records of Science Teaching Methods II course	48 hours (total of 96 hours from two angles)	Transcripts Video analysis Event maps Discourse analysis
	Interviews	24 pre–post, 4 field experience 5 exit interviews for all preservice teachers 1 interview with each instructor	Not analyzed for this study
	Fieldnotes	16 class-sections of science teaching methods II course and 11 class-sections of secondary education clinical application of instruction course	Transcripts Event maps
	Documents and artifacts	22 Rapid Student Survey Tools (RSSTs) for four preservice teachers 12 video analyses of preservice teachers' own discourse – 1 teaching (6) and of Bethany's teaching (6) for all preservice teachers 4 supervisor-feedback for four preservice teachers 24 lesson plans All class materials for science teaching methods II course and secondary education clinical application of instruction course	Transcripts Video analysis Discourse analysis for 12 video analyses. The rest of the documents and artifacts were not analyzed for this study
How do preservice teachers negotiate meaning of ambitious science teaching when they engage in discussions in the first five weeks of methods course?	Fieldnotes	16 class-sections of science teaching methods II course and 11 class-sections of secondary education clinical application of instruction course	Transcripts Event maps
	Video records of Science Teaching Methods II course	48 hours (total of 96 hours from two angles)	Transcripts Video analysis Event maps Discourse analysis

The second author was the instructor of the science teaching methods II course, as well as the dissertation advisor for the first author. The second author, as the instructor of the course, had pedagogical goals to help preservice teachers analyze teaching videos of ambitious science teaching, to have them develop a curricular plan for a unit of instruction, and have them rehearse teaching lessons around the discourse practices. The instructor allowed instructional planning in the classroom to support preservice teachers in designing instruction through in-class and video analysis feedback around their lesson plans and enactment. He saw the big purpose of the discourse practices in ambitious science teaching as being about helping students develop explanations around a phenomenon starting with their own ideas. He aims to support preservice teachers through engaging them in these science practices through tools developed by the University of Washington (https://ambitiousscienceteaching.org/), and through cycles of rehearsal and video analysis and replanning of the practices.

The authors had meetings and conversations throughout the duration of the course to talk about the course and share ideas about students and ongoing analysis. So, both of the authors had an insider view of what was going on in the course.

Data Analysis

It was important to us to have findings emerge from the data we collected, but we also had an a priori perspective on both the practices we wanted to see develop (namely ambitious science teaching) and the practices we expected to describe the process of that development (namely the practices of professional vision). We took a grounded theory approach (Corbin & Strauss, 2007) to analyze the data in this study starting with open coding, grouping the codes, and creating coding categories. With that said, our initial codes originated from the discourse practices of ambitious science teaching practice, and from the core constructs of the professional vision framework. Codes did emerge during the analysis, but we drew from both sociocultural theory and linguistic anthropology to frame key constructs in the study. Within the overall frame of grounded theory, discourse analysis was used to determine the meaning-making and negotiation of professional pedagogical vision from the social interactions and as evidenced in the classroom discourse. So, grounded theory was the overarching approach, and discourse analysis was used within that approach, especially during the open coding process. Kelly (2014b) described how discourse processes are situated in social practice and should be studied in the context of use. Discourse analysis based on interactional sociolinguistics theory (Gee & Green, 1998; Gumperz, 2001; Green & Castanheira, 2012) was used to determine the discourse analytic units. Thus, we wanted to understand how the classroom members negotiate and develop cultural norms in the form of professional pedagogical vision through moment-by-moment discourse interactions.

While the video analysis and creating event maps constituted the macro level analysis of video records, the discourse analysis of the transcription of selected events constituted the micro level analysis of the study. This level of detailed approach helped us *zoom in to understand instances of action* (Kelly, 2014a). During the coding process, we wrote analytical memos to describe the episodes as well as chronologically keep track of emerging code descriptions and example episodes. Writing memos helped us group the episodes in certain codes and write explanations for the code descriptions. Thus, keeping track of codes in a chronological manner helped us *zoom out to view patterns of activity* (Kelly, 2014a) within the discourse over time for the members of the science teaching methods course. We have two main phases of analysis of video records and describe the details of these phases below.

Phase 1: Video Analysis, Creation of Event Maps, and Choosing What to Transcribe

The purpose of the first phase of data analysis was to describe how we sampled the video data to *zoom in* from large video records to decide what the "data" are within the collected video records. Video recordings and fieldnotes constitute the primary data sources for the study. The data analyses for the video recordings include macro and micro level analysis. Macro level analysis includes analyzing videos with Studio Code (https://vosaic.com/products/studiocode) to identify the type and range of events happening in each class, creating event maps at the macro level (Kelly & Chen, 1999; Kelly, Brown, & Crawford, 2000; McDonald & Kelly, 2007), and choosing events to transcribe in detail at the level of spoken discourse and action. A bounded activity around a topic and purpose can constitute the event (e.g., curriculum planning, observing model teacher). The changes in the events can be determined through looking at the changes in purpose, type of activity, and topic (Kelly, 2004). We constructed event maps through our analysis of videos in the Studio Code timelines, shown in Figure 8.1, and through reading the fieldnotes for each day. The event maps were constructed by looking at how time was spent, on what, and for what purpose (Kelly, 2004). We provided a snapshot of a page of an event map in Figure 8.2. The event maps are organized around days of instruction and what assignments preservice teachers were supposed to do for that day, the time stamps devoted for each event, and the list of events. Then we made connections to the coding we have done, which is described in the second phase of the analysis.

After identifying the events, we selected events where the class had discussions around science teaching as a form of purposeful sampling. Because the research questions we are interested in investigating are about preservice teachers' professional pedagogical visions around teaching practices, we did purposeful sampling and transcribed those events where there was discussion of teaching. The selected events are highlighted in Figure 8.2. Thus, macro level analysis also allowed us

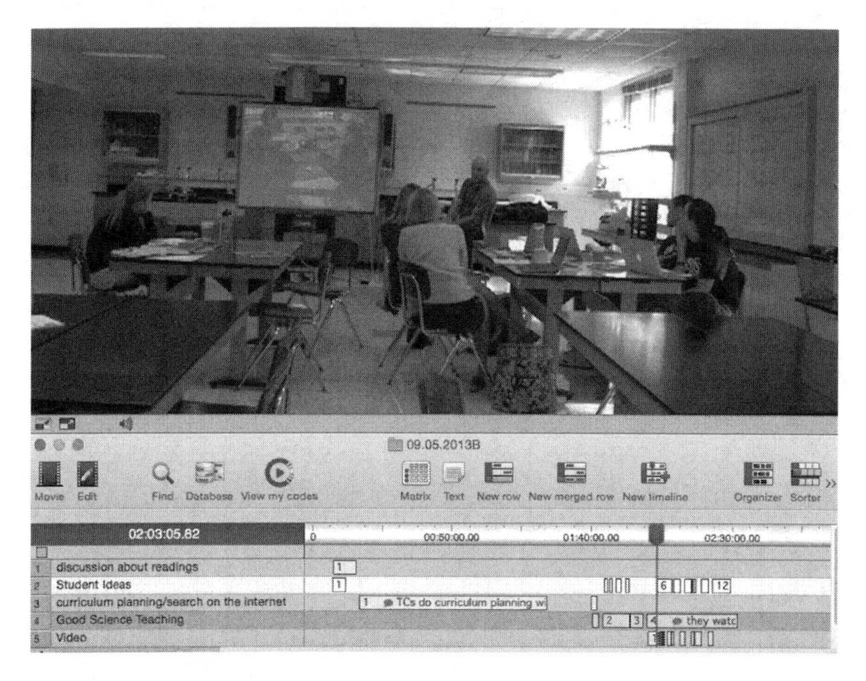

FIGURE 8.1 Example Studio Code timeline.

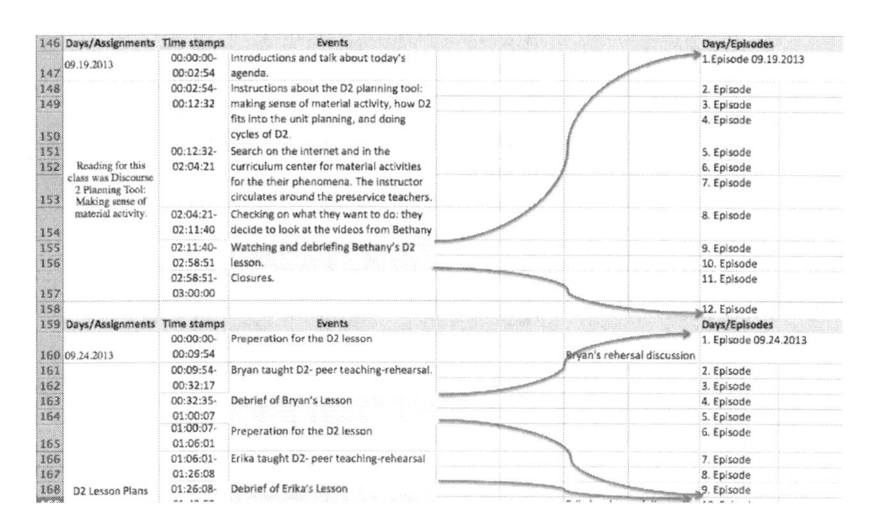

146	Days/Assignments	Time stamps	Events		Days/Episodes
147	09.19.2013	00:00:00-00:02:54	Introductions and talk about today's agenda.		1.Episode 09.19.2013
148		00:02:54-	Instructions about the D2 planning tool:		2. Episode
149		00:12:32	making sense of material activity, how D2		3. Episode
150			fits into the unit planning, and doing cycles of D2.		4. Episode
151		00:12:32-	Search on the internet and in the		5. Episode
152	Reading for this class was Discourse 2 Planning Tool: Making sense of material activity.	02:04:21	curriculum center for material activities		6. Episode
153			for the their phenomena. The instructor circulates around the preservice teachers.		7. Episode
154		02:04:21-02:11:40	Checking on what they want to do: they decide to look at the videos from Bethany		8. Episode
155		02:11:40-	Watching and debriefing Bethany's D2		9. Episode
156		02:58:51	lesson.		10. Episode
157		02:58:51-03:00:00	Closures.		11. Episode
158					12. Episode
159	Days/Assignments	Time stamps	Events		Days/Episodes
160	09.24.2013	00:00:00-00:09:54	Preperation for the D2 lesson	Bryan's rehersal discussion	1. Episode 09.24.2013
161		00:09:54-	Bryan taught D2- peer teaching-rehearsal.		2. Episode
162		00:32:17			3. Episode
163		00:32:35-	Debrief of Bryan's Lesson		4. Episode
164		01:00:07			5. Episode
165		01:00:07-01:06:01	Preperation for the D2 lesson		6. Episode
166		01:06:01-	Erika taught D2- peer teaching-rehearsal		7. Episode
167		01:26:08			8. Episode
168	D2 Lesson Plans	01:26:08-	Debrief of Erika's Lesson		9. Episode

FIGURE 8.2 A section of the event map showing the highlighted transcribed events and episodes within each event. (The figure shows columns with the date and associated assignments on that day, time spent on each event, event names/descriptors. Then, we linked the episodes for the transcribed events. Highlighted/shaded events are transcribed.)

to situate actions in sequences of activity and to select data to help us answer the research questions. We transcribed the classroom discourse of those selected events. This first phase of analysis served as a basis for the more detailed analysis in phase 2 we describe below. We only transcribed discourse at the level of talk and action around teaching. We completed Studio Code video analysis, created event maps, and transcribed selected events for the first five weeks and the last four weeks of the science teaching methods II course.

Phase 2: Coding, Creating Coding Framework, Example Episodes

The purpose of the second phase of data analysis was to describe how we started our analysis with more focused detailed discourse analysis based on transcripts of talk, and then how we *zoomed out* from the detailed analysis to create themes and claims based on the patterns we see in our analysis. Thus, this second phase analysis includes both zooming in with micro-interactional level analysis, and then zooming out to look for larger patterns and themes within the analyzed data.

After transcribing the purposefully selected events, we took grounded theory approach (Corbin & Strauss, 2007) to analyze the transcripts, starting with open coding, then grouping the codes, and creating the categories of codes. Since we were interested in understanding the collective meaning-making of science teaching in the discussions of teaching, we coded for the group conversations including the instructor's input as part of the group. We started with open coding based on what the classroom members said in the discussions of teaching, and as the new codes emerged, we added them in the coding framework table, where we have descriptions and episode numbers. During the open coding process, discourse analysis based on interactional sociolinguistics theory (Gee & Green, 1998; Gumperz, 2001; Green & Castanheira, 2012; Kelly, 2014b; Castanheira, Crawford, Dixon, & Green, 2001) was used to determine the discourse analytic units. While coding, we decided when the focus/content of the conversation changed we would treat it as the end of an instance, thus we chose episodes as the unit of analysis. Also, discourse markers (mostly from the instructor's discourse such as "okay," "so") and paying attention to the instructor's use of video segments to look at the practice of teaching helped us determine the boundary of units. Episodes could consist of one or more turns of talk, which is similar to what other researchers (e.g., Kelly, 2004; Kelly, Crawford, & Green, 2001) identify as sequence units, cohesive thematically tied interactions identified *post hoc* through semantic and contextual cues. Considering episodes as the unit of analysis helped us structure and organize the data and to be able to talk about the content of their discussions in time and how those discussions changed over time. Also considering episodes as the unit of analysis helped us understand how the classroom members made sense and negotiate around and about observed (from model teacher) and experienced (from peer rehearsals) teaching events.

Our coding focused on two components of the discussions: one is around the content and other one is around how the discussions are accomplished and thus represent members' professional vision. For the first round, we coded the content of the discourse of classroom members for three areas: structuring talk, phenomena, and students' ideas and role of prior knowledge. These three areas emerged after coding the first two days of the course in the first round of the analysis process using open coding.

For the second round, we used professional vision practices to describe the interactions among class members. In this part of the coding, our constructs were driven by Goodwin's (1994) professional vision practices: highlighting, coding schemes, and building material representations. Goodwin (1994) describes,

> an event being seen, a relevant object of knowledge, emerges through the interplay between a domain of scrutiny (a patch of dirt, the images made available by the King videotape, etc.) and a set of discursive practices (dividing the domain of scrutiny by highlighting a figure against a ground, applying specific coding schemes for the constitution and interpretation of relevant events, etc.) being deployed within a specific activity (arguing a legal case, mapping a site, planting crops, etc.).
>
> *(p. 606)*

Based on Goodwin's (1994) terms and definitions, in our study, preservice teachers' professional pedagogical vision (constituting a relevant object of knowledge) emerges through looking at the videos of instruction and their experiences in the lessons (constituting the domain of scrutiny), and a set of discursive practices (constituting highlighting, coding, and building material representations) being deployed within a discussion of an instance of teaching (a specific activity). We used these discursive practices of highlighting, coding schemes, and building material representations as constructs for our second round of analysis.

Goodwin's (1994) study of archeologists learning to observe remnants of artifacts described *highlighting* as a social process of coming to "see" a figure against a ground. When preservice teachers state or emphasize a piece of teacher or student talk or behavior from the observed teaching, it indicates they have highlighted it, separating out a figure from the ground in the teaching event. So, as analysts, we coded the instances as highlighting when preservice teachers state a specific instance from the observed or experienced teaching. When they apply a specific meaning, label, or interpretation of the relevant events, it indicates they are using coding schemes. We saw multiple ways preservice teachers use coding schemes for teaching events in the data. Preservice teachers use coding schemes for teaching events by describing the situation, or by connecting and comparing it to other teaching instances either in peers' lessons or exemplar lessons, like Bethany's. This way of comparing to other exemplars is just like when the archeology student compared the dirt with the Munsell color chart in Goodwin's study. Another way that preservice teachers use coding schemes for teaching events is through giving suggestions or alternatives for future implications. Preservice teachers create material representations through analyzing videos in Studio Code, or through developing lesson plans.

Below is an example (08.29. Episode 14) that shows how we coded the episodes:

Transcription	*Code and Research Notes*
1. Instructor: Now, we can probably take a look and see what is she doing. So, let's see. She starts walking around and talking [The instructor is showing the video without sound to fast-forward to come to the instances that preservice teachers marked]	
2. [They watched the video instance]	
3. Debbie: Pressing	Coding of the teacher's practice as Debbie interpreted and labeled the practice as pressing students' ideas
4. Instructor: Hmm? Pressing?	The instructor revoiced Debbie's idea
5. Debbie: Especially for the kid in the jacket	Highlighting the student that Debbie thought the teacher was pressing ideas
6. Instructor: Yeah	The instructor agreed
7. Debbie: To see what he can come up with it	Debbie codes teacher's pressing practice for the purpose of allowing the student to come up with ideas [In the video the student was saying, "I don't know, I have no idea."]
8. Instructor: Yeah, "I don't know, I don't know. I have no idea" [Repeats what the kid said in the video]. Yeah. Anything else she was doing?	The instructor restated the student's idea that Debbie pointed and he agreed with Debbie. Then invited preservice teachers to code (interpret) what else the teacher was doing
9. Kayla: Probing	Kayla coded the practice of probing
10. Bryan: Hm-hmm [Agreeing to Kayla]	Bryan agreed with Kayla's coding
11. Instructor: Probing? Where were the examples of probing?	The instructor wanted evidence of probing and wanted them to highlight an instance
12. Erika: More of the girl. Oh no, I think she said about the steam [The conversation continues to understand what each kid the teacher had conversation with said during the video]	Erika highlighted the student that the teacher probed on. There were three students (two boys and one girl) the teacher had conversation with in the video separately. Erika highlighted the female student that the teacher probed on

One of the tasks for preservice teachers in the science teaching methods class was to observe a video of a model teacher's teaching and code the video with the Studio Code software to look for how the model teacher elicited students' ideas. Eliciting students' ideas is the first discourse practice in the ambitious science teaching practices. After preservice teachers individually coded the same video, the instructor stacked timelines (that show each preservice teachers' coding) allowing preservice teachers to compare each other's analysis and the class watched the same video again together.

At the beginning of this episode, they collectively watched the moments that some of the preservice teachers coded in the timeline. In line 1, the instructor referred to those instances the preservice teachers marked in the timeline. After they watched, Debbie coded teacher's practice as pressing (line 3). Then the instructor revoiced her idea (line 4) and in line 5, Debbie highlighted the student whose idea the teacher pressed. The instructor agreed (line 6). Debbie codes teacher's pressing practice for the purpose of allowing the student to come up with ideas (line 7). In line 8, the instructor restated the student's idea from the instruction that Debbie highlighted and agreed with Debbie's coding, then asked preservice teachers if there is anything else the teacher was doing. Kayla coded (interpreted) that she was probing students' ideas (line 9) and in line 10, Bryan agreed, and the instructor asked where the teacher was probing (line 11), so the instructor wanted evidence for preservice teachers' coding and wanted them to highlight an instance. Then in line 12, Erika highlighted the student whose idea the teacher was probing on by identifying the student from the other students. So, in this instance probing is the coding scheme and within that coding scheme, Erika highlighted the student's idea by emphasizing or attending to a specific student from the instruction. By attending to the student's idea, Erika foregrounded the student against the ground of other students' action and discourse occurring in the video of instruction.

In this episode, preservice teachers and the instructor collectively coded teacher moves and questions, and students' ideas, through labeling and interpreting the ideas. They highlighted parts of instruction through restating the teacher questions or identifying specific students' or the teacher's action or idea from the instruction. The practices that are negotiated among the classroom members in this episode include pressing and probing talk moves. So, the preservice teachers labeled the instances in the observed teaching through interpreting the teacher and student discourse, and they highlighted through restating those specific questions or answers as evidence of their labeling. The instructor also facilitated their highlighting and coding through multiple discourse moves. Preservice teachers and the instructor engaged in discursive practices of highlighting and coding in multiple turns of talk to describe a teaching activity observed in the model teacher's class. So far, we described how we conducted open coding with constructs coming from professional vision and ambitious science teaching.

After completing open coding, we put all the episodes that we coded with the same code and compiled them together. Then, we compiled all these episodes in the memo files and wrote a memo regarding each episode to summarize what is happening in each of them. Compiling all the episodes and writing memos for each one of them helped us check the accuracy and consistency of our coding and allowed us to group some of the similar codes. Then, those memos helped us write a description of the codes and see the trends by looking at the episodes chronologically within each code. We tried to come up with patterns of discursive practices happening for each activity discussion. This process helped us zoom out in order to see the patterns of activity (Kelly, 2014a). Concurrently, we created the final versions of the coding framework tables with descriptions and example episodes from the transcripts, an example page is provided in Figure 8.3.

In this chapter, we aimed to show our logic of inquiry in our use of methods as we analyze preservice teachers' professional pedagogical vision around ambitious science teaching (Tanis Ozcelik, 2016). Using multilayer analysis, we were able to examine how these preservice teachers acculturated into professional pedagogical vision around ambitious science teaching and how they negotiated the meaning of ambitious science teaching. Looking closely at preservice teachers' discussions of teaching events provided us a way to examine how they negotiate ambitious science teaching practices and what tensions emerged as they make sense of those practices (Tanis Ozcelik & McDonald, in preparation-a). We found that the framework of negotiation of professional pedagogical vision as a way of characterizing preservice teachers' learning was productive and provided new insight into the development of sophisticated teaching practices. Preservice teachers identified and negotiated a subset of important practices during initial deconstructions of teaching episodes, and over time, identified additional

Categories	Codes	Description of Codes	Example Episodes
PRESSING (85)	General pressing (8)	Talk is about pressing students' ideas. Preservice teachers identify when the teacher pressed students' ideas, or reflect on when they or their peers as teachers pressed students' ideas. In those episodes, preservice teachers have not included any purposes or justifications of pressing students' ideas.	08.29. Episode 14, 09.05. Episode 5, 09.17. Episode 4, 09.17: Episode 13, 09. 17. Episode19, 09.17. Episode 22, 09.24. Episode 4, 09.26. Episode 13,
	P1: Pressing for clarity on the word meaning (7)	Talk is about pressing for clarity on the word meaning. Preservice teachers identified when the teacher was pressing to make the words the students use clearer, or to get the meaning of the sentences, words, phrases the students used, or to get students' reasoning when they have discussions in small groups.	08.27. Episode 6, 08.29. Episode 29, 09.10. Episode 8, 09.12. Episode 4, *09.12. Episode 12*, 09.26 Episode 2, 09.26 Episode 3.
	P2: Pressing for expanding the idea students have. (Elaboration) (7)	Talk is about asking students to expand or elaborate their ideas. Pressing to expand on the ideas the students have, through asking to say more, or through asking to elaborate on. In these episodes, the purpose is to get more ideas from the students.	08.27 Episode 2, 08.27. Episode 6, 09.10. Episode 20, 09.12. Episode 9, 09.17. Episode 1, 09.17. Episode 17. 09.26 Episode 14
	P3: Adjusting	Talk is about adjusting pressing questions for high	09.10. Episode 15, 09.26. Episode 3.

FIGURE 8.3 Example coding framework table.

practices, as well as negotiated more sophisticated versions of all identified practices to be increasingly aligned with ambitious science teaching practices (Tanis Ozcelik & McDonald, in preparation-b).

Preservice teachers' professional pedagogical vision was negotiated both in-the-moment and over time in their discussions of teaching events (Tanis Ozcelik & McDonald, in preparation-b). Using interactional discourse analysis provided us a way to track how these practices are developed over both of these timescales. The findings provide an example of how detailed, over-time analysis can expose nuanced observations of those preservice teachers as they make sense of teaching practices with their instructor. Thus, the findings have implications for teacher educators in helping preservice teachers to make sense of and develop understandings about teaching practices.

Trustworthiness and Credibility

To ensure credibility we used member checks through soliciting feedback on our emerging findings from some of our participants (Merriam, 2009). The authors had weekly meetings. The nature of those meetings included looking at the transcripts and the videos and discussing each instance and coming to consensus on the codes. We also used peer examination or peer review (Merriam, 2009). Throughout the coding process, the first author shared the analysis with an academic writing group, consisting of a math education graduate student and a science education graduate student in weekly meetings, and asked them whether or not they would agree with the way she coded. She also shared some of the analysis in a discourse analysis group, an informal group consisting of professors and graduate students interested in reading and analyzing discourse in science and engineering education. We also had another science education graduate student code 10 percent of the video recordings. We met and talked about the coding framework, and the first author explained what each code meant and how she was coding. Then one week later we met and discussed his coding. We compared our coding using the percent agreement and found that inter-rater reliability was 71 percent. We discussed the codes that we did not agree on initially and came to consensus in the coding. To ensure dependability, researchers suggest an audit trail. Throughout the analysis process, we kept memos and notes to keep track of how we collected the data, the decisions we made, and how we coded and created the categories.

In a summary of our analysis, we started with theoretical constructs from professional vision and ambitious science teaching as well as used grounded theory approach to analyze the data. We described how we used video analysis, event mapping, and transcribing to zoom in to the "data" within the collected records. We provided example figures showing timelines of video analysis and event maps.

Then, once we purposefully sampled our data, we described how we further zoom in to the micro-interactional level analysis of discourse. We gave example tables showing our discourse analysis in one of the episodes. After discourse analysis, we zoomed out to see the patterns and themes within the analysis. We provided an example coding framework table showing our codes and descriptions of codes as well as example episodes for each code.

Thus far, we described the research design, context, and participants as well as our decisions in selecting data collection and analysis methods, and how we tried to ensure the credibility and trustworthiness of the research.

Methodological Challenges We Faced during the Study

During the study, there were methodological challenges and decisions we made based on those challenges. At the beginning, the study was conceptualized to observe and follow preservice teachers from their first course to the second science teaching methods course including in their field placement schools. We wanted to capture preservice teachers beginning ideas and what they bring from and learn in the first science teaching method class, so we have fieldnotes and classroom documents from that class. Four of the preservice teachers attended the first science teaching methods class together. We tried to follow them in the field placement schools but due to administrative and parent permissions, we were not able to follow them or observe their mentor teachers during their stay in the schools. We have only three days of fieldnotes from two of the mentor teachers' classrooms. We thought it is important to understand what they see in the field placements to understand how preservice teachers develop professional vision. Preservice teachers are in multiple discourse communities during the teacher education program. One of the important discourse communities is their field placement schools including their peers, mentor teachers, principals and their middle and high school students. Due to these circumstances, we collected video data only from the second science teaching methods course when they are in the campus.

Contextual situations including two significant personal problems, also contributed to the complexity of this data set. One was Bryan could not get the clearances to go to the schools, and another problem was Mark was dismissed from the field experience due to some personal problems. These issues were particularly complicating given that the course already was limited to six preservice teachers.

Studying professional vision brings its own challenges. Professional vision is defined by three practices: highlighting, coding, and producing material representations. We studied professional vision from the sociolinguistic perspective by identifying pieces of talk in terms of these professional vision practices. The biggest challenge to studying professional vision was the interpretation of utterances as either highlighting or coding. Highlighting implies marking or outlining. In Goodwin's original example (1994) it is easier to see how the archeology professor physically highlighted the dirt and they coded it through comparisons between the chart and dirt colors. In teacher education, during the discussions of teaching, identifying highlighting and coding as separate practices was difficult. The pieces being highlighted are conceptual and cultural, and they often do not have clear physical manifestations, and thus are open to significant interpretation on their own, which can overlap with the coding for the meaning of the piece being highlighted. Thus, these two practices are very blended and interwoven. The teacher educator also plays a prominent role in highlighting and directing preservice teachers' attention to certain pieces of instruction. In some instances in the data differentiating highlighting from the coding was more clear, especially when the class is re-watching videos the instructor is literally pointing with fingers at the screen. Coding is based on the interpretation of the observed or experienced lessons. Again, making connections to previous teachings from a model teacher or from preservice teachers' own teaching gave reference and intertextual connection to help preservice teachers code. So, they were able to compare one situation to another situation, which is not as clear as how the archeology student compared the color of the dirt to the chart. Teaching is a complex and situated activity. Each moment should be articulated and interpreted carefully based on the situation. Thus, differentiating professional vision practices of highlighting and coding schemes in the teaching context added additional challenge for our data.

Building and articulating material representation is the third piece of professional vision practices. Considering production and articulation of material representations as part of professional vision has not typically been a focus in teacher education research. In this study, material representations in the teacher education context include the lesson plans and assessments preservice teachers developed as part of rehearsals, as well as the Studio Code timelines they generated when coding teaching practice. While the process and discourse of preservice teachers building and articulating their material representations can provide evidence of their developing professional vision, it is difficult to look for evidence of professional vision in the material representations of lesson plans or assessments themselves.

We considered professional vision as collective ways of seeing teaching practices and so the lesson plans, without preservice teachers' embedded reflective statements, do not provide access to the decisions of preservice teachers during the development of the material representations. Thus, the artifacts produced by the preservice teachers are not particularly strong material representations of practice. It could have been possible to investigate collective ways of seeing teaching practices in the lesson plans if we had the opportunity to discuss the lesson plans with preservice teachers before or after rehearsals. As a result, we used video analysis timelines as their material representations. The artifacts created in Studio

Code were brought under the scrutiny of classroom members; preservice teachers were able to look at each other's analysis of videos, re-watched the instances again, and had conversations upon their analysis. However, lesson plans were not shared in a way that enabled analysis or critique of them.

Discussion: Building Professional Pedagogical Vision

In this chapter we aimed to describe our "logic of inquiry" (Green, Dixon, & Zaharlick, 2003) in investigating how preservice teachers develop professional pedagogical vision around ambitious science teaching practices. We tried to reflexively unpack our decisions and methods for how we choose to investigate the research questions within our particular context. We draw from sociocultural and situated learning theories to understand preservice teachers' making sense of ambitious science teaching practices in their discussions within the classroom community. We conceptualized that preservice teachers develop professional pedagogical vision through interactive discourse within and across contexts and time frames. We investigated professional vision through how members of the classroom community discursively develop ideas and practices within and across interactions, times, and events in the science teaching methods course. We draw from Goodwin's idea of professional vision based on anthropological linguistics. In Goodwin's (1994) definition of professional vision, he emphasizes the socially constructed nature of seeing events, in our case educational events, specifically discussions of teaching.

We used ethnographic data collection methods, including participant observation of the science teaching methods course, taking fieldnotes, video recordings of the course, collection of artifacts and documents given during the course. In our description of data analysis, we described the larger data set and how much of that data was analyzed. In order to theoretically ground our methods of coding, we based our analysis in Goodwin's constructs of highlighting, coding and producing, and articulating material representations. In addition to Goodwin's constructs we also used open coding to include what emerges in and from the data. We purposefully sampled data and events within the larger data set in order to answer our research questions. We described our ways of recording, documenting, sampling, and analyzing video data through video and discourse analysis that addresses our research questions to make transparent the logic-in-use informing the methodological decisions of our study (Green, Dai, Joo, Williams, Liu, & Lu, 2015).

We found the framework of negotiation of professional pedagogical vision as a way of characterizing preservice teachers' learning was productive and provided new insight into the development of sophisticated teaching practices. The findings of our study contribute to the understanding of how preservice teachers negotiate the details of ambitious science teaching practices through articulating more detailed sub-practices and thus develop professional vision. We found that preservice teachers' professional pedagogical vision was negotiated both in-the-moment and over time in their discussions of teaching events. With the release of the NGSS (2013), there is an increasing emphasis on developing a more practice-focused pedagogy, such as ambitious science teaching, for science.

Our work is situated in the intersection of teacher education practices (approximation, representation, and decomposition of practice) (Grossmann & McDonald, 2008; Grossman, Compton, Igra, Ronfeldt, Shahan, & Williamson, 2009) as well as science teaching practices (ambitious science teaching). This practice-based emphasis foregrounds discourse-intensive practices in this intersection, where preservice teachers can make sense of the practices within their classroom community. This work can help science teacher educators and professional development facilitators to better understand how to organize science teacher education experiences. In this chapter, we aimed to explain how we studied this discourse-rich context in the teacher education through making visible systematicity in our analysis. This chapter will help educators who investigate complex, multilayered contexts with rich data.

Note

1 One of the tasks for preservice teachers in the science teaching methods II course was to observe a video of a model teacher's teaching and code the video with the Studio Code software to look for how the model teacher elicited students' ideas. Bethany was a chemistry teacher that preservice teachers observed from the ambitious science teaching exemplars.

References

Ball, D. L., & Forzani, F. M. (2009). The work of teaching and the challenge for teacher education. *Journal of Teacher Education*, 60(5), 497–511.

Brown, J. S., Collins, A., & Duguid, P. (1989). Situated cognition and the culture of learning. *Educational Researcher*, 18(1), 32–42.

Castanheira, M. L., Crawford, T., Dixon, C., & Green, J. L. (2001). Interactional ethnography: An approach to studying the social construction of literate practices. *Linguistics and Education*, 11(4), 353–400.

Corbin, J., & Strauss, A. (2007). *Basics of qualitative research: Techniques and procedures for developing grounded theory*. 3rd ed. Thousand Oaks, CA: Sage.

Emerson, R. M., Fretz, R. I., & Shaw, L. L. (2011). *Writing ethnographic fieldnotes*. 2nd ed. Chicago, IL: University of Chicago Press.

Gee, J. P., & Green, J. L. (1998). Discourse analysis, learning, and social practice: A methodological study. *Review of Research in Education*, 23, 119–169.

Goodwin, C. (1994). Professional vision. *American Anthropologist*, 96(3), 606–633.

Green, J. L., Dixon C. N., & Zaharlick, A. (2003). Ethnography as a logic of inquiry. In J. Flood, D. Lapp, J. R. Squire, & J. M. Jensen (Eds.), *Handbook of research on teaching the English language arts* (pp. 201–224). 2nd ed. Mahwah, NJ: Lawrence Erlbaum Associates.

Green J. L., & Castanheira M. L. (2012). Exploring classroom life and student learning. In B. Kaur (Ed.), *Understanding teaching and learning*. Rotterdam: Sense Publishers.

Green, J. L., Dai, Y., Joo, J., Williams, E., Liu, A., & Lu, S. (2015). Interdisciplinary dialogues as a site for reflective exploration of conceptual understandings of teaching-learning relationships. *Pedagogies: An International Journal*, 10(1), 86–103. doi:10.1080/1554480X.2014.999774.

Grossman, P., & McDonald, M. (2008). Back to the future: Directions for research in teaching and teacher education. *American Educational Research Journal*, 45(1), 184–205.

Grossman, P., Compton, C., Igra, D., Ronfeldt, M., Shahan, E., & Williamson, P. W. (2009). Teaching practice: A cross-professional perspective. *Teachers College Record*, 111(9), 2055–2100.

Gumperz, J. J. (2001). Interactional sociolinguistics: A personal perspective. In D. Schiffrin, D. Tannen, & H. E. Hamilton (Eds.), *Handbook of discourse analysis*. Malden, MA: Blackwell.

Heap, J. (1991). A situated perspective on what counts as reading. In A. Luke and C. D. Baker (Eds.), *Towards a critical sociology of reading pedagogy* (pp. 103–140). Amsterdam: John Benjamins. https://vosaic.com/products/studiocode.

Kelly, G. J., Brown, C., & Crawford, T. (2000). Experiments, contingencies, and curriculum: Providing opportunities for learning through improvisation in science teaching. *Science Education*, 84(5), 624–657.

Kelly, G. J., Chen, C., & Crawford, T. (1998). Methodological considerations for studying science-in-the-making in educational settings. *Research in Science Education*, 28(1), 23–49. Special Issue on Science and Technology Studies and Science Education, Wolff-Michael Roth (Guest Ed.).

Kelly, G. J., & Chen, C. (1999). The sound of music: Constructing science as sociocultural practices through oral and written discourse. *Journal of Research in Science Teaching*, 36(8), 883–915.

Kelly, G. J., & Crawford, T. (1997). An ethnographic investigation of the discourse processes of school science. *Science Education*, 81(5), 533–559.

Kelly, G. J., Crawford, T., & Green, J. L. (2001). Common task and uncommon knowledge: Dissenting voices in the discursive construction of physics across small laboratory groups. *Linguistics and Education*, 12(2), 135–174.

Kelly, G. J. (2004). Interim report for the National Academy of Education postdoctoral fellowship 1998–2000.

Kelly, G. J. (2008). Inquiry, activity, and epistemic practice. In R. Duschl & R. Grandy (Eds.), *Teaching scientific inquiry: Recommendations for research and implementation* (pp. 99–117; 288–291). Rotterdam: Sense Publishers.

Kelly, G. J. (2011). Scientific literacy, discourse, and epistemic practices. In C. Linder, L. Östman, D. A. Roberts, P. Wickman, G. Erickson, & A. McKinnon (Eds.), *Exploring the landscape of scientific literacy* (pp. 61–73). New York: Routledge.

Kelly, G. J. (2014a). Analysing classroom activities: Theoretical and methodological considerations. In C. Bruguière, A. Tiberghien, & P. Clément (Eds.), *Topics and trends in current science education: 9th ESERA conference selected contributions* (pp. 353–368). Dordrecht: Springer.

Kelly, G. J. (2014b). Discourse practices in science learning and teaching. In N. G. Lederman & S. K. Abell (Eds.), *Handbook of research on science education* (Vol. 2, pp. 321–336). Mahwah, NJ: Lawrence Erlbaum Associates.

Kelly, G. J. (2016). Methodological considerations for the study of epistemic cognition in practice. In J. A. Greene, W. A. Sandoval, & I. Braten (Eds.), *Handbook of epistemic cognition* (pp. 393–408). New York: Routledge.

Lampert, M., Franke, M. L., Kazemi, E., Ghousseini, H., Turrou, A. C., Beasley, H., & Crowe, K. (2013). Keeping it complex: Using rehearsals to support novice teacher learning of ambitious teaching. *Journal of Teacher Education*, 64(3), 226–243. doi: http://dx.doi.org/10.1177/0022487112473837.

Lave, J., & Wenger, E. (1991). *Situated learning: Legitimate peripheral participation*. New York: Cambridge University Press.

Lemke, J. (1990). *Talking science: Language, learning, and values*. Norwood, NJ: Ablex.

McDonald, M., Kazemi, E., & Kavanagh, S. S. (2013). Core practices and pedagogies of teacher education: A call for a common language and collective activity. *Journal of Teacher Education*, 64(5), 378–386. doi:10.1080/15544800701366563.

McDonald, S. P., & Kelly, G. J. (2007). Understanding the construction of a science storyline in a chemistry classroom. *Pedagogies: An International Journal*, 2(3), 165–177.

McDonald, S. P., & Rook, M. (2014). Digital video analysis to support the development of professional pedagogical vision. In B. Calanda & P. Rich (Eds.), *Video analysis in teacher education*. New York: Routledge.

McDonald, S. P. (2016). The transparent and the invisible in professional pedagogical vision for science teaching. *School Science and Mathematics*, 116(2), 95–103.

Merriam, S. (2009). *Qualitative research: A guide to design and implementation*. 2nd ed. San Francisco, CA: John Wiley & Sons, Inc.

Moje, E. B. (1995). Talking about science: An interpretation of the effects of teacher talk in a high school classroom. *Journal of Research in Science Teaching*, 32(4), 349–371.

National Research Council. (1996). *National science education standards*. Washington, DC: National Academies Press.

National Research Council. (2000). *Inquiry and the national science education standards: A guide for teaching and learning*. Washington, DC: National Academies Press.

National Research Council. (2007). *Taking science to school: Learning and teaching science in Grades K–8*. Washington, DC: National Academic Press.

National Research Council. (2012). *A framework for K–12 science education: Practices, crosscutting concepts and core ideas*. Washington, DC: National Academies Press.

NGSS Lead States. (2013). *Next generation science standards: For states, by states*. Washington, DC: National Academies Press.

Putnam, R., & Borko, H. (2000). What do new views of knowledge and thinking have to say about research on teacher learning? *Educational Researcher*, 29(1), 4–15.

Roth, K. J., Garnier, H. E., Chen, C., Lemmens, M., Schwille, K., & Wickler, N. I. (2011). Video based lesson analysis: Effective science PD for teacher and student learning. *Journal of Research in Science Teaching*, 48(2), 117–148.

Roth, W. M. (1996). Teacher questioning in an open-inquiry learning environment: Interactions of context, content, and student responses. *Journal of Research in Science Teaching*, 33(7), 709–736.

Roth, W. M. (2005). *Talking science: Language and learning in science classrooms*. Oxford, UK: Rowman & Littlefield.

Spradley, J. P. (1980). *Participant observation*. Orlando, FL: Harcourt Brace Jovanovich College Publishers.

Stevens, R., & Hall, R. (1998). Disciplined perception: Learning to see in technoscience. In M. Lamper & M. Blunk (Eds.), *Talking mathematics in school: Studies of teaching and learning* (pp. 107–150). Cambridge: Cambridge University Press. doi:10.1017/CBO9780511571251.007.

Tanis Ozcelik, A. (2016). Science teacher candidates developing professional pedagogical vision around ambitious science teaching practices. (Unpublished doctoral dissertation). The Pennsylvania State University, University Park.

Tanis Ozcelik, A., & McDonald, S. P. in preparation-a. Negotiating tensions: Development of ambitious science teaching practices. To be submitted to *Science Education.*

Tanis Ozcelik, A., & McDonald, S. P. in preparation-b. Developing professional pedagogical vision through the negotiation of ambitious science teaching practices. To be submitted to *Journal of Teacher Education.*

Vygotsky, L. S. (2012). *Thought and language.* Revised and expanded by A. Kozulin. Cambridge, MA: The MIT Press.

Windschitl, M., Thompson, J., & Braaten, M. (2011). Ambitious pedagogy by novice teachers: Who benefits from tool-supported collaborative inquiry into practice and why? *Teachers College Record,* 113(7), 1311–1360.

Windschitl, M., Thompson, J., Braaten, M., & Stroupe, D. (2012). Proposing a core set of instructional practices and tools for teachers of science. *Science Education,* 96(5), 878–903. https://doi.org/10.1002/sce.21027.

Windschitl, M. A., & Stroupe, D. (2017). The three-story challenge: Implications of the next generation science standards for teacher preparation. *Journal of Teacher Education,* 68(3), 251–261.

Yin, R. (2009). *Case study research: Design and methods.* 4th ed. Los Angeles, CA: Sage.

9

ANALYZING THE GENERATIVE NATURE OF SCIENCE TEACHERS' PROFESSIONAL DEVELOPMENT DISCOURSE

Amy Ricketts

Studying Teacher Learning

In lieu of more traditional types of professional development (PD), many teachers are joining together in learning groups within and across schools, sometimes including district administration and university faculty. These groups are sometimes called "professional learning communities" (PLCs). Participants in these groups strive to support their own and each other's learning and development, and ultimately, student learning. These groups engage in a variety of activities, including analyzing student work or videos of classroom teaching, and writing or adapting curriculum. Although different groups may engage in the same activities, *how* the groups engage in these activities may look (and sound) quite different, depending on the particular goals, dispositions, cultural norms, and discourse practices of the group.

Viewed from a sociocultural perspective of learning, the conversations around practice that are constructed in these groups mediate what, the degree to which, and how teachers learn. These conversations include both designed and spontaneous factors that play a role in generating (or constraining) teacher learning opportunities. Few studies have closely investigated teacher groups' discourse to uncover *which* factors matter most, or *how* those factors mediate opportunities for teacher learning. The study described in this chapter addresses this gap in the professional development literature. Considering the calls for substantive pedagogical changes in the *Next Generation Science Standards*, coupled with the burgeoning popularity of engaging in professional learning communities as a form of professional development, this kind of research is crucial to understanding how the talk in those communities might support improvements in teaching practices and, in turn, student learning.

The *Next Generation Science Standards* challenge educators to provide for three-dimensional learning around disciplinary core ideas, crosscutting concepts, and science and engineering practices. This focus on disciplinary knowledge and social practices require new ways of approaching science teaching. To develop such approaches, professional learning communities themselves need new discourse practices that make visible ways of engaging students in disciplinary discourse. Thus, the discourse practices of professional learning communities need to be examined in detail in order to consider the ways that these communities might foster teacher learning. This study set out to answer the following research question: how do conversations around practice mediate educators' opportunities to learn about teaching science?

To address this question, I posed two sub-questions:

1. Which designed and spontaneous factors of the group's conversations around practice accounted for differences in the generative nature of those conversations?
2. How did those factors mediate the generative nature of the group's talk?

In order to understand the goal of the study, it is important to clarify the terms "learning opportunities" and "generative" nature of teacher talk. These constructs refer to the (somewhat abstract) aspects of teacher talk that are *thought to support teacher learning* (i.e. thought to generate "learning opportunities"). Such "generative" talk does not guarantee (nor serve as evidence of) teacher learning, but rather serves as a potential *affordance* for substantive teacher learning and changes in teaching practices. Drawing on the literature in teacher education, I identified four general aspects of "generative" teacher conversations: (a) public, transparent practices, (b) emphasized attention to rationales, (c) theory–practice connections, (d) distributed agency (Horn & Little, 2010; Johnson, 2009; Nelson, Deuel, Slavit, & Kennedy, 2010; Ball & Cohen, 1999; Cochran-Smith & Lytle, 1999). I explain each of these aspects of generative talk below.

Generative Teacher Talk

Generative teacher talk makes classroom practices visible with a great degree of transparency (Horn & Little, 2010). As Barsalou (1999) argued, "comprehension is grounded in perceptual simulations that prepare agents for situated action" (p. 577). Teachers' practices may be made visible through oral accounts such as rehearsals of future teaching or replays of prior teaching (Horn, 2010), and/or through artifacts of practice such as lesson plans, student work, or videos of teaching. Achieving a high degree of transparency frequently involves teachers probing one another for more specific details of classroom procedures and teachers' rationales (Horn, 2010). In the absence of a personal observation of others' teaching, discourse that makes practice transparent can provide the group with another resource for constructing their own models and simulations for taking action in the classroom.

Generative teacher talk includes attention to the rationales behind teaching practices, not just to the procedures involved in those practices (Nelson, Deuel, Slavit, & Kennedy, 2010). Ideally, this attention includes consideration of multiple perspectives and provides a space for revising one's thinking (Ball & Cohen, 1999; Horn & Little, 2010). Teaching is an inherently complex endeavor with no single best solutions appropriate to every context. When teachers articulate their rationales and seek multiple interpretations, they create a space for revising their thinking in substantive ways.

Generative teacher talk connects generalized teaching principles to specific contextual experiences. Horn and Little (2010) argue that these kinds of connections provide "a means of developing teaching knowledge that is deeply rooted in embodied accounts of classroom life, joining important concepts about teaching to particulars of practice" (p. 197). Gee (2008) argued that building models (generalizations) from contextualized experiences allows learners to generate simulations that help them to make sense of specific situations they encounter, and to prepare for action in the world.

Generative teacher talk positions teachers with substantial agency for sense-making and problem solving (Horn & Little, 2010; Ball & Cohen, 1999; Cochran-Smith & Lytle, 1999). It does not position teachers as helpless, or as dependent on the expertise of others. Teachers do not simply advise one another and move on (nor does a facilitator simply advise the teachers and move on). Instead this kind of talk acknowledges teachers' abilities to solve their own problems and answer their own questions, and provides a space for such actions (Horn & Little, 2010). In my analysis, I searched for instances where teachers expressed an experienced or anticipated problem of practice (or a problem of their understanding of a practice) and paid close attention to the degree of agency with which the teacher (or the group) was positioned while the group took up the problem (or question).

Theoretical-Methodological Perspective for Researching Teacher Discourse

Methodologically, the small but growing body of research on teachers' professional conversations has relied heavily on ex-situ accounts supplied by interviews, surveys, self-report logs, and diaries. While these ex-situ methods for generating data are not without merit for understanding aspects of interaction and context, they do not sufficiently capture the detail, nuance, and patterning of social interaction that takes place in teachers' professional conversations. Other approaches to studying interaction in situ rely on the use and analysis of observation protocols, such as the 10-category Flanders Interaction Analysis System (Flanders,

1960, developed for studying classroom interaction. See Simon and Boyer, 1969 for a number of additional examples). While no such interaction analysis system has yet been developed specifically for studying teachers' professional conversations, such systems would not likely capture the complex ways that particular turns function in combination, in sequence, and over time in teachers' professional conversations (Little, 2012). In lieu of these approaches, I used an interactional ethnographic perspective in this study (Green, Skukauskaite, & Baker, 2012; Castanhaiera, Crawford, Dixon, & Green, 2001). Used as a framework for analyzing how teacher learning groups' conversations mediate their learning opportunities, an interactional ethnographic perspective acknowledges the complex, indeterminate (non a priori or assumed) relationship between social practice and learning, while also providing systematic ways to (re)present and analyze that relationship, as situated within its relevant and developing contexts among particular configurations of actors/people (Mitchell, 1984).

Teacher learning groups are situated within unique cultural and historical contexts, which in turn shape the group's social practices. As such, the group's social practices can only be fully understood by examining them within the context in which they are used (Kelly, 2014). Furthermore, the group's discourse both shapes and is shaped by its social practices. For example, this analysis of the group's discourse revealed existing hierarchies of expertise and power in the negotiation of meaning. At the same time, this discourse also constructed, challenged, and reconstructed those hierarchies, which in turn shaped the group's future discourse and meaning making as will be presented in the following sections.

To understand this complex, iterative, recursive, and abductive process in this study, my aim was to develop understandings of the "cultural actions, cultural knowledge, and cultural artifacts that members need to use, produce, predict, and interpret to participate in everyday life within a social group" (Castanheira, Crawford, Dixon, & Green, 2001, p. 394). Specifically, I sought to understand how the complex discourse within a culturally and historically situated group of teachers mediated their opportunities to learn about teaching science. Thus, an interactional ethnographic perspective was most appropriate for investigating this phenomenon, given its orienting logic-of-inquiry that focuses the analyst on tracing the developing dialogic processes across times, configuration of actors, and events.

Studying a teacher learning group in situ required me to make a number of important methodological decisions at every stage of the research process. In Interactional Ethnography (IE) this process is defined as constructing an interactional ethnographic logic-in-use, given that IE is an epistemological perspective and not a method of research (Green, Skukauskaite, & Baker, 2012; see introduction to this volume). In this chapter, I focus on four inter-related decisions that I made while concurrently and recursively generating and analyzing the data. I make transparent the consequences of those decisions in terms of explaining how the teachers' conversations mediated their learning opportunities. These decisions include: (a) identifying and representing key events throughout the data set, (b) defining an emergent analytic focus, (c) identifying and bounding the units of analysis signaled in and through the discourse and actions among participants (Green, Skukauskaite, & Baker, 2012), and (d) constructing explanations from data analyses. Following the next section ("Context of the Study"), I will elaborate on each of the four methodological decisions.

Context of the Study

Teacher learning groups are situated within unique cultural and historical contexts, which in turn shape the group's social practices. As such, the group's social practices can only be fully understood by examining them within the context in which they are used (Kelly, 2014). The learning group in this study included ten middle school science teachers from three middle schools in the Valley School District (VSD), VSD's secondary science curriculum coordinator (Tim), and an associate professor of science education from Mountain State University (MSU).

In the four summers prior to this study (2011–2014), the MSU professor (Sam) facilitated a week-long summer workshop at MSU for middle grades science teachers. Each summer, an increasing number of VSD teachers attended the workshop, beginning with the West middle school teachers (2011–2014), who were joined by some of their colleagues from Central and East in 2014. In August 2014, Tim, Sam, and all the VSD middle school teachers (including two East teachers who had never attended the workshops) agreed to meet as a group throughout the year to support the implementation of the concepts they learned in the summer workshops (described below).

Across the 2014–2015 school year, the group met eleven times, for twenty-two hours total, including four hour-long after school meetings, three half-day inservice workshops, two full-day "Studio Days," and two half-day planning sessions for the Studio Days. (A "Studio Day" is a contemporary professional development context similar to Lesson Study (Lewis, 2002), characterized by cycles of co-planning a lesson, implementing the lesson while colleagues observe, reflecting on and revising the lesson.)

Across the eleven meetings, Sam (MSU professor) facilitated every meeting in which he was present (six total). In Sam's absence, Tim (VSD coordinator) facilitated three meetings. The teachers facilitated themselves during the two planning sessions for the Studio Days (no one person assumed the role of facilitator, and neither Tim nor Sam were present).

The teacher learning group in this study focused heavily on supporting students' explanations for scientific phenomena. In this study, I refer to this kind of non-traditional science teaching as "Explanation-Driven Instruction" (EDI). "Traditional" science teaching generally uses curricula that are organized around individual science "topics" (e.g. Motion, Forces) or "activities" (e.g. designing mousetrap cars), whereas EDI is organized around complex, real-world scientific phenomena (e.g. a lake freezing in winter, the Statue of Liberty "rusting"). Another major difference between these two approaches is the degree to which students are responsible for sensemaking. Traditionally, teachers do the "heavy lifting" in terms of interpreting the results of in-class investigations, revealing the connections between the investigations, and constructing explanations for scientific phenomena. In EDI, students take a much more prominent role in making these connections and in constructing the explanations, with the support of their teacher.

Data Sources and Collection Methods

As the researcher, I collected video, audio, and artifact records and generated data over the course of ten months, from September 2014 to June 2015. During each meeting, I engaged in the group as a passive participant observer (Spradley, 1980). That is, I listened to, watched, and took notes about the interactions of the group, but I did not speak nor interact with the participants during the meetings. I recorded video and audio of the group's conversations at each meeting, using one camera on a tripod, which I placed far enough away from the group to capture all participants in the frame. I moved the camera as necessary when the group's configuration in the room changed. I recorded additional audio using one or two audio recorders, which I placed close to the participants. Following each group meeting, I updated a video log in which I recorded the date, meeting type, facilitator, location, participants, and meeting topics.

During the group meetings I took field notes (typed). In these "raw" field notes I wrote stream of consciousness, moment-to-moment observations (Emerson, Fretz, & Shaw, 2011) along with some 'big picture' descriptions and interpretations of the dynamics and topics of the conversation. These raw notes generated approximately one–two single-spaced pages for each meeting. After each meeting, I reviewed the video and added additional observations to the field notes, usually another one–two pages. As part of my ongoing analyses, I then used these "raw" field notes to write more detailed observations and structured interpretations ("cooked notes") in order to achieve a "thick description" (Geertz, 1973).

In order to better understand the meanings behind the discourse practices of this group, I also conducted semi-structured ethnographic interviews (Spradley, 1979) building on understandings that I was developing throughout the year. As part of these interviews, I used some sort of "grounded stimulus" (ethnographic record) to elicit participants' interpretations: a video clip, transcript excerpt, and/or event map (defined on pp. 212–213) from a previous meeting. To prepare these stimuli, I identified instances of a conversation that I wanted to know more about, from the perspective of the participants. To address these stimuli, I wrote very open-ended questions to pose to the participants. For example, in the September 24 meeting, Tim (the district science coordinator) engaged in the inquiry-oriented discourse practice of "pushing back," by opposing a claim made by Sam (the facilitator). In response to this instance, I wrote the question: "Tell me about what's happening in this clip?" To probe vague responses, I also prepared follow-up questions such as "can you tell me about how you decided to say that?" I tried to phrase these questions as open-ended and judgment-free as possible. Spradley (1979) refers to this as interview conversation which is part of, and based on, an ongoing ethnographic process of inquiry. I audio recorded all interviews.

Methodological Decisions and Analytic Processes

Drawing on Spradley's (1980) Ethnographic Research Cycle, I generated and analyzed data concurrently and recursively throughout fieldwork and writing. As a result of engaging this process over time, my research questions evolved, as did the ways in which I analyzed my data. In the following sections, I describe four important methodological decisions I made during the study, each of which occurred during a different stage of data analysis. These decisions had important consequences for my analysis, allowing me to better deconstruct the "unorganized" raw data corpus into smaller units of analysis, and then to reconstruct those units into a meaningful, organized whole. These analyses allowed me to construct a warranted account and theoretically framed explanation of how the group's conversations around practice mediated its opportunity to learn. To make sense of the group meeting data, I drew on traditions of Microethnographic Discourse Analysis (Erickson, 1992; Bloome, Carter, Christian, Otto, & Shuart-Faris, 2005). There are many variations of discourse analysis (DA), but all discourse analysis approaches attempt to make sense of language in use (Strauss & Feiz, 2014). My approach to discourse analysis focuses on sociocultural aspects of the group's discourse, rather than on linguistic factors. Because this study seeks to understand how various sociocultural aspects of conversation mediate the group's opportunity to learn, discourse analysis is appropriate for this study.

Identifying and Representing Key Events throughout the Data Set

Teacher learning communities construct cultural norms and practices that both build opportunities and impose constraints on the type and nature of professional conversations. Due to the complex nature of this phenomenon (professional conversations), it was important for me to make sampling decisions based on meaningful activity as identified in situ by the participants—as opposed to making those decisions a priori as the analyst. With this in mind, I needed to establish a system that would allow me to both meaningfully organize the data, and identify key events in the data. I decided to use event maps (Green & Meyer, 1991; Kelly, 2004; Brown & Spang, 2008; Kelly & Chen, 1999) to represent the different phases of activity in text form. An event map is an analytical structure used to identify the major and minor events within a data set. Event maps serve as "representations of the phases of activity constructed by participants as they work to accomplish their collective and personal goals" (Kelly, 2004, p. 2). I created event maps at various scales, representing: the year-long collection of meetings and interviews, individual meetings, key conversations ("episodes") within meetings.

To construct the event maps for each individual meeting, I began my analysis by identifying the major phases of activity (which I called "episodes") and the shifts between them. Episodes generally focused on a particular topic, and a change in that topic indicated a shift to a new episode. To facilitate this analysis, I used Studio Code software to create a "timeline" for each meeting. I then created a corresponding event map for each meeting to represent the different episodes in text form (see Figure 9.1). These meeting-level event maps were quite basic, containing just the general topic of each episode, and the times of the shifts between them. Once I had listed each episode, I then identified (in bold, see Figure 9.1) the episodes in which the group talked specifically about some aspect of science teaching practice.

To capture the talk and action, I then created an episode-level event map for those episodes focused on teaching practice. (See Figure 9.2). To capture the talk and action in the event map, I transcribed verbatim speech and any relevant non-verbal data such as gestures. I also included line numbers, episode start times, speakers' names, and episode topics. Within each episode, I then identified smaller sequence units, or "cohesive thematically-tied interactions" (Kelly & Chen, 1999, p. 892). On the event map, I indicated the shifts between each sequence unit and named each sequence (Column E in Figure 9.2). Including these shifts between episodes and sequences on the transcript made visible the ways that talk and action constructed episodes, and in turn, were situated in and framed by the larger units of social meanings. The analytic approach of looking across units of discourse allowed me to identify and represent key events that were interactionally acknowledged and recognized among participants as significant (Bloome & Egan-Robertson, 1993). These were identified analytically as "key events" (Gumperz, 2015).

	Time	Episode title (Focus of Conversation)
1	00:00:00.00	**Experiences Using Claims-Evidence-Reasoning with students**
2	00:22:02.07	**Organizing ideas co-constructed by students during unit**
3	00:25:56.34	**Mystery Powders—West 8's chemistry "phenomenon," part 1**
4	00:37:31.03	**Soap Making—West 8's chemistry "phenomenon," part 2**
5	00:46:03.56	**What constitutes a "phenomenon?"**
6	00:57:15.29	Wacky suggestion box
7	00:58:50.14	Mean girls
8	01:01:02.24	Logistics for next meeting

FIGURE 9.1 Meeting-level event map from the September 24, 2014 meeting.

	A	B	C	D	E
1	Time	Speaker	Verbatim Speech + nonverbal	Episode	sequence units
317	(00:25:56.34)	Tim	So what was the phenomenon you were looking at?	West 8's	new Q
318		Matt	All right, so I kind of feel like we got ourselves into a little bit… I	Chemistry	Beginning new
319			wouldn't call it a mess…	Phenomenon	representation
320		Cheri	Tad bit.		
321		Matt	Just a little bit, but it's a mess. How do we end up with a dual		
322			phenomenon? Which is…		
323		Cheri	We couldn't see it coming.		
324		Matt	So, so here in my mind this is what it is...		
325	(00:26:13:20)	Sam	Wait, before you say that. I just want to be clear. It's always a mess.		expressing
326			Right? This is always a mess. Part of the reason people like the traditional		empathy for
327			way of teaching is it's not a mess. And so, one of the major problems with		challenges of
328			thinking about teaching this way is that it is always a mess, at least for the		shifting to EDI
329			first three to five years. Sew your seatbelt on for that.		

FIGURE 9.2 Excerpt of an episode-level event map of the September 24, 2014 meeting.

Defining an Emergent Analytic Focus

I began my analysis by posing a number of questions to the data, which evolved over time. Knowing that the group included teachers from three different schools, I wondered what kinds of discourse practices would become the norm within this group. For example, would they engage in inquiry-oriented discourse practices such as publicly pushing back on each other's ideas, or would they simply "share" ideas, reserving any critique for private thoughts, which is a much more traditional discourse practice among teachers (Nelson, Deuel, Slavit, & Kennedy, 2010; Grossman, Wineburg, & Woolworth, 2001; Pfeiffer & Featherstone, 1997; Achinstein, 2002; Lieberman & Miller, 2008). Furthermore, would the teachers attempt to enact their school's particular norms when talking to teachers from other schools? What might happen if some teachers attempted to engage in inquiry-oriented discourse practices with other teachers who were used to more traditional, show-and-tell types of teacher-to-teacher discourse?

Knowing that there was a range among the teacher's years of learning about EDI, I was also very curious about whether that range might come into play, in terms of how the group interacted. In schools, teachers frequently advise one another on "best practices." Generally, less experienced teachers seek advice, while more experienced teachers provide advice, and rarely are anyone's advised practices publicly scrutinized, evaluated, or problematized (Nelson, Deuel, Slavit, & Kennedy, 2010; Grossman, Wineburg, & Woolworth, 2001; Pfeiffer & Featherstone, 1997; Achinstein, 2002; Lieberman & Miller, 2008). I wondered if each teacher's (perceived) degree of expertise with EDI would position them as advisers versus advisees, rather than co-learners who are each capable of contributing to other members' learning.

With these wonderings in mind, I began analyzing the first meeting's data about a week after it took place. I began by attending to the episodes that I had identified as "key events." I focused not only on the content of what was said, but also on the kind of "move" that the utterance made in terms of shaping subsequent turns of talk (e.g. posing a question, connecting to previous turns, shifting to a new focus, etc.). Based on my review of the literature regarding teacher-to-teacher discourse practices, I constructed an initial analytic domain (Spradely, 1980) that characterized these moves in a number of ways, including: the degree of certainty, the intent of a question, affirming or opposing others' ideas, the degree to which "exemplars" were scrutinized, acknowledgment of opposing perspectives, the degree of specificity in teachers' representations of practice, and the degree to which turns built on one another. That initial domain analysis is in found Figure 9.3.

As I analyzed the episodes, I also identified instances of conversations that I wanted to know more about, from the perspective of the participants. These instances often included participants engaging in some of the less common inquiry-oriented norms such as "pushing back." During the interviews, I often used video of these instances to elicit participants' interpretations of the interaction.

Like the group meetings, each interview served as a discourse event in which participants engaged in various discourse practices. However, because the interviews served as means of triangulating data from the interactive professional conversations, I was interested in the *content* of what the participants said. That is, I focused on participants' interpretations of the learning group's cultural practices. Given this focus, I did not use the same techniques of discourse analysis that I used with the video recordings of group meetings to interpret the interviews. Instead, I drew on traditions of qualitative thematic analysis (Braun & Clark, 2006).

As the meetings continued and I engaged in the procedures described above, I began to feel as though my focus on discourse practices (defined in Figure 9.3) as the sole factor of the conversation was too narrow. Over time, I began to pay attention to a number of other factors of the group's talk. In ethnographic research, these kinds of changes are common and expected, as the researcher engages the ethnographic research cycle (Spradley, 1980) all throughout data collection and analysis.

In particular, I began to pay more attention to the ways in which the talk positioned individuals in terms of perceived expertise. Specifically, I noted who

Teacher-to-teacher discourse practices	
"Traditional" discourse practice	Inquiry-oriented discourse practice
↑ is a kind of ↑	↑ is a kind of ↑
• Asking technical and clarifying questions • Speaking with certainty, authority • Offering supportive claims, evidence, rationales (affirming) • Denying or characterizing differences as variations of the dominant view • Using evidence as exemplars • Attending to broad issues through stories of classroom practice	• Asking questions that probe rationale • Speaking tentatively, inviting dialogue • Offering alternative claims, evidence, rationales (opposing/pushing back) • Acknowledging and using differences in perspectives productively • Using evidence as object of scrutiny • Attending to specific data from records of practice (student work, lesson plan, video)

FIGURE 9.3 Initial domain analysis.

was posing questions or expressing struggles versus who was providing answers/solutions. I also paid attention to the intended "receiver" of those questions, noting non-verbal aspects such as body positioning and eye gaze. That is, I noted whether questions were posed to the entire group, or to particular individuals. Furthermore, in addition to using the cover terms listed in Figure 9.3 to analyze the *type* of discourse moves in the talk, I began to pay more attention to *who* was using each move.

My increased attention to positioning was based partly on my own observations, but partly based on my analyses of the individual interviews. That is, issues of positioning emerged through my analyses of several early interviews—even interviews in which I did not pose any questions intended to elicit this information. In response to this emergent theme, over time I asked participants questions intended to specifically learn more about how they positioned themselves and others in the group in relation to one another. Thus, the interviews served both as a tool for uncovering an unexpected theme, and as a tool for further investigating that theme.

A structural change in the group's meetings also brought about new wonderings. In the meetings that took place in the fall 2014 semester, the group convened during VSD's middle school science department meetings and inservice days. The vast majority of this time was focused on learning about EDI and thus facilitated by Sam. But in the spring 2015 semester, Sam's teaching schedule at MSU conflicted with VSD's established schedule for the middle school science department meetings. Thus, the responsibility for facilitating those meetings shifted to Tim, the district science coordinator (who had facilitated those meetings in the three years prior to the meetings' focus on EDI). In order to continue to support the teachers outside those meetings, Sam designed and facilitated two Studio Days, one for each grade level.

These changes resulted in a number of new wonderings for me. First, Tim and Sam were very different facilitators, in terms of the kinds of expertise they brought to the group—not just in terms of EDI, but also in terms of facilitating inquiry-oriented discourse. I wondered how the variation between facilitators would impact the conversations. Second, I noticed that the Studio Days created a very different context for the conversation. For example, the nature of planning a Studio Day lesson together meant that the practices that the group discussed were "shared" by everyone in the conversation, whereas conversations that took place in the fall meetings tended to focus on a single teacher's practice, or practices shared by a small number of teachers in the group. Furthermore, the inservice workshops and afterschool meetings tended to reflect on practices that teachers used in their classes in the recent past, whereas the Studio Day conversations also required the group to look forward to practices in the immediate future. These different contexts for conversations also required different degrees of consensus from the group. That is, the nature of a Studio Day requires teachers to come to consensus (somewhat quickly) about how they will revise the lesson for the next class. Perhaps most importantly, the Studio Day structure gave every teacher in the group live, first-hand access to the teaching practices under discussion. In contrast, conversations that took place during the inservices and afterschool meetings centered around teachers' *representations* of their practice, which usually took the form of narratives.

As the meetings progressed throughout the spring, I also noticed that some episodes of teacher talk were more "generative" than others. That is, some episodes made teachers' practices public and transparent, while others left them private or very opaque. In some episodes, the group focused simply on pedagogical procedures, while in other episodes they probed the rationales underlying those procedures. In some episodes, the groups spoke about the theories underlying EDI, and/or their teaching practices, but did not necessarily attempt to connect the two. In other episodes, those connections were made explicitly. Finally, in some conversations, agency for sensemaking and problem solving was distributed across the members of the group. In other episodes, participants who were perceived as "more expert" (usually Sam or the teachers who had attended the summer workshops multiple times) seemed to be positioned as the sensemakers and problem solvers, whereas those perceived to be "less expert" were positioned as the recipients of those solutions.

At the same time, I began to ask myself, "So what?" That is, I realized that my wonderings tended to be descriptive, but not necessarily explanatory. While descriptive studies of teacher discourse are important, I wanted to move beyond description in order to construct an explanation of *how* the complexities of the teachers' conversation mediated their opportunities to learn. I needed to pay attention to the four aspects of generative teacher talk, and figure out if and how the quality of the talk was mediated by the variety of conversational factors that had piqued my interest.

As I attended to new factors of the group's conversations, I added new domains to my analysis. Having widened the scope of my investigation, I revised my research questions to identify which factors (not just discourse practices) accounted for differences between more- and less-generative talk, and to explain *how* those factors constructed more- or less-generative talk.

Identifying the Relevant Unit of Analysis

As I analyzed the group's talk over time, I began to feel that the small grain size of my analysis—on individual moves—was constraining my ability to explain how the conversation mediated the group's learning opportunities. Specifically, I struggled to characterize the generative nature of the conversation, especially the distribution of agency across the group's members. To understand the ways that meanings were constructed through part–whole relationships, I decided to "zoom out" to the level of the "conversational routine" as my unit of analysis. Horn and Little (2010) define a conversational routine as "the patterned and recurrent ways that conversations unfold within a social group. Routines are constituted by moves, turns of talk that shape the interaction's progress by setting up and constraining the response of the subsequent speakers" (p. 184). They argued that in the study of teachers' conversations, "distinctions at the level of routines are most useful in understanding opportunities to learn" (p. 184). Zooming out to this meso-level unit of analysis allowed me to tie together multiple discourse moves and instances of positioning into a single factor (the conversational routine) in a way that was more meaningful than focusing on either of these micro-level practices individually. Zooming out to the level of the conversational routine also made it easier to identify aspects of more- and less-generative talk. I added four categories of codes, based on my review of the literature: transparency of practices; attention to rationales; theory–practice connections; and agency. (See the previous section titled "Generative Teacher Talk.")

As I made each of these changes throughout the year, I went back to the beginning of the data set to update my analysis of previous meetings, using the new codes for consistency across the data corpus. As a result, I reviewed the developing data set several times, including a pass of the full data set (after the school year ended) extending from the very first to very last meeting. As a result of this process, I settled on five factors of the teachers' conversations that seemed important to pay attention to: (a) the context in which the conversation occurred, (b) the tools that participants used to represent their practices, (c) the stance (improving versus proving) with which participants represented their practice, (d) the resources that participants drew upon while engaging in conversation, and (e) the conversational routines in which the group engaged when taking up practice. (The different varieties of these factors are listed under "Mediating Factors" in Figure 9.4 and in the bottom half of Figure 9.5. See Ricketts (2017) for more details about these factors.) The various units of analysis that I used throughout the study (episodes, routines, moves, practices) are embedded within one another. For example, a single episode (the largest unit) may include one or more conversational routines that include multiple speakers. These routines are composed of multiple, connected moves (made by individuals), each of which embodies one or more discourse practices. The five factors I identified as mediating the generative nature of the conversation were apparent at different levels. For example, the impact of the context and conversational routines became apparent at the episode level. The resources that participants drew on became apparent at the level of conversational routine. Stance and tools were apparent in individual moves.

Constructing Explanations from Data Analyses

Following the pass of the full data set, I created an event map spanning the entire school year that identified all of the conversations around practice in each meeting. To help me identify relationships among the data, I added to the event map: (a) cover terms for all the potential mediating factors that I observed (context, tools, stance, resources, conversational routines), (b) my codes for all of the aspects of more- and lessgenerative talk. An excerpt of this event map is found in Figure 9.4.

Laying out the analysis in this way allowed me to characterize each episode as overall more generative or less generative (including episodes of "mixed" generativity). I then reorganized the order of the episodes listed in the year-long event map, shifting from chronological order to degree of generativity. That is, I ordered the episodes from least to most generative. I then compared the mediating factors of all the conversations within a particular category ("more-generative talk," "less-generative talk" or "mixed talk") to identify the varieties of each factors that they generally had in common. Then I compared those sets of factors across the three categories to better understand how they differed. Thus, the event map served not only as a useful organizational tool, it also served as an analytical tool. Using these techniques, I identified the varieties of each factor associated with more-generative talk, and the varieties of each factor associated with less- generative talk. These associations are represented in Figure 9.5.

While these associations were useful in terms of description, they still did not answer the question about *how* the conversation mediated the teachers' learning opportunities (or in other words, how the factors constructed more- or less-generative talk). I needed to find a way to shift the analysis from description to explanation. To facilitate this process, I created a skeleton concept map that contained the five factors that I identified as mediating the generative nature of the conversation (context, tools, stance, resources, and conversational routines), along with the four aspects of more- and less-generative talk (transparency of practices, attention to rationales, theory–practice connections, agency) as a tool for making sense of *how* these constructs related to one another.

	A	B	C	D	E	F	G	H	I	J	K	L	M	N	O	P	Q	R	S	T	U	V	W	X	Y	Z	AA
1			MEDIATING FACTORS																	LEARNING OPPORTUNITIES							
2	Meeting Date	Episode "name"	Stance Improving Proving		Tools Narrating Artifacts		Contexts					Conversational Routines for Take-up					Resources Expertise: Contextual Theoretical Facilitation			More Generative Talk (Learning Opportunities Afforded)				Less Generative Talk (Learning Apportunities Constrained)			
3			I	P	N	A	Plan shared pract	Revise shared pract	Reflect on unshare pract	Check in	Imagine future pratice	Min/No Take Up (NTU)	Affirm & Elab (AE)	Quick Advice (QA)	Probe & Advise (PA)	Coll Sense Making (CSM)	C	T	F	Transp. Practice	Att'n to Ration.	Theory-Practice Connect	Distr. Agency	Opaque Practice	Emph. on Proced.	Theory OR Practice	Imbal. agengy
4	09/24/14 Sept Monthly Meeting	Using CER		P	N				Reflect								C							Opaque	Proc	Pract	Imbal
5		Organizing ideas	I		N				Reflect						PA		C	T	F	Transp	Ration	Connect					Imbal
6		Mystery Powders	I		N				Reflect					QA			C	T	F	Transp	Ration	Connect					Imbal
7		Soap Making	I	P	N				Reflect					QA			C	T	F	Opaque	Ration	Connect	Distr*				Imbal*
8		What's a phenom	I		N				Reflect							CSM	C	T	F		Ration	Connect		Opaque			Imbel
9	10/28/14 Oct monthly meeting	reluct to part.	I		N				Reflect						PA		C	T	F					Opaque	Proc	Pract	Imbal
10		pressing vocab		P	N				Reflect				AE				C	T	F					Opaque	Proc	Pract	Imbal
11		Lack of Engagmt	I		N				Reflect							CSM	C	T	F					Opaque	Proc	Pract	Imbel
12		fit ideas together	I		N				Reflect						PA		C	T	F					Opaque	Proc	Pract	Imbal
13		illusion rigor	I		N				Reflect				AE				C	T	F					Opaque	Proc	Pract	Imbal
14		stu's dominate	I		N				Reflect			NTU					C	T	F					Opaque	Proc	Pract	Imbal
15		means to know	I		N				Reflect						PA		C	T	F					Opaque	Proc	Pract	Imbal
16	10/31/14 Oct inservice	EDI overview		P	N	A					Imagine				PA		C	T	F		Ration	Connect		Opaque			Imbal
17		Group assess	I		N						Imagine				PA		C	T	F	Transp	Ration	Connect	Distr				
18		D3 scaffolds	I		N						Imagine				PA		C	T	F	Transp	Ration	Connect	Distr				
19		Video - D1	I			A			Reflect						PA		C	T	F	Transp	Ration	Connect	Distr				
20		Acorn to Oak I		P	N				Reflect						PA		C	T	F					Opaque	Proc	Pract	Imbal
21		Acorn to Oak II	I		N				Reflect							CSM	C	T	F		Ration	Connect	Distr	Opaque			
22		problematizing EDI	I		N				Reflect					QA	PA		C	T	F					Opaque	Proc	Pract	Imbal

FIGURE 9.4 Excerpt from year-long event map with codes.

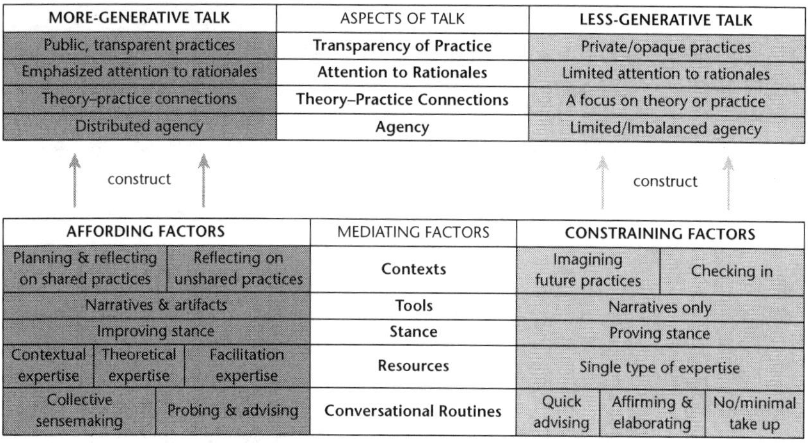

MORE-GENERATIVE TALK	ASPECTS OF TALK	LESS-GENERATIVE TALK
Public, transparent practices	**Transparency of Practice**	Private/opaque practices
Emphasized attention to rationales	**Attention to Rationales**	Limited attention to rationales
Theory–practice connections	**Theory–Practice Connections**	A focus on theory or practice
Distributed agency	**Agency**	Limited/Imbalanced agency

↑ construct ↑ (more-generative talk) ↑ construct ↑ (less-generative talk)

AFFORDING FACTORS	MEDIATING FACTORS	CONSTRAINING FACTORS
Planning & reflecting on shared practices; Reflecting on unshared practices	**Contexts**	Imagining future practices; Checking in
Narratives & artifacts	**Tools**	Narratives only
Improving stance	**Stance**	Proving stance
Contextual expertise; Theoretical expertise; Facilitation expertise	**Resources**	Single type of expertise
Collective sensemaking; Probing & advising	**Conversational Routines**	Quick advising; Affirming & elaborating; No/minimal take up

FIGURE 9.5 Conversational factors that construct associated with more- and less-generative talk.

As I reviewed an episode's transcript, I filled in details about the mediating factors, and I drew arrows between the mediating factors and the various aspects of generative talk. On those arrows, I wrote specific examples of how the constructs related to one another. Figure 9.6 shows a completed concept map from a very complex episode that took place during the September 2014 meeting.

As I looked across the collection of concept maps of the episodes, what stood out most to me were the ways in which the mediating factors *interacted with each other* to construct more- or less-generative talk. That is, there was rarely a simple path connecting a single mediating factor to a single aspect of generative talk. Rather, the factors tended to influence each other (which can be seen in Figure 9.6). Most interestingly, the mediating factor of stance was not directly related to any of the four aspects of more- or less-generative talk. But in every episode, stance interacted with the other factors to mediate the generative nature of the talk (see Figure 9.6). These interactions and the ways in which they constructed the talk are explained in greater detail in the analysis of the "Chemistry Phenomena" episode that follows.

Illustrative Example of Analysis of Professional Learning Discourse

In the first official meeting of the group (September 2014), the participants negotiated a common understanding of the construct of "phenomenon," in terms of the anchor for constructing a scientific explanation. The transcript excerpts below powerfully illustrate the ways in which five factors (context, tools, stance, resources, and conversational routines) interacted with one another to mediate

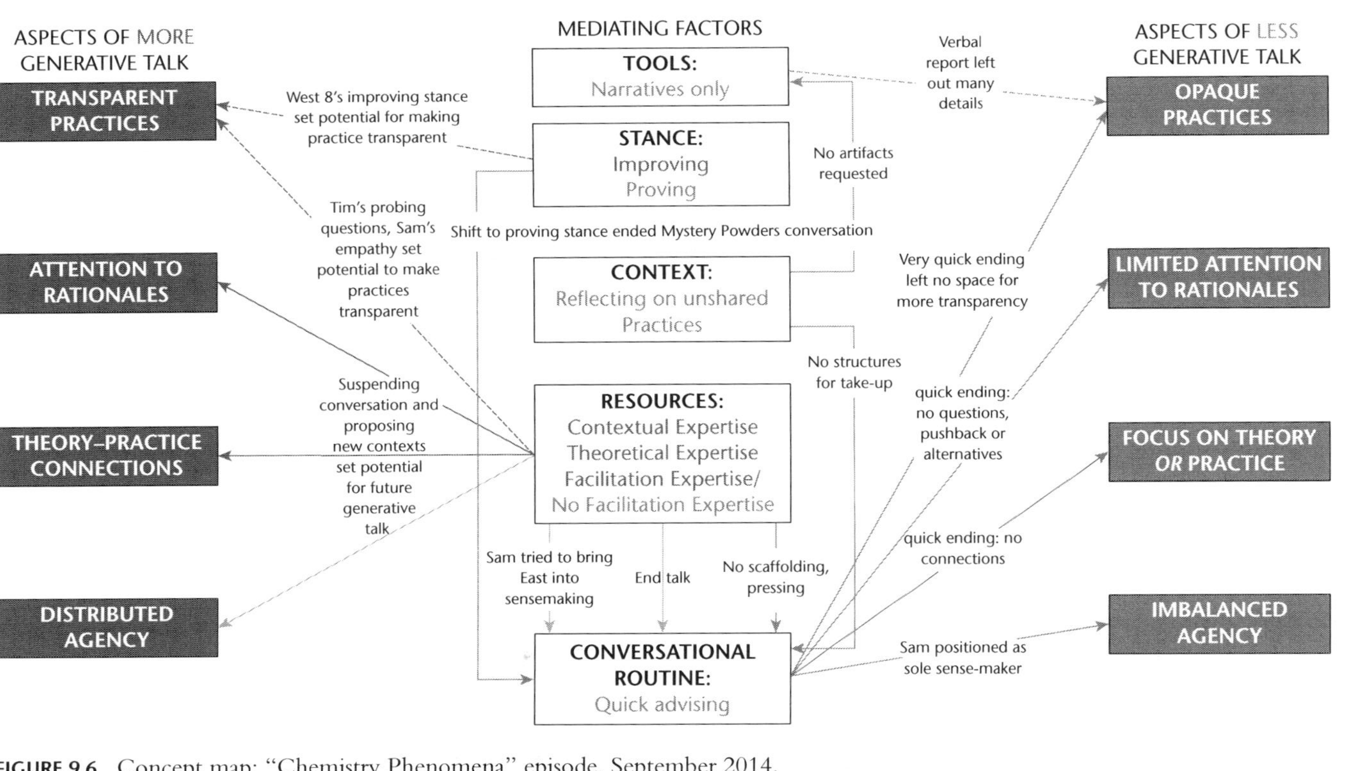

FIGURE 9.6 Concept map: "Chemistry Phenomena" episode, September 2014.

the generative nature of the group's talk (transparency, rationales, theory–practice connections, agency; see Figures 9.5 and 9.6).

Tim (district science coordinator) posed a question to West teacher Matt that began the episode:

317	Tim:	So what was the phenomenon you were looking at?
318	Matt:	So I feel like we got ourselves into a little bit. . . I wouldn't call it a mess . . .
319	Cheri:	Tad bit.
320	Matt:	Just a little bit, but it's a mess.
321	Cheri:	We couldn't see it coming.
322	Matt:	So, in my mind this is what it is . . .
323	Sam:	Wait, before you say that. I just want to be clear. It's always a mess. Part of the
324		reason people like the traditional way of teaching is it's not a mess. So one of
325		the major problems with thinking about teaching this way is that it's always a
326		mess, at least for the first three to five years.
327		*[Matt describes the day-to-day activities in the Mystery Powders unit, to including the explanation that the students construct—distinguishing between*
356		*eight white powders in a mixture]*
357	Sam:	[*2 second pause*] So again, I'm, so . . .
358	Matt:	Go ahead, just let it fly. That's what we do usually.
359	Cheri:	We started with something else. And that's what . . .
360	Matt:	Yeah, we did but . . .
361	Cheri:	But that's why, Matt . . .
362	Matt:	Yeah, just talk about it.
363	Sam:	Okay, so here would be my argument. What you have chosen is not a
364		phenomenon.
365	Matt:	I knew it! [*laughs*]
366	Cheri:	But we . . .
367	Sam:	What you have chosen is a task that's assigned in schools to accomplish a goal.
368		I'm not saying it doesn't accomplish that goal, but where in life do you encounter
369		eight white powders mixed together and you have to figure out what they are?

This excerpt demonstrates the evolving nature of the group's conversation. In lines 317–326, the group set off on a trajectory toward generative talk. This trajectory can be attributed to three important factors: context, resources, and stance.

The free-form nature of the context allowed any participant to pose questions to any other, supporting distributed agency. In line 317, Tim (who was not the designated facilitator) used the resource of facilitation expertise to pose an important question. This question created an opportunity for theory–practice connections because it grounded the group's previous theoretical talk about "phenomena" in the West teachers' actual practice. Because Tim was not the designated facilitator, his question also supported distributed agency by encouraging others to engage as co-sense-makers. In lines 318–322, both Matt and Cheri represented their practice with an improving stance. Specifically, Matt acknowledged the limitations of their practice, referring to the West 8 teachers' shared chemistry phenomenon as "a mess" (lines 318 and 320), which Cheri affirmed ("tad bit," line 319). Cheri also pointed out the uncertain nature of trying out something new, saying, "We couldn't see it coming," (line 321). In lines 323–326, Sam drew on the resource of facilitation expertise, empathizing with the teachers' struggles. His comment further encourages the group's improving stance. Their improving stances set the tone for the group to ask questions and take up the West teachers' practice in a conversational routine of collective sensemaking, which can create opportunities for making practices transparent, attending to rationales for practice, making theory–practice connections, and distributing agency for sensemaking.

In lines 327–356 (omitted for presentation), that trajectory began to shift toward less-generative talk, including opaque practices, limited attention to rationales, imbalanced agency, and no explicit theory–practice connections. This shift can be explained by the interaction of a number of factors, including context, tools, resources, and conversational routine. The shift begins in lines 327–356, when Matt provided a very general description of the Mystery Powders unit, without using any visual tools such as student work, classroom video, or lesson plans. Following his turn, the free-form nature of the context served to constrain learning opportunities. That is, although the participants were free to take up Matt's representation in any way they wanted, there were no structures in place to encourage that take-up (i.e. a Critical Friends Group conversation protocol, National School Reform Faculty, 2018). Without these structures in place, Sam was positioned as the sole sensemaker (lines 357, 363–364, 367–369). While his contributions drew on the valuable resource of his theoretical expertise, no one drew on facilitation expertise to ask the teachers questions that clarified their teaching practices, probed their rationales, or gave any kind of feedback. The reliance on narratives as the sole tool for representing practice, combined with the free-form nature of the context and the lack of facilitation expertise left the teaching practices opaque, rationales for practice and theory–practice connections unexplored, and the agency for sensemaking imbalanced.

It is also important to note the variety of stance taking in lines 358–369. Throughout these lines, Matt maintains an improving stance, inviting the group to "let it fly" (line 358), "just talk about it" (line 362), and laughing at his own error in judgment about what counts as a phenomenon (line 365). Sam's responses took a strong proving stance, assessing the West 8 teachers' practices in very certain terms ("what you have chosen is not a phenomenon," lines 363–364), and assessing the goals of the Mystery Powders unit as inconsistent with EDI (lines 367–369). The certainty of his stance (in combination with the lack of conversation structures) may have further constrained others' sense of agency for contributing to the group's sensemaking process. In all three of Cheri's turns (359, 361, 366), she began to shift the focus of the talk to a different practice. Cheri's turns represent a proving stance because they explicitly turned *away from* the Mystery Powders, and toward "something else," in an effort to prove the West 8's teachers' effectiveness with EDI.

The important role of this stance taking became more apparent in the dialogue that followed:

370	Cheri:	All right Brent, tell him what we did. Tell him what we originally did.
371		We had a phenomenon. We thought.
372	Brent:	I'm not sure if the other one is a phenomenon either.
373	Cheri:	Brent, tell him. Tell him what we did. I want you to tell him.
374	Matt:	Tell him what we did. Sam's probably going to say, "Yeah, it's a phenomenon."
375	Cheri:	It's better, I think.
376	Brent:	So I don't still think it is, because of the way we framed it.

Here, the interaction of stance, context, and conversational routine continued the group's shift toward less-generative talk. Cheri's turns (lines 370–371, 373, 375), attempt to shift the conversation away from talking about the Mystery Powders, and instead focus on what they "originally did" (370). Cheri asserts that they "had a phenomenon" (line 371) which is "better" [than Mystery Powders] (line 375). In one sense, turning away from the Mystery Powders and toward their "original" phenomenon demonstrates a stance of proving the effectiveness of the practices. This shift in stance and focus—perhaps in response to the strong proving stance of Sam's assessment of their practices—took advantage of the "free-form" nature of the context. In terms of resources, no member of the group used facilitation expertise to return the group to the original topic (Mystery Powders). Thus, when Cheri turned away from Mystery Powders, the rest of the group followed along. As a result of these interactions (context, stance, resources), the conversational routine around "Mystery Powders" ended abruptly (known as "quick advising"), thereby constraining all four aspects of generative talk. It is important to reiterate that it was the interaction of multiple factors (contex, tools, stance, resources, conversational routine)—rather than any one factor or person—that constrained the group's learning opportunities.

Viewed from a different perspective, Cheri's turns also demonstrate an improving stance, because they reveal the tentative nature of Cheri's assertions—"we thought" (line 371) and "I think" (line 375). This tentativeness may indicate Cheri's openness to improving (rather than proving) the effectiveness of this practice. In Brent's two turns during this negotiation (lines 372 and 376), he maintains an improving stance, using tentative language ("I'm not sure," "I don't think"), and acknowledging the possibility that "the other one" does not constitute a phenomenon in the context of EDI. A mixture of stances can send mixed signals to a group, making it difficult for them to decide how to respond. (Improving stances generally invite questions, pushback, tentative alternatives, etc., whereas proving stances often invite silence or equally strong proving (defensive) stances (Nelson, Slavit, & Deuel, 2012).)

The ways in which the group would take up West's "other" phenomenon were further shaped by the role of positioning during this negotiation. In lines 370–374, Cheri and Matt explicitly position Sam as the evaluator of their practices. Cheri nominates Brent to "tell him" [Sam] about their practices five times: twice in line 370, and three times in lines 373. Matt affirms Sam's position, specifically naming Sam as the evaluator in line 374. This positioning can potentially construct a conversational routine of "advising," which generally constrains the distribution of agency within a group. In contrast to Cheri and Matt, during this negotiation Brent did not position Sam as the sole evaluator of the West 8 teachers' practices. For example, rather than telling Sam about their other phenomenon, Brent pushed back against Cheri's interpretation of the phenomenon's alignment with EDI (lines 372 and 376), and began to provide a rationale ("because of the way we framed it" line 376). These turns positioned Brent as a capable interpreter of his own practice, pushing the conversation toward collective sensemaking (as opposed to advising).

Instead of engaging with Brent's rationale, in the next turn (line 377) Matt began to narrate the West 8 teachers' practices to Sam:

377 Matt: So we mixed sodium hydroxide with coconut oil.
378 Cheri: But we didn't tell them what it was.
379 Brent: We just said it was coconut oil being added with something.
380 Cheri: And they saw something happen.
381 Brent: And I got these two [inaudible] at the end that look a lot alike, and basically the
382 question is "What do we have here? Is the coconut oil just together with some
383 other stuff, just mixed up?" Some think that it's something different. And we have
384 to be able to develop the skills to quantify what's different about them. We kind of
385 use the "Fat versus Soap" from elementary that they did. But this is expanding it

386 to trying to describe the differences between them in a more quantitative chemical
387 level. And then we can use that to talk about later on what changes [inaudible].
388 Sam: Okay now stop, I got that.
389 [inaudible side conversation begins—Jill, Brandon, and Kathy from East]
390 Brent: But the framing for it I haven't been able to—'cause it's also not the kind of
391 thing that you just come across somebody mixing.
392 Sam: Yeah, especially those two particular things.
393 Brent: If you call it Soap Making. . .

In this excerpt, the conversational routine continues to take shape, due to the interaction of multiple factors. In line 388, Sam takes advantage of the free-form nature of the context, interrupting the West teachers' co-representation of their practices ("Okay now stop, I got that"). In this turn the interaction of context and resources begins to constrain the generative nature of the group's talk. In the absence of structures for taking up West's practices (context), Sam did not draw on facilitation expertise (resource) to invite the other teachers to pose any clarifying questions, nor did he check in with others in the group to assess whether they also "got that." This move nudged the conversation toward a routine of advising, and potentially constrained two aspects of generative talk: the transparency of West's practices, and the agency of other teachers in the group to make sense of those practices. (Note that following this turn, the East teachers began a quiet side conversation, rather than participating in the existing conversation. This choice serves as evidence of constrained agency.) Brent's turns in lines 390 and 393 resist Sam's position as primary sensemaker, by contributing a rationale for the framing of the classroom activities as "Soap Making" (lines 393) but also critiquing the alignment of those activities with the tenets of EDI (lines 390–391). Brent's critique of his own practices also demonstrates his improving stance. Brent's turns thus shift the conversation toward a routine of collective sensemaking and toward multiple aspects of generative talk: distributed agency for sensemaking within the group, attention to rationales for practice, and (dis)connections between those practices and the underlying theory of EDI.

Noticing the East teachers' side conversation, Sam then drew the East teachers into the whole group conversation:

394 Sam: Wait. I want to know what these guys [Jill, Brandon, and Kathy] are asking.
395 Jill: Well, I was just saying that if you're covering in eighth grade chemistry—atoms,

396		periodic table, reactions, acids, and bases—that's your chemistry unit, right?
397		So find an everyday chemical reaction that does that. But you know, why does
398		this happen? How does it happen?
399	Matt:	Yeah, that crossed our mind, but just in our defense. . .
400	Sam:	You don't have to defend yourself.
401	Matt:	Well, I know. One of the things we were worried about was that we didn't
402		want to have something that was too big, that went on forever. So we
403		decided let's make the phenomenon—that we thought was a phenomenon
404		—basically long enough that we can keep coming back to it, without it
405		dragging on and everyone just getting bored of the whole idea.
406	Sam:	Right, because that can lead to the kids wanting to gouge their eyes out
407		because they're like, "Again?!"

Here, the conversational factors interacted in even more complex ways to mediate the group's learning opportunities. On the one hand, the group's talk positioned multiple members as contributors to the sensemaking process. For example, when Sam interrupted the West 8 teachers' representation (line 394), he was likely trying to draw out the East teachers' interpretation of the West 8 teachers' practices. While she did not specifically evaluate whether the "Soap Making" activities constituted a phenomenon, Jill considered the range of the eighth grade chemistry standards (lines 395–398) and suggested a (somewhat general) alternative to "Soap Making" as a phenomenon (397–398.) In this way, Jill positioned herself as a potential contributor (albeit around a slightly different imagined practice). After Jill's turn, Sam remained quiet, allowing Matt to take up Jill's advice (line 399). When Matt drew the group's attention to West's rationale for their practices (lines 401–405), he also positioned himself as a co-sensemaker. The talk in lines 394–407 then, constructs a conversational routine approaching collective sensemaking, in which agency is distributed more equally across the group.

On the other hand, the interaction of resources and context constrained other aspects of generative talk. In Sam's first turn (line 394), he drew on the resource of facilitation expertise, unifying the two parallel conversations that were occurring. This move had had potential for calling attention to others' interpretations of the "Soap Making" practice (rationales for practice). Instead it introduced yet another (but related) topic—Jill's advice to "find an everyday chemical reaction," and explain "why does this happen? How does it happen?" (lines 397–398). Here, the free-form nature of the context overpowered

Sam's attempts to use facilitation expertise, constraining the group's opportunity to reason about whether "Soap Making" represented a phenomenon in the terms of EDI (connecting theory and practice). Although Matt's response ("that crossed our mind," line 399) acknowledged Jill's advice, he did not take up her contribution any further. Instead, the free-form context allowed Matt to return to the West teachers' Soap Making practices (lines 401–405). Although his turn shifted away from an opportunity to learn by talking about Jill's advice, in turning back to the Soap Making practices, Matt drew on his contextual expertise (experience in the classroom trying EDI) to focus the group's attention on the West teachers' rationale for choosing Soap Making as a phenomenon (wanting to avoid a phenomenon that was "too big, that went on forever," lines 401–402).

Sensing the limitations of the current conversation's generative nature, Sam drew the conversation to a close:

408 Sam: Okay, so part of the problem that we're going to have here is that—it's
409 like having conversation in Italian with a bunch of people at the table
410 who don't speak Italian. So let me think about this, because as much as I
411 think, for me and maybe for you [West teachers], this idea of "What is a
412 phenomenon?" and "What is the correct grain size phenomenon to select
413 for this sort of task?" I think that's an interesting conversation. But if
414 we're going to talk as a whole group, I don't think that's a productive
415 question. So I'm going to recommend a couple of possibilities. So the
416 University of Washington just put out a video that is summary of how
417 they think about science teaching. It gives you an idea of what this stuff
418 looks like, what the purposes are. The other thing we can do, is start with
419 something smaller, so that you don't feel like there's this huge thing that
420 you have to do. Because it is a mess and it can be disconcerting to feel
421 like you—or your class—is out of control. You don't want to feel like,
422 "My kids don't understand what's going on. I don't understand what's going
423 on. We've gone off the rails into this territory where I don't know how to
424 get us back." And that is not a place that I think anybody wants to be in.

In this excerpt, Sam used facilitation expertise to draw the conversation about the West 8 teachers' practices to a close, by: (a) pointing out the varying levels of understanding about EDI across the group (lines 411–413), (b) emphasizing the need for the talk to be productive for everyone in the group (lines 413–415), and (c) suggesting two possible choices for future conversations (lines 415–420). In lines 420–424 he also demonstrates facilitation expertise by empathizing with the "disconcerting" messiness of shifting to EDI. Although these moves temporarily closed the opportunity to learn from talking about the "Soap Making" practice, it opened future possibilities for this opportunity to learn in a more intentionally designed future context. His suggestion of watching the video from the University of Washington (lines 415–418) potentially supports a conversation in which practices are made transparent ("it gives you an idea of what this stuff looks like," lines 417–418), teachers attend to the rationales for EDI practices ("what the purposes are," line 418), make connections between the underlying theory of EDI and actual classroom practices ("how they think about science teaching," lines 416–417). He also suggests that they "start with something smaller" (lines 418–419), which would allow everyone to engage in collective sensemaking, thereby distributing agency for sensemaking across the group.

Summary: "Mixed" Talk around the Mystery Powders "Phenomenon"

Overall, this episode can be characterized as two rounds of "quick advising" around two of West 8's chemistry "phenomena": Mystery Powders and Soap Making. ("Quick advising" is a conversational routine that begins with a teacher expressing a problem that is then taken up by one or more group members in the form of advice or solutions—as opposed to collectively negotiating potential solutions.) In the talk around both phenomena, the group's initial trajectory toward more-generative talk was disrupted by interacting mediating factors, thereby constraining the generative potential of the conversation. Those shifts occurred in different ways.

In the talk around Mystery Powders, although Matt and Cheri relied on narratives, their improving stance combined with Sam's facilitation expertise (empathy) set the conversation on a potential trajectory toward some aspects of generative talk. That trajectory was interrupted when Sam pushed back against the West 8 teachers' practices as "not a phenomenon." At that point, a combination of factors—the "free-form" nature of the context and one participant's shift to a proving stance—allowed the topic of the conversation to shift abruptly (to Soap Making). When no one drew on facilitation expertise to draw the group's focus back to the Mystery Powders that part of the conversation ended, constraining any potential opportunities to learn from examining that practice.

In the talk around Soap Making, Brent's improving stance and his attention to rationale again set the group on a potential path toward more-generative talk. But this time, that trajectory was interrupted by the "free-form" nature of the context, when the East teachers began a parallel conversation. This time, Sam drew on facilitation expertise to draw the East teachers into the conversation, which potentially could have helped the group to engage in collective sensemaking around whether and why "Soap Making" constituted a "phenomenon" in the terms of EDI. But in practice, that facilitation move had the opposite effect. It instead introduced yet another (though closely related) topic into the mix (Jill's advice to find a common everyday chemical reaction). The free-form context allowed the topic to shift again, when Matt turned away from Jill's advice and instead turned toward the topic of an appropriate "grain size" for phenomena. Sensing a trajectory toward imbalanced agency, Sam drew on facilitation expertise to close the conversation and propose a different context for the group's next meeting. Although that move constrained the group's immediate opportunity to learn, it opened possibilities for opportunities to learn in a different future context.

Conclusion

Teachers' professional conversations are becoming more common, thanks in part to the growing popularity of engaging in professional learning communities as a form of professional development. While these conversations hold great potential for supporting teacher learning, too little is known about how the designed and spontaneous factors of these conversations mediate teachers' learning opportunities. More research is needed to better inform the design and facilitation of these groups, but that research requires methods that can sufficiently capture and make sense of the complex nature of the conversations.

Teacher learning groups are situated within unique cultural and historical contexts, which in turn shape the groups' social practices. Thus, the interaction within these groups is nuanced, subtle, and complex. To date, ex situ accounts of this interaction (such as interviews, surveys, self-report logs, and diaries) have not sufficiently captured this complexity. While in situ approaches that rely on observational protocols have not been used widely to study teachers' professional conversations, they too are unlikely to account for the conversations' subtlety and nuance, or to explain how the groups' talks shape and are shaped by their social practices.

Instead, an interactional ethnographic perspective—coupled with the strategic methods of discourse analysis—is better suited to capturing and explaining such a complex, situated phenomenon. In this study, these methods provided me with tools to investigate the phenomenon in different "grain sizes," and to understand how those differently sized units of analysis interacted with one another, and with the context. For example, in the episode analyzed above, it was important for me to look at very small units (such as individual turns) to understand stance taking and representational tools. But I had to zoom out to the level of conversational routine to understand how the participants drew on their varying types of expertise as resources in the conversation, and how their turns positioned one another with varying degrees of agency. Looking even more broadly at the episodes in whole allowed me to understand the influence of the designed context on the kinds of conversational routine that unfolded. It was also important for me to learn about the group's history and the cultures of its subgroups to better understand the patterns of positioning that unfolded over the year (see Ricketts, 2017 for year-long patterns of positioning).

Investigating this teacher learning group through an interaction ethnographical perspective provided an approach that incorporated a systematic, conceptually framed approach to discourse analysis. This allowed for close attention to the ways in which the relationships and knowledge were (co)constructed in the moment. In addition, by understanding the cultural and historical context of teacher professional development, and the specifics of this group, I was able to identify *which* designed and spontaneous factors mediated the conversation's potential for generating learning opportunities. Through these analyses, I was able to construct explanations of *how* those factors interacted in complex, patterned ways to construct more- or less-generative talk. In order to better inform the design and facilitation of teachers' professional conversations, future studies of this phenomenon should draw on a similar logic-of-inquiry, using the multi-faceted levels of discourse analysis within an ethnographically informed perspective of interaction.

References

Achinstein, B. (2002). Conflict amid community: The micropolitics of teacher collaboration. *The Teachers College Record, 104*(3), 421–455.

Ball, D., & Cohen, D. (1999). Developing practice, developing practitioners: Toward a practice-based theory of professional education. In G. Sykes & L. Darling-Hammond (Eds.), *Teaching as the learning profession: Handbook of policy and practice* (pp. 3–32). San Francisco: Josey-Bass.

Barsalou, L. W. (1999). Perceptual symbol systems. *Behavioral and Brain Sciences, 1999*(22), 577–660.

Bloome, D., Carter, S. P., Christian, B. M., Otto, S., & Shuart-Faris, N. (2005). *Discourse analysis and the study of classroom language and literacy events: A microethnographic perspective* (p. 328). Mahwah: Lawrence Erlbaum Associates.

Bloome, D., & Egan-Robertson, A. (1993). The social construction of intertextuality in classroom reading and writing lessons. *Reading Research Quarterly, 28*(4), 304–333.

Braun, V., & Clarke, V. (2006). Using thematic analysis in psychology. *Qualitative Research in Psychology, 3*(2), 77–101.

Brown, B. A., & Spang, E. (2008). Double talk: Synthesizing everyday and science language in the classroom. *Science Education, 92*(4), 708–732.

Castanheira, M. L., Crawford, T., Dixon, C. N., & Green, J. L. (2001). Interactional ethnography: An approach to studying the social construction of literate practices. *Linguistics and Education, 11*(4), 353–400.

Cochran-Smith, M., & Lytle, S. L. (1999). Relationships of knowledge and practice: Teacher learning in communities. *Review of Research in Education, 24*, 249–305.

Emerson, R. M., Fretz, R. I., & Shaw, L. L. (2011). *Writing ethnographic fieldnotes*. 2nd ed. Chicago: University of Chicago Press.

Erickson, F. (1992). Ethnographic microanalysis of interaction. In M. G. LeCompte, W. L. Millroy, & J. Preissle (Eds.), *The handbook of qualitative research in education* (pp. 201–225). San Diego: Academic Press.

Flanders, N. A. (1960). *Interaction analysis in the classroom*. Minneapolis: College of Education, University of Minnesota.

Gee, J. P. (2008). A sociocultural perspective on opportunity to learn. In P. S. Moss, D. C. Pullin, J. P. Gee, E. H. Haertel, & J. L. Young (Eds.), *Assessment, equity and opportunity to learn* (pp. 76–108). Cambridge: Cambridge University Press.

Geertz, C. (1973). Thick description: Toward an interpretive theory of culture. In *The interpretation of cultures: Selected essays* (pp. 3–30). New York: Basic Books.

Green, J. L., & Meyer, L. (1991). The embeddedness of reading in classroom life: Reading as a situated process. In C. Baker & A. Luke (Eds.), *Toward a critical sociology of reading pedagogy* (pp. 141–160). Amsterdam: John Benjamins.

Green, J. L., Skukauskaite, A., & Baker, W. D. (2012). Ethnography as epistemology: An introduction to educational ethnography. In J. Arthur, M. Waring, R. Coe, & L. V. Hedges (Eds.), *Research methodologies and methods in education*. London: Sage.

Grossman, P., Wineburg, S., & Woolworth, S. (2001). Toward a theory of teacher community. *The Teachers College Record, 103*(6), 942–1012.

Gumperz, J. J. (2015). Interactional sociolinguistics: A personal perspective. In D. Schriffrin, D. Tannen, & H. E. Hamilton (Eds.), *The handbook of discourse analysis* (2nd ed., pp. 309–323). West Sussex, UK: Wiley.

Horn, I. S. (2010). Teaching replays, teaching rehearsals, and re-visions of practice: Learning from colleagues in a mathematics teacher community. *Teachers College Record, 112*(1), 225–259.

Horn, I. S., & Little, J. W. (2010). Attending to problems of practice: Routines and resources for professional learning in teachers' workplace interactions. *American Educational Research Journal, 47*(1), 181–217.

Johnson, K. E. (2009). *Second language teacher education: A sociocultural perspective*. New York: Routledge.

Kelly, G. J. (2004). Discourse, description, and science education. *Interim report for the National Academy of Education postdoctoral fellowship 1998-2000*.

Kelly, G. J. (2014). Analyzing classroom activities: Theoretical and methodological considerations. In C. Bruguière, A. Tiberghien, & P. Clément (Eds.), *Topics and trends in current science education: 9th ESERA conference selected contributions* (pp. 353–368). Dordrecht: Springer.

Kelly, G. J., & Chen, C. (1999). The sound of music: Constructing science as sociocultural practices through oral and written discourse. *Journal of Research in Science Teaching, 36*(8), 883–915.

Lewis, C. C. (2002). *Lesson study: A handbook of teacher-led instructional change*. Philadelphia, PA: Research for Better Schools.

Lieberman, A., & Miller, L. (2008). *Teachers in professional communities: Improving teaching and learning*. New York: Teachers College Press.

Little, J. W. (2012). Understanding data use practice among teachers: The contribution of micro-process studies. *American Journal of Education, 118*(2), 143–166.

Mitchell, J. (1984). Typicality and the case study. In R. Ellen (Ed.), *Ethnographic research: A guide to general conduct* (pp. 237–241). London: Academic Press.

National School Reform Faculty. (2018). *NSRF protocols and activities . . . from A to Z*. Bloomington, IN: National School Reform Faculty. www.nsrfharmony.org/protocols/.

Nelson, T. H., Deuel, A., Slavit, D., & Kennedy, A. (2010). Leading deep conversations in collaborative inquiry groups. *The Clearing House, 83*(5), 175–179.

Nelson, T. H., Slavit, D., & Deuel, A. (2012). Two dimensions of an inquiry stance toward student learning data. *Teachers College Record, 114*(8), 1–42.

NGSS Lead States. (2013). *Next generation science standards: For states, by states*. Washington, D.C.: The National Academies Press.

Pfeiffer, L. C., & Featherstone, H. J. (1997). *Toto, I don't think we're in Kansas anymore: Entering the land of public disagreement in learning to teach*. East Lansing: National Center for Research on Teacher Learning, Michigan State University.

Ricketts, A. (2017). Conversations around practice: Mediating opportunities to learn about teaching science. Unpublished doctoral dissertation.

Simon, A., & Boyer, E. (Eds.). (1969). *Mirrors for behavior: An anthology of classroom observation instruments*. Philadelphia, MA: Research for Better Schools.

Spradley, J. P. (1979). *The ethnographic interview*. New York: Holt, Rinehart and Winston.

Spradley, J. P. (1980). *Participant observation*. New York: Holt, Rinehart and Winston.

Strauss, S., & Feiz, P. (2014). *Discourse analysis: Putting our worlds into words*. New York: Routledge.

10

COMMENTARY

Constructing Transparency in Designing and Conducting Multilayered Research in Science and Engineering Education – Potentials and Challenges of Ethnographically Informed Discourse-Based Methodologies

Audra Skukauskaite

When I received the invitation to contribute to the book on science and engineering education, initially I was surprised because I do not have a background in STEM fields. However, as dialogues with the editors and review of the table of contents and the introductory chapter revealed, the focus of this volume is more on research methodologies as ways of understanding the construction of science and engineering in classrooms, rather than on the content of science or engineering itself. As an ethnographer and a professor of qualitative research methodologies, I accepted the challenge to write this chapter as an opportunity for me to learn how scholars in a field new to me, construct research utilizing the ethnographic, discourse analysis, and interactional ethnographic approaches with which I am familiar. Entering the field of science and engineering education provided me with an opportunity to step back from my own interests in order to "fight familiarity" (Delamont, 2013) and thus look at research in an unfamiliar field to examine the potentials of research methodologies represented across chapters in this book.

In *Key Themes in the Ethnography of Education*, a British sociologist and ethnographer of education, Sara Delamont proposed six strategies to fight familiarity:

1. Revisiting 'insightful' educational ethnographies of the past.
2. Studying learning and teaching in formal education in other cultures.
3. Taking the standpoint of the researcher who is 'other' to view the educational process, for example, by doing ethnography from the standpoint of participants from a different social class, a different race or ethnicity, a different gender, or a different sexual orientation.

4. Taking the viewpoint of actors other than the commonest types of 'teachers' and 'students' in ordinary state schools. This can mean focusing on unusual settings in the school system, such as schools for learning disabled pupils, or the deaf or blind, or in the UK Welsh or Gaelic medium schools, or 'other' actors in ordinary schools such as secretaries, laboratory technicians, campus police, cooks.
5. Studying learning and teaching outside formal education settings.
6. Using intermediate theoretical concepts from other areas of the discipline to re-energise educational ethnography.

(Delamont, 2013, pp. 15–16)

These six strategies of fighting familiarity emphasize the need for researchers to explore unfamiliar settings, theories, and points of view in order to make the familiar strange and strange familiar (Heath & Street, 2008), thus re-envision education and ways of studying the complexities of educational processes, practices, and outcomes. *Stepping into new disciplinary fields* offers another strategy to fight familiarity.

Underlying this challenge of fighting familiarity by entering new fields are ethnographic principles of setting aside ethnocentrism (Green, Skukauskaite, & Baker, 2012; Heath, 1982) or suspending known categories (Green & Bridges, 2018), employing a contrastive perspective (Green, Dixon, & Zaharlick, 2003) and constructing new ways of knowing and representing (Green & Bridges, 2018), or translating (Agar, 2011) the local ways of knowing to the broader audiences. In this way, this chapter also follows Kelly's (2006) arguments for examining conversations within theory groups in order to build knowledge that transcends the local group and becomes a resource for dialogues across disciplines and theoretical and methodological positions (see Chapter 1 in this volume).

Approach to Reading within and across Chapters

In taking up the challenge of examining what can be learned from ethnographically informed discourse analysis studies in science and engineering education, I draw on the ethnographic reading tradition developed in the extended research community of interactional ethnographers and education researchers (Green, Castanheira, Skukauskaite, & Hammond, 2015; Green & McClelland, 1999; Green & Skukauskaite, 2008; Skukauskaite & Green, 2004, 2010, 2012). Drawing on the ethnographic epistemology (Agar, 2006; Anderson-Levitt, 2006; Green *et al.*, 2012), we view texts as artifacts of a cultural group. As artifacts, texts have the potential to make visible what counts as valued and appropriate ways of constructing knowledge, doing research, writing, and representing the research processes that make visible particular aspects of the work of students and teachers in educational settings. In viewing texts as artifacts of the research group's culture-in-the-making, the reader-as-analyst (Green *et al.*, 2015) seeks to make visible what the insiders in the group do, in what ways, with whom, where, for what purposes, and with what outcomes, as they write about their ethnographically informed discourse-based studies in science and engineering education.

Building on my research community's and my individual work on reading across traditions and asking ethnographically informed questions (Green *et al.*, 2015; Green *et al.*, 2017; Skukauskaite & Grace, 2006), in addressing the challenge of exploring what the chapters in this volume make visible about researching educational processes and practices in science and engineering classrooms, I posed the following questions to guide my analyses:

1. *What* is studied as science and engineering education? In other words, what are the phenomena studied and how do the authors conceptualize these phenomena?
2. *How* do they research science and engineering education? Or, what data and analysis methods are utilized to examine the processes and practices of science and engineering education?
3. *So what?* Or, what knowledge is constructed and what does it contribute?

The first question focuses on choosing *what* to study, the second on *how* to study, and the third on the contributions of the study, or the *so what?* As a researcher, research consultant, and professor of research methodology, I use these three questions in my work and teaching to emphasize that the *what*s and the *so whats* of our research are highly dependent on *how* we construct our studies and how we represent our designs and logic-in-use in transparent ways to the larger research and practice communities. Even if a study's findings may be interesting and relevant to the areas we study, issues in research design and methodological transparency may invalidate the study and make it unusable. Therefore, in reviewing and analyzing the chapters in this volume, I focused on the transparency in *how* the researchers constructed their studies and made visible their logic-of-inquiry (design) and its iterative and recursive nature in the process of conducting the research (logic-in-use).

In the next section I explore the actions researchers took in constructing their research studies. I then focus on two actions *conceptualizing the phenomenon* and *analyzing at multiple levels of scale*, to answer the *what* and *how* questions. In focusing on these questions, I seek to examine and make transparent the processes and practices of researchers who conduct ethnographically informed discourse-based studies in science and engineering education. The final section builds on these analyses to explore the *so what* question and make visible what the studies in this volume contribute to research in science and engineering education.

Constructing Ethnographically Informed Discourse-Based Studies in Science and Engineering Education: Researcher Actions in Constructing the Logic of Inquiry

Research is a systematic way of examining phenomena and constructing knowledge about those phenomena. As such, research involves researcher actions that are shaped by and shape researcher interests, social, political, theoretical, historical, disciplinary, and interpersonal experiences, knowledge, intentions, and ways of conceptualizing and examining phenomena of interest. These actions are never neutral and are always consequential for what can be known about educational and social processes studied. Through an ethnographic lens, actions of a cultural group have the potential of making visible what members of the group need to know and do in order to participate in group-appropriate ways. Applying this lens to the analysis of the chapters in this book, I sought to understand what actions the researchers took as they conducted research in science and engineering classrooms.

In exploring the researcher actions within and across the eight empirical chapters in this volume (Chapters 2–9), I constructed a domain analysis following Spradley's (1980/2016) developmental research sequence and *x is a kind of y* semantic relationship. As represented in Figure 10.1, *x* was an included term that described the actions and constituted the cover term *y*. The seven actions listed in Figure 10.1 are kinds of *y* – the researcher actions in constructing the logic-in-use represented across chapters in this volume. Figure 10.1 is based on my analyses of what the researchers did as they constructed their studies represented across the eight chapters. In constructing the figure, I followed the interactional ethnographic principle of practice of representing actions in gerunds plus object to signal intentional activity by the actor (researcher, in this case).

The seven actions in Figure 10.1 make visible the relationship between the research design, or, in the language of interactional ethnography, logic-of-inquiry, and the situated nature of researcher actions that are constructed in the process of conducting the study, or logic-in-use. In the next two sections I examine in

x		y
1. **Conceptualizing phenomena to be studied**		
2. Formulating and (re)formulating research questions		
3. Gaining and (co)maintaining access to purposefully selected research sites		
4. Locating self and co-constructing and re-constructing researcher roles and reflexivity	is a kind of	Researcher action in constructing a logic-in-use
5. Constructing archives and datasets		
6. **Analyzing at multiple levels of scale**		
7. **Constructing knowledge**		

FIGURE 10.1 Researcher actions (*x* is a kind of *y*).

more depth the actions of *conceptualizing phenomena* (1) and *analyzing at multiple levels of scale* (6), and return to action (7), *constructing knowledge*, in the final section of this chapter. Given that there is not sufficient space in this chapter to analyze each action in detail, I chose to focus on these three particular actions because they are often missed, taken for granted, or underdeveloped in many research publications. In focusing on specific actions in more depth, I demonstrate how a reader-as-an-analyst can uncover what writers make possible for other readers to learn within and across each chapter about systematic ways of researching educational processes and practices in science and engineering classrooms.

Transparency in *What* Is Studied: What Phenomena Are Studied in Science and Engineering Education and How Are These Phenomena Conceptualized?

Determining what to study involves conceptualizing a phenomenon, formulating a research question, and selecting a research site and gaining access (actions 1–3 in Figure 10.1). Most research methods books indicate that research starts with the formulation of a research question. This advice obscures the processes and practices as well as ontological and epistemological assumptions and decisions that inevitably are part of choosing the question. The authors of this volume make visible that before the question can be asked and research site selected, phenomena to be studied need to be conceptualized. In this section, I analyze the work the authors of this volume undertook to determine what was important to study and in what ways. The ways they conceptualized the phenomena informed their research questions and selection of research sites, while negotiations regarding gaining and maintaining access within those sites in turn informed the formulations and reformulations of research questions.

To examine what is involved in conceptualizing the phenomenon to be studied, I returned to the eight individual chapters and re-read their introductory pages focusing on the first two paragraphs. I call this return to the text with an analytic purpose in mind an *analytic pass* through the text. I focused on the first two paragraphs as a site in which the author locates the self, the context for the study, and starts conceptualizing the phenomenon of focus. The conceptualization continues beyond the two paragraphs, but the beginning of the text, like the first day in classrooms, signals what insiders choose to foreground as they begin the journey of knowledge construction.

In this analytic pass with the focus on conceptualizing phenomena, I looked at what information, ideas, or resources the authors discursively referenced as significant for their processes of choosing and understanding phenomena to study. I utilized Spradley's "means-end" semantic relationship, *x is a way to do y*, to identify included terms that were a way to conceptualize the phenomenon to be studied. Using this analytic pass, I started with the first empirical chapter by Alicia McDyre and began to identify what she considered in conceptualizing her study of "Making science and gender in kindergarten." I entered her actions in the first column, continuing to use gerunds to indicate intentional practices.

Reading from the beginning of the first empirical chapter, I started to construct a matrix represented in Table 10.1. As I continued through each individual chapter, I added a column for the next author. I used author initials to construct the columns in the table. Throughout the analyses, I refer to the authors by their initials. Upon identifying new actions as ways to conceptualize the phenomenon to be studied, I added those actions in the first column, *x*, then returned to the previous chapters to see if the other authors also signaled that action, albeit less directly. For direct actions, I used a checkmark √, and for indirect (implied) actions included in conceptualizing the phenomena to study, I used a small v.

For example, in the first sentence, Alicia McDyre (AM) noted that television, news stories, and advertising "are more likely" to connect women or girls "to STEM related images now than in the past." Through this one sentence, McDyre inscribes actions of the society as well as historical shifts that influence how science and gender phenomena she intends to study are conceptualized. Thus, I added "noting actions or historical shifts in society" in Table 10.1 to mark ways of conceptualizing research phenomena of interest. McDyre starts the second sentence with the pronoun "we," thus identifying personal interest as well as marking herself as a member of a group who "hears about women's accomplishments." The second part of this sentence also marks the "changing political society" as well as "women demanding to be heard" as aspects of the phenomenon. I added "signaling political shifts" to the actions column to represent her idea related to politics as an influence in conceptualizing the phenomena for research. Later, this action was changed to "political and policy" shifts to include related references to policies signaled by other authors of the volume. I did not add an action for "women demanding to be heard" in this table since, through the lens of contrastive analysis, I compared and contrasted this idea with those noted before and determined that it could be subsumed in the action of "noting actions in society." However, as I read the first sentence of the second paragraph, I did add the action of "marking science reform documents," given that my prior readings of the introductory and other chapters in this volume identified the new science standards as a significant influence on ways of conceptualizing science and engineering research. While it could be included under "political and policy shifts" the dominance of the Next Generation Science Standards as a key policy marked across the chapters warranted a separate action that was influential in how the authors conceptualized the phenomena they chose to study.

I continued this logic of reading sentence by sentence and adding actions signaling ways of conceptualizing phenomena researched. After identifying ways of conceptualizing phenomena proposed by Alicia McDyre in the first two paragraphs of her chapter, I followed this analysis of the other individual chapters in the order listed in the table of contents. The first row of Table 10.1 marks the initials of chapter authors and the first column indicates actions uncovered

TABLE 10.1 *x* is a way to conceptualize the phenomenon to be studied

x	*AM*	*CV*	*MJ*	*PL*	*EH*	*ASB & RM*	*ATO& SM*	*AR*
1. Noting actions or historical shifts in society	√			√			v	
2. Identifying personal interest, background or stance	√		√			√		
3. Marking membership in a community interested in the phenomenon	√		√				v	
4. Signaling political or policy shifts	√	√	v	√			v	
5. Marking social justice issues	√			v				
6. Referencing prior literature	√	√		√	√	√	√	
7. Identifying gaps in the literature	√	√		v	√			√
8. Marking science reform documents (NGSS)	√	√	√	√			√	√
9. Identifying an epistemological stance of classrooms and/or science/engineering as socially constructed	√		√				√	
10. Noting disciplinary practices of science and/or engineering	√	√	v	√	√	√	√	
11. Marking classroom as context	√	√	v	√	v	v	v	
12. Aligning self with particular theoretical and epistemological stances or research community	√		v				v	
13. Explaining orienting theories of the phenomenon	√	√			√		√	v
14. Signaling level of education as context for understanding phenomenon	v	√				v		
15. Making visible intersections and/or differences between science and engineering		√						
16. Signaling a "large" video archive			√					
17. Indicating methodological focus			√	√				v
18. Marking teachers and/or students as key actors	√	√	√	√		v	√	√
19. Foregrounding language and discourse	v			√			√	√
20. Drawing on interdisciplinary scholarship, beyond science and engineering education	v			v	√			
21. Emphasizing the human aspects of science	√				√	√		
22. Identifying challenges or requirements for teachers			v	v		v	√	√
23. Explaining the US context	v			√			√	v
24. Focusing on learning in groups								√

across the chapters sequentially, in the order of chapters analyzed. For example, in analyzing the second empirical chapter by Carmen Vanderhoof (CV), I added actions 13-15 and entered check marks for the actions that were already identified by analyzing McDyre's chapter.

Drawing on the contrastive logic of ethnographic analysis, I proceeded through all eight chapters, recursively returning to previous chapters as I added new actions in the first column. Initially, in constructing the table, I did not use the numbers for the actions, but I added the numbers to aid in describing my analytic processes. By maintaining the sequence of analysis, this table enables seeing the actions constituting ways of conceptualizing phenomena. Additionally, reading of the checkmarks down the column also makes visible which actions each author foregrounded as important for their particular conceptualizations of the phenomena studied.

Representing the sequential logic of analysis enables seeing author actions in choosing particular aspects significant in conceptualizing research phenomena in science and engineering education. However, this table with the sequential listing of actions across and within chapters obscures the larger patterns underlying these actions. To make the patterns visible, I conducted pair-wise contrasts across items, grouping them based on the main aspect each action emphasized as important in shaping how the phenomenon was conceptualized. Domain analysis in Figure 10.2 makes visible the kinds of aspects (*x*) influencing the conceptualization of a phenomenon to be studied (*y*)

Figure 10.2 includes seven kinds of actions that influence what authors draw upon as they conceptualize the phenomena they choose to study. In this figure the numbers next to each aspect indicate the actions from Table 10.1. Taken together, they make visible that choosing what to study in science and engineering education requires knowing the field, understanding the national and policy contexts, considering educational settings and actors in those settings, identifying appropriate theories and methodologies, and locating self in the study and the larger field.

These aspects not only impact what phenomena are chosen to study and in what ways, but also position the authors as members of a research community in particular ways. Reading across chapters and conducting this analysis helped

Personal or epistemological stance	(2, 3, 12)		
National and policy contexts	(1, 4, 5, 8, 23)		
Educational settings	(11, 14)	is an	**conceptualizing the**
Actors in the educational setting	(18, 22, 24)	aspect	**phenomenon to be**
Scholarship in the field	(6, 7, 10, 15, 20, 21)	of	**studied**
Theoretical framework	(9, 13)		
Methodological considerations	(16, 17, 19)		

FIGURE 10.2 *x* is a kind of aspect influencing conceptualizing phenomena to be studied.

me, as a reader and an outsider to the science and engineering community, to see the coherence and complementarity of the phenomena studied across chapters. Focusing on the actions in conceptualizing the phenomena to study also made visible that the authors of this volume are not only science and engineering education researchers, but researchers of a larger educational community, of which I am a member. This larger community beyond the local theory group consider similar aspects of conceptualizing phenomena as listed in Figure 10.2.

While researchers across fields consider most of these aspects, ethnographic and interactional ethnographic researchers pay particular attention to the actors and personal and epistemological stances, including the focus on discourse and other theoretical perspectives. Inclusion of actors and personal stance in conceptualizing what and how to study a phenomenon of interest is critical in interactional ethnographic research. Interactional ethnographers seek to enter people's everyday worlds and learn with and from the local actors about the local processes, practices, and discourse that constitute life and learning in a particular educational setting. Reflexivity in locating self and identifying the epistemological stance is a necessary part of an ethnographer learning to step back, fight familiarity, and continuously contrast their ways of seeing and understanding with those of the local members of a group (Green & Bridges, 2018).

Once conceptualized, *what* is studied and what is learned by focusing on the chosen phenomenon is dependent on *how* the study is conducted. Therefore, having examined the actions and influences that shape how phenomena to be researched are conceptualized, I returned to the chapters with a new *analytic pass*, seeking to make visible the multiple layers of analytic scale the authors of this volume utilized.

Transparency in Methodology, the *How*: Exploring What Data and Analyses Are Utilized to Examine the Processes and Practices of Science and Engineering Education

Analysis is a systematic way of working with the information, of parsing things into smaller parts, and looking for multiple connections among the parts, with the goal of constructing grounded explanations of the patterns that provide insights into the work of actors in the social settings being studied. Analyzing is an ongoing process that begins as researchers conceptualize their phenomena to study, select research questions, sites and participants, negotiate access and relationships, reflexively analyze their roles, and construct datasets for purposeful in-depth analyses intended to answer research questions. Analysis is often the most difficult and at the same time the most exhilarating aspect of the ethnographic and qualitative research process, since it involves discovery, creativity, and divergent thinking and systematic work with various sources of information. In well-developed studies, analysis is both theoretically grounded and reflexively constructed through the creativity and logic-in-use of the researcher. Analysis is one of the aspects of research that is often invisible or lacks transparency in published research reports, obstructing other researchers' learning of the ways of conducting complex studies in educational settings.

While many research reports make it look like analysis begins after the data are collected, ethnographic and qualitative researchers have argued that analysis needs to be considered from the very beginning, while the study is being conceptualized (Brinkman & Kvale, 2015; Heath & Street, 2008; Maxwell, 2013). Considering analytic choices from the start can influence the questions asked, the records collected, and data generated as well as the knowledge constructed through the analyses. Analysis is never neutral nor "emerging" as if by magic from the data. It is always constructed by the researcher, in dialogue with the data, the participants, the theories, the goals of the particular research study, as well as with the precepts of the research community of which the writer is or seeks to be part (Green *et al.*, 2015). Heath and Street (2008) argued that "ethnographic work is dialogic between existing explanations and judgments (whether held by scholars, outsiders, or insiders) and ongoing data collection and analysis" (p. 57). These dialogues, and the ways they impact researcher analytic decisions, are clearly visible in this volume as a whole, from the introductory chapter to the appendices.

Uncovering Theoretical Principles and Implicated Actions for Researchers

To uncover how and why the authors of the empirical chapters constructed analyses at multiple levels of scale, I began by revisiting the introductory chapter, in which Kelly and Green laid out the goals and the theoretical foundations for this volume. My decision to start with the first chapter was guided by the abductive processes of ethnography and the practices of employing the *if . . . then* logic (Green *et al.*, 2012) to uncover relationships between the volume's goals and the underlying theories and analytic practices of authors within and across the chapters. Below is a statement from the introduction about the central premise for this volume (emphasis mine):

> This book provides a set of selected studies each of which examines some of the current practices in science, engineering, and teacher education. At the center of this volume is an understanding that whether focused on students' engineering design challenges, identity construction as a scientist, or development of teachers' professional vision, *everyday educational events are, and have always been, constructed through discourse processes, within the cultural practices of life within these and related settings* (e.g., home, community, laboratories, social spaces).

Embedded in the underlined sentence are theoretical propositions (Table 10.2), each of which implies a particular kind of action the researchers need to take.

That is, *if* the statement in the first column of Table 10.2 is taken as true and as a premise for research, *then* the researcher needs to engage in a range of actions listed in the second column. The actions in Table 10.2 are derived from the actions the authors of the empirical chapters of this volume represented in uncovering their logic-in-use when constructing analytic representations of the social and discursive accomplishment of science and engineering in educational settings.

Table 10.2 makes visible that theoretical premises suggest particular analytic actions, which in turn require particular forms of analyses for developing grounded warrants about what is learned through analyses of the social and discursive construction of everyday events in science and engineering classrooms. In ethnography (and, I would claim, any research), analytic processes are inseparable from underlying theories, be they tacit or extant (Skukauskaite, 2012). The theories, in turn, are linked to the epistemological and ontological

TABLE 10.2 *If . . . then* logic that demonstrates the link between theoretical propositions and implicated actions

If: *theoretical propositions*	Then: *implicated actions for researchers*
Everyday educational events are constructed	• Focusing on the everyday, naturally occurring events in educational settings; focusing on the "mundane" • Documenting how the events are constructed (not given) by actors in the event • Choosing social construction theories that help uncover the processes of construction
Everyday educational events have always been constructed	• Accounting for the histories of educational events as constructed • Building on prior knowledge • Documenting event construction over time
Everyday educational events are constructed through discourse processes	• Conceptualizing discourse • Analyzing processes of event construction • Analyzing discourse as actions through which events are constructed
Everyday educational events are constructed within the cultural practices of life	• Analyzing the cultural nature of practices • Analyzing how cultural practices constitute life • Examining how the cultural practices of life are a site within which educational events are constructed
Cultural practices are within settings	• Locating practices in a particular setting • Examining the consequential interrelationships between settings and cultural practices
Cultural practices happen in related settings	• Identifying related settings • Backward and forward tracing of links between and among cultural practices constructed in different settings • Conducting multi-sited research or accounting for sites impacting the cultural practices brought to and constructed by members as significant in the local setting

conceptualizations of the phenomena studied. After all, as Heath and Street (2008) argued, "Ethnography . . . is a theory-building and theory-dependent enterprise," in which:

> ethnographers construct, test, and amplify theoretical perspectives through systematic observing, recording, and analyzing of human behavior in specifiable spaces and interactions for the co-occurrence of language, literacy, and modalities for any situation or context selected as field site(s)
>
> *(p. 38)*

Having noted the theory, implicated action relationships signaled in the introductory chapter and represented in part in Table 10.2, I returned to the eight empirical chapters to analyze how the authors constructed their analyses to uncover the discursive and cultural practices that constitute what counts as science and engineering in varied educational settings.

Constructing and Representing Datasets for a Research Study

Given the goals of this volume to create transparency in uncovering the logics-in-use in conducting multilayered studies of science and engineering practices, in this analytic pass through the empirical chapters, I focused on the analyses the authors conducted, the tools they used, and the records they drew on to select data for the analyses. I began by constructing a table of the kinds of records researchers needed to uncover the discursive and cultural patterns of teaching and learning in science and engineering focused educational settings. In reading the chapters, I noticed that most of the authors noted video records, artifacts, and interviews they used, but there was no common framework for presenting how the archives were constructed or the data chosen for purposeful analyses. A few of the authors, such as Asli Sezen-Barrie and Rachel Mulvaney (ASB & RM) as well as Arzu Tanis Ozcelik and Scott McDonald (ATO & SM), provided explicit tables that made visible the data and analysis utilized in their studies. Other authors, such as Elizabeth Hufnagel (EH) and Peter Licona (PL) embedded the information about the data within the text, linking analyses to specific sources of information chosen for analyses. As a reader and analyst, I found the tables helpful in creating the transparency and providing a quick overview of the records and resources needed for conducting multilayered analyses. Building on Tanis Ozcelik and McDonald's Table 8.2 as an example, I constructed a similar table, in which I sought to capture the sources of information the authors drew on to construct their empirical analyses.

In examining data sources across the chapters, I also looked for how the authors inscribed the larger programs of research or data archives on which they drew to construct purposeful datasets for the studies reported in these chapters. I identified the need for paying attention to the archives by following the referential trails within each chapter and across chapters. For example, McDyre mentioned a prior video study group as a larger context for her study, while Vanderhoof, Hufnagel, Tanis Ozcelik, and McDonald mentioned their doctoral dissertations. Johnson, Vanderhoof, and Sezen-Barrie and Mulvaney referred to larger multi-state or multi-site projects with extensive data archives, while Ricketts and McDyre also referred to their histories in relation to the groups studied. Paying attention to how transparent the authors were about the sources of their data, I noticed a challenge that arose across the chapters. Some authors referred to their data as data, while others talked about records and explained how they purposefully constructed datasets for the specific analyses represented in this volume. Other scholars in the interactional ethnographic research community have argued that data and records are not interchangeable terms and that data can be derived from the records through theoretical sampling and purposeful selection based on researcher epistemological decisions and research goals (Baker, Green, & Skukauskaite, 2008; Green, Skukauskaite, Dixon, & Córdova, 2007). Therefore, further theorizing of what counts as records or data could enhance the transparency of the sources of information used in the eight empirical chapters in this volume.

Focusing on the data and records used for these studies, as an outsider to the field, I sought to understand what kinds of information were needed to examine the processes and practices of science and engineering education. The amount of video records ranged from 20 to 139 hours, and in all studies video was the primary source of records for data analyses. Other data sources included interviews with participants, audio recordings, student and curricular artifacts, emails, reflections, as well as fieldnotes of observations in the science and engineering learning environments. What this analysis made visible to me, as a reader, an ethnographer, and an analyst of texts of a cultural group of researchers engaged in discourse-based studies of science and engineering, was that multiple sources of information were needed to examine complex research questions posed in these studies.

This analysis also demonstrated that while video was a necessary component for discourse-based ethnographically informed studies, video alone was not enough to construct warranted claims about the complex work and interactions among teachers, students, material resources, and contextual layers, which shape and are shaped by the actors in these settings. The more transparent the authors were in documenting the kinds and amounts of records available for their studies and reporting which of the available records were transformed into data, the easier it was for me as a reader to visualize the study, the setting, and the kinds of actions taken to create warranted claims. Transparency in data sources contributed to developing the trustworthiness of the studies. In other words, the details opened doors for outsiders like me to gain a better understanding of the field and to learn in deeper ways from and with the authors of this volume.

Examining Ways Data Were Analyzed to Construct Multifaceted Accounts of Science and Engineering Phenomena Studied

After examining the sources of data the authors used, my next analytic pass focused on how the data were analyzed. Initially, I attempted to construct a visual representation of the layers of analyses the authors undertook for each study with rows representing separate analytic layers. However, maintaining my ethnographic perspective and seeking to uncover the insiders' ways of researching, I chose to follow the authors' inscriptions of their analytic logic as abductive, iterative, and recursive. A number of the authors mentioned that throughout their analyses, they had to zoom in and zoom out multiple times, from the micro moments of interaction to examining the cycles of activity in the science and engineering setting across a semester, a year, multiple years, or a particular episode. Therefore, there was no linear way of constructing representations of these complex layers of analyses in one table or figure.

Most of the authors started with analysis of video to construct event maps that represented the big picture view of what occurred in the setting over time. Then, as represented in Table 10.3, they used various methods of analysis to examine the in-the-moment discursive interactions and over time patterns through which science and engineering was co-constructed by the actors in the setting. Analyses also included making visible how the actors utilized particular resources and created specific ways of doing, being, and knowing in these cultural science and engineering spaces. The methods listed in Table 10.3 are representative of the kinds of analytic approaches used within each chapter; however, given that the authors used these methods in multiple ways iteratively and recursively throughout their studies, the listing does not represent an exhaustive account or a chronological order of the analytic processes.

In "analysis methods" column in Table 10.3, I noted the methods each author described in uncovering their analytic logic-in-use. Reading across chapters and the methods column in this table makes visible that while there are some common methods of analysis, including event mapping and discourse analyses, authors present the common methods in different ways. They also use a variety of other methods, including concept mapping, coding, domain analysis, transcribing as analysis, tallying, and descriptive statistics. Each author, in their individual chapters, presented a transparent logic of why and how they utilized a particular method of analysis for examining particular layers of the discursive and cultural construction of science and engineering phenomena.

In the "units of analysis" column of Table 10.3 I sought to identify the units of focus for analysis. However, since not every author mentioned units of analysis explicitly, the units captured in Table 10.3 are my interpolations based on the authors' descriptions of their logic. Conversations with authors would be needed to construct a more comprehensive and representative account of the focal units of analyses used within each chapter. The lack of transparency in what the units

TABLE 10.3 Analysis methods and technological tools

	Analysis methods	*Units of analysis*	*Technological tools*
AM	• Event maps • Message, action, interaction, sequence units • Sociolinguistic analysis • Coding for practices of science, positioning, and authoring • Discourse analysis to look for patterns of science discourse • Case study girls' interactions	• Identities-in-practice • Positioning	Microsoft Excel (visible in analyses, but not specified in the chapter) Pen, paper, colored markers
CV	• Event maps, sequences • Constructing analytic transcripts • Interactional sociolinguistic and microethnographic analyses • Multimodal social semiotics analyses	• Speech events	Microsoft Excel Transana 3.0
PL	• Event maps, interactional spaces • Coding for classroom activities and scientific practices • Constant comparative method • Open coding • Discourse analysis	• Events • Classroom activities • Scientific practices • Language practices • Teacher translanguaging	Windows Media Player Microsoft Word Microsoft Excel
MJ	• Event maps, phases, sequences, action units • miroanalysis of transcripts • Descriptive statistics • Coding of failure types, causes, teacher reactions, intersecting aspects • Comparison of average scores	• Discourse events • Failure types, causes • Teacher reactions to students' failed designs	Transana Multiuser 3.0 software
ASB & RM	• Event maps • Phases, sequences, intertextuality, backward mapping • Discursive moves • Coding guided by climate science concepts	• Epistemic practices • Assessment practices • Cycles of interaction	Word tables and drawing tools (visible in figures, but not specified in the chapter)
EH	• Event maps • Coding the corresponding events and written artifacts • Discourse analysis (of written and spoken discourse) • Frequencies • Coding contrastive cases	• Emotional expressions	Spreadsheet software

ATO & SM	• Event maps • Transcripts • Discourse analysis based on interactional sociolinguistics • Coding using GT (grounded theory) methods, including open coding, grouping the codes, and creating coding categories	• episodes as units of analysis • Discursive practices of highlighting, coding schemes, and building material representations	Studio Code
AR	• Event maps • Domain analysis • Coding based on review of literature • Micro-level discourse/ individual moves • Meso-level conversational routines • Concept map of key episodes	• Episodes, routines, moves, practices (embedded within one another)	Studio Code (to identify episodes) Excel (visible in tables presented, but not specified in the paper)

of analyses are and how to bound them presents a challenge for other researchers who may want to learn how to conduct discourse-based ethnographic studies and select appropriate units to analyze. As an outsider seeking to understand the ways of studying science and engineering education, I would need to engage in further dialogues with the insiders (researchers and participants) in order to be able to select appropriate analytic units.

In reviewing the chapters to identify units of analysis, I noticed a detail that I did not consider in my previous analytic pass that focused on methods of analysis. The detail related to the technologies utilized, so I added a column to Table 10.3 and labeled it "technological tools" to make a distinction between the methods of analysis used as part of the logic-in-use to uncover aspects of the phenomenon studied and the software that may have aided in the analyses or representations of the analyses. Reviewing technologies used, I noted that there was no one tool used by all authors. Two of the authors used Studio Code software and two used Transana for video analysis. The software was used to create video frame grabs and construct the event maps at different levels of scale. One author mentioned Windows Media Player as a tool used for listening to the records to construct transcripts, while the rest did not mention the audio or video software used for playback or transcription. Three authors mentioned the use of Excel, and one mentioned spreadsheet software, but did not specify which. Only one author mentioned Microsoft Word as a tool; however, the use of this tool was visible in all the chapters – not only in the texts and transcripts, but also in the ways analyses were represented in tables or figures.

Including this column about technological tools made visible that researchers may need to be more transparent about the software and technologies they use, including the everyday tools such as Microsoft Office or iOS products such as Word, Excel, Numbers, Pages, and others that are often taken for granted. I chose to make this point visible because with the increasing popularity and ubiquity of Computer Assisted Qualitative Data Analysis (CAQDA) packages, both novice and experienced researchers can easily forget that it is the researcher, not the software, who constructs the analytic logic, and that many everyday technologies, including computer software, pen, and paper, can aid in constructing transparent analytic logic that maintains the theoretic and analytic grounding of the claims. Naming the software used is not enough; accounting of the analytic processes and practices is needed to make the logic-in-use transparent and accessible to outsiders who seek to learn from the insider researchers about how to do this kind of work.

In ethnography and qualitative research, the researcher is the "instrument" (Heath and Street, 2008) through whose eyes and actions the logic-in-use is constructed for a particular study. As Kelly and Green argue in the introductory chapter of this volume, transparency in this logic is necessary for constructing trustworthy accounts of complex educational processes and practices in science and engineering and all other educational and social settings of everyday life. In other words, as stated in the introduction of this chapter, transparency in *what* phenomena are chosen to study and *how* they are conceptualized and studied, is consequential for the *so what*, i.e., what can be learned from the study and what it contributes to the larger field(s).

In this section I focused on transparency in *how* the studies were constructed methodologically. As described above, multiple analytic methods were used in all chapters, demonstrating that understanding the complexity of teaching, learning, and other phenomena, such as identity construction or representation of emotions, in science and engineering, requires engagement with the data in a variety of ways. As an outsider to the science and engineering field but an insider to the interactional ethnographic epistemology, analyzing methods used across the chapters made me realize that understanding epistemological and methodological choices for analysis of complex datasets can provide a pathway of entering any field and examining what insiders in the field need to know and do to be and act as a member of the group.

Transparency in *So What*: What Knowledge Is Constructed in Ethnographically Informed Discourse-Based Studies in Science and Engineering Classrooms and What Does it Contribute to the Field?

Transparency of epistemological and methodological processes and practices represented within each chapter and across the volume as a whole provides an opportunity to understand science and engineering education as a complex and multifaceted field that is shaped by layers of external and internal factors that play a part in who can say, do, and learn what, when, where, in what ways, with whom or what resources, for what purposes, and with what outcomes or consequences. The authors of this volume demonstrated that science and engineering are complex, living fields that are constructed through the in time and over time interactions among actors, contexts, and resources in specific settings. What counts as science and engineering is not a given but is developed by students, teachers, other human actors, as well as multimodal texts and technological tools. The interactions among these actors enable or constrain particular ways of being, doing, and knowing science and engineering in specific local learning environments, which are also part of larger community, national, policy, and practice contexts that impact the local learning situations in visible and invisible ways (Couch, Estabrooks, & Skukauskaite, 2018; Green & Heras, 2011).

This volume provides evidence that science and engineering, like other "everyday educational events are, and have always been constructed, through discourse processes, within the cultural practices of life within these and related settings" (Kelly & Green, this volume). Whether authors study girls' positioning (AM), student decisions (CV) and failures (MJ) in classrooms, the importance of emotions (EH), formative assessments (ASB & RM) or translanguaging (PL), or examine teacher pedagogical vision (ATO & SM) and generative talk (AR), they make visible that science and engineering concepts, processes, and practices are situated and discursively constructed by members in interaction at particular moments in time and over time. Through the multilayered analyses the authors demonstrate that learning science and engineering involves complex actions and interactions that can be made visible through over time observation and analysis of video, audio, and other materials.

Using ethnographic principles, researchers of this volume constructed ethical, responsive, and collaborative research in which participants were not just "subjects" of research but were instrumental in shaping what access to the site and knowledge was granted, what records were constructed, what research questions could be asked, and what knowledge developed within the setting and in the research represented in this volume. Analyses were responsive to the people, the data utilized, and were shaped by researcher reflexivity and over time engagement in the field and with the data. There were a variety of influences that shaped what analyses were conducted and represented across chapters. Analyses were chosen based on dialogues with participants, advisors, and research collaborators (e.g., chapters by AM, PL, ASB & RM) and over time engagement in the field (e.g., AM, AR) as well as dialogic interactions and iterative-recursive revisiting of video records and other data sources (e.g., AM, CV, MJ, PL, EH, AR, ATO & SM), theories, and literature (e.g., AM, AR, MJ, EH, ATO & SM, AR) and interactional ethnographic principles of practice (e.g., AM, EH). Researchers not only followed their research questions (e.g., AM, MJ, ATO & SM), but also continuously asked questions of what they saw in the field, in the data analysis, and in the processes of reflecting on their own positions and developing understandings (e.g., AM, CV, AR, EH). The reflexive stance, the ethnographic goal to uncover the insider meanings, and the interactional ethnographic focus on discursive construction of everyday life, make visible that the ethnographic logic-of-inquiry represented across this volume can become visible through enacted logics-in-use in each study. Taken as a whole, the chapters in this volume create a pathway to understanding the nonlinear, dynamic, iterative, abductive, and recursive nature of ethnographically informed discourse-based studies. Given the wide range of possibilities for what and how to study through the interactional ethnographic lens, it is critical that researchers make transparent their analytic processes, practices, changes, and decision-making processes that are woven together in creating and reporting studies that are trustworthy and provide value to the field.

Kelly (2014) provided five criteria that help make visible the value of discourse-based ethnographic studies (see Kelly & Green, this volume). The authors of this volume address these criteria in multiple ways through disclosing their decision-making processes, grounding claims in analyses, and making visible the theoretical, methodological, and epistemological foundations of their work. Each chapter provides numerous examples of how other researchers could construct transparent and grounded accounts of the processes and practices of studying science and engineering or other educational settings. In Table 10.4 I have chosen to highlight a few practices from each chapter that can serve as exemplars for other researchers interested in conducting ethnographic discourse-based studies.

The practices highlighted in this table are utilized by most of the authors across the volume, but I offer this list as a heuristic for other researchers seeking to learn and explore ways of constructing transparent and warranted research accounts.

In reading the chapters of this volume through an ethnographic lens, I sought to make visible how an outsider like me can enter a new field and, by focusing on what and how the insiders research, construct new understandings not only of the unfamiliar field, but also of the ways unfamiliar fields can be studied. In fighting familiarity by entering a new field, I developed a deeper appreciation of the interdisciplinary potentials of interactional ethnography and learned about the multiple nuances that constitute science and engineering education. Learning about women's positioning, curricular and assessment practices, emotions, group dynamics, the role of language, and the impact of policy (among other phenomena) in learning and constructing knowledge in science and engineering, expanded my vision about the varieties of aspects that need to be considered when studying educational and other interactions within and across any other disciplinary fields.

Examining ways of studying one field opens doors to understanding other fields. To refer to Kelly's (2006) arguments about knowledge construction within theory groups, in discourses for public reason, and through hermeneutical conversations across fields, the varied contributions of the theory group in this volume created opportunities for dialogues across all these levels of dialogue – within group, in the field of science and engineering education, and in other disciplines beyond. *Entering an unfamiliar field with an ethnographic lens*

TABLE 10.4 Exemplars of transparent research practices

Author	*Exemplary research practice*
AM	• Accessing and continuously co-negotiating access • Reflexivity and examining own bias and positions • Demonstrating systematic use of everyday tools in constructing the logic-in-use
CV	• Uncovering the iterative-recursive processes over time of the research study • Constructing purposeful transcripts • Purposefully choosing data and analysis methods to address research questions • Making visible theoretical grounding for methodological decisions
PL	• Accessing the research site • Employing a co-expertise model of co-researching with participants • Making visible continuously shifting participant–researcher roles
MJ	• Ensuring participant protection and confidentiality • Constructing purposeful transcripts • Relating questions to analyses • Using locally defined, emergent definitions of key constructs ("failure")
ASB & RM	• Making visible the contributions and challenges of the interdisciplinary team • Transparently demonstrating data sources • Anchoring analyses in interrelated rich points
EH	• Triangulating video data with interviews and written artifacts • Anchoring analyses in frame clashes
ATO & SM	• Constructing a visual representation of question–data–analysis logic • Mapping and maintaining interrelationships among events, episodes, and analytic codes
AR	• Conducting contrastive analyses to uncover nuances of discourse • Conceptually connecting multiple layers influencing teacher talk

and *focusing on transparency in reporting of research* presents two additional strategies to fight familiarity beyond those proposed by Delamont (2013) and presented in the introduction of this chapter. While Delamont, through a sociological lens, focused on going outside familiar fields, literature, and common educational settings, in this chapter I made visible that an ethnographic perspective and a systematic focus on transparency of methodology as well as the entry in a new field with the goal of learning from the people also provide opportunities to develop new and multifaceted understandings of educational processes, practices, contexts, and research methodologies.

This volume is a significant contribution not only to science and engineering education and education more generally, but also to research methodology in education and other social sciences. Discourse-based ethnographic and qualitative research approaches have made important contributions to education over the past six decades, yet they largely remain invisible in research publications, including in texts on research methodology (Skukauskaite, Rangel, Rodriguez, & Ramon, 2015). This volume makes visible how the discourse-enabled and ethnographically informed approaches such as interactional ethnography and related approaches used across the chapters get closer than any other approach to seeing and documenting what actually takes place in classrooms moment by moment and over time. As a whole, this volume demonstrates the importance of examining discourse and social construction of everyday life to understand the multilayered processes, practices, and outcomes of learning and living in complex educational and social environments.

References

Agar, M. (2006). An ethnography by any other name . . . *Forum Qualitative Sozialforschung/ Forum: Qualitative Social Research*, 7(4). Retrieved from www.qualitative-research.net/fqs.

Agar, M. (2011). Making sense of one other for another: Ethnography as translation. *Language & Communication*, *31*(1), 38–47. doi:10.1016/j.langcom.2010.05.001.

Anderson-Levitt, K. (2006). Ethnography. In J. L. Green, G. Camilli, & P. B. Elmore (Eds.), *Handbook of complementary methods in education research* (pp. 279–296). Mahwah, NJ: Lawrence Erlbaum for AERA.

Baker, W. D., Green, J. L., & Skukauskaite, A. (2008). Video-enabled ethnographic research: A microethnographic perspective. In G. Walford (Ed.), *How to do educational ethnography* (pp. 77–114). London: Tufnell Press.

Brinkman, S., & Kvale, S. (2015). *Interviews: Learning the craft of qualitative research interviewing* (3rd ed.). Los Angeles, CA: Sage.

Couch, S., Estabrooks, L. B., & Skukauskaite, A. (2018). Addressing the gender gap among patent holders through invention education policies. *Technology & Innovation: Journal of the National Academy of Inventors*, *19*, 735–749.

Delamont, S. (2013). *Key themes in the ethnography of education: Achievements and agendas*. London: Sage.

Green, J. L., & Bridges, S. M. (2018). Interactional ethnography. In F. Fischer, C. E. Hmelo-Silver, S. R. Goldman, & P. Reimann (Eds.), *International handbook of the learning sciences* (pp. 475–488). New York: Routledge.

Green, J. L., Castanheira, M. L., Skukauskaite, A., & Hammond, J. (2015). Exploring traditions studying discourse and interaction in classrooms: Developing transparency, reflexivity, and multi-faceted research designs. In N. Markee (Ed.), *Handbook of classroom discourse and interaction* (pp. 26–43). Hoboken, NJ: Wiley.

Green, J. L., Dixon, C. N., & Zaharlick, A. (2003). Ethnography as a logic of inquiry. In J. Flood, D. Lapp, J. R. Squire, & J. Jensen (Eds.), *Handbook of research on teaching the English language arts* (2nd ed., pp. 201–224). Mahwah, NJ: Lawrence Erlbaum.

Green, J. L., & Heras, A. I. (2011). Identities in shifting educational policy contexts: The consequences of moving from two languages, one community to English only. In G. López-Bonilla & K. Englander (Eds.), *Discourses and identities in contexts of educational change* (pp. 155–194). New York: Peter Lang.

Green, J. L., Joo, J., Dai, Y., Hirsch, T., Chian, M., & David, P. B. (2017). Challenges in understanding different epistemologies for studying learning: A telling case of constructing a new research agenda. *International Journal of Educational Research*, *84*, 119–126. doi:https://doi.org/10.1016/j.ijer.2016.08.005.

Green, J. L., & McClelland, M. (1999). What difference does the difference make? Understanding difference across perspectives. *Discourse Processes*, *27*(2), 219–230. doi:10.1080/01638539909545059.

Green, J. L., & Skukauskaite, A. (2008). Comments on Slavin: Becoming critical readers: Issues in transparency, representation, and warranting of claims. *Educational Researcher*, *37*(1), 30–40. doi:10.3102/0013189x08314828.

Green, J. L., Skukauskaite, A., & Baker, W. D. (2012). Ethnography as epistemology: An introduction to educational ethnography. In J. Arthur, M. J. Waring, R. Coe, & L. V. Hedges (Eds.), *Research methodologies and methods in education* (pp. 309–321). London: Sage.

Green, J. L., Skukauskaite, A., Dixon, C. N., & Córdova, R. (2007). Epistemological issues in the analysis of video records: Interactional ethnography as a logic of inquiry. In R. Goldman, R. Pea, B. Barron, & S. J. Derry (Eds.), *Video research in the learning sciences* (pp. 115–132). Mahwah, NJ: Lawrence Erlbaum.

Heath, S. B. (1982). Ethnography in education: Defining the essentials. In P. Gillmore & A. A. Glatthorn (Eds.), *Children in and out of school: Ethnography and education* (pp. 33–55). Washington, D.C: Center for Applied Linguistics.

Heath, S. B., & Street, B. V. (2008). *On ethnography: Approaches to language and literacy research*. New York: Teachers College Press.

Kelly, G. J. (2006). Epistemology and educational research. In J. L. Green, G. Camilli, & P. B. Elmore (Eds.), *Handbook of complementary methods in education research* (pp. 33–56). Mahwah, NJ: Lawrence Erlbaum for AERA.

Kelly, G. J. (2014). Analyzing classroom activities: Theoretical and methodological considerations. In C. Bruguière, A. Tiberghien, & P. Clément (Eds.), *Topics and trends in current science education* (pp. 353–368). Netherlands: Springer.

Maxwell, J. A. (2013). *Qualitative research design: An interactive approach* (3rd ed.). Los Angeles, CA: Sage.

Skukauskaite, A. (2012). Transparency in transcribing: Making visible theoretical bases impacting knowledge construction from open-ended interview records. *Forum Qualitative Sozialforschung/Forum: Qualitative Social Research*, *13*(1). Retrieved from http://nbn-resolving.de/urn:nbn:de:0114-fqs1201146.

Skukauskaite, A., & Grace, E. (2006). On reading and using the volume: Notes to students. In J. L. Green, G. Camilli, & P. B. Elmore (Eds.), *Handbook of complementary methods in education research* (pp. xxi–xxiii). Mahwah, NJ: Lawrence Erlbaum for AERA.

Skukauskaite, A., & Green, J. L. (2004). A conversation with Bakhtin: On inquiry and dialogic thinking. *Journal of Russian and East European Psychology*, *42*(6), 59–75.

Skukauskaite, A., & Green, J. L. (2010). Research as social action: Constructing critical dialogue as a complex social and educational phenomenon. In L. B. Jennings, P. C. Jewett, T. T. Laman, M. Souto-Manning, & J. L. Wilson (Eds.), *Sites of possibility: Critical dialogue across educational settings* (pp. 143–171). Creskill, NJ: Hampton Press.

Skukauskaite, A., & Green, J. L. (2012). Review essay: On transparency, epistemologies, and positioning in writing introductory qualitative research texts. *Forum Qualitative Sozialforschung/Forum: Qualitative Social Research*, *13*(1). Retrieved from www.qualitative-research.net/index.php/fqs/article/view/1768/3274.

Skukauskaite, A., Rangel, J., Rodriguez, L. G., & Ramon, D. K. (2015). Understanding classroom discourse and interaction: Qualitative perspectives. In N. Markee (Ed.), *Handbook of classroom discourse and interaction* (pp. 44–59). Hoboken, NJ: Wiley.

Spradley, J. (1980/2016). *Participant observation*. Long Grove, IL: Waveland Press, Inc.

11

COMMENTARY

Research Methods for the Advancement of Possibility Knowledge and Practice in Science and Engineering Education

Kristiina Kumpulainen

It was in the year 2005 when I first heard a children's story on *Seven Blind Mice* by Ed Young (1991) in connection to a talk given by Dr. Ralph Cordova at the University of California, Santa Barbara. The story retells in verse the Indian fable of the blind men discovering different parts of an elephant and arguing about its appearance. This metaphorical story created an important rich point for me academically to further my personal learning journey in searching, developing and making sense of different ways of researching and understanding discourse, knowledge and social practice in educational settings, and the possibilities and limitations each strand of research entails for informing educational theory and practice (see also Green, Camilli & Elmore, 2006). Most importantly, this story inspired me to explore research approaches in education whose logic-of-inquiry would allow researchers to move beyond a narrow and one-sided focus of analysis, towards acknowledging part–whole relationships and micro–macro level dynamics of educational processes and the opportunities such an approach can afford for unpacking engagement, learning and identity building among the participants.

All those who have conscientiously read the chapters of this volume are most likely to agree that the studies and their logic-of-inquiry create a set of compelling academic narratives for educational researchers interested in the study of everyday life in science and engineering classrooms as situationally constructed in and across space and time. The studies zoom in and out of the everyday life of science and engineering classrooms conveying insights regarding specific cultures of learning – how they are relationally and iteratively constructed into being, maintained and transformed in situ and over time. Altogether, the studies illustrate the expressive potential (Strike, 1974) of the so called *interactional ethnographic* approach (Green & Castanheira, 2012) to address many complex goals and challenges of contemporary science and engineering education. This approach takes serious and systematic account of part–whole relationships and micro–macro level analyses of educational processes, somewhat similar to the story of seven blind mice and their collective sense-making and discovery of the strange Something, the elephant.

This rich set of studies of discourse discussed in this volume make visible how classroom interactions are sites of social construction of science and engineering content, processes and practices. Grounded in ethnographically informed logic-of-inquiry, interactional sociolinguistics and sociocultural theories of learning that account for the interactional ethnographic approach, each chapter of this volume approaches science and engineering education as interactional accomplishments situated in sociocultural contexts with a goal of shedding light into how, in what ways, for what purposes, and with what outcomes and consequences science and engineering education and learning are socially, discursively and conceptually constructed in and across space and time.

Altogether, the studies of this volume create powerful narratives that convey insights into the everyday activities, practices and cultures of science and engineering classrooms, and how these are interactively and iteratively designed, implemented and maintained. We can view these studies from the perspective of *chronotopes* that direct attention to times and spaces through which particular types of educational processes and opportunities are made possible in the continuum of the past, present and future. The notion of chronotope originates from the works of Mikhail Bakhtin (1981), a dialogic literary scholar, who used the concept to describe the contextual grounding of events in a literary narrative, that is, the unity of time and space. Here, space and time are not seen as neutral abstractions or as a background or a passive context in which activity occurs but as socially constructed, intrinsically interconnected and imbued with cultural meanings and practices, values and ideology (Morson & Emerson, 1990). Hence, chronotopes are actively constructed in social interactions within and across sociocultural contexts. In sum, drawing on Bakhtin (1981), we can define chronotopes as socially constructed time-space configurations with a specific narrative character that represent cultural practices and values, and that operationalize the framing of the interactional situation and its actors (Kumpulainen & Rajala, 2017). Specifically, chronotopes index the relative changeability of the social world, the opportunities for individual agency and the relations of social and individual development as each chronotope relates actors, actions and contexts in specific ways, as illuminated by the studies of this volume.

The study of McDyre addresses a timely and societally relevant chronotope to science and engineering education that is to do with the ways in which females are positioned in science education. Drawing on interactional ethnography the study shows how young kindergarten children participated in science, which norms were established in the classroom and how girls were positioned in terms of learners of science. Her empirical data consist of longitudinal, two year-long video-recordings of student discourse, student interviews, ethnographic field notes, photographs of student science notebooks and additional artifacts, teacher informal interviews and a guardian questionnaire. These multiple methods were deemed pivotal in order to gain an emic understanding of the dynamic interactional processes for students' positioning and identity building. Alike to the other studies of this volume, characteristics of this work is its generative nature resulting in new questions and insights in conceptualizing, understanding and researching girls positioning, identity building and educational opportunity in science.

In the chapter of Vanderhoof, research attention is directed to investigating how young children attending third grade (8 years old) negotiate uncertainty in their groups in situ and over time in civic engineering. The study pays specific attention to how the children's positioning of self and others affected their decision-making processes in a group. Informed by interactional ethnography which is enriched by a multimodal approach, the study entailed careful reading and inductive, interactive and recursive analysis of rich multimodal data from different angles and timescales. Each phase and layer of analysis added extra background knowledge about the participants, their changing group roles and the developing final project. In doing so, the study unpacks the chronotopic character of the students' management of uncertainty, resulting in nuanced and situated research knowledge about the opportunities for these children's science learning. Overall, the study challenges those methodological approaches that draw upon pre-defined and de-contextualized categorizations of productive/unproductive dichotomy in understanding educational opportunity.

The study of Licona communicates a compelling narrative of the chronotope of equal educational opportunity in reform driven science education among culturally and linguistically diverse students. Drawing on interactional ethnography, the study narrates the implementation of a socio-scientific approach to science education coupled by a scientific argumentation framework in an English–Spanish dual language middle school science classroom. The study demonstrates multiphase, recursive and consequential data collection and analysis processes, entailing macro level analyses that zoom over the norms and expectations of the communicative settings, and micro level analyses of selected interaction episodes. The study speaks to the importance of creating inclusive interactional spaces for diverse learners to engage in and learn about scientific and epistemic practices and their discourses, and the meaning of teacher translanguaging in this process. In addition, the study shows how interactional ethnography transformed the role of the researcher and the teacher, resulting in a co-expertise model in which research on the classroom culture was done "with" the teacher, instead of "on" the teacher.

The study by Johnson illustrates the expressive potential of interactional ethnography accompanied by the sociomaterial perspective to investigate the social construction of failure and improvement as they are socially constructed into being in the interactions of students, teachers and materials in the context of engineering design projects. The study draws on longitudinal research data involving large video data sets of classroom interaction, discourse and student journals. The chronotope addressed by this study deals with the contextual grounding of failure and its consequential negotiation for improvement at the nexus of discourse, social practice and use of material artifacts. Not only does this study demonstrate how failure and improvement take place in situ but also contribute to a nuanced understanding of the meaning and value of failure in the learning of science and engineering, and how teachers can build on failure as a learning opportunity.

In their chapter, Sezen-Barrie and Mulvaney take us to an ethnographic research journey on how teachers and students draw from an interdisciplinary area of climate science to make sense of human-caused contemporary climate change, namely the uses of alternative energy sources. The study looks into the discursive interactions among a team of professionals, namely a scientist, a mathematics instructor and educational researcher, during their joint development of a mini-unit on climate change as part of a university level course for secondary education majors. Research attention was directed to discursive interactions manifested in written reflections and feedback, and email exchanges within the development team, and how these interactions supported or constrained decision making in incorporating interdisciplinary knowledge and practices into the unit. Another set of data in this study is embedded in the actual classroom implementation of the mini-unit, entailing video-records of classroom interactions, records of instructional tools, formal assessment probes, students' written artifacts and field notes. The iterative, recursive and consequential analyses of these diverse data sets reveal a chronotope that illuminates how frame clashes between diverse interdisciplinary discourses not only diminish but can also enhance conceptual and epistemic coherence in making sense of climate science and climate change.

In her chapter, Hufnagel introduces yet another chronotope by focusing on the social construction of emotions within the collective action and cultural norms of the science education classroom in the context of climate change. Hufnagel argues that although emotional sense-making is an important component of making sense and taking action on climate change, science is still often characterized objectively with little attention directed to emotional ties between humans and nature. In order to study emotional sense-making in an environmental science course on climate change, she directs her research attention to students' *emotional expressions* in situ, investigating how these are conveyed in talk and text through interactional, contextual and intertextual features at the nexus between the individual-collective and the individual-within-the-collective scale. Similar to the other studies of this volume, the logic-of-inquiry was grounded in the ethnographic research cycle (Spradley, 1980) that entailed investigating the culture of the classroom as a participant observer through an abductive, iterative and recursive process, attending to the cultural behaviors, cultural knowledge and cultural artifacts within the class community (Agar, 1994). This study also makes visible how this project and its goals developed and shifted over time generating new data sets to answer further questions.

The chapter of Ozcelik and McDonald discusses how preservice teachers and their instructor co-constructed a new, reform-based teaching model in science education. In specific, the study communicates a chronotope that unpacks how preservice teachers develop a professional vision for ambitious science teaching. Drawing on interactional ethnography, the data collection included following preservice teachers across several science teaching methods classes and field experiences over time, and relying on a number of data sources including participant observation, ethnographic field notes, video-recordings, interviews and collected artifacts and documents from the courses. These data sources were analyzed at macro and micro levels, zooming in and out of the data to unpack complex and multi-layered contexts of professional growth across space and time. Altogether, this study sheds contextual light into chronotopes that mediate preservice teachers' construction of professional vision.

The chapter of Ricketts deals with professional discourses in science teacher learning groups. In particular, the study is motivated to generate research knowledge on how teachers' conversations around practice mediated their opportunities to learn about teaching science, with a specific focus on generative teacher talk. By harnessing interactional ethnography, the chapter makes visible the cultural actions, knowledge and artifacts that teachers use, produce, predict and interpret during their engagement in the teacher learning group. The analyses of longitudinally collected video-records of the teacher group meetings, teacher interviews and observational field notes proceeded iteratively and recursively. The analysis consisted of identifying and representing key events, defining emergent analytic focuses, identifying relevant unit of analyses and constructing explanations relevant to this specific sociohistorical and cultural context (Kelly, 2014). This study and its logic-of-inquiry allow us to gain access to designed and more serendipitous aspects that mediated the construction of generative talk and learning opportunities in teacher groups. These findings account to the chronotope of teacher learning as relational, situated and consequential.

The studies introduced in this volume communicate rich, contextual stories about the uses and possibilities of interactional ethnography to advance our language, knowledge and understanding of contemporary science and engineering classroom cultures and how these create opportunities for engagement, learning and identity building among diverse students and their teachers. The collective force of these academic narratives and their chronotopes evoke a more humane and nuanced approach to the investigation and understanding of educational processes and learning opportunities in science and engineering in situ. Rather than treating culture as a container, as an independent variable that influences engagement and learning, these studies treat culture as an interpretative and localized meaning-making process that enables participants to engage in different collective activities. In this approach, culture is defined as a situated resource—a fund of knowledge and a repertoire of practice—that learners draw upon in order to make sense of their social and material worlds and to participate in them. These studies also move away from individualistic and trait-like explanations of learning success and failure, to consider cultural continuities and discontinuities in situ, across space and time. By emphasizing both processes of acculturation and transformation, many of the chapters in this volume are positing an agentic learner whose capacities are afforded and constrained by the discourses, knowledge, cultural practices and tools they can access within their social setting. The studies also imply how science and engineering education is always a normative and ethical endeavor, affording or constraining access to value-laden discourses, practices and resources that affect the level and kinds of participation that individuals might achieve (Kumpulainen & Renshaw, 2007; Renshaw, 2013).

Whilst following Bakhtin's formulation of chronotope, Kamberelis and Dimitriadis (2005) have pointed out that all research efforts arise through human activity within a particular time and place that:

> delimit the objects worthy of investigation, the research questions that may be asked, the units of analysis that are relevant, the analyses that may be conducted, the claims that may be made about the objects of investigation, and the forms of explanation that may be invoked.
>
> *(Kamberelis & Dimitriadis, 2005, p. 24)*

In this volume, we are introduced to a set of empirical studies of contemporary science and engineering education, whose logic-of-inquiry rests on the interactional ethnography approach. Whilst each study is also unique in its focuses, and addresses different topical issues in science and engineering education, a common thread across the studies is their attempt to coordinate analysis of both individual actions and collective practices across space and time, as well as their efforts to make sense of part–whole relationships and micro–macro level dynamics of educational processes as situated and socioculturally framed. Each study is characterized by multiphase, recursive and consequential data collection processes and analyses which are reported in systematic and transparent ways, resulting in generative and reflexive accounts guiding their way to the formulation of new research questions. Hence, these studies based on interactional ethnography open up new possibilities for discourse, knowledge and social practice in researching and understanding science and engineering education processes. The studies also highlight how the interactive ethnographic approach challenges the traditional role of the researcher and those taking part in research, illuminating the delicate and challenging processes of constructing an emic perspective of the research context(s) and the research phenomenon in question, and developing more co-participatory research relationships and arrangements with the research participants.

Drawing upon Bakhtin's notion of addressivity, we can ask "What audiences are addressed by the academic narratives shared in this volume?" Clearly, one prime audience of this volume is educational researchers interested in the study of discourse, knowledge and social practice in contemporary science and engineering classrooms, and the possibilities and consequences of these studies to advance educational theory and practice. The volume also speaks to teachers, curriculum developers and policy-makers about the situated conditions and processes of the construction of science and engineering concepts, processes and practices in diverse classrooms and among diverse students and teachers. As such, the volume creates powerful narratives for professional development and educational change. At the same time, this volume illuminates what it entails to conduct educational research based on the interactional ethnography approach, and the expressive potential of its language, concepts and social practices for educational research, educational opportunity and educational change (Strike, 1974). The chapters also make clear that there is a history to each of these articles reflecting personal and professional journeys of the authors in their production, thus making educational research human and situational.

While my interest is not to attempt to judge any of the studies and their merits, nor to argue in favor of the interactional ethnography over other research approaches, I would like to conclude my commentary by underscoring one feature in these studies and the whole volume what I find highly compelling and important, and worthy of attention. This is to do with the notions of stabilization knowledge and possibility knowledge, and their use and production in educational research on science and engineering education (see also Engeström, 2007).

Stabilization knowledge accounts for knowledge that is constructed and used by individuals and collectives in order to make sense of complex reality that is constantly shifting and changing. Stabilization knowledge is typically used to access and categorize a phenomenon so that it can be registered and dealt with. An illustrative example of stabilization knowledge in use is the labeling of handicapped students, as pointed out and challenged in the classical study of Mehan and his colleagues (Mehan, Hertweck & Meihls, 1986). Although such narrow and one-sided categorizations are at times needed—just like in the story of seven blind mice who all came up with their solution to the strange Something—these categories unfortunately often turn into fixed and simplified labels for phenomena, including human beings, social practices and learning.

Possibility knowledge, on the other hand, emerges when objects and/or phenomena are approached in ways that allow access for their situated meanings as part of everyday interaction, movement and transformation. The generation and use of possibility knowledge has the power to destabilize knowledge and put it in movement which can again open up new possibilities for discourse, knowledge and social practice. In this sense, possibility knowledge is agentive, future-oriented and generative (Engeström, 2007). As the studies in this volume demonstrate, interactional ethnography has many characteristics that offer potential instrumentality to educational research towards the generation of possibility knowledge in science and engineering education. The logic-of-inquiry of interactional ethnography invites researchers to take seriously the local ways in which discourses and social practices and their meanings are constructed over time in classrooms and their cultures, reflected in recognized ways of talking, being and knowing (Green & Castanheira, 2012). The research knowledge generated by interactional ethnography not only offers complimentary methods to study and makes sense of science and engineering education but creates an expressive and reflexive language of justice and hope.

References

Agar, M. (1994). *Language shock: Understanding the culture of conversation.* New York: William Morrow & Company.

Bakhtin, M. (1981). *Dialogic imagination: Four essays.* Austin, TX: University of Texas Press.

Engeström, Y. (2007). From stabilization knowledge to possibility knowledge in organizational learning. *Management Learning, 38*(3), 271–275.

Green, J., Camilli, G. & Elmore, P. (Eds.) (2006). *Handbook of complementary methods in education research.* Mahwah, NJ: Lawrence Erlbaum Associates.

Green, J., & Castanheira, M. L. (2012). Exploring classroom life and student learning: An interactional ethnographic approach. In B. Kaur (Ed.), *Understanding teaching and learning: Classroom research revisited* (pp. 53–65). Rotterdam, NL: Sense.

Kamberelis, G. & Dimitriadis, G. (2005). *Qualitative inquiry: Approaches to language and literacy research.* New York: Teachers College Press.

Kelly, G. J. (2014). Analysing classroom activities: Theoretical and methodological considerations. In C. Bruguière, A. Tiberghien, & P. Clément (Eds.), *Topics and trends in current science education: 9th ESERA conference selected contributions* (pp. 353–368). Dordrecht: Springer.

Kumpulainen, K., & Rajala, A. (2017). Negotiating time-space contexts in students' technology-mediated interaction during a collaborative learning activity. *International Journal of Educational Research, 84,* 90–99.

Kumpulainen, K., & Renshaw, P. (2007). Cultures of learning. *International Journal of Educational Research, 46,* 109–115.

Mehan, H., Hertweck, A., & Meihls, J. L. (1986). *Handicapping the handicapped: Decision making in students' educational careers.* Stanford, CA: Stanford University Press.

Morson, G. S., & Emerson, C. (1990). *Mikhail Bakhtin: Creation of prosaics.* Stanford, CA: Stanford University Press.

Renshaw, P. (2013). Classroom chronotopes privileged by contemporary educational policy: Teaching and learning in testing times. In S. Phillipson, K. Y. L. Ku, & S. N. Phillipson (Eds.), *Constructing educational achievement: A sociocultural perspective* (pp. 57–69). London: Routledge.

Spradley, J. P. (1980). *Participant observation.* Orlando, FL: Harcourt Brace Jovanovich College Publishers.

Strike, K. (1974). On the expressive potential of behaviorist language. *American Educational Research Journal, 11*(2), 103–120.

Young, E. (1991). *Seven blind mice.* New York: Puffin Books.

Appendix A

HOW WE LOOK AT DISCOURSE

Definitions of Sociolinguistic Units

Judith L. Green and Gregory J. Kelly

Throughout the chapters in this book, the authors drew from interactional ethnography to examine the various ways that science and engineering were socially constructed in educational settings. Across the studies, the interpretation of the relevant cultural practices and discourse processes were informed by tracing the roots and intertextual relationships among discursively and socially constructed events across levels of analyses. Interactional ethnography recognizes the ways that discourse shapes, and is shaped by, the cultural practices of social groups. Across levels of analyses, different aspects of these cultural, social, and discursive processes and practices are rendered visible and made subject to analyses and interpretation from the perspective of the participants constructing the activity. We call the process of creating (re) presentations across levels mapping of the events. These structuration maps provide insights into ways that members of social groups propose, recognize, acknowledge, and interactionally accomplish what is academically, socially, interpersonally, and interculturally significant. By considering multiple angles of analysis, from the collective to individuals within the collective, interactional ethnography also provides a basis for tracing individuals across times, events, and configurations of actors. Through this process, interactional ethnography supports the developing of warranted claims about what members collectively and individually need to know, understand, produce, and predict to engage in learning what constitutes science and engineering knowledge in particular areas of study.

Structuration maps at multiple levels of analytic scale (transcripts, event maps, cycles of activity) are constructed through analysis of the moment-to-moment and over time interactions of the participants. The particular level of a map is created by identifying how and in what ways, when and where, and for what purpose(s), particular configurations of members of the classroom (whole class, small group, individual with texts) orient to the topics being constructed as well as to each other. The basis for analyses of interaction(s) are videotaped records of classroom life, which form the basis for constructing ethnographic data sets that may include formal and informal interviews and artifacts from the community of participants to support the development of emic (insider) understandings of the ways of knowing, being, and doing everyday life in the particular social group.

The discourse analytic units that form the basis of transcribing developing events and intertextual ties among events are based on interactional sociolinguistic theory developed by Green and her colleagues (Green & Dixon, 1993; Green & Meyer, 1991; Green & Wallat, 1981). This approach to discourse analysis identifies ways members of a social group (a class, small group, or other configuration of actors) interactionally mark and interpret contextualization cues (pitch, stress, pause, juncture, kinesics, proxemics, lexicon, grammar, gesture, eye gaze) to construct thematically tied units, divergences from these units, and thematic shifts in topics and activity. This form of discourse analysis traces the episodic nature of the instructional (and other) conversations for analysis purposes.

The following descriptions of discourse analysis units are offered to make visible the logic underlying this approach to discourse analysis; however, the research methods are best understood through application to particular cases where analyses of discourse processes provide examples of the procedures. Each unit of analysis is part of a *reflexive process* that makes visible how the ethnographer *produces data* for analysis (Ellen, 1984) as well as the data set designed from an archive of recorded events in social spaces.

The units that follow constitute an *orienting theory* for the initial analysis of the particular record (video) to be analyzed for a particular purpose within an ongoing ethnography. The units are based on the understanding that the events of life within a social group are being socially, interactionally, and dialogically constructed by particular configuration of actors, in particular social spaces, to achieve particular social intentions (e.g., teaching, learning, identity building, power relationships, academic content presentations, among others). Interpretation of these units and what they are accomplishing occurs post hoc, after the transcribing process and the process of (re)presenting the actions, interactions, and accomplishments of participants. Once these units are mapped, then the ethnographer is able to identify patterns of interaction and/or activity that can then be examined using *explanatory theories* from literature written by others.

Units of Analysis for Discourse Analysis within an Interactional Ethnographic Research Project

Message units (MU) are the smallest unit of sociolinguistic meaning (Bloome & Egan-Robertson, 1993; Green & Wallat, 1979, 1981; Kelly & Crawford, 1996; Kelly & Chen, 1999). Message units are defined post hoc by identifying boundaries of utterances, "bits" of talk or social action that are identified as cues to contextualization, e.g., pitch, stress, intonation, pause structures, gesture, kinesics, lexicon, grammar, physical orientation, proxemic distance, and eye gaze (Gumperz, 1982, 1992). This is typically done directly from the videotape as the non-verbal cues are important in identifying the message units. The message unit is (re)presented as a "bit/burst" of talk on a single line of a transcript and is the basis for identifying action units. McDyre (this volume) provides an example of a transcript using message units.

Action units (AUs) are comprised of one or more message units that show a semantic relationship among message units and represent an observed intended act by a speaker (Kelly & Crawford, 1996, 1997; Kelly & Chen, 1999). Action units, like message units, are identified post hoc, with consideration of contextualization cues, as well as the topical content of the talk, as together these features of discourse are used and make available to the analysts the message intent, meaning, message boundaries, and messages ties (discourse or social action). Action units tie within a speaker's turn-at-talk/action. These are illustrated in McDyre and Johnson (this volume).

Turn units (TUs) are tied sequences of action units of speakers signaled by a change in speakers and/or shift in what topic by a particular speaker, signaling a continuing turn-at-topic/actions proposed by the speaker. For example, a tutor may appear to maintain his/her turn while observing the actions (non-verbal) of the tutee; however, if the non-verbal cues are considered, a turn may continue verbally but when actions of the recipient are examined as a co-present element of the developing conversation, those receiving the action units may make visible how they are receiving, interpreting, and taking actions based on the developing conversational processes. Turn units, therefore, when analyzed from a video record are dialogic in nature leading to or signaling interpretive processes in a speaker–hearer process (Bakhtin, 1986). Speaker turn units also signal (make visible) how the speaker is processing what is happening and how they are signaling to others their right to continue holding the floor (Goffman, 1974). There are a number of examples of turn units provided in the chapters in this volume including Vanderhoof, Hufnagel, and Licona.

Interaction units (IUs) are sequences of actions (i.e., comprised of message units) tied to turn exchanges as signaled by participants through message and action cohesion and determined by the social, semantic, and contextual cues. For example, an interaction may be a question–answer sequence, or a chain of intertextually tied messages in which turns-at-talk are exchanged. However, like the message and actions units, these are constructed post hoc through careful observing and listening to the cueing occurring in the conversations, and to what participants are orienting, but are not pre-defined (e.g., by turn or a set of turns) (Green & Wallat, 1979, 1981). McDyre (this volume) made use of interaction units.

Sequence units (SUs) are cohesive thematically tied interactions identified post hoc through semantic and contextual cues (Green & Wallat, 1981; Kelly & Crawford, 1997; Kelly, Crawford, & Green, 2001). These units may be thematically tied or may show potential divergences from the developing theme. For example, if a student asks a question while a theme is being developed, that action unit (of tied messages) has the potential for taking the developing coherence of this theme away from the current focus. How the speaker accepts, redirects, or does not address such units forms a basis for identifying the dynamic and developing nature of the social norms for participation as well as for individual actors' contributions to the developing sequence. This form of analysis requires two (or more) transcript columns to map the flow of the developing dialogic processes and how the event is being discursively proposed and socially constructed. Sequence and phase units are illustrated in a number of chapters in this volume including chapters by Tanis Ozcelik and McDonald, Ricketts, and Sezen-Barrie and Mulvaney.

Phase units/sub-event (PUs) represent sequences of tied SUs that form the foundation of the developing activities marking the ebb and flow of concerted and coordinated action among participants. Phase units reflect a common content and activity focus of the group (Green & Wallat, 1981; Kelly & Brown, 2003; Santa Barbara Classroom Discourse Group [Floriani, A., Heras, A. I., Franquiz, M., Yeager, B., Jennings, L., Green, J. L., & Dixon, C.], 1995). Phase units were presented in a number of the chapters in this volume including chapters by Johnson, Sezen-Barrie and Mulvaney, and Tanis Ozcelik and McDonald.

Event units (EUs) refer to a bounded activity around a particular topic and purpose, often undertaken at a particular time in the flow of a larger social time of the configuration of actors in a particular social space. Changes in events are marked by a shift in purpose, type of activity, and topic (Santa Barbara Classroom Discourse Group [Floriani, A., Heras, A. I., Franquiz, M., Yeager, B., Jennings, L., Green, J. L., & Dixon, C.], 1995). Events may be represented in "event maps" showing phases of activity constructed by participants as they work interactively to accomplish their collective and personal goals. An event map is constructed by observing how time was spent, with whom, on what, for what purpose, when, where, under what conditions, and with what outcomes (Green & Wallat, 1979; Green, Weade, & Graham, 1988; Green & Meyer, 1991; Kelly, Crawford, & Green, 2001; Spradley, 1980). Actions of actors in developing events may be added to the boundaries to capture the flow of activity within an event. These actions are written as present continuous verbs (when presented in English) with the object of action/activity and form a *running record* of the processes and their object of action (Castanheira, Crawford, Green, & Dixon, 2001; Green, Castanheira, & Yeager, 2011; Kelly, Crawford, & Green, 2001; Baker & Green, 2007). For example, a teacher may signal the following actions – ringing the chimes for shift in activity, proposing the new focus, presenting steps in activity, signaling future activity in the day (or other times). This level of mapping the developing focal objects and processes provides a more macro level transcript of actions than is (re)presented in a transcript of message units, action units, turn units, sequence units, and phase units. Event units are represented in a variety of ways. References to events and event maps are found across the chapters in this volume.

Cycle of activity units (CAUs) are comprised of a set of intertextually tied events, interactionally bound and centered around a specific theme (Green & Meyer, 1991). A cycle of activity denotes a set of intercontextually tied activities initiated, enacted, and bound interactively by the participants with common thematic content (Baker & Green, 2007; Baker, Green, & Skukauskaite, 2008; Bloome, 1992; Bloome & Egan-Robertson, 1993; Bloome, Carter, Christian, Otto, & Shuart-Faris, 2005; Fairclough, 1992; Floriani, 1993).

Timelines (TLs) make visible contexts for developing events, social processes, and discourse practices. For example, to trace when in time an event was developed, or to seek to develop an historical progression of developing events, the interactional ethnographer constructs a timeline of the macro boundary of the times that the social group's activity (e.g., a class, a game, or other) was undertaken (Kelly & Chen, 1999). At the level of the developing curriculum with a particular group of participants, this permits a macro–micro relationship to be made visible. The largest timeline shows the boundaries of the group for a particular actor, a boundary that may differ for teachers and for students. The primary timeline, therefore, serves to anchor a whole–part relationship across years, within years, or within small units. This form of part–whole analysis requires that timeline two (small unit of time) be linked to timeline one (the boundary of the phenomena being studied from a particular actor's point of view (e.g., teacher, policy maker, student)). Each level of timeline, therefore, is anchored in the larger social contexts that led to the current construction (Kelly & Chen, 1999). This form of part–whole analysis draws on previous analyses at particular levels of analytic scale to construct a history of developing messages/actions/interactions/sequences/phases/event (Baker, Green, & Skukauskaite, 2008; Green, Skukauskaite, & Baker, 2012; Kelly, 2014). The chapter by Sezen-Barrie & Mulvaney (this volume) provides an example of a timeline.

References

Baker, W. D., & Green, J. L. (2007). Limits to certainty in interpreting video data: Interactional ethnography and disciplinary knowledge. *Pedagogies: An International Journal, 2*(3), 191–204.

Baker, W. D., Green, J. L., & Skukauskaite, A. (2008). Video-enabled ethnographic research: A microethnographic perspective. In G. Walford (Ed.), *How to do educational ethnography* (pp. 77–114). London: Tufnell Press.

Bakhtin, M. (1986). *Speech genres and other late essays.* Austin, TX: University of Texas Press.

Bloome, D. (1992). A special issue on intertextuality. *Linguistics and Education, 4*(3–4), 255–256.

Bloome, D., Carter, S. P., Christian, B. M., Otto, S., & Shuart-Faris, N. (2005). *Discourse analysis and the study of classroom language and literacy events: A microethnographic perspective.* New York: Routledge.

Bloome, D., & Egan-Robertson, A. (1993). The social construction of intertextuality in classroom reading and writing lessons. *Reading Research Quarterly, 28*(4), 305–333.

Castanheira, M. L., Crawford, T., Dixon, C., & Green, J. L. (2001). Interactional ethnography: An approach to studying the social construction of literate practices. *Linguistics and Education, 11*(4), 353–400.

Ellen, R. F. (1984). *Ethnographic research: A guide to general conduct.* New York: Academic.

Fairclough, N. (1992). *Critical language awareness.* New York: Longman.

Floriani, A. (1993). The construction of understanding in a sixth-grade bilingual classroom. *Linguistics and Education, 5*(3–4), 241–274.

Goffman, E. (1974). *Frame analysis.* Boston, MA: Northeastern University Press.

Green, J. L., Castanheira, M. L., & Yeager, B. (2011). Researching the opportunities for learning for students with learning difficulties in classrooms: An ethnographic perspective. In C. Wyatt-Smith, J. Elkins, & S. Gunn (Eds.), *Multiple perspectives on difficulties in learning literacy and numerac* (pp. 49–90). New York: Springer.

Green, J. L., & Dixon, C. (Eds.). (1993). Santa Barbara classroom discourse group [Special issue]. *Linguistics and Education, 5* (3&4).

Green, J. L., & Meyer, L. (1991). The embeddedness of reading in classroom life: Reading as a situated process. In C. Baker & A. Luke (Eds.), *Toward a critical sociology of reading pedagogy* (pp. 141–160). Amsterdam: John Benjamins.

Green, J. L., Skukauskaite, A., & Baker, W. D. (2012). Ethnography as epistemology: An introduction to educational ethnography. In J. Arthur, M. Waring, R. Coe, & L. V. Hedges (Eds.), *Research methodologies and methods in education* (pp. 309–321). London: Sage.

Green, J. L., & Wallat, C. (1979). What is an instructional context? An exploratory analysis of conversational shifts over time. In O. Garnica & M. King (Eds.), *Language, children and society.* New York: Pergamon.

Green, J. L., & Wallat, C. (1981). Mapping instructional conversations: A sociolinguistic ethnography. In J. L. Green & C. Wallat (Eds.), *Ethnography and language in educational settings* (pp. 161–205). Norwood, NJ: Ablex.

Green, J. L., Weade, R., & Graham, K. (1988). Lesson construction and student participation: A sociolinguistic analysis. In J. L. Green & J. O. Harker (Eds.), *Multiple perspective analyses of classroom discourse* (pp. 11–47). Norwood, NJ: Ablex.

Gumperz, J. J. (1982). *Discourse strategies.* Cambridge: Cambridge University Press.

Gumperz, J. J. (1992). Contextualization and understanding. In A. Duranti & C. Goodwin (Eds.), *Rethinking context* (pp. 229–252). Cambridge: Cambridge University Press.

Kelly, G. J. (2014). Analysing classroom activities: Theoretical and methodological considerations. In C. Bruguière, A. Tiberghien, & P. Clément (Eds.), *Topics and trends in current science education: 9th ESERA conference selected contributions* (pp. 353–368). Dordrecht: Springer.

Kelly, G. J., & Brown, C. M. (2003). Communicative demands of learning science through technological design: Third grade students' construction of solar energy devices. *Linguistics and Education, 13*(4), 483–532.

Kelly, G. J., & Chen, C. (1999). The sound of music: Constructing science as sociocultural practices through oral and written discourse. *Journal of Research in Science Teaching, 36*(8), 883–915.

Kelly, G. J., & Crawford, T. (1996). Students' interaction with computer representations: Analysis of discourse in laboratory groups. *Journal of Research in Science Teaching, 33*(7), 693–707.

Kelly, G. J., & Crawford, T. (1997). An ethnographic investigation of the discourse processes of school science. *Science Education, 81*(5), 533–559.

Kelly, G. J., Crawford, T., & Green, J. L. (2001). Common tasks and uncommon knowledge: Dissenting voices in the discursive construction of physics across small laboratory groups. *Linguistics and Education, 12*(2), 135–174.

Santa Barbara Classroom Discourse Group [Floriani, A., Heras, A. I., Franquiz, M., Yeager, B., Jennings, L., Green, J. L., & Dixon, C.] (1995). Two languages, one community: An examination of educational opportunities. In R. F. Macias & R. G. Garcia Ramos (Eds.), *Changing schools for changing students: An anthology of research on language minorities, schools & society* (pp. 63–106). Berkeley, CA: UC Linguistic Minority Research Institute.

Spradley, J. P. (1980). *Participant observation.* New York: Holt, Rinehart, & Winston.

INDEX

Locators in **bold** refer to tables, those in *italics* refer to figures